# AMERICAN USAGE: THE CONSENSUS

Books by Roy H. Copperud:

*Words on Paper,* 1960

*A Dictionary of Usage and Style,* 1964
(paperback edition, 1967)

*American Usage: The Consensus,* 1970

# Roy H. Copperud

# AMERICAN USAGE: THE CONSENSUS

**VNR** VAN NOSTRAND REINHOLD COMPANY
NEW YORK  CINCINNATI  TORONTO  LONDON  MELBOURNE

# PREFACE

This is an age of dictionaries. Two major new works, the Third Edition of Webster's New International Dictionary and the Random House Dictionary of the English Language, both falling into the category loosely described as unabridged, have been published since 1961. And in the last dozen years, more than a half-dozen complete revisions of dictionaries of the so-called collegiate or desk size have appeared.

It is also an age of keen concern with the choice and arrangement of words, if we can judge from the fact that in the same period no fewer than nine more or less comprehensive dictionaries of usage have been published. This seems to indicate an unprecedented interest in the subject, when one considers that from 1926 to 1942 there was only one such book (the formidable Fowler) and that from 1942 to 1957, with the addition of Partridge, there were only two. Widespread preoccupation with usage was also reflected in the reception given the Third Edition of Webster in 1961. Reactions ranging from indignation to outrage resulted from the fact that this work accepted as standard many usages that had been and still are widely criticized. The editors could have spared themselves much obloquy if they had only given some indication of this criticism, which need not have interfered with their own judgments. The rebellion against Webster III reached such a pitch that the American Heritage Publishing Company attempted to buy out Merriam-Webster, the publisher of Webster III, and point its lexicography in a new, more prescriptive direction. This attempt failed, and instead American Heritage joined forces with Houghton-Mifflin to bring out the American Heritage Dictionary of the English Language (1969), a $4,000,000 project clearly intended as an antidote to Webster.

Considering the existence of all these works, representing every reasonable point of view on usage, some special justification is necessary for yet another one. That justification arises out of the very plenitude of such books, and the fact that their judgments often differ. There is an unspoken assumption, even among those who in more analytical moments know better, that "correct" usage is a matter of revealed truth; that somewhere, perhaps on Cloud Nine, there is an expert, or perhaps a board of experts, on the subject whose taste is impeccable and whose judgments are irrefutable. The fact is, of course, that there is no final authority.

The American Heritage Dictionary appointed a panel of more than 100 presumed experts—writers, editors, teachers, and officials—to give judgments on disputed points. They divided all the way from 50–50 to 98–2 per cent. In an introductory essay to the dictionary entitled "Good Usage, Bad Usage, and Usage," Morris Bishop commented, "It is significant that on specific questions, the Usage Panel disagreed more than they agreed, revealing a fact often conveniently ignored—that among those best qualified to know, there is a very considerable diversity of usage. Anyone surveying the panelists' various opinions is likely to conclude that good usage is indeed an elusive nymph, well worth pursuing but inconstant in shape and dress, and rather hard to back into a corner." In making hundreds of judgments, the panelists were unanimous only once, to the effect that *simultaneous* may not be used as an adverb ("The referendum was conducted simultaneous with the general election").

Considering, then, the divided state of even expert opinion on usage, it occurred to me that a useful purpose would be served by presenting the consensus of authorities on disputed points. That is the purpose of this book, which compares seven current dictionaries of usage as well as the leading conventional dictionaries. The reader thus may discover not only where the weight of opinion lies, but also what his favorite authority, if he has one, thinks, and he may choose the opinion he likes best. Every authority on usage, after all, is offering what he believes to be the educated consensus; none of them would admit that he is attempting to impose his own idiosyncrasies on readers. This book, then, presents what is truly the consensus—or comes as close, at least, as it is possible to get.

The dictionaries of usage compared for this book are:

*The Careful Writer,* by Theodore M. Bernstein (Atheneum, 1965)

*Current American Usage,* by Margaret M. Bryant (Funk & Wagnalls, 1962)

*A Dictionary of Usage and Style,* by Roy H. Copperud (Hawthorn, 1964)

*A Dictionary of Contemporary American Usage,* by Bergen Evans and Cornelia Evans (Random House, 1957)

*The ABC of Style,* by Rudolf Flesch (Harper & Row, 1964)

*Modern American Usage,* by Wilson Follett and others (Hill and Wang, 1966)

*A Dictionary of Modern English Usage,* by H. W. Fowler, Second Edition, revised by Sir Ernest Gowers (Oxford University Press, 1965)

In addition, comparisons have been made as appropriate (particularly of definitions) with the unabridged Webster III and Random House dictionaries. Because it gave unprecedented attention, for a conventional dictionary, to usage, the judgments in the American Heritage Dictionary have also been included. Nearly always, these are the opinions of the Usage Panel as recorded in usage notes—judgments, it may be noted, with which the editors of that dictionary did not always agree, as indicated by the way they are sometimes reported. The description of a usage in this book as having been approved or rejected by American Heritage means that it either received or failed to receive a majority vote from the Usage Panel. Usages that the panel may have voted down are nevertheless entered among the definitions in American Heritage, together with instructions to see the usage notes appended to the entries, in which the panel's views are given. Some of the usage notes were written by the editors, and are not based on Usage Panel decisions.

From time to time, as it seems useful, other works are cited. They include the Standard College Dictionary (Funk & Wagnalls, 1963); the American College Dictionary (Random House, 1957); Webster's New World Dictionary (World Publishing Company, 1960); and the Oxford Universal Dictionary (Oxford, 1955) and the Concise Oxford Dictionary (Oxford, 1964), both abridgments of the great Oxford English Dictionary, which itself is occasionally cited. Mentions of Perrin refer to that indispensable handbook *Writer's Guide and Index to English*, by Porter G. Perrin (Scott, Foresman and Company).

There are two notable exclusions from the list of dictionaries of usage surveyed here. One is *Usage and Abusage* by Eric Partridge, which was omitted partly because of age, since its basic text dates back to 1942, and partly because it is British. British views are considered adequately represented by the revision of Fowler. The other work omitted is *A Dictionary of American-English Usage* by Margaret Nicholson (1957), an earlier version of Fowler that is regarded, for the present purpose, as having been superseded by Gowers' revision.

The authorities being compared on a given point are listed in alphabetical order by their last names. Dictionaries of usage are cited first, and then conventional dictionaries.

Some brief comments on the dictionaries of usage surveyed for this book may be pertinent. Bernstein's *The Careful Writer* grew out of *Winners & Sinners,* the in-house critique of the content of the New York *Times* that he has produced for many years. In his judgments on usage, Mr. Bernstein tends to be strict and traditional, though he has noticeably softened some views expressed in *Winners & Sinners.*

Bryant's *Current American Usage* is directed more at scholarly than at general use. Yet it resembles this book, in that it offers a consensus—not of other authorities on usage, but one based on the work of researchers who conducted surveys on how various expressions are actually used. This approach is surely the most scientific, if one concedes that language changes, and that actual practice governs acceptability. Unfortunately, the book covers very little ground, in comparison with other dictionaries of usage.

My own *Dictionary of Usage and Style* grew out of the column, "Editorial Workshop," that I have conducted in the magazine *Editor & Publisher* since 1954, and it was preceded by another book, *Words on Paper* (1960). Probably no one can accurately define his own position in these matters, but if I were to attempt it, I would say that my views tend to the middle of the road.

Bergen and Cornelia Evans' *Dictionary of Contemporary American Usage,* published in 1957, is the oldest of the books surveyed. Its judgments tend to be liberal, or permissive.

Flesch's *ABC of Style* is extremely idiosyncratic and not very comprehensive. The author often describes expressions as ugly or as sounding awkward, and often asserts flatly without explanation that certain words "shouldn't be used." He is opposed on principle to what he considers long words. Most of these are judgments of a kind to be found in no other dictionary of usage. Dr. Flesch is perhaps the most liberal of the authorities surveyed, and often shows keen perception in pointing out criticized usages that have become established.

Follett's *Modern American Usage* was not complete when its author died, and the book was completed by a committee headed by Jacques Barzun. As some of the reviews pointed out, this is the kind of book that lends itself least to committee authorship. Mrs. Follett complained bitterly that the book failed to carry out the intention of her late husband. Its judgments tend to be traditional and restrictive, and it neglects to take up many commonly disputed usages.

H. W. Fowler was the great Cham of usage; his dictionary, published in 1926, was the first. And it was, as Sir Ernest Gowers remarks in the preface to the revised edition, an epoch-making book. Fowler was exceedingly doctrinaire by today's standards, but perhaps not at all by the standards of his time, and surely not by the standards of Britain, which have always been more exacting than those of the United States. Like all works on usage, his dictionary was left behind by changes in the language, though much of it remains surprisingly pertinent. Even so, a revision was long overdue when Sir Ernest brought one out in 1965. Sir Ernest, following the spirit of the original and no doubt his own inclination as well, is still pretty doctrinaire. He retained unchanged a great deal—some might say too much. Yet he is intelligently receptive to change, and particularly to Americanisms, which Fowler was likely to reject out of hand. "The English way," Fowler wrote (under -*our* & -*or*), with his tongue perhaps only part way into his cheek, "cannot but be better than the American way; that is enough." Sir Ernest kept this comment; the revision, like the original, is still British, and does not deal with many expressions peculiar to America. Its judgments, with a few startling exceptions, tend to be traditional.

The surprising and disappointing thing about nearly every book on usage is its omissions—not of rare, abstruse points, but of commonly disputed ones. Conversely, most such books offer considerable discussion of errors that appear to have been noticed only by the author, and to have obsessed him. It is easy to collect nonce-errors of all kinds, but a book that attempted to include them all would have no point and no end. A review of a book on usage characterized such entries as "obtrusive pet peeves." The test that was used for inclusion of a point in this book is its appearance in two or more of the works compared. This not only fulfills the declared purpose of this book as offering the consensus, but also insures that the points taken up are significant enough to have been noticed by more than one authority. Obviously prevalent errors that have been dealt with by only one authority have been included, however.

Scrupulous care has been exercised not to misrepresent the views of any authority. The examples are my own, and so, of course, are the summations and unattributed judgments. An effort has been made too to avoid long discussions and repetitious examples, which the reader may find tiresome and which may tend to obscure the point being made. This book is aimed at writers, editors, teachers, and students who are seeking readily accessible answers to their questions rather than discursive lectures.

Making judgments in this field is largely a matter of deciding whether new or divergent usages have become acceptable. Some new usages establish themselves quickly among educated people; others win acceptance by slow degrees; still others are aspersed for decades, and may never come to be regarded as standard. Some usages that were once standard are revived under a cloud of disapproval. It is easy to see that judgments on usage depend a good deal on the education and temperament of the judge. Since language is constantly changing, a principle that all writers on usage give at least lip-service to, their verdicts are useful only if they are observant, are reasonably receptive to change, and are not resolved to die with the notions they acquired about words in grammar school. Insistent rejection of usages that have gained widespread acceptance on a cultivated level may result in failure to convey exactly what is intended, and is both misleading and impractical.

Writers on usage, even the most dogmatic of them, do change their minds as they observe, over a period of time, that usages they found reprehensible when they were new have won wide and educated acceptance. Some authorities are readier than others to accept change; that is, they decide at an earlier date than the others that the time for acceptance has come. Such authorities are sometimes damned by the more conservative as permissive and as corrupters of the language. On the other hand, the conservatives may be scorned as pedantic. In any event, there is no infallible test that may be applied to determine whether the hour of acceptance has arrived. Derivation, contrary to widespread opinion, is of little help in deciding questions of usage; many words have departed far from their original senses. Nor is logic a good guide. It all comes down to the taste of the person making the judgment. And taste, it was established long ago, is not a fit subject for disputation.

Some of the material in this book was adapted from my earlier ones. And, as when those books were published, I want to thank Jerome H. Walker, executive editor of the magazine *Editor & Publisher*, for permission to reprint, sometimes in different form, material that first appeared there.

I want to express appreciation too to Ted Johnson, whose perception as an editor made this a better book, and to Paul Sargent Clark, for the benefit of his editorial expertise. Once again, I am indebted to my wife, Mary, for having typed the manuscript and having helped me otherwise in putting the book together; not least for her unflagging confidence and encouragement at times when they were needed.

Roy H. Copperud

January 1970

# AMERICAN USAGE: THE CONSENSUS

# A

**a, an.** The chief difficulty is deciding which form of the article to use with certain words beginning with *h* (notably *history, hotel, humble, hysterical, habitual, hallucination*) and with some others that begin with vowels that are pronounced with consonant-sounds (*unique, utopia, eulogy*). Bernstein, Copperud, Evans, Flesch, Follett, and Fowler agree that *a* is preferable when the consonant is sounded in pronunciation: *a* (not *an*) *historian, hotel, humble,* etc. Similarly *a* is desirable with *utopia, eulogy,* etc. The persistence of usages like *an hotel, an humble, an historical* reflects the fact that at one time the *h* was not sounded, or was sounded lightly.

Phrases like *a 100 miles* and *a 1,000 tankloads,* often seen in print, are disjointed, and do not take account of the fact that the numbers are read *one hundred, one thousand,* not simply *hundred* and *thousand.*

Follett and Fowler discourage misplacement of *a, an* in such sentences as "Can anyone suggest more valuable a book?" (*a more valuable*). This error seems rare. Fowler and American Heritage call the article superfluous in such constructions as *no more striking a triumph* and *no brighter an hour.* See also THE.

**Abbreviations.** Flesch calls the idea that abbreviations are inappropriate in serious writing a superstition. Copperud cautions against abbreviating the month without the date ("last Dec.") or the state without the city ("The factory is in Ala.") and against abbreviation of proper names (*Robt., Wm.*) by anyone but their owners. Clipped forms like *Ed* do not take a period (Copperud, Evans). See also ACRONYMS; ALPHABETICAL DESIGNATIONS; LB., LBS. for plural forms.

**abdomen.** See BELLY.

**ability, capacity.** Ability is acquired; capacity is innate (Bernstein, Evans). American Heritage, Random House, and Webster, however, say ability may be either native or acquired.

**abjure, adjure.** Often confused, warn Bernstein and Evans, though the first means *forswear* and the second means *admonish.*

**ablutions.** Evans and Fowler discourage its facetious use and say its only serious use is in religious connections.

**abode.** Facetious or pretentious in modern use as the term for a dwelling (Evans, Flesch).

**abolishment, abolition.** Bernstein, Follett, and Fowler suggest that the second is preferable as the more usual form.

**about.** Often used redundantly with figures spanning a range, as in "The victims were described as about 45 to 50 years old," or with other indications of approximation, such as "The number of beans in the jar was estimated to be about 6,000."

Bernstein calls such expressions as *about the head* (in reference, for example, to blows) police or newspaper lingo; Copperud calls them standard. (Webster III gives "here and there upon: *the knife wounded him about the face and throat.*" The Standard College Dictionary gives "on every side"). The consensus is that the usage is standard. See AT ABOUT; NOT ABOUT TO.

**above.** Approved by Bryant, Evans, Fowler, Random House, and Webster in the sense *previously mentioned* or *cited;* that is, *above* may be used as an adverb, adjective, or noun ("the statement above"; "the above statement"; "repeating the above"). Follett disapproves; American Heritage approves the adjective but not the noun ("correct the above to say").

**Absolute Comparatives.** Such comparatives as "the better stores" and "older automobiles," as used when no specific comparison is being made or even implied, are regarded by Copperud as an idiosyncrasy of advertising prose. Bryant finds this usage informal standard English.

**Absolute Constructions.** Fowler warns against the first comma in such constructions as "The day, having dawned brightly, the weather soon grew dull and cloudy." (The second comma is correct, however.) Flesch makes a blanket criticism of absolute constructions as sounding clumsy in written English, and recommends avoiding them entirely by recasting.

**Absolutes.** For comparison of absolutes, such as *more unique, most complete,* etc., see COMPARISON 3.

**abysmal, abyssal.** Formerly synonyms, but in modern use the first means *deep* in a figurative sense (*abysmal ignorance*), and the second has become a technical term of oceanography (Evans, Fowler). The definitions in American Heritage, Random House, and Webster corroborate this distinction.

**Academe.** Criticized by Evans as pompous and by Fowler as wrong in reference to a school (except for "the Grove of Academe").

**accelerate, exhilarate.** Described by Bernstein and Evans as sometimes confused; they explain that *accelerate* means *speed up, exhilarate* means *gladden.*

**accent, accentuate.** Evans concurs in Fowler's conclusion that *accentuate* now predominates in figurative senses (*emphasize, draw attention to*) and *accent* in literal senses (*stress in speaking or writing*), but says this usage is chiefly British. Evans adds that Americans who observe this distinction should reserve *accentuate* for small matters. Current dictionaries do not recognize any distinction, treating the words as synonyms.

**Accent Marks.** Their use has all but disappeared in English, except when foreign words are introduced. Even the native dieresis (as in *coöperate*) now tends to be dropped. Precision is advised in the use of foreign accents with words that require them. Flesch, on the other hand, counsels avoidance of foreign terms entirely in favor of their English equivalents. See also DIACRITICAL MARKS.

**acceptance, acceptation.** Evans, Follett, Fowler, American Heritage, Random House, and Webster agree that the first is the act of accepting, the second now the interpretation or usual meaning of something; for example, a concept, word, or doctrine, though there is some overlapping.

**access, accession.** Evans and Fowler caution that the first means an opening or opportunity, the second ascent or attainment. The correct phrase for assumption of royal power is *accession* (to the throne), not *access*. Copperud notes that *access* has newly become a verb in computer technology ("Any one of 235 cards can be randomly accessed") and has won considerable popular acceptance. This sense is yet to be found in any dictionary.

**accident, mishap.** Bernstein and Evans agree that chance is the primary attribute of an accident, and that *mishap* implies undesirability or misfortune. Bernstein restricts *mishap* to what is unimportant. Dictionaries, as he concedes, do not associate the idea of small scale with *mishap*, however. The Standard College Dictionary offers the comment, "*Mishap* and *mischance* suggest a single unforeseen occurrence: a *mishap* on the road interrupted our

trip." Webster cites *a great mishap*, such as a landslide.

*Mishap* is a favorite among newspaper headline writers because of its convenient length, and the distinction insisted on by Bernstein is often disregarded by them.

**accidentally, accidently.** Although Webster now sanctions the second spelling, it is unusual enough so that it is likely to be considered an error; Random House does not include it.

**accommodate.** Often misspelled *accomodate*.

**accompanist, accompanyist.** Copperud, Evans, and Fowler agree that the first is now the predominant form, though Fowler regrets that *-nier* or *-nyist* did not win popular favor.

**according to, accordingly.** *According to* in attribution is discouraged by Copperud as casting a shadow on the credibility of the speaker. Flesch criticizes the expression *accordingly* (and also *in accordance with*) as clumsy.

**accrue.** Bernstein and Evans advise saving the word for legal and financial contexts.

**accumulative, cumulative.** The second is preferable to and has nearly displaced the first (*a cumulative development*) (Copperud, Evans, Fowler).

**accused.** Descriptives like *the accused spy, the suspected murderer* are best avoided because they imply guilt at a time before it has been established (Bernstein, Copperud). See also ALLEGE. *Accuse* takes *of*, not *with*.

**acid test.** A cliché (Evans, Fowler).

**acquaintanceship.** Superfluous beside *acquaintance* (Evans, Fowler).

**acquiesce.** Bernstein, Follett, American Heritage, Random House, and Webster agree that *in* is preferable with this verb (*acquiesce to* is now old-fashioned).

**Acronyms.** The term applies only to abbreviations that form words, such as Jato (for *jet-assisted takeoff*). Bernstein, Copperud, and Follett warn against the indiscriminate use of such expressions when they may not be familiar to the reader, a favorite practice among newspaper writers in their headlong urge to compress.

**act, action.** Though one will do where the other will not, the vagaries of idiom affecting the choice make it difficult to formulate any really useful rule, as discussions in Copperud, Evans, Fowler, and American Heritage show. All point out, however, that only *action* has a collective sense; that is, more than one act may make up an action. *Act* in modern usage also generally indicates the thing done, and *action* the doing of it.

**activate, actuate.** The first, in ordinary contexts, means to make active, the second to cause to move (Evans, Fowler). Dictionaries do not recognize any such hard and fast distinction.

**actual, actually.** Criticized by Copperud, Evans, and Fowler as used for a meaningless emphasis, especially in conversation: "No sooner had the Reds appeared when they were actually pelted with tomatoes";

"The stocks were sold at prices above actual market prices." Omission of *actually* and *actual* from these sentences has no effect on the meaning.

**ad.** Standard for *advertisement* (Bernstein, Copperud, Flesch, Evans, Random House, and Webster; American Heritage calls it informal, and Fowler withholds judgment).

**A. D. (anno domini).** Bernstein and Copperud point out that the designation cannot be correctly used with centuries, since it translates "in the year of our Lord." A.D., unlike B.C., precedes the year so designated: A.D. 566. Webster, however, allows the application to centuries, and in this instance approves also placement after the century designated; American Heritage calls both usages informal.

**adage.** See OLD ADAGE.

**adapted.** Evans calls the word inappropriate as a synonym for *suitable* because *adapted* implies *changed* (to meet a requirement, for example). This view conforms with dictionary definition.

**add an additional.** A common and careless redundancy (Copperud, Fowler).

**addicted.** Bernstein and Evans advise reserving the term for what is harmful, and criticize its facetious use for what is not (*addicted to grapes*). Random House concurs. Webster, however, quotes Galsworthy: "addicted to pleasure."

**addition.** See IN ADDITION (TO); NUMBER IN ADDITION.

**additionally.** Clumsily used for *also:* "Additionally, he had acquired three houses and two cars." *He had also acquired . . .* (Copperud, Evans).

**address.** Discouraged by Flesch as pompous where *speech* will do; described by Evans as more formal than *speech,* together with *lecture.*

**adequate.** A euphemism of reviewers, who employ it in praising faintly (Copperud, Follett). See also IMPECCABLE; CONSUMMATE.

**adequate enough.** Redundant (Evans, Follett).

**adhere.** Copperud discourages such expressions as *adhere to a plan,* but Follett and Fowler consider this usage standard, as do American Heritage, Random House, and Webster. Follett and Fowler recognize *give adhesion* in political connections, but this usage is not common in the U.S.

**adjacent.** Means *near,* not necessarily *touching* (Copperud, Fowler). Flesch prefers *next to* as simpler, and Fowler prefers *near* or *close.*

**adjectivally, adjectively.** The first is preferable (Evans, Fowler).

**Adjectives.** All the usage books being compared, except for Bryant, contain discussions of the misuse of adjectives. Since this is primarily a matter of rhetoric rather than usage, strictly speaking, and since the discussions are too long and involved to yield satisfactorily to summary, only a listing of the problems considered is included here:

Bernstein deals with placement, sequence of comparatives or superlatives, adjectives as nouns, and adjectives with con-

dition of health (mainly in newspaper headlines).

Copperud deals with comparison, participial modifiers, placement, piled-up adjectives, limiting adjectives, nouns as adjectives, repetition of defining modifiers.

Evans deals with comparison, formation, kinds of adjectives, order in a series, adjectives as adverbs, and adjectives as nouns.

Flesch deals with nouns as adjectives and stuffing irrelevant modifiers into a sentence in the style of much journalistic writing.

Follett deals with erroneous punctuation of adjectives.

Fowler deals with nouns as adjectives, superfluous and mischosen adjectives, and adjectives as clichés.

For comparison of adjectives, see COMPARISON 2; see also MODIFIERS.

**adjure.** See ABJURE, ADJURE.

**adjust, readjust.** See EUPHEMISMS.

**administer, administrate.** Synonyms, though *administrate* is an Americanism and may be considered unnecessary beside *administer* (Copperud, Fowler).

**admission, admittance.** Bernstein, Evans, and Fowler agree that *admission* predominates. Bernstein says that *admittance* denotes physical entry, *admission* the allowance of certain rights and privileges, a distinction maintained by American Heritage, the Standard College Dictionary, the American College Dictionary, and Webster; Follett describes the distinction as disappearing. Copperud, Evans, Random House, and Webster's New World Dictionary give the terms as synonymous. Opinion is thus divided.

**admit, admit to.** *Admit to* is criticized by Copperud, Follett, Fowler, and American Heritage in the sense *confess*. (*He admitted to having stolen the money*). Evans says the addition of *to* to *admit* has a weakening effect, and implies that this is deliberate; as *admit to* is used in journalistic writing particularly, however, it is obviously intended as an exact synonym of *admit*.

**admonishment, admonition.** Bernstein and Fowler suggest that the second is preferable as the more usual form. This view seems unarguable.

**Adolf (Hitler).** Perhaps the most misspelled of names in recent history; often given *Adolph*.

**adopt.** Bernstein and Evans warn against confusion with *adapt*.

**adopted, adoptive.** Evans says that while the common American use is *adopted* in reference to parents, the British *adoptive* is preferable, and Fowler and American Heritage also favor this form. Bernstein warns that *adoptive* may be regarded as overcorrect, and Random House and Webster consider the forms interchangeable.

**adumbrate.** Formal, literary, and unsuitable for ordinary contexts (Evans, Fowler, Flesch).

**advance, advancement, advanced.** The first is preferable for the general idea of progress, the second for promotion (Evans, Follett, Fowler).

*Advance* is redundant with *warning, planning, prepara-*tions; sometimes it erroneously displaces *advanced*, as in *advance writing classes* or *advance degree* (Bernstein, Copperud, Follett, American Heritage).

**Adverbial Genitive.** The term describes such expressions as *days* in "He worked days" and *afternoons* in "They slept afternoons." Bryant reports the form well established in informal standard expression (as against such alternatives as *during the day, every day, in the afternoon*). Evans calls such forms standard usage in the United States but obsolete in Britain.

**Adverbs.** An erroneous idea that compound verbs (like *have seen, will go*) should not be separated by adverbs (*have easily seen, will soon go*) has become widespread, and is perhaps most firmly established among newspaper journalists. Most commentators agree that it is apparently an offshoot of the prohibition against splitting an infinitive, which in its absolute and arbitrary form is also a superstition (see INFINITIVES 1). Some examples in which the verb is split by an adverb (italicized): "The budget was *tentatively* approved"; "The matter was *automatically* delayed"; "Experts are *now* pinning their hopes on the House." In many sentences, the adverb falls naturally among the parts of the verb, and in negative sentences it is impossible to place the adverb (*not*) anywhere else: "He would not concede the election"; "The decision will not block action." The desirability of placing the adverb within the compound verb is agreed on by Bernstein, Copperud, Evans, Follett, and

Fowler, who says that placing the adverb anywhere else requires special justification. Newspaper copy editors are particularly assiduous in plucking out the word *also* from between parts of a compound verb. Thus "He was also singled out for commendation," which says that among other things, he was singled out, is likely to be changed by them to read "He also was singled out for commendation," which alters the sense to "He in addition to others . . ."

An adverb should not intervene between a verb and its object: "He said every chance would be given to complete *satisfactorily* the negotiations"— *complete the negotiations satisfactorily;* "An applicant for a federal job should have a chance to explain *informally* derogatory information"—*to explain derogatory information informally* (Copperud, Evans, Follett, Fowler). This and related problems are discussed at length by Bernstein under *Adverbs, Placement of;* by Copperud under *Verbs;* by Evans under *Sentence Adverbs;* by Follett under *Adverbs, Vexatious;* and by Fowler under *Position of Adverbs.* See also MODIFIERS.

**adverse, averse (to).** The expression is *averse to* ("She was not averse to a drink before dinner"); not *adverse* (Bernstein, Copperud). Evans says *averse to* is preferable but allows *averse from.* British usage differs; Fowler insists on *to* with *adverse,* and allows either *to* or *from* with *averse.* Random House and Webster give *averse to;* this is the con-

sensus; American Heritage says usually *to,* less often *from.*

**advert to.** Obsolete for *refer to* (Flesch, Fowler).

**advise.** Criticized when it displaces *say, tell, write, inform,* especially in business correspondence ("Beg to advise . . .") (Copperud, Evans, Flesch). Often inexactly used in attribution (see ATTRIBUTION). *"The meeting will be postponed,"* he advised. Journalese; *said.* But American Heritage approves.

**adviser, advisor.** Copperud comments that insistence on *-er* is one of the peculiarities of journalism; both forms are standard and in wide use. Bernstein says *-er* is preferred. Perrin says *advisor* is now probably predominant, by analogy with *advisory.* All dictionaries give both forms as standard.

**ae, e; oe, e.** The digraphs are being abandoned in favor of *e* alone in such words as *archeology (archaeology), esthetic (aesthetic), encyclopedia (encyclopaedia), esophagus (aesophagus), fetus (foetus)* (Copperud, Flesch, Fowler). Fowler's comments show, however, that British usage is somewhat more conservative than American in this respect.

**aegis.** Criticized by Bernstein as used in the sense of *jurisdiction, surveillance,* without the connotation of protection. Dictionary definitions generally corroborate this view.

**aero-, air-.** Copperud and Evans say that *aeroplane* has disappeared in the U.S. in favor of *airplane,* and Fowler despairingly reports that even in Britain, the prefix *aero-* is being forced to the wall by American influence.

**affect, effect.** As verbs, perhaps the commonest confusion of them all. It is unanimously denounced by Bernstein, Copperud, Evans, Fowler, and American Heritage. It seems almost superfluous to explain that *affect* means *influence* ("The moon affects lovers") and *effect* means *accomplish* ("A merger was effected").

**affiliated (associated, identified) with.** Society-page pomposities for *belongs to, works for* (Copperud, Evans, Flesch).

**affirmative, negative.** Pretentious for *yes, no* ("He answered in the affirmative") (Copperud, Flesch, Fowler). A newsmagazine reported that secretaries at the Manned Space Center in Houston, under military influence, have taken to saying "negative" over the telephone where other people would say "no."

**afflict, inflict.** See INFLICT, AFFLICT.

**aforementioned, aforesaid.** Unsuitable for ordinary contexts (Copperud, Flesch).

**Afrikaner, Afrikander.** Evans, American Heritage, Random House, and Webster give the forms as applying interchangeably to a South African of European descent, and in some instances the meaning *a breed of cattle* is added. In *Inside Africa* John Gunther says *Afrikander* is an old-fashioned term applied now only to the breed of cattle.

**after.** In Irish dialect, it does not mean *about to* but *have just done* (Evans, Fowler). (*I am after taking a walk* = *have just taken,* not *intend to take*).

**aftermath.** The word should be reserved for what is disagreeable, and not used for what merely follows upon something else (Evans, Fowler). The distinction is supported by American Heritage, the Standard College Dictionary, and Random House, but Webster cites the *New York Times* in "a gratifying aftermath." The consensus favors the distinction.

**afterward, afterwards.** Interchangeable in the U.S.; only *afterwards* is used in Britain (Evans, Fowler).

**age, aged.** Expressions like *at age 65* and children *aged 9 to 12* sound actuarial and old-fashioned, respectively; *at the age of 65; 65 years of age* (or *old*). Copperud and Flesch advise that the numbers indicating age can as well be used without the descriptive words: *at 65, children 9 to 12.*

**agenda.** Unanimously described as a standard English singular ("the agenda includes . . .") though it is technically a Latin plural, which sometimes causes pedants to attempt to revive *agendum* as the singular. The plural is *agendas.* (Bernstein, Bryant, Copperud, Evans, Fowler, American Heritage, Random House, Webster).

**aggravate.** Bernstein insists on the traditional view that the word can properly mean only *make worse,* and not *annoy, irritate.* Copperud, Flesch, Follett, and Fowler say that the time has come to accept the sense *annoy;* Evans calls it colloquial (that is, informal). The consensus is that the struggle to limit *aggravate* to the traditional sense has been lost. Both Random House and Webster regard the new sense as standard; American Heritage calls it informal.

**ago.** Redundant with *since:* "It is only 20 years ago since the treaty was signed." (Bernstein, Copperud, Follett, Fowler, American Heritage).

**Agreement.** See SUBJECT-VERB AGREEMENT.

**ah, aw.** Copperud says *ah* should be reserved to express delight, relief, and *aw* to express regret, contempt, incredulity etc.: "Ah, this is a splendid wine"; "Aw, we have lost the game." Random House and Webster concur on *aw* but assign both sets of meanings to *ah*, as does American Heritage, which gives only this form.

**ahold.** Not standard for *hold*, with *get* or *take*: "I'd like to get ahold of that information." *get hold.* (Copperud, Random House, Webster).

**aid, aide.** Loosely interchangeable in the sense of *assistant. Aide* has been retained in military connections, however, and more or less also in diplomacy and nursing. Newspaper headlines would be less ambiguous if *aide* were used invariably as the noun. (Copperud, Random House, Webster). Flesch objects to the shortening of *aide* (the original form) to *aid.* Current dictionaries, however, uniformly give *aid* in the sense of *assistant* or *helper.*

**aim to.** Bernstein calls this standard in the sense *intend,* but concedes some consider it dialectal. Random House calls it chiefly dialectal; Webster and American Heritage consider it standard. Fowler says that the usage originated in America and somewhat surprisingly adds that it has established itself as acceptable in Britain. Evans evidently considers it standard, since it is cited without qualification. This is the consensus.

**ain't.** Bernstein calls *ain't* illiterate and Bryant calls it nonstandard. Copperud, Evans, and Fowler regret that it is not acceptable for *am not,* since there is no other contraction for this form; Copperud and American Heritage deplore *aren't I* but Fowler calls it "colloquially respectable," reflecting a difference between British and American usage that is corroborated by Evans. Bryant says *aren't I* is relatively rare and that cultivated speakers prefer *am I not.* Flesch says *ain't* is on its way in. All his examples, however, are either quoted speech, or jocular.

The fact is that *ain't* is sometimes boldly used in writing by those who are sure of themselves, though most people consider it the hallmark of the uneducated. *Ain't* for *am not* is considered nonstandard by Random House and American Heritage, but acceptable in speech by Webster; all consider it nonstandard for *have not.* The consensus is that it is best avoided in writing.

**air.** Unexceptionable for *broadcast.* May be ambiguous in newspaper headlines, however, where the word also means *expose, discuss, explore.*

**à la.** Not *ala; à la* (in the style or manner of) *Hollywood.* The French grave accent over *a* is pretty much disregarded in English text, but is required in carefully edited matter.

**albeit.** Considered archaic a generation ago; now being revived (Fowler; both unabridged dictionaries give it as standard).

**Alger, Horatio.** The name is often used to characterize a successful man ("The Horatio Alger of the insurance business, a millionaire who once supported himself as a newsboy"). In fact, Horatio Alger was the name of the author, not of any of the heroes, of his rags-to-riches tales (Bernstein, Copperud).

**alibi.** The technical meaning in law is a defense against a criminal charge by a plea of having been elsewhere (the meaning of *alibi* in Latin is *elsewhere*). The term is in common use in the sense of *excuse;* Evans points out that one of Ring Lardner's best-known characters was Alibi Ike, who won the sobriquet by perpetually having ready some extenuation of his shortcomings. *Alibi* in this sense is sometimes bitterly criticized, particularly by lawyers who consider the extended sense a corruption, and Fowler stands with them. This must be regarded as a British view, however; Bernstein, Copperud, and Evans all approve the popular sense, and it is admitted, sometimes with the qualification "informal" or "colloquial," as standard by all current American dictionaries. American Heritage admits it as informal, though only 41 per cent of its usage panel approved. Sir Ernest Gowers, Fowler's reviser, might be dismayed to discover that even the Oxford Universal Dictionary, a modern abridgment of the great Oxford English Dictionary, approves the popular sense.

**align, aline.** Both versions are in use, but the first is by far the more frequent (Copperud) and is the correct one (Fowler).

**alive.** See LIVE.

**all-around, all-round.** Bernstein favors *all-round* as more logical in such phrases as *all-round athlete;* Copperud says both forms are in common use and the distinction is footless. The Standard College Dictionary cites *all-around athlete,* and the other current American dictionaries unanimously equate *all-round* and *all-around.* American Heritage, however, adds that *all-round* is preferable. The consensus is that the forms are interchangeable.

**allege, alleged, allegedly.** Bernstein says that while *alleged* strictly must apply to a deed and not a person, journalistic necessity makes it acceptable in the sense of *supposed* or *presumed.* Copperud and Evans point out that it is a delusion among journalists that the word confers immunity from suit for libel. Some authorities point out, however, that it may have a mitigating effect even if it does not offer the protection often assumed. See also ACCUSED.

**allergic.** Disapproved by Bernstein, Evans, and Follett in the nonmedical, often facetious sense (*allergic to televi-*

*sion*); Fowler approves of this sense as useful; the Standard College Dictionary calls it informal (as does American Heritage) and cites *allergic to work*. Random House and Webster admit it without qualification; this is the consensus.

**all is not** . . . See NOT ALL, ALL . . . NOT.

**Alliteration.** The repetition of sounds at the beginnings of words or in accented syllables: *after life's fitful fever*. Bernstein and Evans caution that this literary device should be employed with care. Flesch calls it silly in ordinary prose. Often prized and flaunted in journalistic and advertising writing; otherwise, generally scorned these days (Copperud).

**all of.** Copperud and Fowler object to *of* with *all* where it is unnecessary, as in *all (of) the papers, all (of) the money.* Bryant says *all* is much more frequent than *all of* where *of* is optional, as in the examples cited. Bernstein and Evans approve *all of* in such circumstances by analogy with *none of*, though Bernstein concedes *of* may well be omitted as superfluous when it is optional. Flesch says a good writer or editor automatically changes *all of* to *all* (presumably he means only when *of* is optional, for there are instances, as with pronouns [*all of them*] when it is essential). Random House and Webster accept both forms; American Heritage gives a slight preference to *all* where *of* is dispensable. This is obviously a morass of conflicting opinion. The point is hardly an important one, since the choice has no effect on meaning and

is unlikely to be noticed by the reader.

**allow of.** Admitted by Evans and Fowler in specified senses; Copperud says *of* is superfluous here, but American Heritage, Random House, and Webster accept it.

**all right, alright.** Although often seen in print, *alright* is regarded as nonstandard by Bernstein, Copperud, Evans, Fowler, American Heritage, and Random House. Flesch expresses confidence it will establish itself, and Webster says it is in reputable use though not so common as *all right*, which is favored by the consensus.

**all-round.** See ALL-AROUND, ALL-ROUND.

**all that.** *All that* as in "If things were all that bad he would have heard about it" (or, more commonly, in the negative, as "The speech wasn't all that bad") is criticized by Bernstein, Copperud, and American Heritage. Bernstein says *all* used in this way is unnecessary and inappropriate to writing; Copperud calls the phrase a Briticism that sounds affected in the U.S. As for its native habitat, Fowler calls the use of *all* as an adverb, of which *all that* and *not all that* are examples, a colloquialism that is approaching literary acceptance. The consensus is against it. *Not that* ("He's not that rich"), when no basis for a comparison has been stated, is similar.

**all the (easier, etc.).** *All* with a comparative is confirmed as standard English by Bryant and Evans, a judgment that may surprise many to whom it would never have occurred that such confirmation was necessary. American Heritage and Random House give the usage as standard, but Webster calls it chiefly dialectal. The consensus is that it is standard. Bryant and Random House say *as far as* is preferable to *all the farther* ("This is all the farther I can go").

**all-time record.** See RECORD.

**all together, altogether.** Often confused; *all together* means *in a group; altogether* means *entirely:* "We will go all together"; "The idea is altogether ridiculous" (Bernstein, Copperud, Evans, Fowler, American Heritage, Random House). See also IN THE ALTOGETHER.

**all told.** Bernstein would restrict the phrase to counting or enumeration, as in *all told, there were 50 crows in the tree,* and considers it wrong as used to indicate a general summation. Webster III, however, cites *all told, it had been one of the most frustrating experiences imaginable;* American Heritage also gives the general senses.

**allude, refer.** To allude to is to suggest without naming the thing specifically; to refer to is to name specifically. *Allude* is often misused for *refer* (Bernstein, Copperud, Evans, Follett, Fowler, American Heritage; definitions in Random House and Webster corroborate this view).

**allusion, elusion, illusion.** Copperud and Evans warn against the frequent confusion of the terms. (*Allusion* is *suggestion* or *unspecific reference; elusion*—a rarity—is *avoidance* or *escape; illusion* is *deception.*) The adjectival forms *allusive, elusive,* and *illusive* are sometimes confused. Flesch is critical of the device of literary allusion; that is, incorporating in one's prose fragments of well-known quotations with the aim of dressing it up. Bernstein says literary allusions are useful but that the writer should beware of making them too esoteric; Fowler concurs.

**almost.** *Almost* as an adjective modifying a noun, as in *an almost accident,* is sanctioned as standard and well established by Evans, Fowler, and Webster. Despite this, however, the construction is likely to be regarded as an error in America. Neither American Heritage nor Random House recognizes it. Perhaps it may best be classified as literary and British. *Almost* is described by Evans as designating a shorter space than *nearly,* a distinction that no other authority suggests, much less corroborates. *Almost* is often unnecessarily hyphenated, like adverbs ending in *-ly: an almost-open break* (Copperud). This applies also to *less, more, most, much, nearly, once, sometimes.* See also MOST.

**almost more, less (better, worse, etc.).** Flat contradictions in terms and thus nonsense. A condition is either almost, equal to, or more than another; it cannot be two at once. *Almost* and *more* taken together, if they mean anything, cancel each other out precisely on the line of equality. "The whole orchestra is used with almost more than the composer's usual adroitness." What did the writer mean? More adroitness?

No, not quite. Less? No, more than that. The composer's usual adroitness? We can only guess. "Direct intervention, if it had been successful, would have been almost less harmful than failure." *Perhaps less harmful* would have made the sense aimed at and missed. Fowler concurs with this criticism by analogy, citing *almost quite* under the heading *Incompatibles.* For a similar incongruity, see TIMES LESS, TIMES MORE.

**along with.** See WITH.

**Alphabetical Designations.** Copperud and Follett criticize the largely journalistic trick of following an unfamiliar designation (e.g., International Monetary Fund) with its alphabetical abbreviation (IMF), and thereafter referring to it by the abbreviation alone, as confusing to the reader, especially when more than one such abbreviation figures in the same account. In such instances reference by a general term is preferable, calling the International Monetary Fund *the fund,* the International Organizations Employees Loyalty Board *the board,* rather than *the IOELB.*

**alright.** See ALL RIGHT, ALRIGHT.

**also.** Disapproved as a conjunction in writing: "A typical picnic menu includes wieners, buns, beer, also potato salad." *and;* or possibly *and also.* "The automobile needs repair; also it must be repainted." Such errors usually can be corrected by adding *and,* substituting *moreover, in addition, besides,* or by shifting the position of *also* to make it function as an adverb (Bernstein, Copperud, Follett, Fowler, American Heritage).

Random House and Webster, however, admit *also* as a conjunction. Copperud and Follett add that *also* at the beginning of a sentence or clause is wrong except in such constructions as "Also on the agenda are . . ." where *also* is used as an adverb but has been taken out of its normal position: "are *also* on the agenda." See also INVERSION.

**alternate(ly),    alternative(ly).** The noun and adjective forms *alternate* and *alternative* are often confused. *Alternate* has the sense *in turns, one after the other; alternative* has the sense of a choice. An alternate course of action is exchanged with another; an alternative is a substitute. The idea that *alternative* may apply to a choice between two and no more is a pedantry (Bernstein, Copperud, Evans, Follett, Fowler, American Heritage, Random House, Webster). Flesch says *choice* is preferable to *alternative* for the sake of simplicity.

**although.** See THOUGH, ALTHOUGH.

**altogether.** See ALL TOGETHER.

**aluminium, aluminum.** The first form is British, the second American (Copperud, Evans).

**alumnus, etc.** The correct forms are *alumna,* feminine singular; *alumnae,* feminine plural; *alumnus,* masculine singular; *alumni,* both masculine and mixed plural. These are among the few Latin terms that have not acquired English plurals. *Alumni* is substandard for the singular: "He is an alumni of the state university" (Copperud, Evans, Follett, American Heritage). Evans, however, allows *alumnus* in reference to a woman, and Random House and Webster support this by asexual definitions, though Webster says it usually refers to a male.

**a.m., p.m.** Such phrases as *6 a.m. in the morning* and *9 p.m. tonight* are redundant, since the letters designate the half of the day (Copperud, Evans).

**Ambiguity.** The greater part of any book on usage deals with ambiguity of one kind or another. Fairly long discussions of ambiguity in general are to be found in Evans and Fowler. In this book ambiguities are dealt with under more specific headings, including PRONOUNS, MODIFIERS, DANGLING MODIFIERS, FALSE COMPARISON, MEANING, RESTRICTIVE AND NONRESTRICTIVE CLAUSES, and, of course, in numerous entries having to do with misapprehensions of meanings.

**ambiguous, equivocal.** The words are roughly synonymous, but the second suggests deception (Bernstein, Evans).

**ambivalence, ambivalent.** Criticized by Bernstein and Follett as often used to describe duality in general, rather than a conflicting or contradictory attraction and repulsion, and by Fowler as too technical for ordinary contexts. The connotation of conflict is supported by dictionary definitions.

**ameliorate.** Criticized by Copperud as bookish and by Flesch as the long word for *improve.*

**amend, emend.** See EMEND-(ATION).

**America(n).** Despite frequent complaints, the application of the terms to the U.S. and its inhabitants is so well established and so well understood as to be beyond reasonable criticism (Copperud, Evans, Fowler). Dictionary definitions corroborate this view. The objection, of course, is that the term is geographical, and thus includes Canada, Mexico, and Central America.

**Americanisms.** A long list of terms for which different British and American versions persist despite the strong tendency toward coalescence may be found in Fowler under this heading.

**amid, amidst.** Criticized as bookish or literary by Bernstein, Evans, Fowler, and Flesch. See also AMONG, AMONGST, AMID.

**amok.** See AMUCK, etc.

**among, amongst, amid.** *Among* is generally used with plurals of three or more countable things: *among my friends, among the audience, among the trees.* With singular nouns that are not collectives, *amid* is preferable; *amid the wreckage, amid the confusion* (Bernstein, Copperud, Evans, American Heritage; though Bernstein disapproves of *among the news* and Copperud approves of it). Bernstein and Copperud agree that *amongst* is quaint in America; Evans calls it overrefined in the U.S. Evans and Fowler agree that it is standard in Britain, and Fowler devotes some space to differentiating *among* and *amongst* as used there. See also BETWEEN 1.

**amoral.** See IMMORAL, AMORAL.

**amount.** Not good usage in reference to what is countable, as in *a large amount of people* (Bernstein, Copperud, Evans). Flesch calls *in the amount of* usually unnecessary for *of* or *for: A check in the amount of $10.*

**Ampersand (&).** Should be used only in the names of businesses that use it themselves: *Wellington & Co.* It was one of H. W. Fowler's endearing idiosyncrasies that he used it abundantly in place of *and* in ordinary text, and also in the form *&c.* (for *et cetera*), presumably to save space, but more likely to assert his spiky individuality. In his revision of *Modern English Usage,* Sir Ernest Gowers swept away the ampersands and substituted *ands* without a word of explanation, nor did he even include *Ampersand* as an entry. Margaret Nicholson, in her revision of Fowler (*A Dictionary of American-English Usage,* Oxford University Press, 1957), was not so venturesome. She not only left the ampersands bespangling such of the original text as she retained, but used ampersands in her own additions. It is hardly necessary to say that ampersands are not considered acceptable outside firm names, formulas, and other abridged matter.

**ample, enough.** *Enough* is enough, but *ample* is more than enough; *ample* should not be used where *enough* is wanted (Bernstein). Evans, however, allows the terms to be used interchangeably, and so do Follett, Random House, and Webster. The weight of opinion is that *ample* may mean either *enough* or *more than enough.*

**am to, are to.** See INFINITIVES 3.

**amuck, berserk.** *Amuck* is the preferred spelling, rather than *amok* (Copperud, Evans, Fowler). *Amuck* is stronger than *berserk; amuck* connotes murderousness, *berserk* merely means enraged.

**an.** See A, AN.

**anachronism.** A misplacement in time, as, for example, describing Victorians as having watched television. Often misused for *contradiction, anomaly, paradox* (Bernstein, Copperud); Random House and Webster corroborate this.

**analysis.** *In the final* (or *last* or *ultimate*) *analysis* is criticized as pretentious by Flesch and Fowler.

**and.** There is no reason why sentences should not begin with *and* (Bernstein, Bryant, Copperud, Flesch, Follett, Fowler). Copperud and Flesch add that when this is done, *and* should not be followed by a comma. Nor should a comma follow the conjunction that begins a clause: "They have found it pays, and, we have too." But the comma is required after the conjunction to set off a parenthetical element (italicized): "They have found it pays, and, *I must admit,* we have too." See also COMMA 8. For displacement of *and* by commas see COMMA 13.

**and (but) which, and (but) who.** Bernstein and Copperud agree that, in general, *and which* is either wrong or undesirable unless it comes after a parallel *which:* "Most Italians believe that the loot, *which* is known as the Dongo Treasure, and *which* has been valued at $32 million . . ." The comments on this subject apply equally to *but which, and who, but who; and who, but who* must, of course, be preceded by *who*. Fowler devotes ten columns of small type, filling five pages (under the entry *Which with and or but*) to modifying the rule cited above, and to demonstrating at length six methods by which faults involving *and which* may be cured. He also cites exceptions to the rule that he considered permissible. The reasoning is involved, however, and his general conclusion corresponds with the principle stated here. Partridge agrees with this principle, and it is observable that careful writing follows it. Often *and which* and *and who* are used where *which* or *who* or *and* alone would be smoother, as will be illustrated in' examples to follow.

In revising *Modern English Usage*, Sir Ernest Gowers retained Fowler's discussion almost verbatim, except for some subheadings. Margaret Nicholson's revision of Fowler, *A Dictionary of American-English Usage*, cut the discussion approximately in half, omitting the methods of cure. Curiously, neither Bernstein nor Fowler recognizes that *and (but) who* presents the same problem as *and (but) which*. In summary, it may be said that nearly all Fowler's examples are disagreeably involved or quaint to the modern ear, and would likely be stated today in ways that would not cause the *and which* problem to arise.

Flesch's prescription is to cross out *and* in *and which*,

and if this does not work, cross out *which*. He deals with *and who*, recommending that *and* be deleted.

The examples that follow are intended to present as simply as possible the problems likely to arise and the easiest means of solving them:

"Life has two strikes on children deserted by their parents and who never experience the love and home life adoptive parents can give them." Either *who have been deserted by their parents and never experience* or *who have been deserted . . . and who . . .*

"Production of European-type grapes, which are grown almost exclusively in California and Arizona, and which account for most of this year's crop . . ." This conforms with the rule but *and account for* would be simpler.

"Most men entering their eighty-ninth year and who have won wealth and fame might be content to sit back at ease." *who are entering . . . and have.*

"Fritz Weaver, who played Hamlet last summer, and who is one of the most versatile actors in the American theater, is shockingly believable as the haunted weakling." *summer and is one.*

"The Copts are a forgotten people but who made interesting contributions to art." *people, who made* or *people, although they made.*

**and/or.** Discouraged as a legalism with varying degrees of vehemence by Bernstein, Copperud, Flesch, Follett, Fowler, and American Heritage. Most of them point out that usually *or* would suffice when *and/or* is used.

**anent.** Denounced variously as quaint, pretentious, or heavily humorous by Bernstein, Copperud, Evans, Follett, and Fowler. Sometimes misspelled *annent*. Random House and Webster recognize it as standard for *concerning*.

**anesthesiologist, anesthetist.** The distinction is that the first is a physician trained in the specialty of administering anesthetics.

**angle.** Mildly criticized by Evans and Flesch when used as a noun in the sense *approach, point of view, position* ("He had a peculiar angle on the situation"), Evans saying it is overworked in journalism, and Flesch that it sounds slangy but has no entirely satisfactory substitute. Sir Ernest Gowers, however, in *The Complete Plain Words*, criticizes this usage for imprecision. Random House, Webster, and most desk dictionaries give *viewpoint, standpoint, point of view* as standard senses of *angle*. The conclusion may be drawn that this sense of *angle* is under a faint shadow that is fast disappearing.

**anoint.** Often mispelled *annoint*.

**another.** "Eighteen persons were summoned as witnesses, and another six were interrogated." This use of *another* is a favorite journalistic construction, sometimes criticized, as by Bernstein, on the ground that *another* means *one more of the same kind*, and that thus the sentence could not be correct unless the second number were the same as the first. Current dictionaries, however, all give one sense of *another* as an adjective as *different, distinct,* or *not the same,* which appears to invalidate the criticism. In many sentences of the kind cited, however, *another* is simply superfluous. See also OTHER.

**anticipate.** Criticized by Bernstein, Copperud, Flesch, and Fowler when it displaces *expect,* as in "Agricultural officials anticipate production will be about the same as last year" and "The principal anticipated normal attendance." *Anticipate,* in the strict view, has the sense of *preceding, forestalling, going before.* This cause appears lost, however, since all current dictionaries give *expect* as a synonym. Follett, curiously enough, considering his usual resistance to change, accepts *anticipate* for *look forward,* and so does American Heritage. Discriminating writing nevertheless continues to observe the distinction. Perhaps the best advice to anyone who wants to follow suit is that nearly always the word wanted is *expect,* and that if it fits, it should be used. *Anticipate* is seldom required, and when *expect* will do, *anticipate* sounds pretentious.

**anxious, eager.** Bernstein, Follett, and American Heritage hold that *anxious* connotes foreboding, and that it should not be used in the sense of *eager* in such sentences as "We are anxious to see the play." Evans and Fowler, however, say *anxious* for *eager* is fully established, and Random House and Webster regard this sense as standard. This is the consensus.

**any.** For *of any, than any* (*other*) see COMPARISON 1; see also THAN ANY, THAN ANYONE.

**any and all.** Trite and pompous (Bernstein, Copperud).

**anybody, anyone, etc.** *Anybody* is one word as a pronoun (Bernstein, Copperud, Fowler). References to *anybody, anyone, each, either, everybody, everyone, neither, nobody, no one, somebody,* and *someone,* all of which are technically singular, are nevertheless often in the plural (*they, them, their*) when the reference is indefinitely to both sexes: "Everybody shouldered their pack and moved on"; "Anyone who fails the examination can lose their license." Bryant, Evans, Flesch, and Webster find the plural reference acceptable; Bernstein, Copperud, Follett, Fowler, and American Heritage are indulgent toward it in speech and disapproving of it in writing. Random House calls it nonstandard. See also OF ANY, OF ANYONE; THAN ANY, THAN ANYONE; PLURAL AND SINGULAR; See ELSE for *anyone's else, anyone else's.*

**any more.** Misused in positive statements, like "They certainly have good television programs any more" and "One can get terribly discouraged by reading the newspapers any more." *Any more* properly requires a negative context or implication: "We hardly see her any more"; "They don't go there any more" (Bernstein, Bryant, Copperud, Evans). Bryant and other authorities say *any more* in a positive sense is standard in certain parts of the country, however. Preferably two words, though *anymore* is given by both American Heritage and Webster.

**anyone.** One word as a pronoun: "Any one of the crowd will testify" (adjective plus pronoun) vs. "Anyone may apply" (Bernstein, Copperud, Fowler, American Heritage). With *they, their, them,* see ANYBODY, ANYONE.

**any other.** See COMPARISON 1.

**anyplace.** Disapproved by Bernstein and Bryant as colloquial for *anywhere,* accepted by Fowler as a U.S. usage, and considered standard by Evans and Flesch. Among the dictionaries, Webster and American Heritage accept it as standard, but Random House calls it informal. Here, as in other instances when the authorities fall out, the writer may safely make his own decision.

**anyway, any way, anyways.** One word in the sense *regardless* ("We'll go anyway"); otherwise, in the sense *at any rate,* two words: "We did not understand him in any way" (Bernstein, Copperud, Fowler; American Heritage adds that the forms are interchangeable in the sense *in any manner:* "The books were scattered anyway [or *any way*] on the floor." *Anyways* for *anyway* is substandard (Bryant, Bernstein, Copperud, Evans, American Heritage, Random House, Webster).

**anywheres.** Substandard in writing (Bernstein, Bryant, Evans).

**Apostrophe.** See CONTRACTIONS; PLURAL AND SINGULAR; POSSESSIVES.

**appear.** Often ambiguous with an infinitive, and to be avoided in sentences like "The budget was approved after no one appeared to protest," which can be taken to mean either that no protesters appeared, or that statements made about the budget apparently were not protests.

**appendix, appendices, appendixes.** Either *appendices* (the Latin form) or *appendixes* is correct; in nontechnical contexts, *-ixes* probably predominates (Copperud, Evans, Fowler). Both unabridged dictionaries recognize both plural forms as standard.

**Appositives.** The distinction between restrictive appositives, which are not set off by commas, and nonrestrictive appositives, which are, is often neglected. An example: "He has been married to his wife Ethel for twenty-six years. Their daughter, Eve, is married to a Harvard man." Since Ethel was the only wife, the name should have been set off by commas. Setting off *Eve* by commas indicates she was the only daughter; "their daughter Eve is married . . ." would have indicated the existence of other daughters (Copperud, Evans). The distinction is similar to that between RESTRICTIVE AND NONRESTRICTIVE CLAUSES, which see. See also DANGLING MODIFIERS; MODIFIERS 1; FALSE TITLES.

**appraise, apprise.** Often confused. *Appraise* means *set a value on,* as "appraise a property"; *apprise* (usually with *of*) means *inform, tell,* or *notify,* as "apprise him of danger" and "apprise us of the circumstances." "I don't care to comment," the lawyer said, "until I have been appraised of the

conditions." *apprised.* (Copperud; the distinction is clear in definitions in both Random House and Webster.)

**appreciate.** Bernstein approves the sense *be grateful for,* which is given by American Heritage, Random House, and Webster; Evans considers it grudging and dishonest, and Flesch calls it overworked. Apparently this meaning is not used in Britain, for Fowler criticizes *appreciate* only as overdone for *understand* or *recognize* in business letters, especially with an indefinite subject: "It is appreciated that . . ." Follett has an ambiguous discussion that leaves it unclear whether he wants the original sense of *evaluate* preserved or is willing to accept *like, enjoy.* The consensus is that *be grateful for* is acceptable.

**approximately.** Criticized by Flesch as pretentious and by Follett as inappropriate for *about;* Fowler calls it the formal displacement of *about,* and adds that it connotes more precision. Webster gives *about* as a synonym. The consensus is that when *about* will do, it is preferable.

**apropos.** Takes *of,* or no preposition at all, not *to.* "This is apropos to the controversy." *of.* (Bernstein, Copperud, Evans, Fowler, American Heritage, Random House, Webster). Fowler warns against confusion of the term with *appropriate; apropos* means *pertinent, with reference to; appropriate* means *fitting.*

**apt, liable, likely.** *Apt* and *likely* are often used interchangeably in the sense *prone to:* "It's apt to be cold on the pier." Copperud and Evans recommend *apt* for the senses *fit* or *suited:* "His reply was sarcastic, but it was apt." All current dictionaries, however, including Webster and Random House, equate *apt* with *likely;* the consensus is that the words are interchangeable. *Liable* is often loosely used for *likely:* "At this rate, we are liable to win the award." But discriminating use generally applies *liable* only to what is undesirable: "An overheated radiator is liable to explode." Current dictionaries generally concur in this distinction, giving the sense *likely* as colloquial or informal. *Liable* is also used in the sense *exposed to legal action:* "If a stair is broken, the householder may be liable." Bernstein and Evans concur in these general distinctions; Fowler offers some additional ones reflecting British usage.

**Arab, Arabian, Arabic.** *Arab* pertains to Arabs, *Arabian* to Arabia, and *Arabic* to matters of language and writing (*Arabic numerals*). *Gum arabic* is an exception (Evans, Fowler).

**arbiter, arbitrator.** Fowler says the arbiter has absolute power, whereas the arbitrator is answerable for his decisions, but this is a British distinction. The terms are interchangeable in the U.S., as indicated by Random House and Webster, except that *arbitrator* is the usual one in labor disputes, and *arbiter* in other connections, e.g., fashions, philosophy, literature. See also ARBITRATE, MEDIATE.

**arbitrate, mediate.** An arbi-

trator's decision is binding; the mediator merely attempts to help disputants come to an agreement, and has no authority over them (Bernstein, Copperud). Evans describes *arbitrator* as if it meant *mediator.*

**Archaisms.** Evans, Fowler, and Flesch warn against the use of archaisms in ordinary contexts, especially by unpracticed writers. Some examples: *anent, aught, yclept, derring-do, howbeit, parlous, perchance, betwixt, quoth, spake, betimes, illume, forsooth.*

**arcing, arcking.** *Arcing* is the usual form for *traveling in an arc* ("The power was arcing across the lines"), but the conventions of English pronunciation make it seem as if it should be pronounced *arsing,* which is not only wrong but unseemly. Dictionaries give *arcking,* but this spelling is seldom seen. The answer to the problem may be *arching* in some contexts (Copperud, Bernstein, Fowler).

**area.** Criticized by Copperud, Flesch, and Follett as a vague fad word displacing *field, problem, issue,* or *question.* "But the whole area has been clouded with misunderstanding." *Area* in this and similar general senses where a more specific term is called for is pretentious and has become tiresome.

**aren't I.** See AIN'T.

**are to, am to.** See INFINITIVES 3.

**argot, jargon.** *Argot* is the language peculiar to a group, as for example thieves' cant; *jargon* was originally any unintelligible speech, but now the term is applied to a special vocabulary, for example of a profession, art, etc. The distinctions between these and related terms are detailed in Fowler under *Jargon*. The list includes *argot, cant, dialect, gibberish, idiom, jargon, lingo, lingua franca, parlance, patois, shop* (*talk*), *slang, vernacular*. A shorter discussion, covering *argot, jargon, lingo,* and *slang,* appears in Bernstein under the entry *Inside Talk*. Follett uses the term *educationese* to criticize what is sometimes called pedagese, and also takes up *argot* and *jargon* under those headings.

**arithmetical, geometrical.** Often inaccurately used with *progression* and *ratio*. An arithmetical progression is a sequence that grows by addition of the same quantity: 2,4,6,8, for example, in which the added quantity is 2. A geometrical progression grows by multiplication by the same quantity: for example, 2,4,8,16, in which the multiplier is 2 (Copperud, Fowler).

**aroma.** Bernstein and Evans warn that the term is properly applied only to what is pleasant, and should not displace *odor* or *smell* unless the writer intends to be facetious.

**around.** Bernstein criticizes *around* for *about* ("around three o'clock") as casual; Evans says the usage has been standard in the U.S. for seventy-five years. The Standard College Dictionary and American Heritage call this usage informal, and the American College and Webster's New World dictionaries designate it colloquial. Merriam-Webster and Random House equate *around* with *about*. The consensus is narrowly that *around* for *about* is not fully acceptable in formal contexts. See also ROUND.

**arrant, errant.** See ERRANT.

**Articles.** See A, AN; THE; APPOSITIVES.

**as.** The uses of *as,* both by itself and as part of phrases like *as of, as such, as to,* occupy considerable space in most dictionaries of usage. When such points are comparable, they have been dealt with in this book, but some considerations involving *as* and its combinations have been taken up by only one or another of the authors, and the reader is referred to the books compared for further details on the subject. Entries in this book, to be found in their alphabetical places (which means that the *as*-entries are not all together), are AS (PREP.), below; AS . . . AS, SO . . . AS, NOT SO . . . AS; AS VS. BECAUSE, SINCE; AS (SO) FAR AS; AS FOLLOWS; AS HOW; AS IF, AS THOUGH; AS IS, AS ARE; AS IS WELL KNOWN; AS VS. LIKE; AS LONG (FAR) AS, SO LONG (FAR) AS; AS OF; AS REGARDS; AS SUCH; AS THOUGH; AS TO; AS WELL AS; AS WITH.

**as (prep).** As a preposition, *as* is unnecessary after such verbs as *named, appointed, elected*: "He was appointed as vicar." *appointed vicar* (Copperud, Follett).

**as . . . as, so . . . as, not so . . . as.** The second of the pair *as . . . as* is sometimes carelessly omitted: "The critic said the play was as good or better than last season's hits." *as good as. So* is not necessarily required with a negative statement: "The moon is not so large as it was last night." *Not as large as* is equally correct. In a positive statement, *as . . . as* is preferable to *so . . . as:* "This leader is likely to run the show as (not *so*) long as he lives" (Bryant, Copperud, Evans, Follett, American Heritage). Bernstein and American Heritage hold that locutions like "His word was good as his bond" require *as good as;* Evans considers it acceptable to drop the first *as.*

**as vs. because, since (causal as).** *As* in the sense of *since* or *because* is avoided in careful writing; partly, perhaps, because sometimes it may be confused with the sense *during the time that,* but mostly because it grates on the well-tuned ear as unidiomatic. "As the door was locked, he turned and walked away" is ambiguous, for *as* may be understood as conveying either *during the time that the door was being locked* or *because the door was locked.* "Porter's design is called the Revised Springfield, as he made it while living in Springfield, Mass." *because* or *since.* (Copperud, American Heritage; Flesch concurs that this use of *as* is unidiomatic; Follett and Random House consider it weak; Fowler says the causal *as* is acceptable if it comes early in the sentence, but is unpleasant if it comes late. This apparently is British idiom; according to this reasoning, the first example in this entry would be acceptable and the second unacceptable.) Bryant says the causal *as* is infrequent but considers it standard, as do Evans and Webster. The consensus is that it is questionable usage.

**as everyone knows.** See OF COURSE.

**as (so) far as . . . is concerned.** It has become a journalistic mannerism, or perhaps inadvertency, to leave off *is* (or *are*) *concerned* from this construction: "Many of the nation's gridiron experts have nothing to say as far as candidates for the All-America squad." *are concerned* (Bernstein, Copperud, Fowler). Flesch and Fowler discourage the whole expression as an unnecessary inflation in such constructions as "The increase in price does not seem to have had any effect as far as the customers are concerned." *on the customers.* Those who have trouble filling out the *as far as . . .* construction might consider using *as for* or *as to* instead.

**as follows.** Always in the singular; never *as follow.* The idiom is inflexible even though a series of items succeeds: *The tools used by the mason are as follows: the trowel, the plumb line, the level, and the groover* (Copperud, Evans, Fowler, American Heritage).

**as for.** See AS TO.

**as good (as) or better.** See AS . . . AS.

**as how.** Considered substandard for *that* ("He explained as how the pump was broken") by Bernstein and Evans. Bernstein puts *being as how* and *seeing as how* in the same category.

**Asian, Asiatic.** Fowler says *Asiatic* has a derogatory connotation. American editors have settled on *Asian flu* in prefer-

ence to *Asiatic flu,* which was
sometimes used when the disease first appeared. Random
House and Webster agree that
*Asiatic* may be considered offensive.

**as if, as though.** Bernstein
and Fowler say they are interchangeable. Evans and Fowler
agree that they must be followed by the conditional form
of the verb in a statement contrary to fact: "The liquor tastes
as if it were (not *is* or *was*)
watered." Flesch flatly disagrees and cites a long list of examples, apparently from newspapers, using the indicative.
See also SUBJUNCTIVE; and
LIKE, AS 2 for the substitution
of *like* for *as if, as though.*

**as is, as are (than is, than
are), etc.** The device of making
a comparison by putting *as* or
*than* in front of a misplaced
verb is both artificial and unnecessary; "The defendant—as
did everyone in the courtroom
—knew the verdict was coming." Clumsy and unnatural.
*The defendant, like everyone
else in the courtroom* . . . "The
President is probably as popular as was his predecessor after
his first month in office." *as
his predecessor was after.* "Obviously the people of the United
States are as anxious as are the
people of Russia for peace and
friendship." Drop the second
*are* (Copperud). Fowler classifies this construction as a variety of inversion after relatives
and comparatives, and concludes that the straightforward,
uninverted version is preferable.

**as is well known.** See OF
COURSE.

**as long (far) as, so long as.**
Bryant finds the forms used

with about equal frequency:
"I have no objection as (so)
long as it's a step forward";
"As (so) far as he knew, the
matter was closed." Evans considers *as long as* unacceptable
for *since* in formal writing: "As
long as it is raining, we may as
well stay." Bryant, however,
cites reputable authors and pe-
riodicals in this use. *So long as*
also occurs, she finds, but less
often. Here too reputable
sources are cited for examples.

**as of.** The expression is sometimes criticized as a pomposity
or a legalism in constructions
like *as of the first of the month.*
Copperud, Flesch, and Follett
say it can easily be omitted or
avoided by using other prepositions; in the example, *on.* All
criticize *as of now,* variously
suggesting *now, right now, at
present* instead.

**as regards.** See REGARD.

**assaulted.** See ATTACK(ED).

**assay, essay.** Sometimes confused as verbs. To assay is to
analyze or evaluate; to essay is
to attempt (Copperud, Evans,
Fowler).

**assess.** Bernstein says the
word means *evaluate,* or *impose a levy upon,* and thus is
misused in the simple sense
*impose,* as in "A jail sentence
was assessed." This view is corroborated by the definitions in
Random House and Webster.

**assist, assistance.** Criticized
by Flesch and Fowler when
they displace *help.*

**associated with.** See AFFILI-
ATED WITH.

**as such.** Follett and Fowler
point out that the expression is
sometimes used meaninglessly:
"The horse, as such, played an

important role in the development of civilization." In these instances, there is no possibility that the thing modified by *as such* can be considered in any other role than its own. The test of its utility is to leave the expression out and decide whether anything is lost.

**assume, presume; assumption, presumption.** The first forms are tentative, the second more positive (Bernstein, Fowler).

**assure.** Takes an object: "The United States, the president assured, will always be willing to discuss the question." *assured the conference,* or whatever (Copperud, Random House, Webster).

**Asterisk.** Used to indicate a footnote; placed at the end of what is to be footnoted, and at the beginning of the footnote, though it is sometimes supposed that it should come at the beginning of the footnoted sentence. Often misleadingly used in advertising, merely to attract attention when there is no footnote (Copperud, Evans). Often misspelled *asterick,* as a consequence of mispronunciation. See also ELLIPSIS 6.

**as the crow flies.** Criticized by Bernstein and Evans as a cliché and an archaism.

**as though.** See AS IF, AS THOUGH.

**as to.** Bernstein, Follett, and Fowler say the phrase is useful to focus attention at the beginning of a sentence on some element that otherwise would have to be postponed: "As to Jones, his conduct was unexceptionable." Bernstein, Copperud, Flesch, Follett, and Fowler point out that *as to* is often superfluous: "There is some question as to who came in next." *As to whether* is perhaps the most frequent offender: "There was some question as to whether he had eaten dinner." *whether. As to* is also criticized for fuzzily displacing other prepositions, including *about* or *concerning* ("There was some doubt as to the proper pitch"); *of* ("peculiar ideas as to conduct"); *on* ("The children were lectured as to behavior"). Bryant concludes that *as to, as to whether,* and similar combinations are standard English even though they add nothing to the meaning.

Bernstein says it is a superstition that *as to* is preferable to *as for* in constructions like "As for me, I'm quitting." All this seems like much ado about (or as to) very little.

**astronomical.** Criticized by Copperud, Follett, and Fowler as overused and inappropriate to convey the idea of a large number: "The odds against detection in the act are astronomical." Dictionaries, however, give this sense as standard.

**as well as.** The connective does not change the number of the verb: "John as well as Jane was (not *were*) late for dinner" (Bernstein, Follett, American Heritage). See also WITH.

**as with.** See LIKE, etc., 3.

**at vs. in.** Bernstein, Copperud, and Fowler agree that there is no workable rule to govern the choice here in such expressions as *in (at) San Francisco, at (in) the Municipal Auditorium.* Often the prepositions are interchangeable, and when they are not, idiom rather than any definable principle controls the choice. Evans warns that such constructions as "Where is the ball at?" are ungrammatical because *at* requires an object and *where*, as an adverb, cannot serve. American Heritage points out that *where . . . from* is acceptable, but says that *where . . . at* and *where . . . to* are not. Evans and Fowler, together with Webster III, point out that *in* is usual to express the idea of containment (*traffic in the city*).

**at about.** Criticized by Bernstein, Copperud, and Follett as redundant for *about* ("At about 6 p.m."). Evans defends the phrase on the ground that *at* is often followed by *almost*, *nearly*, and *exactly*, and with Follett points out that sometimes *at about* is inescapable, as in "The meat was sold at about $2 a pound." Bryant concludes that *at about* is normal in informal contexts, even though *at* may be omitted without changing the sense, and compares it with *at almost, at around, at approximately,* and *at exactly.*

**athletic, -ics.** See -IC, -ICS.

**at present, at the present time.** The second is excessive for the first (Bernstein, Copperud) and both are excessive for *now.* Bernstein points out that any indication of time is often unnecessary in a sentence whose verb is in the present tense. See also PRESENTLY.

**at that.** In the sense *nevertheless, even so, notwithstanding* ("The car cost $5000 and did not run well at that") the expression is described by Fowler as a convenient idiom and given as standard by Webster. Sometimes confused with *with that* (*at that point, as a consequence, then*): "They told him he was not qualified for the job. With that (not *at that*) he jammed on his hat and left."

**at this point, etc.** Perhaps the newest of the pomposities is *at this point* (or *moment*) *in time*, which inexplicably displaces *now.* It is as if *at this particular point on the earth's surface* were to supplant *here.*

**atop.** Use of the word as a preposition is called journalese by Evans (*atop the mountain*), and other criticisms of this construction are occasionally heard. The disapproval apparently arises from the fact that this was once an American usage, not ordinarily heard in Britain. But no current dictionary questions *atop* as a preposition, not even the British Concise Oxford Dictionary.

**attack(ed).** A newspaper euphemism for *sexually assaulted:* "The woman's arm was broken, her ear cut off, and her cheek slashed, but she had not been attacked" (Copperud). Fowler has a similar example (under *Euphemism*) in which the word is *assaulted.*

**attorney, lawyer.** Bernstein, Copperud, and Evans point out that an attorney is not necessarily a lawyer, but merely one who has been authorized to act for another; that is, one who has been given power of attorney. Bernstein and Copperud agree that in the U.S. *attorney* is the genteel word for *lawyer,* the workaday term for one who is licensed to practice law. See also COUNCIL, etc.

**attorney general.** See GEN-ERAL.

**attractive.** Criticized by Copperud and Flesch as the catchall in journalism for *beautiful, lovely, handsome, pretty, comely, fair, good-looking,* and other descriptives for women.

**Attribution. 1.** Inversion in Attribution. Use of such forms as *said he, declared she, questioned Mr. Smith,* in place of *he said, she declared, Mr. Smith questioned,* is a tiresome device for gaining variety. H. W. Fowler said the writer who employs it makes a damning admission that he is afraid of boring his readers. Fowler's reviser, Sir Ernest Gowers, has decided that inversion with *said, replied,* or any other inconspicuous word is now unobjectionable, as long as the attribution comes at the beginning and not at the end of the sentence. Evans considers the normal order (*he said*) preferable.

**2.** Misleading Attribution. Some ill-advisedly chosen forms of attribution have the effect of associating the writer or the publication in which they appear with the statement being made. *Pointed out* implies that the statement is true: "The senator has an ugly record of broken promises, his opponent pointed out" (Bernstein, Copperud). So do *admitted, noted, conceded, explained,* and *cited the fact that.* Possessives carelessly used may have the same effect: "The couple were indicted as spies by a grand jury but have denied their guilt." *Their* convicts them; *denied guilt. According to* (like *said he believes*) may suggest doubt of credibility; apart from this,

it is a clumsy and overused displacement of *reported, announced, said.* Copperud and Flesch agree that *disclose* and *reveal* are appropriate only in reference to what has been concealed.

**3.** Excessive Attribution. In giving the substance of reports it seems superfluous to tack *the report said* or something of the kind onto every sentence unless the statements are questionable or damaging (Copperud, Evans).

**4.** Utterance by Proxy. The purported utterance of words by smiling, grimacing, frowning, laughing, and other methods is criticized by Copperud, Flesch, and Fowler: " 'Romance seems to be out of fashion these days,' he grimaced"; " 'I'd rather work from the neck up,' the actress smiled"; " 'This equipment is not included in the budget,' the auditor frowned." H. W. Fowler traced this idiosyncrasy back to Meredith, and cited examples of verbs used in attribution, including *husked, fluted, defended,* and *surrendered.* Without putting them in a different category, he also criticized some attributive verbs that come close to describing actual utterance, such as *scorned* and *denied.* Flesch cites *blushed, needled, dimpled, tch-tched, shrugged.* Writers who employ this trick should be aware that it is conspicuous and regarded by some critics as tiresome. The alternative is the normal *he said grimacing, she said smiling;* and *she said, frowning.*

**5.** Speech Tags. Copperud and Flesch criticize breaking into quotations awkwardly with the attribution, as in *"I," the producer said, "will not accept* *this responsibility." The producer said* fits comfortably at the end; the example also lays meaningless emphasis on *I*. See also SAY, SAID; QUOTATION; CLAIM; CONTEND; INSIST.

**audience.** Bernstein would restrict the word to listeners, in accordance with its derivation, or to those who are both listeners and spectators, as for example those attending a circus. Copperud and Evans allow *audience* to be applied to spectators alone. The distinction now may be pedantic because Random House, Webster, and most desk dictionaries give *listeners* and *spectators;* further blurring results from (correctly) applying *audience* to the readership of a book. The consensus overwhelmingly favors the broader application.

**audit.** Criticized by Bernstein when it displaces *listen* or *hear.* No dictionary recognizes this sense, though undeniably it appears in print.

**aught.** Criticized by Evans, Flesch, and Fowler as archaic in modern contexts and thus, perhaps, pretentious.

**augment, supplement.** Follett argues, with corroboration from Webster, that augmentation is the addition of more of the same thing; thus, rain may augment a stream, but, in contradiction to Random House, commissions may not augment a salary, but rather supplement it.

**au naturel.** Oftenest used in the sense *nude,* and sometimes misspelled *au natural.* The writer who resorts to foreign phrases is showing off and must take special care to get them right (Copperud, Follett).

**authentic vs. genuine.** Evans and Fowler concede that the words are often synonymous, but also offer examples of distinctive uses. No attempt will be made to strain the reader's powers of discrimination by citing these here. The most useful conclusion appears to spring from Fowler's comments that the distinction is artificial and by no means universally observed. When a distinction is necessary, the right form will probably come by instinct. No one would call a novel *genuine,* rather than *authentic,* to describe its fidelity to historical background, for example. Both Random House and Webster give *genuine* as a synonym of *authentic,* thus bearing out Fowler.

**author.** Disapproved as a verb ("He has authored several books") by Copperud, Follett, Flesch, and American Heritage. The usage is considered standard, however, by Random House and Webster.

**authoress.** See FEMININE FORMS.

**authoritative.** Sometimes misspelled *authoritive* or *authorative* (Copperud, Fowler).

**automation, mechanization.** Automation does not mean simply the substitution of machinery for hand labor; it refers, rather, to the automatic control of machines. A thermostatically controlled heating system is an example of automation; a mechanical coal stoker that does the job of a man is not. Dictionary definitions bear this out. Fowler complains that both *automate* and *automation* are barbarisms (that is, words improperly formed) but concedes it's too late now.

**avenge, revenge, vengeance.** Bernstein, Evans, Fowler, and American Heritage agree that in general *avenge* and *vengeance* have to do with justice, *revenge* with getting even.

**aver.** Objectionable as a variant of *say* (Bernstein, Copperud, Flesch).

**average, median, mean.** *Average* is sometimes loosely interchanged with *median* and *mean.* The average of a group of quantities is their sum divided by the number in the group; the average of 6, 10, 14, and 2 (which add up to 32) is 8 (32 divided by 4). The median of a set of quantities is the one above which and below which an equal number of quantities occur; if the median pay rate is $3.40, there are as many rates higher than $3.40 as lower. The mean, in ordinary use, is the midpoint; the mean temperature on a day when the maximum was 90 and the minimum 60 would be 75 (Bernstein, Copperud). In nonstatistical use, Evans says, *average* should not be used as a synonym for *common, ordinary, typical,* or *mean,* and adds that *common* or *ordinary man* should be used instead of *average man.* Bernstein and Follett, however, say *average* is commonly used to mean *ordinary* or *typical,* a judgment concurred in by all current dictionaries.

**averse.** See ADVERSE.

**avert, avoid vs. prevent.** *Avoid* sometimes usurps the place of *avert* or *prevent,* when *keep from happening* is the sense wanted. "The firemen fought to avoid flying sparks setting fire to neighboring roofs." *to prevent . . . from.* "No expedient could have avoided the flood after the dam broke." *averted, prevented.* *Avoid* has the sense of *sidestep* (Bernstein, Copperud). This view is borne out by dictionary definitions.

**aviatrix.** Now seldom used. See FEMININE FORMS.

**avoid.** See AVERT, AVOID VS. PREVENT.

**aw.** See AH, AW.

**away, way.** See WAY, AWAY.

**aweigh.** See UNDER WAY.

**awful(ly).** Through frequent use of *awful* to describe what is merely unpleasant or disagreeable, and of *awfully* for *very,* the words have been devalued from the original sense of *awe-inspiring* ("The weather is awful"; "We were awfully cold"), Bernstein, Copperud, Evans, Fowler, and Random House agree. Webster regards this use as standard, and Flesch finds it common in academic and literary prose. American Heritage does not even give the original sense. Other words have suffered a like fate, such as *dreadful(ly), terrible (-bly).*

**awhile, a while.** Often confused. *Awhile* is an adverb— "We loafed awhile"—and *a while* are article and noun— "We loafed for *a while.*" This makes *a while* wrong in the first example and *awhile* wrong in the second (Bernstein, Copperud, American Heritage, Random House). Flesch concludes that *awhile* for *a while* is establishing itself, and Evans admits that the confusion is widely reprobated but feels indulgent toward it. Webster regards the usage as standard. The consensus favors the distinction.

# B

**Back-formation.** The term, which appears occasionally in this book, is used to describe the formation of a word from what is mistakenly assumed to be its derivatives. Generally it applies to verbs formed from nouns: *donate* from *donation, diagnose* from *diagnosis, drowse* from *drowsy.* Such terms are objectionable only when new and recognizable as back-formations; many, like the examples given, have long since graduated into standard usage. The process is continuous, and usefulness is what wins them acceptance.

**background.** Criticized by Flesch and Fowler as pretentious for *origin, cause, reason, qualifications, history,* or some other more precise term.

**back of, in back of.** Discouraged by Bernstein, Copperud, and American Heritage in the sense of *behind;* Fowler regards *back of* as an Americanism. Bryant concludes that both forms have advanced from colloquialisms to informal standing in both speech and writing, but that *behind* is still preferred in formal prose. Webster considers *back of* colloquial and *in back of* standard; Random House calls both informal. Evans considers both standard. The consensus is that there is no serious objection to either form.

**bad off.** Considered standard, together with *badly off,* by Random House and Webster in such contexts as "The town isn't as bad off as many of us like to think in our bluer moments"; Copperud approves only *badly off.*

**bad, badly.** *Bad* as an adverb for *seriously, severely* ("He was beaten up bad"; "Her head ached bad") is described by Evans as often criticized, rejected by American Heritage, and considered informal by Random House and substandard by Webster. *Badly* for *very much (badly in need of repair)* is approved by American Heritage, Random House, and Webster. See also FEEL BAD, BADLY.

**bail, bale.** *Bail* means *to dip water out of* or *post a bond; bale* means to tie in a bundle. Boats and prisoners are bailed; hay is baled (Copperud, Evans), Fowler says that British usage prefers *bale* for dipping water and for jumping from an airplane; the American form for the latter sense is *bail (out).*

**balance.** Discouraged in the sense of *rest* or *remainder* in nonfiscal contexts ("The balance is silence") by Bernstein, Copperud, Evans, Follett, and Fowler. American Heritage discourages it too, though 53 per cent of its Usage Panel approved.

**balding.** Denounced by Bernstein as needless; considered useful and standard by Copperud and Flesch. A new word, to be found only in American Heritage (which specifically approves the usage), Webster, and the Standard College among current dictionaries.

**band, orchestra.** See ORCHESTRA, BAND.

**bank, banker.** Carelessly and improperly applied to savings and loan associations and their officials, which operate under different laws from banks. Savings and loan associations are very sensitive to the distinction, and in some states it is illegal to refer to them as banks. With respect to another sense, the left and right banks of a river are determined by imagining oneself as facing in the direction the water flows.

**banquet.** Highflown as used to describe present-day public dinners (Bernstein, Copperud, Evans).

**barbecue, barbeque.** Both forms are standard but the first is predominant and also closer to the generally assumed derivation, from the American-Spanish *barbacoa* (Random House, Webster).

**barbiturate.** Often misspelled *barbituate.*

**barely.** See HARDLY.

**bar sinister.** Evans and Fowler point out that the correct form of the heraldic term to denote illegitimacy is *bend* or *baton sinister,* not *bar.* Considering the widespread use of *bar,* however, Fowler regards correction of the term as pedantry; Evans recommends using *bastard* instead, advice not likely to be widely followed. Random House calls *bar sinister* erroneous for the heraldic designation; Webster describes the popular interpretation as suppositious. But both give one sense as an indication of illegitimate birth.

**basal, basic.** The original edition of Fowler pointed out that both words were relatively newly coined technical terms relating to botany, chemistry, and architecture, and recommended that *fundamental* be used in other connections. The revised Fowler, however, together with Bernstein and Evans, concedes that *basic* is probably here to stay and is preferable in most contexts to the clumsy *fundamental.* Evans restricts *basal* to technical connections (most commonly, *basal metabolism*); Random House agrees but Webster gives *basic* as a synonym of *basal.* See also ON THE BASIS OF; FUNDAMENTAL.

**based on.** See DANGLING MODIFIERS; ON THE BASIS OF.

**basically.** The correct form; *basicly,* though sometimes seen, remains unrecognized. *Accidently* and *incidently,* however, have found their way into Webster but not into Random House.

**base, bass.** Sometimes confused; perhaps because *bass* (*deep-toned*) is pronounced *base.* "The adventure had the nation all but wired to its communications systems, listening for the next base-voiced announcement." *Bass-,* unless the voice was ignoble. It's always *bass* in musical connections:

*basses, bass viol, bass clarinet, bass clef* (Copperud, Random House, Webster).

**basis.** See ON THE BASIS OF.

**bastion.** Bernstein says the term must be limited to a projection from a fortification, or a fortified outpost. Current dictionaries unanimously recognize a second general sense of *strong point* or *stronghold* or *fortified place* as exemplified by the common and figurative *bastion of democracy*.

**B.C.** See A.D.

**beauteous.** Decried by Flesch as an ugly, barbaric, unnecessary synonym for *beautiful*. The original Fowler described it as a poetic form suitable only for exalted contexts. Webster defines it as laying stress on sensual aspects of beauty; Random House considers it literary. The word has also been known to be regarded as having a derogatory tinge. When encountering it, the reader is probably aware that *beautiful* has been sidestepped, and is likely to assume that this has been done for a reason, perhaps to dilute the tribute.

**beauty.** The term has become popular in such constructions as "The beauty of the arrangement was that it was cheap," and Bernstein criticizes this use. Current dictionaries, however, give as standard senses of *beauty* "any very attractive feature," "a pleasing excellence," "the quality that pleases and gratifies." Webster cites "the beauty of this mathematical demonstration" and Random House has a corresponding example. The con-

sensus is that the extended sense, going beyond esthetics, is standard.

**because.** See AS VS. BECAUSE; REASON IS BECAUSE.

**become.** See GET.

**behalf.** Bernstein, Copperud, and American Heritage agree that in strict usage *on behalf* means *representing* or *as the agent of; in behalf* means *for the benefit* (or *advantage*) *of*. But the distinction has been blurred beyond recovery by indiscriminate use. It is preserved by Webster's New World and the American College Dictionary; the Standard College Dictionary says it tends to disappear in modern usage; Random House and Webster ignore the distinction, and so does British usage. The consensus appears to be that it is rapidly fading if it has not already been done in.

**being as how.** See AS HOW.

**believe.** See FEEL.

**belly.** Bernstein, Copperud, Evans, and Fowler agree that as applied to people *belly* is unexceptionable but shunned as vulgar, somehow. Bernstein holds that *stomach,* as the name of an internal organ, is an inexact substitute, but Random House, Webster, and all current desk dictionaries sanction it for *abdomen* or *belly* (though Webster's New World calls this application loose). Fowler is ready to admit *stomach* in this sense and Copperud does so. *Abdomen,* as used in place of *belly,* is somewhat technical or clinical (Bernstein, Copperud, Evans). *Tummy,* used by others than children, is deplored by Bernstein, Evans, and Fowler.

**benedict.** Society-page lingo, probably less used now than formerly, for *newly married man.* Strictly, it should be *benedick,* from the character in *Much Ado About Nothing* (Copperud, Evans, Fowler). But the consensus is that *benedict* is well established.

**berserk.** See AMUCK, BESERK.

**beseeched, besought.** Flesch prescribes *beseeched,* as the newer form, but this contradicts Evans, Fowler, and observable usage, which is all but invariably *besought.* Random House does not give *beseeched;* American Heritage and Webster give *besought* as predominant.

**beside, besides.** *Beside* means *at the side of:* "We stood beside the canyon." *Besides* means *in addition to:* "Besides the lecture there was a concert" (Bernstein, Copperud, Evans, Fowler).

**bet, betted.** Both forms are standard as the past tense for the word meaning *wager,* though *bet* tends to be preferred in the U.S. (Evans, Fowler, Random House; Webster considers them equal). Follett insists on *betted.*

**bête noire.** *Bête noir* is an error (Evans, Flesch, Fowler).

**betted.** See BET, BETTED.

**better** (stores, etc.) See ABSOLUTE COMPARATIVES.

**better.** The word has been frequently criticized in the sense of *more,* as *better than a week, better than fifty dollars.* This sense is recognized as standard by all current dictionaries, including the Concise Oxford. American Heritage, while recording this sense, reports that 69 per cent of its Usage Panel disapproved of it.

**better.** For *had better* (or *had best*)—"You better watch out"—described by Bryant and Webster as informal, by Evans as unacceptable in writing, and by Flesch as an incipient idiom. The consensus is that it is not open to serious criticism.

**between.** 1. vs. *among.* No one would use *among* with only two objects ("among you and me") but there is a misguided though prevalent idea that *between* cannot be correctly used with more than two: "Agreements were reached between six nations." The proper use of *between* does not depend on the number of objects but on whether they are being considered in pairs. Even this is open to question as an absolute rule, though Follett insists on it. The Oxford English Dictionary specifies that *between* may be used of relations between two or more things: "It is still the only word available to express the relation of a thing to many surrounding things severally and individually; *among* expresses a relation to them collectively and vaguely . . ." The foregoing comments summarize the views of Bernstein, Bryant, Copperud, Evans, Fowler, and American Heritage.

2. *Between you and I.* Considered questionable by Flesch, and wrong by Bernstein, Evans, Fowler and American Heritage; most of them concede that there are many (bad)

examples of the expression in literary classics.

3. *Between each, every.* Considered unacceptable by Bernstein, Copperud, Follett, Fowler, and American Heritage, and acceptable by Evans. Here, too, many classical authors are cited as having used the construction.

4. *Between . . . and, to, or.* *And,* not *to* or *or,* follows *between* in such constructions as "Reporters on Florida newspapers were receiving between $40 to $150 weekly." *and* (Copperud, Evans, Follett, Fowler).

**bi-.** In such expressions as *biennial(ly)* and especially *bimonthly* and *biweekly,* bi- has become ambiguous; the reader cannot be sure whether it means *every two* or *twice a.* It is safer to say *every two years* (*months, weeks*) or *twice a year* (*month, week,* etc.), or *semiannual(ly), semimonthly, semiweekly,* as appropriate (Bernstein, Copperud, Evans, Fowler; American Heritage holds that *bi-* means *every two,* but since 16 per cent of the panelists did not concur in this, the warning given here gains validity).

**bid.** The word has a number of senses; the one in which it is usually criticized is that of *try* or *attempt,* and this use is generally resorted to in newspaper headlines because of the need to save space: "Navy Flight Bids to Save Russian." Copperud recommends that this use be avoided when possible; Evans regards it as standard; Fowler regards it as headlinese. Current dictionaries, including American Heritage, all recognize *bid* as a noun in the sense

of *attempt* without restriction ("A bid to succeed"); only American Heritage recognizes it in this sense as a verb, as in the headline cited. The consensus is that *bid* for *try* as a verb is nonstandard.

In the sense of making an offer or a proposal, the form of the past and past participle is *bid;* in other senses, *bade* and *bidden.*

**bid in.** A technical term that means topping a bid on behalf of the owner of the property; sometimes mistakenly used as a synonym for *bid* (Bernstein, Copperud, Random House, Webster).

**billion.** All the more regrettably in these days when the term has come into such common use, it means different things in the United States, France, and Germany on the one hand, and Britain and its imitators in linguistic matters on the other. The American billion is a thousand million; the British, a million million. The American billion is the British milliard. The disparity persists throughout the names of other large numbers ending in *-illion: trillion, quadrillion, quintillion,* etc. Both systems are set forth in detail in a table accompanying the definition of *number* in Webster III (Copperud, Evans, Fowler).

**birthday anniversary.** Some stylebooks insist that one can have only one birthday—the day on which he was born—and that recurrences of this date must be his *birthday anniversary.* The idea is pedantry, unsupported by either dictionaries or usage.

**bit.** As used in such expressions as *the whole bit, the liberal bit,* meaning *an instance of behavior,* the term is rejected by Copperud and American Heritage, and labeled slang by the Standard College Dictionary, the only other book that gives the word in this sense.

**black.** An old term for *Negro,* in the past considered more or less derogatory. That connotation appears to have come from its use by whites, dating from the colonial era in Africa, to refer to native bearers and other servitors; at best, it was patronizing. Inexplicably, it was seized upon during the civil rights confrontations of the 1960s by many Negroes as the designation they preferred. At first, this preference was expressed mainly by militants, but later Negroes came to apply *black* more generally to themselves. Some of them demanded that the term be used by others, and pretended to see something derogatory in *Negro.* Before long, the term became a more or less neutral variant of *Negro,* and is now often to be seen in general use. Nevertheless, *Negro* remained the preferred form of reference among members of that race, according to a poll published by *Newsweek* on June 30, 1969. *Negroes* was the term liked most by 38% of the sampling; *colored people* was second, with 20%, and *blacks* a close third, with 19%. On the other hand, the terms liked least were *colored people* (31%) and *blacks* (25%).

**blacken acres.** The journalistic stereotype in reference to forest and brush fires; almost invariably used in place of *burn, burn over,* etc.

**blame for, on.** *Blame on* ("Don't blame it on him") is denounced as wrong by Bernstein and Fowler, and defended as standard by Copperud, Evans, Flesch, and American Heritage. Bryant finds that both forms occur in standard English with about equal frequency. The expression is extremely common in carefully edited writing, and few people are aware that a question of correctness arises here. Every current American dictionary cites the form *blame on* without qualification, and so the criticism of it must be dismissed as pedantry.

**blatant, flagrant.** Bernstein appears to conclude that *blatant* should be limited to connections involving noise, because of its derivation. Evans says the meaning *obtrusive* is a natural extension, a conclusion in which all current dictionaries concur. American Heritage, however, adds that *flagrant* connotes wrong or evil. *Blatant* is often used where *flagrant, offensive, rank, gross, glaring,* or other terms would be more exact.

**blaze, blazon.** Sometimes confused. A trail is blazed; *blazon* means to make public, proclaim, display prominently (Bernstein, Evans).

**blink (at).** "Democratic politicians aren't blinking at the fact that his popularity gives them a slight chance of recapturing the legislature." The idiom is *blink the fact,* not *blink at.* One blinks at a strong light; *not to blink* something undesirable (the usual form of the expression) means to take it into account (Copperud, Fowler, American Heritage, Random House, Webster).

**bloc, block.** The first spelling is preferred for the political alignment (Bernstein, Copperud, Evans, Random House, Webster).

**blond, blonde.** *Blonde* should be reserved for women; *blond* may be used of either sex. Fowler in the original recommended that *blond* should displace *blonde;* his reviser concludes that *blonde* is usual in reference to a woman. All current American dictionaries concur (Copperud, Evans, Flesch, Follett, Fowler). The consensus is that *blond* may apply to either sex, but *blonde* is applied only to women. These comments apply to *blond(e)* as a noun ("The shapely blonde in the front row of the chorus"; "Like most Swedes, he was a blond"). As an adjective ( *a blond girl; blond veneer*), *blond* is preferable for either sex, Evans, Flesch, and Follett agree; Fowler prefers *blonde* as applied to women. American Heritage, Random House, and Webster give the adjective form *blond* as predominant, though the first two acknowledge that *blonde* is often used of women ( *the blonde waitress*).

**boast.** Copperud questions the use of the word to mean *take pride in possession of,* in such statements as "Such clubs now number more than a thousand and boast assets in the millions." This sense is recognized as standard by American Heritage, Random House, and Webster; but 45 per cent of the

American Heritage panel disapproved of it.

**boat.** Bernstein, Copperud, and Evans agree that strictly speaking the term applies to a small craft. Restricting it to this sense is a naval fetish; it is established in reference to ocean liners, a usage Bernstein will permit in conversation but not in writing. Both Random House and Webster equate *boat* with *ship*. The consensus is that *boat* for *ship* is standard.

**bona fide, bona fides.** The first is the adjective, the second the noun, and it is singular, not plural: "Our *bona fides* was (not *were*) under suspicion" (Evans, Fowler, Random House, Webster).

**boost.** Criticized by Bernstein and Copperud in the sense *increase, raise: a boost in pay*. This sense is considered standard by both Random House and Webster, however.

**born, borne.** *Born* is sometimes used where *borne* is called for as the participle of the verb *bear* that means *carry* ( *the burdens were borne patiently*): "Helicopter-born commando troops were landed." *borne*. The reference to birth is always *born* except in such constructions as "She had borne four sons" or "Four sons were borne by her" (Copperud, Fowler).

**bosom(s).** A euphemism when used for *breasts* (Copperud, Evans, Follett).

**boss.** Described as colloquial by Evans, and as slang or colloquial by Bernstein in the sense *employer, supervisor, political leader*. Random House and Webster recognize it as standard, but most desk dictionaries designate it as informal or colloquial.

**both.** 1. Redundantly used. Since *both* indicates duality, it is redundant with such words as *equal, alike, agree, together:* "Both are equally deadly." *They are . . .* "Both appeared together." *They appeared . . .* "Both looked alike." *They looked alike.* "Both agreed." *They agreed. Both* is also redundant with *as well as;* in this instance, *both* should be omitted or *as well as* changed to *and* (Bernstein, Copperud, Follett, Fowler, American Heritage).
2. Placement with prepositions. *Both* is often misplaced before, instead of after, prepositions that govern the two elements it modifies: "Foreign policy, both under the present and preceding administrations." *under both* (Bernstein, Copperud, Follett, Fowler, American Heritage). However, *both under the present and under preceding administrations* (repeating the preposition) is correct.

**Brackets.** Brackets, [    ], should be differentiated from parentheses, ( ). The principal uses of brackets are to set off words inserted by someone other than the writer, and to indicate parenthetical material within parentheses. Parentheses are often referred to as brackets in common parlance, but this can create unnecessary confusion (Copperud, Evans).

**brand.** Bernstein is sharply critical of the term in a noncommercial sense, such as *kind, variety* ("His peculiar brand of humor"), and Evans is equivocal. Among current dictionaries, only Webster recognizes this sense, which is probably figurative.

**breach, breech.** Like *affect* and *effect,* often confused. In their commonest sense as nouns, a *breach* is a place that has been broken open (*a breach in the dike*), and a *breech* is the back end of a gun. As a verb, *breach* means *break open* (*breach a cask*). *Breech* as a verb has no current sense (Copperud, Evans).

**break, broke.** It has been seriously argued, usually by newspaper stylists, that "Mrs. Jones broke her arm" is improper and absurd unless she did so intentionally. This is good, unmistakable idiom, however, and recognized as standard by both Random House and Webster with the explicit example "He broke his leg." See also SUSTAIN.

**breakdown.** Bernstein objects to the term in the sense *analysis* or *itemization* ("a breakdown of the supplies on hand"), a view apparently borrowed from that captious critic of American English, Lord Conesford. Fowler, concurred with by Evans and Follett, warns that the term may sound ludicrous when used in the analytical sense concerning something that can be physically broken down (*the buildings were broken down by age and use*). He adds, however, that when this danger is avoided, the term is unexceptionable in the analytical sense. American Heritage, Random House, and Webster recognize it as standard.

**breakthrough.** Criticized by Bernstein and Fowler as overworked. Copperud points out that it is sometimes erroneously hyphenated or given as two words, *break through,* which is the proper form for the verb but not for the noun.

**break up.** In the sense *to be* (or *cause to be*) *overcome by laughter* ("His witticisms broke up the speaker"), considered slang by Copperud and American Heritage and standard by Random House. Webster does not give this sense, which appears to be theatrical cant that has newly percolated into general use.

**bring, take.** *Bring* indicates motion toward the speaker or agent, and *take* motion away from him. Webster's Dictionary of Synonyms cites as an illustration of their use: "a mother asks a boy setting out for school to *take* a note to the teacher and to *bring* home a reply." The words are often confused in these senses (Bernstein, Copperud, Evans, American Heritage).

**Britain, British.** See GREAT BRITAIN.

**Briticism.** In an entry retained intact from the original edition of 1926, Gowers' revision of Fowler (1965) complains that this term, which is often used in this book, is a barbarism, and that only the forms *Britannicism* or *Britishism* are acceptable. *Briticism* is considered primary and standard, however, by all dictionaries, including the British Concise Oxford Dictionary (1964). The term was, in fact, given as primary and standard in the British Oxford Universal Dictionary (like all the Oxford series, an abridgment of the great Oxford English Dictionary) in 1933.

**broadcast, broadcasted.** Bernstein, Copperud, Follett, and Fowler all prefer *broadcast* for the past tense, though both forms are correct. Evans regrets that "the broadcasters have now made *broadcasted* standard, but *broadcasted* is rarely heard or seen. See also *forecast, telecast.*

**brother, sister.** Fraternal cant in reference to members of an organization, and therefore unsuitable except among the members themselves, who have chosen to address or refer to each other in this way. This mannerism has been taken up by labor unions. Sometimes regarded by others as a simpleminded and hypocritical device (Copperud, Evans).

**brunet, brunette.** As with *blond, blonde,* the first was formerly the masculine form exclusively. *Brunet* is now sometimes applied to women. (Random House says the term is usually applied to a male, but Webster no longer recognizes a sex distinction.) *Brunette* continues in wider use than *blonde* and is the feminine form (Copperud, Follett).

**bug.** In the sense of *eavesdropping,* considered standard as a noun ("They found a bug behind the picture") and as a verb ("The agents bugged the hotel room") by American Heritage and slang by Random House and Webster.

**bugger.** Widely enough known in the sense of *sodomite* to be offensive in its alternate sense as a term of affection ("a cute little bugger"). *Bugger* as a verb ("bugger—or *bugger up* —the works"), meaning to confuse or frustrate, suffers from the unsavory associations of *bugger* in the sexual sense (Copperud, Evans).

**bulk.** See LARGELY.

**bulk of.** *Most of*, or something else, is generally preferable in nonphysical connections, when *bulk of* is inappropriate (Copperud, Evans, Fowler). Bernstein defends *bulk of* as preferable to *majority* when indefiniteness is indicated. In the press, *bulk of* has all but displaced the more natural *most of*.

**bullet, cartridge, shell, round.** *Bullet* is often loosely used for *cartridge*. The bullet is the lead missile that leaves the gun; the cartridge comprises both the shell containing the explosive charge and the bullet. *Cartridge* and *round* are interchangeable (Bernstein, Copperud). Random House and Webster, however, recognize *bullet* as the equivalent of *cartridge*. It may be concluded that this latter is general usage, and that the distinction is technical.

**burgeon.** Bernstein argues that the word can mean only *put forth buds;* Random House and Webster, however, also recognize the senses *flourish, expand, grow,* which it must be confessed are now predominant though probably newer. These senses were popularized by *Time* magazine. Flesch recognizes the sense *grow* but discourages *burgeon* as fancy in any sense. The American Heritage panelists narrowly (51 per cent) rejected *grow* but approved figurative applications of *put forth buds: his burgeoning talent.*

**burglarize.** Criticized by Evans as journalese and defended by Bernstein as economical and thus justified. Grudgingly accepted by Flesch. Considered standard by both Random House and Webster. Objections to the term are thus pedantry. See also -IZE, -ISE.

**burglary.** Means *breaking and entering.* One should distinguish between it and *robbery,* taking away by force or threat; *theft,* taking what belongs to someone else; and *holdup,* which is essentially the same as robbery but involves the use of a weapon. Under the common law, burglary is defined as forcible entry into a dwelling at night with intent to commit a felony. Thus the nouns *robber, burglar, thief* are not interchangeable (Bernstein, Copperud, Evans).

**burst, bust.** The past tense of *burst* is *burst:* "The water main burst last night" (Bryant, Evans). *Bust* as a verb is slang: "They busted the door down" (Bryant, Copperud, Evans, Fowler, Random House, though Webster considers it standard), but as a noun meaning *failure* ("The corporation was a bust") is standard (Bryant, Random House, Webster).

**bus.** As a verb in the sense *transport by bus*—"The children are being bussed (also *bused*) across town"—narrowly rejected for writing by American Heritage but considered standard by Random House and Webster.

**but.** 1. *But what, but that.* Bernstein disapproves of *but* *what* for *but that* ("I do not doubt but what society feels threatened by the homosexual"); Bryant finds *but what* standard usage for *but that,* and it is also so recognized by Webster. Copperud considers *but* excessive in *I do not doubt but that.* The question concerning *but that, but what* sometimes is directed at the fact that these locutions necessarily occur in sentences already containing negatives, and thus it is asked whether the use of *but* does not create a double negative. Evans says this double construction is established literary idiom. American Heritage rejects both versions. See also CANNOT (HELP) BUT; NOT . . . BUT.

**2.** *But however, but nevertheless.* Both expressions are redundant; use either *but, however,* or *nevertheless* alone (Bernstein, Copperud, Fowler, American Heritage).

**3.** *But* as Conjunction or Preposition. *But* may be regarded as either a preposition or a conjunction; the question arises when it is followed by a pronoun in such constructions as "They were all educated but (me, I)"; and "All but (us, we) received tickets." Bernstein and Fowler agree that either form of the pronoun may be considered technically correct. Evans and Follett consider *but* a preposition in such examples, which would call uniformly for *but me, but us.* Bernstein, following Webster, and concurred with by American Heritage, prescribes considering *but* as a preposition when the pronoun comes at the end of the sentence, and putting the pronoun in the same case as the word

it is linked with when it comes earlier ("All but we received tickets"; "From all but him came dissent"). The distinctions seem hairsplitting; instinct will probably lead most of us to the more agreeable choice here. The most famous occurrence of this locution undoubtedly is in Felicia Dorothy Hemans' poem *Casabianca,* in reference to the boy standing on the burning deck "whence all but he had fled." Early editions of *Bartlett's Familiar Quotations* carried a footnote saying, "The first American edition of Mrs. Hemans' *Poems* (1826) gave this line 'whence all but him had fled.' English editions and subsequent American editions seem evenly divided between 'but him' and 'but he.' The last edition published while Mrs. Hemans was still living and presumably approved the contents gives 'but he.' "

**4.** *But* Followed by Comma. As a conjunction, *but* (like other conjunctions) is often wrongly followed by a comma: "The wood was dry, but, the fire wouldn't light." The rule also applies when *but* begins the sentence: "But, there were some objections." Omit the commas. There is no reason, incidentally, why *but* (or any other conjunction) should not begin a sentence (Bryant, Copperud, Follett, Fowler). See also COMMA 8.

**5.** *But which.* See AND (BUT) WHICH, AND (BUT) WHO.

**6.** *Buts* in Succession. Copperud and Fowler warn against constructions like "But the storm continued through the night, but the river did not rise dangerously" (*The storm continued . . . but . . .*) in which *but* cannot do its job of indicating a contrast. Follett and Fowler also criticize the use of *but* when there is no contrast: "The snake was not venomous, but its bite did no serious harm." *venomous; its bite* . . .

**buy.** As a noun in the sense of *a bargain* (*It was a good buy*), described as informal by Bryant and as not standard by Evans. Copperud and Flesch consider it standard, as do American Heritage, Webster, and the Concise Oxford Dictionary; Random House calls it informal, and so does the Standard College Dictionary. Webster's New World and the American College Dictionary designate it colloquial. The consensus here appears to be that the term is well on the way to formal acceptance if it has not already arrived there. The use of *buy* as a noun for *purchase* (as distinguished from *bargain*), though sometimes questioned, is regarded as nonstandard only by Evans (*a sensible buy*). *Buy* for *accept* or *believe* ("I won't buy that idea") is slang, American Heritage, Random House, and Webster agree.

**by means of.** Usually redundant for *by* or some other preposition alone: "The fish were caught by means of a net." *in* or *with* (Bernstein, Copperud).

**by the same token.** See TOKEN.

# C

**cablegram.** Criticized by Bernstein as applied to messages sent from ships, which are necessarily radiograms (Random House and Webster concur); and by Fowler when used as a verb displacing *cable*.

**caesarian.** See CESAREAN.

**calculate.** Dialectal for *suppose, assume:* "I calculate it will rain" (Bernstein, Copperud, Evans, Follett, Fowler; Random House and Webster consider it a Northern regionalism).

**caliber, calibre.** Designations of caliber of pistols and rifles should be preceded by decimal points since they indicate hundredths of an inch (*.22 caliber; .45 caliber*). *Caliber* is the preferred spelling in the U.S., *calibre* in Britain (Copperud, Fowler).

**callous, callus.** The adjective is *callous,* the noun *callus: a callous attitude; a callus on the finger* (Bernstein, Copperud, Evans, Fowler, American Heritage). *Calloused* and *callused* as adjectives are interchangeable, according to Webster, the only authority that deals with this point, though here too the general distinction that only the *-ous* form indicates emotional insensitivity must apply.

**Calvary, cavalry.** Often ignorantly or carelessly confused. Calvary was the place of the crucifixion; cavalry are troops mounted on horses, a vanishing breed except for ceremonials (Copperud, Evans).

**came.** Criticized by Flesch and Fowler as an affectation in such constructions as *came the war, came the dawn.*

**campus.** Formerly reserved for colleges; now often applied to high schools, especially in the West (Copperud, American Heritage, Random House, Webster).

**can, may.** Bernstein holds that except in informal English *can* in the sense of *be able* should be used to indicate possibility. American Heritage holds to the strict usage of *can* for possibility, *may* for permission except in negative or interrogative statements, where *can't* is inconsistently preferred to *mayn't.* Bryant finds *can* is used to express permission on all levels, but that *may* is used in formal, written English. Copperud, Evans, and Flesch say *can* is interchangeable with *may.* The Standard College Dictionary says *can* is acceptable for *may* informally; the American College Dictionary and Webster's New World call this use colloquial; and Random House and Webster recognize it as standard though Random House says *may* is preferred in asking permission. The consensus favors *can* as standard for *may;* the authorities are unanimous that this use is informally acceptable.

**can but, cannot but, cannot help but.** *Cannot but* and the more usual *cannot help but* have been criticized on the ground that they contain a double negative (*but* plus *not*). Bernstein calls *cannot help but* the usual and acceptable form;

Bryant, citing a number of studies, says it has been used by cultivated writers for more than fifty years; Copperud says the prejudice against it is a superstition; Evans says it is preferred and irreproachable in the U.S., adding that a double negative is not actually formed; Flesch sees no reason why it should not be used; American Heritage approves both forms; Follett, however, disapproves of *cannot help but* as "a grammarless mixture," and Fowler calls it indefensible. The weight of authority overwhelmingly favors the legitimacy of *cannot help but.* Curme cites a number of quotations from literary classics where it occurs. Webster recognizes it as standard; Random House warns it is common but frowned on. *Can but* (= *can only*) and *cannot but* (= *cannot help*) sound literary and are unlikely to be used except by the self-conscious. Follett approves *cannot help* (doing, or whatever), *cannot but,* and *can but.* Those who are offended by *cannot help but* may write *cannot help* (*going,* or whatever, omitting *but*); Bryant finds this form more frequent in formal written English, and it has Fowler's approval too. See HELP.

**candelabra.** Technically the plural (of *candelabrum*). Its use as a singular is recognized by Copperud and Evans but disapproved by Fowler in a criticism picked up unchanged from the original 1926 edition. *Candelabra* as a singular (with the plural *candelabras*) is given by all current dictionaries, including the British Concise Oxford Dictionary.

**canine.** As a variant for *dog,* the term is called journalese by Copperud and discouraged by Evans and Flesch.

**cannibalize.** This term, in the sense *use as a source of spare parts,* was derided by Henry George Strauss, Baron Conesford, a captious critic of American prose, and subsequently defended by Copperud. Fowler regards it as felicitous, as indeed it is (the term originated in the Army). It is given without qualification in all current dictionaries, including the Concise Oxford.

**can't hardly.** Substandard (Bryant, Copperud). See also HARDLY.

**can't help but.** See CAN BUT, etc.

**can't seem.** The expression has often been criticized as illogical, but it is considered idiomatic and acceptable by Bryant (in standard conversational English), Bernstein, Evans, Flesch, American Heritage, and Webster.

**canvas, canvass.** Often confused. The heavy cloth is *canvas;* solicitation from door to door and the verb for doing so are *canvass.* Certain forms of the verb are especially liable to errors: *canvasses* (not *canvases*) *the neighborhood; canvassing the town* (Copperud, Evans, Fowler).

**capital, capitol.** The capital is the city, the capitol the building.

**Capitalization.** All the usage books being compared in this one have entries under this heading, some of them long and detailed. Apart from such conventions as are universally observed, as that sentences and proper names begin with capitals, there is a wild diversity of practice. Capitalization beyond this point is a matter of style or preference, not of right or wrong. Most publications have stylebooks setting forth the rules they follow. American dictionaries (but not the British Oxford dictionaries) indicate preferred capitalization. The writer who is uncertain of his own preference and not governed by a stylebook is advised to make a selection from among reference works or stylebooks to serve as his guide. A dictionary is likely to be most satisfactory for this purpose because it will cover the most ground. Even publications having their own stylebooks, after laying down general and special rules arising out of their own fields, are well advised to refer their staffs to a specified dictionary for instances not covered. The important thing is that consistency should be observed; inconsistency in this and other mechanical matters distracts and perhaps annoys and puzzles the reader. It may leave him with the impression that the writers and editors of the publication are careless or confused, and thus may create a general mistrust toward the content.

**caption.** Fowler (in the original) objected to the use of the term for a title or heading. Other critics have insisted it should apply only to the heading that stands above a picture, and not to the legend beneath. Universal usage even on publications, including newspapers (which, incidentally, are notoriously inexact in their own technical terminology), applies *caption* indifferently to headings and explanatory matter, regardless of position. Copperud and Follett, together with current dictionaries, including the new Concise Oxford, recognize this usage as standard. The insistence that a caption should be a heading arises from a mistaken idea that the word derives from *caput* (head); it comes instead from *capere* (take).

**carat, caret.** The first is the unit of weight for precious stones and metals, and the second the mark (∧) used to indicate an insertion in written or printed material. *Carat* is sometimes spelled *karat*.

**care less.** See COULDN'T CARE LESS.

**careen, career.** To *careen* is to *heel over, lean,* or *sway:* a sailboat careens. To *career* is to *move at high speed*; the word may also connote erratic movement (Bernstein). Fowler notes that Webster allows "lurch or toss from side to side" for *careen.* When *careen* is applied to automobiles it is difficult to establish the writer's intention; a wildly driven automobile does sway. American Heritage approves *careen* for fast and erratic movement regardless of swaying. Perhaps the best that can be said is that *career* does not suggest swaying or leaning. Follett regards *career* as having displaced *careen* in modern American usage.

**cartridge.** See BULLET.

**case.** The use of this word in various phrases was unforgettably ridiculed in the lecture "Interlude: On Jargon" by Sir

Arthur Quiller-Couch in *On the Art of Writing.* Somehow, these expressions seem immune to attack, which has come from all directions. We have *in case,* which displaces *if; in most cases* (*usually*); *if that were the case* (*if so*); *not the case* (*not so*); *in the case of* (which often may be omitted entirely, and if not, replaced by *concerning*); and *as in the case of* (*like*). "It is possible that this material may become mixed with clouds in some cases and produce rain sooner than otherwise would have been the case." Stripped of excrescences: "This material may become mixed with clouds and produce rain sooner" (Bernstein, Copperud, Evans, Flesch, Fowler). Follett concurs generally in these criticisms, but argues plausibly that *case* for *instance, the event of,* for example *in case of fire,* is idiomatic and beyond criticism.

**cast, caste.** The spelling is *cast* (*moral cast, cast of temperament*) in all senses except that of the social stratification in India, or something analogous, which is *caste* (Evans, Fowler).

**casualty.** Although the term originally meant only *accident,* the sense *victim* (of fighting, accident, etc.) is standard (Evans, Fowler, Random House, Webster).

**catastrophes.** Often erroneously *-phies.*

**catchup, catsup, ketchup.** Fowler calls *ketchup* the established spelling, and Evans says it predominates in the U.S., a conclusion that seems at least doubtful, since *catsup* is also common. *Catchup* is unusual, but all forms are recognized as correct.

category. Use of the term in other than scientific or philosophical connections, when *class* will do, is discouraged as pretentious by Bernstein, Copperud, Fowler, and Evans, though Evans concedes the sense *class* is now standard in the U.S.; both Random House and Webster concur.

Catholic. The term *Catholic* does not belong exclusively to Roman Catholics although spokesmen for their church have been known to insist that it does. There are several varieties of Catholics, and *Roman Catholic* should be used when differentiation is called for (Copperud, Fowler). Evans says, with good reason, that *Catholic* is always taken in the U.S. to mean *Roman Catholic*.

Caucasian. Evans (writing before the great civil rights crises of recent years) says the term is vulgar and offensive as a euphemism for *white*. Newspapers, often enthusiastic devotees of the long or technical term in spite of an avowed preference for simplicity, have seized upon *Caucasian*, though probably not as a euphemism. Whatever the reason, *white* is certainly to be encouraged in racial connections as the word everyone uses when not trying to put on airs.

cause is due to. Redundant ("The cause of the flood was due to heavy rain in the foothills"). Either *cause was heavy rain* or *the flood was due to*. See also DUE TO; REASON IS BECAUSE (Bernstein, Copperud, Fowler).

cavalry. See CALVARY, CAVALRY.

cease. Tends to be formal, pretentious, or poetic for *stop* (Copperud, Flesch, Fowler).

ceiling. Evans and Fowler complain that the term in its relatively new use designating the upper limit (*price ceilings*), as well as *floor*, tends to be overworked and sometimes figures in mixed metaphors.

celebrant, celebrator. Bernstein and Evans hold that the original distinctions of the words should be maintained: that *celebrant* should be reserved for one who takes part in a religious rite, and *celebrator* for one who celebrates in the sense of having a good time. Copperud acknowledges the difference but fears it is being done in by careless interchange of the terms, a view that is supported by current dictionary definitions. The Standard College Dictionary gives as the first sense of *celebrant* "One who participates in a celebration." Similar definitions are given by Webster, Random House, and the American College Dictionary; American Heritage approves *celebrant* for *celebrator* by a narrow margin. Webster's New World, however, holds to the distinction.

'cello, cello. The apostrophe is now unnecessary and old-fashioned (Copperud, Fowler).

cement, concrete. Technically, cement is the powder that is one of the ingredients of concrete, the finished product. Copperud says *cement* is interchangeable with *concrete* for the finished product (*cement sidewalks*); Evans grants this use colloquial standing. Dictionaries are not explicit on the distinction. Webster III, however, equates *cement* with *concrete.*

**censor, censure.** Often confused. To *censor* is to *prohibit* or *suppress;* to *censure* is to *disapprove* or *criticize strongly.* People may be *censured* but not *censored;* writings, speeches, and other forms of expression may be either *censored* (prohibited in whole or in part, or examined with a view to possible prohibition) or *censured* (condemned) (Copperud, Evans).

**center about, around.** These expressions, rather than *center on, in, at,* are declared wrong by Bernstein, Follett, Fowler, and American Heritage; Copperud and Flesch concede that they are illogical but regard them as established idiom. Webster cites *a hamlet that was centered around a church* and *centered around the political development,* among several other examples, and specifies that *center* as a verb is used with *in, at, upon, about,* or *around.* Random House calls all the questioned versions informal. The Concise Oxford gives as the definition of *center* "be concentrated *in, on, at, round, about.*" The consensus clearly accepts *center about, around.*

**Centuries.** These are confusingly designated by a number one higher than seems right at first glance; 1863 was in the nineteenth century, 1963 in the twentieth, etc. (Copperud, Fowler).

**ceremonial, ceremonious.** What is ceremonial pertains to a ceremony; what is ceremonious is marked by ceremony or ostentation (a ceremonious manner, tone of voice, gesture) (Bernstein, Copperud, Flesch, Fowler, American Heritage). Random House and Webster generally bear this out but give *ceremonial* as a synonym for *ceremonious.*

**cesarean, caesarean, etc.** The operation known as *cesarean section,* which effects delivery by cutting through the walls of the abdomen and uterus, is commonly supposed to have taken its name from the legend that Julius Caesar, like Macduff, "was from his mother's womb Untimely ripp'd," but this is disputed. It has also been held that the term comes from the Latin *caedere,* to cut. At any rate, the preferred spelling now, and the one generally used in medical circles, is *cesarean.* The terminations *-ean* and *-ian* are both acceptable, but *-ean* tends to be favored for the operation, and *-ian* for the adjective meaning *pertaining to Caesar* (*Caesarian ambition*). It has been the practice for some time not to capitalize the name of the operation however spelled (Copperud, Random House, Webster, though Random House gives *Caesarean* as the preferred form).

**chafe, chaff.** Sometimes confused. To *chaff* is to *tease good-naturedly;* to *chafe* is to *irritate,* literally or figuratively. A man's wrists might be chafed by handcuffs, or he might be chafed by chaffing. "The mayor was chaffing at his confinement in the hospital." *chafing. Chafe* rhymes with *safe* and *chaff* with *laugh* (Copperud, Evans).

**chain reaction.** A technical term often misused. Webster defines it as "a series of events so related to each other that each one initiates the succeeding one." Thus a flood of telephone calls to the police, prompted by an explosion, would not be a chain reaction, but merely a simple case of cause and effect (Bernstein, Copperud, Fowler).

**chair, chairman.** *Chair* as a verb is primarily journalese ("Mrs. Adams chaired the meeting") and is disapproved by Bernstein and Copperud, though American Heritage, Random House, and Webster give it as standard. *Chairman* is even more disagreeable in this use: "Smith chairmanned the meeting" (Copperud; but once again, the dictionaries approve).

**chaise longue.** The erroneous form for this term (French for *long chair*) has now been recognized by Random House and Webster: *chaise lounge.* The practical effect may not be as outrageous to precisians as it could be, since usually the term is clipped to *chaise* (Copperud and Evans accept the new form; Follett and American Heritage insist on the original).

**chaperon, chaperone.** Both spellings are correct and recognized by American dictionaries, but the first predominates (Bernstein, Evans); Fowler calls *chaperone* wrong, reflecting British usage.

**character.** Often used in phrases where it has a mushy effect: *the delicate character of the music* (*delicacy*); *activities of a public-spirited character* (*public-spirited activities*); *con-centration of an intermittent character* (*intermittent concentration*); "It is regrettable that an incident of this character (*an incident like this, of this kind*) has occurred" (Bernstein, Copperud, Flesch, Follett, Fowler). See also NATURE.

**charges.** See PLURAL AND SINGULAR.

**chastise.** Often misspelled *chastize* (Copperud, Fowler).

**check into, up on.** Legitimate and useful expressions. A critic cited as examples "He is kept busy checking into developments" and "She had asked someone to check into such rumors," saying *into* was unnecessary. But *check* without *into* would have been ambiguous, for *check* alone might have been understood in the sense *retard* (Copperud, Evans). Follett regards *check up on* as excessive for *check*, and Bernstein says *into, on, out, over,* and *up* are usually superfluous with *check.* There is no question here of general acceptability; all such combinations with *check* are considered standard by both Random House and Webster.

**chief justice.** The federal title is *chief justice of the United States* (not *of the Supreme Court*).

**childish, childlike.** As applied to adults, the first denotes the disagreeable, the second the appealing qualities of childhood (*a childlike trust*). *Childish* is not, however, invariably disparaging: *a childish treble* (Bernstein, Copperud, Evans, Fowler).

**Chinaman.** Considered derogatory; neutrally, *Chinese,*

which as a noun is both singular and plural: *A Chinese operated the laundry; numerous Chinese* (Bernstein, Copperud, American Heritage, Random House, Webster). Evans says *Chinaman* is accepted in Britain, but Fowler says no.

**chinchy, chintzy.** In the senses *cheap, unfashionable, chintzy* overwhelmingly predominates. *Chinchy* is not listed in the Wentworth and Flexner's Dictionary of American Slang; Random House and Webster give it as a Southern and Midwestern regionalism for *miserly, stingy;* in this sense, *chintzy* is regarded as a variant of *chinchy.*

**chord, cord.** Although these words have the same ancestor and both can mean *string, chord* in its commonest sense means a group of tones sounded together in a pattern. The folds in the throat that produce the sound of the voice are vocal *cords,* not *chords;* also spinal *cord* (not *chord*) (Bernstein, Copperud, Evans, Fowler).

**Christian name.** Evans and Fowler point out that the expression is not applicable to those of other than the Christian faith. Evans recommends instead *first name;* Fowler advocates *forename,* a form rarely used in the United States. *Given name* is perhaps at least as common as *first name* and also disposes of the objection to *Christian name.*

**chronic.** Means *long-continued, habitual;* misused in the sense *severe* (Evans, Fowler, Random House, Webster).

**circumstances.** Both *under* (and *in*) the *circumstances* are

correct. Fowler called the objection to *under* puerile; Bernstein, Copperud, Evans, and Flesch concur. Fowler refines matters by limiting *in* to statements of condition and *under* to situations affecting action, and Bernstein agrees.

**civilian.** Among dictionaries, only Webster recognizes the term as contrasting those not on military duty, and extends it to contrasting those who are not members of police or firefighting forces. Copperud says the use of *civilian* to contrast with those in any kind of uniform, as for example policemen, is questionable. Bernstein allows the extension to designate those not in police or fire forces, but protests further stretching. The consensus appears to be that any stretching beyond a contrast with the military is questionable.

**clad.** Criticized by Evans, Flesch, and Fowler as bookish and archaic for *clothed.* A favorite affectation of journalism. Flesch also objects to *unclad* as a euphemism for *nude,* which has been objected to as a euphemism for *naked.*

**claim.** Bernstein and Copperud object to the term in the sense *say* or *assert* ("He claims the weather is too cold"); Fowler goes a step farther and allows it in demanding belief for the improbable: "She claims to have heard a ghost." All three trace the loose use of *claim* for *say, assert, declare,* etc., to the press. Flesch is willing to allow *claim* in any of these senses, saying common usage does not recognize any distinction. The current dictionaries do not go much beyond Fowler in this instance; though some, like American Heritage, allow *claim* for *assert* (especially in a context indicating insistence or argument), none can be understood as loosely permitting it for *say* or its variants. See also ATTRIBUTION.

**classic, classical.** Copperud, Evans, Fowler, and American Heritage agree that the choice (when the reference is to the literature of Greece and Rome, and derivative senses) is a matter of idiom. *Classical* is usually acceptable even when *classic* is more idiomatic: *Classical works of ancient Rome.* But *classical* is necessary with *education, allusions.* The term for *outstandingly important* is *classic: a classic game of chess.*

**Clerical Titles.** See REVEREND.

**clew, clue.** *Clue* is preferred in the sense (*piece of evidence*) for which the forms are interchangeable (Copperud, Evans, Fowler).

**Clichés.** A dictionary definition of *cliché* is "a trite phrase; a hackneyed expression." This leaves wide open the question, trite or hackneyed to whom? Language is full of stock phrases, many of which are indispensable, or at least not replaceable without going the long way around. The expressions that draw scorn as clichés, however, are generally those that attempt a special effect —usually drama or humor. Whether a particular expression is regarded as a cliché depends on the discrimination of the regarder, and sometimes on the context. A good way to acquire an extensive and acute awareness of clichés is to read Frank Sullivan's reports from his cliché expert, Magnus Arbuthnot, as set down in such books as *A Pearl in Every Oyster, A Rock in Every Snowball,* and *The Night the Old Nostalgia Burned Down.* Every book on usage has an entry on the subject, some of which point out that the use of clichés is by no means the worst literary fault that can be committed, and that the conspicuous avoidance of a cliché can be worse than the cliché itself.

Since there is no limit to the number of clichés, and since what constitutes a cliché is to some extent a matter of opinion, no space has been wasted on collecting and exhibiting them in this book. Hundreds of them may be found as entries in Evans, and the subject is also explored in Fowler under the headings *Cliché, Battered Ornaments,* and *Hackneyed Phrases;* and in Follett under *Set Phrases.*

Ill-read and dull-witted writers will always be proud of having picked up expressions that the finer-grained despise. Even on the upper levels of ability, opinions will differ whether a particular expression is overworked. George Orwell once fiercely proposed that a writer should rigorously excise from his work every turn of phrase he did not invent himself. This may be going too far. Writing that contained nothing familiar or at least recognizable in this respect might leave the reader ill at ease. In any event, no writing exists that does not contain clichés by one standard or another. This state of affairs was once described in verse:

If you scorn what is trite

I warn you, go slow
For one man's cliché
Is another's *bon mot.*

*Cliché* is often redundantly qualified by *old, usual* (*the usual parting clichés*). Conceivably there are old and new clichés, but *old* is superfluous unless clichés are being differentiated on the basis of age. See also JOURNALESE, etc.

**client.** Best reserved for the customers of professionals, particularly lawyers, but not doctors, who have *patients* (Copperud, Evans, Flesch).

**climactic, climatic.** The first refers to a climax, the second to climate (Copperud, Evans).

**climate (of opinion, etc.).** The figurative extension of *climate* as in the phrase cited is considered acceptable by Evans but criticized by Fowler as a cliché and by Flesch as a fad. Random House and Webster both consider it standard.

**climax.** Bernstein insists, on the basis of the Greek derivation, that the term properly can mean only an ascending gradation, not the apex, acme, or culmination. This is a technical sense applicable to rhetoric. Evans and Fowler acknowledge that in popular use *climax* means *culmination,* a sense recognized as standard by every current dictionary, including the Concise Oxford.

**climb down.** Defended by Bernstein and Evans as standard despite criticism; recognized as standard also by every American dictionary and by the Concise Oxford Dictionary.

**close (closed) corporation.** Both forms are correct (Copperud, Random House, Webster).

**close proximity.** Redundant for *close, near, in proximity to* (Evans, Flesch).

**cloture.** Bernstein holds that the form is an affectation beside *closure,* and in defining the term Fowler uses only *closure.* Whatever the merits of this, journalists in the U.S. are addicted to *cloture,* which has the advantage of being distinctive and unmistakable in the parliamentary sense; both Random House and Webster give *cloture* as the primary form. Both forms are correct.

**clue.** See CLEW.

**coal oil.** See KEROSENE.

**cohort.** Criticized by Bernstein, Copperud, Evans, Follett, Flesch, and American Heritage in the sense of *colleague, associate,* or *companion.* In the Roman Army a cohort was one of the ten divisions of a legion, and in fastidious modern usage the word means a band of people. Follett says it is appropriate only for members of a large group engaged in a contest of some kind. All but the American College Dictionary now recognize the criticized usage, which indicates that popular acceptance is carrying the field. Flesch considers the term contemptuous, but there is no evidence for this. Those who have studied Latin are likely to be most critical of the new sense.

**Coined Titles.** See FALSE TITLES.

**collective.** The use of the adjective is ridiculed by Copperud as pretentious and meaningless in such contexts as the following: "The industry has its collective eye on Washington"; "Local experts merely cocked their collective eyebrow at the prediction"; "The committee seemed to have its tongue in its collective cheek." The last example is even more absurd than the others; how a collective cheek without a collective tongue? *Collective* in this sense means *shared by a group* (*the collective opinion of the faculty*). The misuse almost invariably applies to parts of the body, which it is preposterous to think of as being shared. No dictionary definition gives any warrant for the usage criticized here. The American Heritage panel was asked its opinion, but for some reason the verdict was not reported in the dictionary.

**Collective Nouns.** Terms like *couple, group, team, crowd, committee, class, jury,* and *herd* take either singular or plural verbs depending on how the writer regards them, and on logic: "A score were injured in the wreck"; "The crowd was dispersed"; "The crowd were waving their programs." Consistency should be observed in the selection of pronouns: don't use *their* after saying *The team is;* say *its* (Bernstein, Copperud, Follett, Fowler, American Heritage). Bryant and Evans concur in the basic principle affecting the choice of number. Ordinarily, nouns for organizations considered as an entity, like *company,* are referred to by *it,* not *they;* "The company redefined its (not *their*) policy on retirement." Sums of money, distances, and the like are logically considered singular, not plural: "The delinquency was $55 million, of which $44 million was (not *were*) owed by the Communist bloc"; "Twelve miles was (not *were*) covered the first day."

**collide, collision.** A *collision* must involve two moving objects; two objects described as *colliding* must both be in motion. A moving object, however, may be described as *colliding with* a stationary one: *the waves collide with the shore*; but not *the waves and the shore collide,* nor *there is a collision of waves and shore* (Bernstein, Copperud).

**Colloquialisms.** *Colloquial* means *characteristic of spoken* (rather than written) *expression.* Webster has been at pains to explain (in the introduction to the Second Edition) that *colloquial* is not a derogatory descriptive, and that terms so described are standard and acceptable. Nevertheless, there is no overcoming the stigma that has attached itself to the term. When it was in widest use, *colloquial* was counterpoised to *formal,* and though *formal* was not susceptible of precise definition as applied to writing, the inescapable implication was that what was colloquial was loose if not worse. As the result of this stigma, writers on language now tend to avoid *colloquial* as misleadingly pejorative. Webster III does not use the label *colloq.* nor any equivalent; the editors hold that what is colloquial is standard. Other dictionaries and works on usage have adopted such substitutes for *colloquial* as *informal, familiar, conversational, casual,* none of them entirely satisfactory. The confusion has been heightened by the fact that in the last generation written expression for all purposes has veered sharply toward the informal (Bernstein, Copperud); it is difficult today to identify a category of writing that would invariably fit the description *formal*, apart, perhaps, from legal documents and proclamations, both of which preserve the archaic, and neither of which is likely to be a satisfactory model for the writer of anything else. It may be useful to give here the definitions of *informal* as presented in the two principal dictionaries that use it as a status label. American Heritage says, "The label must not be taken to imply ignorant or inferior usage. It describes what has been called the 'cultivated colloquial,' that is, the speech of educated persons when they are more interested in what they are saying than in how they are saying it. Informal terms may, of course, appear also in writing when the flavor of speech is being sought." The foregoing appears in the introduction. The applicable definition in the lexicon runs, "Belonging to the usage of natural spoken language but considered inappropriate in certain cultural contexts, as in the standard written prose of ceremonial and official communications." (Presumably, once again, proclamations, legal documents, and government and academic prose.) Random House says of *informal*, "Suitable to or characteristic of casual, familiar, but educated speech or writing." The inescapable conclusion here is that what is informal is standard and acceptable in any context that is not deliberately

stiff. The interpretation of *colloquial* is further confused by the fact that no well-defined line can be drawn between colloquialisms and slang. *Colloquial* can no longer be contrasted with *literary;* contemporary literature is nothing if not colloquial. See also STANDARD.

**collusion.** Not to be confused with *cooperation, collaboration, concert,* all of which neutrally refer to joint action; *collusion* connotes a fraudulent or dishonest purpose (Copperud, Evans, Fowler).

**Colon.** The main uncertainty is whether a complete sentence following a colon should begin with a capital letter. Copperud and Flesch say no, Bernstein says yes, Evans says the writer may choose.

The colon is mistakenly used to introduce a series that immediately follows the verb: "Members of the committee are: Jane Doe, Oscar Zilch, Perry Moore, and Lucinda Knight."

**colossal.** Facetious use of the word in the senses *entertaining, delightful, terrible,* or as an intensive to indicate qualities other than size, is sharply criticized by Bernstein, Evans, and Fowler. This use was a fad now sharply on the wane.

**combine.** As a term for a combination of people or interests, may have a derogatory connotation and should be used with care (Bernstein, Copperud). Bryant discusses the term as standard and neutral in this sense, but concedes that it sometimes conveys the idea of intrigue.

**comic, comical.** Copperud and Fowler say the basic distinction is that what is comic is intentionally amusing, and that what is comical is amusing whether or not that is the intention. Both also concede, however, that the distinction is obscured by interchangeable use, and no sign of any such differentiation is to be found in any current dictionary. The terms are, in effect, synonyms; rhythm or idiom may govern the choice.

**comity.** Evans, Follett and Fowler point out that though the word means *courtesy,* it is often misused in the sense of *company, association, league, federation.* The *comity of nations* is a code of civilized conduct, not an association.

**Comma. 1.** Adverbs and Commas. The modern tendency is to use fewer commas, and it is encouraged by Bernstein, Copperud, Evans, Flesch, and Fowler. It is especially noticeable in the trend away from setting off adverbial modifiers: "We know that, in the individual man, consciousness grows." (Huxley). The tendency today would be not to set off *in the individual man.* The commas setting off the adverbs are also unnecessary and somewhat old-fashioned in these examples: "There[,] he ogles pretty girls"; "Finally[,] the president took action"; "In the machine shop[,] alone, 26 windows have been broken." Opinion is divided on setting off such adverbial elements as *of course, therefore,* and *however* (Bernstein, Copperud).

**2.** Adjectives and Commas. Commas are often also superfluously used to separate adjectives that apply cumulatively

rather than separately: *a hard[,] second look; a balky[,] old sultan; two[,] short, gloomy acts.* The test is whether the word *and* can be substituted for the comma; if not, the comma is excessive. There is a tendency, however, to leave out all commas from a series of adjectives: *a short exciting chase; a hot dusty road.* Commas are better omitted from such constructions entirely than used where they don't belong. See also 6, below.

**3.** One-Legged Comma. Elements that must be set off require two commas (unless they occur at the beginning or the end of the sentence). Often the comma is placed at one end of such an element but left off the other: "All New Orleans schools were closed as a precaution but the storm, *bringing winds of 64 miles per hour*[] passed the city without causing much damage"; "Dr. Manilo Brosio, *Italian ambassador to Britain*[] flew to Rome yesterday." The first is a participial phrase, the second an appositive; both must be set off. Some appositive constructions are ambiguous because they are faultily punctuated: "The publication will be edited by Dr. William Ney, conference secretary, and a member of the faculty." This implies two men will do the editing. One man: *Dr. William Ney, conference secretary and a member of the faculty.* "Severe storms[] accompanied by hailstones up to three-quarters of an inch in diameter, pounded western Texas"; "A 47-year-old man[] who had just been released from jail for drunkenness, was found burned to death beside a fire." These examples require two commas or none, depending on whether the writer regards the modifying clauses as nonrestrictive or restrictive (Copperud, Fowler).

"This, obviously[] was a planned diversionary movement." Once again, two commas or none, depending on whether it is desired to set *obviously* off. As explained under 1., the modern tendency is away from setting off single adverbs.

**4. Comma with Reflexives.** Commas setting off reflexives are excessive: "A few lawgivers, themselves, call it the biggest boondoggle in Washington history." *A few lawgivers themselves call . . .*

**5. False Linkage.** The comma is desirable between coordinate clauses unless they are very short, and even then clarity of sense should govern: "He was a man of action[] and words interested him less than deeds." The comma is necessary for ease of comprehension (Bernstein, Copperud, Fowler).

**6. Serial Comma.** Opinion is divided on whether the comma should be used before *and* in a series; the parade, led by newspapers, is turning away from it. Meticulous writing and editing preserves this comma; care in this matter is advocated by Copperud and Fowler; Bernstein and Evans consider the serial comma optional. Usually its absence does not affect meaning, but sometimes it does: "They had brown, green, gray and blue eyes." *Gray eyes and blue eyes* is meant, but *gray-and-blue* eyes may be understood without the comma.

**7.** Comma with Nouns of Address. The comma is necessary but is sometimes neglected: "Johnny says: 'I'd like to take photography Mr. Counselor.'" *photography, Mr. Counselor* (Bernstein, Copperud).

**8. Comma After Conjunctions.** Often seen, but superfluous, whether the conjunction starts a sentence or a clause: "So[,] I took him up on it"; "They have found it pays, and[,] we have too." But the comma is required after the conjunction to set off a parenthetical element (italicized): "They have found it pays, and, *I must admit,* we have too." Commas are oftenest unnecessarily used after *and, but, so, or* (Copperud, Fowler).

**9. Commas with Suspensive Modifiers.** These are desirable: "Ancient Ostia is near, but not on[] the sea."

**10. Qualifiers with *but*.** Need not be set off: "Notables from neighboring[,] but friendly[,] provinces."

**11. Comma with Dash.** This combination is old-fashioned: "They jar the ear of some,—the soul of others." Either mark alone should be used. If a dash is used to set off one end of a phrase, a dash (not a comma) should be used at the other end: "Hoses were played on the structure—a wooden frame building of three stories, from all angles, but smoke rose stubbornly." *stories—from* (Copperud, Evans). Fowler holds that a comma that would be used if the parenthetical phrase set off by dashes were not there should be used: "If we had seen him—whether or not he saw us—, things would have turned out differently." This usage is rare in the U.S., and even Fowler concedes that it is often regarded as fussy.

**12.** Separation of Subject and Verb. One of the commonest of errors: "A barefoot, tattered boy[,] leads two pet black goats down a concrete street"; "On July 5, she and eight other American students[,] set sail for Southampton" (Copperud, Fowler). A similar error separates modifiers from modified: *white, ragged, fluffy*[,] *clouds* (Evans).

**13.** Comma for Period or Semicolon. This fault is sometimes described as the comma splice: "German land investments have sent values rocketing in some areas, good farms of 200 acres now cost twice as much." *areas. Good . . .* or *areas; good . . .* (Bernstein, Copperud, Follett, Fowler).

Sometimes *and* is displaced by the comma: "Here visitors can get information about roads, weather conditions, sightseeing." This may be either an oversight or a stylistic mannerism, generally considered objectionable.

**Commandments.** Confusion and accusations of ignorance repeatedly arise from the fact that there are two ways of dividing Exodus 20:2–17 (and Deuteronomy 5:6–21) into sets of ten commandments. To Catholics and Lutherans, the sixth prohibits adultery and the seventh theft, while to most other denominations the seventh deals with adultery and the eighth with theft. The moral is that reference to a commandment by number alone is likely to be ambiguous and to generate arguments.

**commence.** Considered old-fashioned and inappropriate when it displaces *begin* or *start* (Copperud, Flesch, Fowler).

**commentate.** "Mrs. Jones will commentate [on] the fashions being shown." This does not mean *comment,* but *function as a commentator. Commentate* is a revival, rather than a neologism; the Oxford Universal Dictionary traces it back to 1859. American Heritage roundly rejects it. Among other current dictionaries, only Webster gives it.

**common.** See MUTUAL.

**communicate, communication.** *Communicate* is a new pomposity for *tell,* and *communication* is an old one for *letter* (Copperud, Flesch, Follett).

**Comparative, Absolute.** See ABSOLUTE COMPARATIVES.

**comparatively, relatively.** Use of these expressions in the senses *somewhat* or *fairly,* when no basis of comparison has been stated or implied (*It was a comparatively trivial matter;* comparative to what?), is criticized by Bernstein, Evans, and Fowler. *A comparatively few* is criticized by Copperud and Fowler as not standard; *a comparative few, comparatively few.*

**compare to, with.** *Compare to* means to state similarities; *compare with* to examine with a view to noting differences or similarities (Bernstein, Copperud, Evans, Follett, Fowler, American Heritage). Perrin notes, however, that in the common construction with the past tense, *with* and *to* are used indiscriminately. Current desk dictionaries note the distinction, but Random House and Webster do not. The consensus is that it still holds good.

**Comparison. 1.** Illogical Comparison. Expressions like "the longest bill of any bird"; "the worst storm of any last year"; "the smartest lawyer of anyone I know" are often criticized as illogical on the ground that *any* includes the thing compared in the group it is being compared with; American Heritage rejects them. Bryant, however, says that such forms date back to Chaucer and have been used by writers of such standing that they defy criticism and must be regarded as standard; Bernstein also approves of *any* here. Bryant finds that illogical comparison with the comparative, rather than the superlative, as in "He is more popular than any [other] financial writer in New York," is rare; Bernstein, Copperud, Perrin, and American Heritage recommend *any other*. See also FALSE COMPARISON.

**2.** Comparison of Adjectives. Strictly, forms like *better, richer, smarter* (comparative adjectives) are used for comparing two things, and *best, richest, smartest* (the superlative forms) are used for comparing three or more. This nicety tends to be disregarded, however, and the superlatives are used indifferently in both circumstances: *the best (smartest, richest) of the two*. Copperud (quoting C. C. Fries) and Evans defend this practice as standard; Bernstein and Fowler say that while it should normally be avoided there are admissible exceptions. Bryant finds it frequent in speech and in informal English, but rare in formal written English.

What may be called the suspended comparative, that is, one lacking a specified or clearly implied positive, is oftenest found in advertising: *the better stores, a more refreshing beer*. Sometimes it is a euphemism: *older homes* (instead of *old*). This usage is commented on by Copperud without judgment as a curiosity; Bryant calls it informal standard. See also ALL THAT.

**3.** Absolutes. *Perfect* and *unique* are often cited as terms incapable of comparison, and Bernstein and Follett so cite them. The expressions usually criticized are *more unique* and *most unique*, on the ground that what is unique is *sui generis*. Bryant finds such comparisons acceptable as informal English, while Copperud and Evans defend them as standard. Fowler and American Heritage will not allow *more, most,* or *less* with *unique*, but will allow *quite, almost, nearly, really, surely, perhaps, absolutely*. Webster accepts *more unique* and *most unique*, but Random House will not admit any comparison. The current desk dictionaries are divided on whether *rare, unusual* (which admit of comparison) are standard or informal senses of *unique*. The consensus is that *unique* is now comparable, at least in informal expression. See COLLOQUIAL; A, AN.

Fowler says, of the doctrine that *perfect* cannot be compared, that logic is an unsure guide to usage, and cites with approval *a more perfect character*, which seems flatly inconsistent with his judgment on *unique*. Bryant cites *a more perfect union* in the Constitution; Bernstein cites and flouts it.

*Complete* is also sometimes described as not comparable, but Bryant, Evans, and American Heritage permit comparison. American Heritage also approves comparison of *certain* and *equal,* which are sometimes considered absolutes.

4. Forms of Comparatives. Most monosyllables (like *loud, soon*) are compared by adding *-er, -est; loud, louder, loudest; soon, sooner, soonest. More loud* is not wrong; the form *louder* is preferable and predominant. Many disyllables are compared by adding *-er, -est,* but here there is more of a choice: *nobler, holiest, narrower; more noble, most holy, more narrow.* Longer words are seldom compared other than with *more, most. Beautifuler* is something a child still getting a grip on the language might say, but it would not ordinarily be written except by the unpracticed or the affected. Fowler cites such forms as examples of disagreeable stylistic tricks when they are used intentionally (*delicater, admirablest,* etc.).

These comments reduce the principles of comparison to their simplest form. More detailed rules may be found in Fowler under the heading *-er and -est, More,* and *Most,* and in Evans under the heading *Comparison of adjectives and adverbs.* These analyses, however, put one in mind of the rules governing English spelling: it is easier to learn to spell than to learn the rules. In general, the ear is the best guide to the formation of comparatives. When in doubt, use the form that sounds more agree-able, or agreeabler. Comparative forms are given in dictionaries. See also FALSE COMPARISON; ABSOLUTE COMPARATIVES.

**compendious, compendium.** Not all-embracing, as is commonly assumed; a compendium, or that which is compendious, is a brief compilation, list, summary, or outline (Bernstein, Copperud, Evans); the definitions in Random House and Webster concur.

**compensate.** In the sense *make up for* ("His tactlessness was compensated by his kindness"), approved by American Heritage and considered standard by Random House and Webster.

**competence, -cy.** Interchangeable in the U.S. in the sense of *ability,* though the first predominates, and Flesch finds it preferable. In Britain, according to Fowler, *competence* is favored for ability and *competency* for modest means; Random House and Webster equate them in the first sense.

**competent.** As used in criticism, the equivalent of ADEQUATE (which see).

**complacent, complaisant.** Sometimes confused; the first means *self-satisfied,* the second *eager to please* (Copperud, Evans, Fowler).

**complected.** An error for *complexioned,* as in *a dark-complected woman* (Bernstein, Copperud, Evans, Flesch); Webster reports it is not often in formal use; Random House does not label the term but, like American Heritage and Webster, regards it as irregularly formed.

**complement, compliment.** To complement is to complete or fill out; to compliment is to praise. "The jacket complements her ensemble"; "She was often complimented on her taste in clothes" (Copperud, Evans).

**complete.** For *more complete,* etc., see COMPARISON 3.

**complex.** For *fixed idea* or *obsession,* criticized as a misapplied technical term by Bernstein, Evans, and Fowler: a *complex about racing.* But Random House and Webster recognize this sense as standard.

**compose.** See COMPRISE.

**Compound Modifiers.** See HYPHENS.

**Compound Nouns.** See HYPHENS.

**Compound Verbs.** Divided, see ADVERBS.

**comprise.** The whole *comprises* the parts; thus *is comprised of* is wrong. "The district comprises three counties and part of a fourth," not "Three counties and part of a fourth comprise . . ." (Bernstein, Copperud, Evans, Follett, Fowler, American Heritage). By this reasoning *comprised of* should be *composed of* and parts that are said to be *comprising* the whole in fact *compose* it. Random House and Webster, however, allow the parts to comprise the whole—"Three counties comprise the district"—and Random House also allows *comprised of.* The consensus favors the principles first stated in this entry.

**concede.** See ATTRIBUTION.

**concept.** Criticized by Bernstein, Flesch, and Fowler as a fad for *idea, rule, plan, design, program,* etc. The basic sense is more or less technical, belonging to philosophy and science, and is that of an abstract idea generalized from particular instances. All current dictionaries, however, also recognize as standard one or more of the senses *thought, general notion, idea.* It is the fate of technical terms, if they catch the public fancy, to be enthusiastically taken up and distorted from their original senses, and then finally to be recognized as standard in the distorted senses. The process often generates indignation and sometimes outrage. See also NTH.

**concertize.** Sometimes aspersed by being classed with verbs unnecessarily created by affixing *-ize. Concertize* is entirely reputable, however, like many another established word in *-ize* (Copperud, Random House, Webster). See also -IZE, -ISE.

**conciseness, concision.** Synonyms, though *concision* is newer. Evans accepts both on equal terms; Fowler considers *concision* something of an affectation, and he and Follett reason that *concision* connotes the process of cutting down, *conciseness* the quality of being concise. Random House and Webster both equate *conciseness* and *concision* in the literary sense, and both also regard the sense *cutting up* or *off* or *down* as obsolete.

**conclave.** Bernstein holds, and most current dictionaries concur, that the term applies to a secret or private meeting, specifically that of the cardinals to elect a pope. Newspapers use *conclave* as a random variant for *convention* or *conference,* and this sense is recognized by Webster; Random House gives a similar sense as standard. The consensus, however, is heavily against this usage.

**concrete.** See CEMENT, CONCRETE.

**concretize.** Standard in the sense *make specific* (Copperud, Random House, Webster). Users of the term should be aware that it bears some of the same opprobrium as *finalize* (which see) and other new verbs in *-ize,* and will be disdained by many as gobbledygook.

**condemn, contemn.** *Contemn* is not a fancy synonym for *condemn,* as is sometimes assumed; it means treat with scorn or contempt (Evans, Random House, Webster). *Condemn* is close enough to *damn* so that the association should be kept in mind. The usual error is to use it as a synonym for *criticize* or *blame.* The writer of a letter of recommendation said, for example, that he did not believe the subject should be condemned for having changed jobs, and made his beneficiary cringe.

**condition.** Copperud criticizes the term as used in *heart condition, lung condition* as a faceless euphemism for *ailment, disease;* the criticism is common in newspaper circles. American Heritage and Webster sanction this sense as standard; American Heritage acknowledges the criticism of it; Random House does not recognize it.

**confess to.** Clumsy and not idiomatic for *confess:* "He confessed to an interest in the occult" (Copperud, Evans). But American Heritage, Random House, and Webster consider it standard. See also ADMIT, ADMIT TO.

**confidant, confidante.** Fowler says *confidant* is masculine; in the U.S., however, as pointed out by Evans and Flesch and confirmed by current dictionaries, though *confidante* is feminine, *confidant* is bisexual.

**congratulate, congratulations.** Almost always mispronounced *conGRADulate, conGRADulations* over the air and often elsewhere. The dictionaries unanimously give *conGRACHulate, conGRACHulations,* and this is the version used by educated talkers. Whatever the origin of the mispronunciation, it is comparatively new, dating perhaps from no later than the late 1950s. The error is so prevalent it might be expected to have given rise to the corresponding misspelling, but there is no sign of this.

**Congressional Medal of Honor.** A misnomer oftener applied than the correct designation (Medal of Honor) to the nation's highest military award.

**Conjunctions.** See the entry for the specific word (AND, BUT, etc.); COMMA.

**connection.** See IN CONNECTION WITH.

**connive.** Bernstein points out that the word is often misused to mean *conspire,* rather than *shut one's eyes at* (usually, an evil). This view is supported by three current desk dictionaries, though American Heritage, Random House, and

Webster also give *conspire, intrigue.*

**connote, denote.** What a word denotes is what it specifically means; what it connotes is what it suggests (Bernstein, Evans, Fowler). Follett discusses connotation at length under that heading.

**conscience'(s) sake.** See SAKE.

**consensus of opinion.** Redundant for *consensus,* which, incidentally, is often misspelled *concensus* (Bernstein, Copperud, Evans, Flesch, American Heritage.)

**consequential.** Rejected by American Heritage in the sense *important, significant* (*consequential findings by the grand jury*) but considered standard by Random House and Webster.

**conservative.** After earlier indignation, Fowler now grudgingly admits *conservative* in the sense *moderate* with such words as *estimate;* Evans defends it, and Flesch derides it. This sense, however, is specifically sanctioned by all current dictionaries.

**consider.** In the sense RE-GARD (which see), not idiomatic with *as:* "He was considered [as] a coward" (Copperud, Fowler, American Heritage). *Consider* implies deliberation, and is inappropriately used for *believe, think, feel, suppose;* it does not idiomatically have a clause as its object: "The general considers the art work is obscure" (omit *is*); "The office of public information does not consider that bias or distortion has been shown." *think, feel, believe,* etc. (Bernstein, Copperud).

**considerable.** Not standard for *considerably:* "He was considerable put out by the criticism" (Bryant, Copperud, Evans, American Heritage). American Heritage, Random House, and Webster all recognize *considerable* as a noun ("He has done considerable for the university"), though American Heritage and Random House consider this informal.

**consist in, of.** To *consist in* is to inhere or reside in: "The value of the advice consists in its honesty"; to *consist of* is to be made up, or composed, of: "The cake consists of flour, milk, eggs, and other ingredients" (Bernstein, Copperud, Evans, Fowler, Random House, Webster).

**consummate.** Loosely used by music critics; *consummate* as an adjective means *perfect,* and conveys the kind of praise that should be too seldom bestowed to give rise to the cliché that *consummate artistry* is (Bernstein, Copperud).

Society writers and others often mistake *consummate* for *perform* or *solemnize* as a verb, and write that a marriage was consummated. The term in this connection has to do with sexual intercourse, and is a legal consideration. *Consummate* is sometimes misspelled *consumate.*

**contact.** Still sometimes criticized as a verb for *get in touch with* ("I'll contact him"). Now considered fully acceptable by Bryant, Copperud, Evans, Flesch, Follett, and Fowler; Bernstein remains doubtful of it and American Heritage rejects it. Random House and Webster both recognize it as standard;

this is the overwhelming consensus.

**contagious, infectious.** Diseases that are contagious are transmissible by contact; those that are infectious are transmissible by organisms, and may or may not also be contagious (Bernstein). Evans says that in popular use the terms are interchangeable, but all dictionaries maintain the distinction and the Standard College Dictionary explains it.

**contemporary.** Bernstein, Follett, and Fowler say that the word can mean only existing at the same time, and thus a thing must be said to be contemporary with something else. This rules out applying the term to one thing alone (*a contemporary fashion*) in the sense *current, modern, of today.* This use, however, is widespread and clearly understood. Evans explicitly accepts it, and so do American Heritage, Random House, and Webster.

**contemptible, contemptuous.** These deserve to be told apart, as much as *infer* and *imply.* What is contemptible is deserving of contempt: *a contemptible evasion.* What is contemptuous expresses contempt: *a contemptuous smile* (Copperud, Evans, Fowler).

**contend.** See INSIST.

**continual, continuous.** Strictly speaking, *continual* means recurring at intervals and *continuous* means going on without interruption. The distinction is set forth by Bernstein, Evans, Follett, Fowler, and Random House. Copperud and Follett believe that careless interchange is destroying its usefulness, and Bryant, writing in

*Word Study,* has cited statistics to show that even literary writers are using the terms interchangeably. Most current dictionaries, including Webster, give one as the synonym of the other, but American Heritage and Random House maintain the distinction. The consensus is that the distinctiveness has been lost for any practical purpose. Writers who know the difference may carefully choose between the terms, but they will be wasting their effort since the difference will not be perceived by any but a small minority of readers. The writer who wants to be sure of conveying his meaning will do better to use *intermittent* than *continual* and *incessant* or *uninterrupted* than *continuous.*

**continue on.** Redundant for *continue* (Bernstein, Copperud).

**Contractions.** Contractions (*I'll, we've he'd, it's*) are sometimes aspersed, but their use is described as standard and as an aid to readability by Bryant, Copperud, and Flesch. Flesch says that words not contracted in speech should not be contracted in print (but gives no examples), and that an impression of stiffness may be given by writing *is he not* rather than the more natural *isn't he.* See also POESY. Fowler (under the heading *Elision*) takes a skeptical view of contractions, saying that while on the one hand they follow the pattern by which *es* became *'s* to form possessives, "the printing of these elided forms in serious prose will no doubt continue to grate on some old-fashioned ears." The consensus is that contractions, judiciously used, are desirable and in key with the generally informal tone of today's writing.

**contractual.** Sometimes misspelled *contractural* (Bernstein, Copperud).

**controversial.** ". . . we have changed the meaning of the word *controversial*. It now means something (or someone) about which we cannot afford to engage in controversy—virtually the opposite of the former meaning. Even for lawyers, controversy is made to sound like a disreputable thing, as this description suggests: 'His background has not prevented him from building a lucrative practice, mainly with respectable trade unions but with some controversial ones as clients.' "—Jacques Barzun, *The House of Intellect*. In a similar vein, Follett deplores the wide use of *controversial* to mean not, in its original sense, *engaging in controversy*, but rather *disapproved of* or *causing criticism*. Thus *a controversial figure* might be intended to mean merely one who arouses controversy or debate, not necessarily one who engages in controversy. Random House, however, gives *subject to controversy; debatable*, and Webster defines the term similarly. Considering this, and the fact that the word in the criticized sense is in such wide use, Follett's distinction seems useless and hairsplitting. See also NON-CONTROVERSIAL ISSUE.

**convince.** Bernstein, Copperud, Follett, and American Heritage hold that *convince* followed by the infinitive is unidiomatic; in this construction *convince* displaces *per-suade:* "The director of the museum had convinced Brancusi to part with the sculptures for a while." *persuaded;* or *convinced Brancusi that he should.* Flesch says *convince* with *to* is a new idiom, but neither Webster nor Random House recognizes it. The consensus overwhelmingly disapproves of *convince to.*

**cooperate, co-operate, coöperate.** Copperud, Evans, and Fowler recommend *cooperate;* this is also the preferred version of Random House and Webster. But the clipped version is preferably *co-op* (Evans, Fowler). See also DIACRITICAL MARKS.

**coordinate, co-ordinate, coördinate.** Copperud, Fowler, Random House, and Webster recommend *coordinate.*

**cop.** For *policeman*, the evaluations of this term in current dictionaries run the gamut from slang through informal to standard. In any event, *cop* cannot be considered formal. Opinions differ on whether the term is disparaging. Many newspapers ban it on the assumption that it is; others use it freely. The term is also in general use among policemen themselves, even though they sometimes object to its use by others.

**cope.** Until recently, *cope* was invariably used with *with* and an object in the sense *contend:* "He did his best to cope with the situation." Sometimes, however, it stands alone: "He was unable to cope," a construction that is recognized as standard by Copperud (but described as likely to be considered an error) and Webster and considered casual by Bernstein. Random House and three of the four current desk dictionaries give only *cope with;* American Heritage rejects *cope* without *with.* This is the consensus.

**cord.** See CHORD, CORD.

**corn.** The difference between British and American usage sometimes causes confusion. In the U.S. corn is Indian corn (or maize); in Britain it is wheat or oats (Copperud, Evans).

**corporal, corporeal.** The term is *corporal* (i.e., bodily) *punishment; corporeal* usually relates to the body in contradistinction to the spirit (Evans, Fowler).

**corps.** Pronounced *core;* singular and plural are identical. Sometimes ignorantly given *corp* in such designations as *Corps of Army Engineers* and *corps of cadets* (Copperud, Evans).

**couch.** For *say, express (the offer was couched in extravagant terms),* criticized as pretentious in ordinary contexts by Evans and Flesch.

**couldn't care less.** A vogue expression that has not only grown tiresome, but also apparently has fatigued some of its users to the point that they cannot get it all out, and end by reversing its sense. The distinguished chancellor of one of the country's leading universities said, for example, in a speech: "They use the word *obscene* to describe rat-bitten children in Chicago. They could care less about the striptease joints in the same city." *couldn't care less.*

**council, -sel, -cilor, -selor, consul.** A council is a governing or consultative body (*city council; council of elders*). *Counsel* is a noun meaning advice (*good counsel is often ignored*); the designation of one who advises (*the defendant was represented by counsel*—in this case, a lawyer); or a verb meaning *to advise (we were counseled to change our plans).* "He preached a council of moderation" is wrong; *counsel.* A modern consul is a government official who looks after commercial interests. *Councilor* and *counselor* may both be spelled with two *l*'s. A councilor is a member of a council, although sometimes the term is used as the title of an office without reference to a council. A counselor is one who counsels or gives advice; there are, among other varieties, investment counselors, camp counselors, and student counselors. *Counselor* is also a term of address applied, usually by judges in a courtroom, to a lawyer serving as counsel. Applied to a lawyer in other circumstances, it usually is jocular. A county council is a governing body; a county counsel is a legal adviser (Bernstein, Copperud, Evans, Follett, Fowler).

**couple.** In reference to people, preferably takes a plural verb: *The couple are* (not *is*) *honeymooning* (Bernstein, Copperud, Evans, American Heritage); Bryant says either singular or plural may be used with the word in this sense. See also COLLECTIVE NOUNS.

Copperud and Evans say the omission of *of* after *couple,* as in *a couple halfbacks, a couple rounds,* is not standard.

**course (in, during the course of).** Redundant for *during, at,* etc.: "During the course of the questioning." *during the ques-*

*tioning* (Bernstein, Copperud, Flesch). See also OF COURSE.

**court-martial.** Here the adjective stands in the unusual position after the noun, rather than before; a court-martial is a martial court. All authorities except Fowler agree that the term is hyphenated as both noun and verb. There is inconsistency among the authorities on formation of the plural. Bernstein, Copperud, American Heritage, and Random House prescribe *courts-martial* for the plural form, but *court-martials* is approved by Evans, Fowler, and Webster. Thus opinion is divided on the point, making it appear that either form is at least acceptable. See also GENERAL for titles formed with it.

**Court of St. James's.** The strictly correct form for the place to which ambassadors to Great Britain are accredited; knowledge of this and of the spelling *restaurateur* (rather than *restauranteur*) was for many years what marked the distinction between cubs and more experienced reporters on such American newspapers as attempted any discriminations. Evans and Random House say that now, however, *Court of St. James* is acceptable. But American Heritage gives only *James's.*

**cowardly.** Evans and Fowler criticize the term as applied to acts where fear is not present, and where *bullying, arrogant, overbearing, cruel, mean, unsportsmanlike,* etc., would be more appropriate.

**crack.** Worn out and journalese as applied to trains, regiments, divisions, etc. (Copperud). Fowler notes the term without aspersion. As a clipped form of *wisecrack,* see QUIP.

**craft.** As a verb for *make, design, produce,* etc. ("We proudly craft every cabinet"; "Two plays were crafted by Mr. Halley"), *craft* is considered superfluous by Bernstein and Follett but is regarded as established beyond cavil by Copperud, who points out that this is a revival, not a new invention. Most desk dictionaries do not yet contain *craft* as a verb, but it is given as standard in both Random House and Webster. *Craft* is both singular and plural in reference to a plane or boat, though *crafts* is also correct; in reference to a skill, the plural is *crafts* (Bernstein, Copperud, Evans).

**crass.** Bernstein points out that the word is often misused. His examples and observed usage indicate that what the writers often have in mind is *cheap, mercenary, greedy.* There is no warrant for this; dictionaries are agreed that the meaning is *stupid, coarse, thick, obtuse.*

**credit.** Bernstein and Evans hold that *credit* is improperly used in the sense of *attribute* in connection with unfavorable or discreditable things. Current dictionaries corroborate this opinion.

**credulous, credible, creditable.** Both *credulous* and *credible* have to do with belief; *credulous* applies always to people, and means *willing to believe.* It generally connotes simplemindedness. *Credible* means *believable, worthy of belief,* and applies usually to statements and the like, though it may apply to people: *The explanation was credible; a credible witness.*

*Creditable* may be synonymous with *credible,* but it also has the more usual sense of *worthy of credit, suitable, acceptable:* "The orchestra gave a creditable performance." In such contexts, *creditable* is the faint praise that, like *adequate* and *competent,* damns (Copperud, Evans).

**criterion, criterions, criteria.** *Criterions* is acceptable as the plural; so is *criteria,* the original Latin form. *Criteria* should not be used in the singular: "This is the criteria that has been set up." *criterion* (Bernstein, Copperud, Evans, Follett, American Heritage).

**critique.** Criticized by Evans, Flesch, and Fowler as pretentious for *criticism, review, notice.*

**crochet, crotchet, crotchety.** *Crochet* (cro-SHAY) is needlework; a *crotchet* (CROT-chet) is a quirk. *Crotchety* (cranky) is often misspelled *crochety* (Copperud, Evans).

**crumby, crummy.** The slang term meaning *shoddy* is *crummy;* inconsistently, a fellow held in low esteem is a *crumb* (Copperud, Evans, Random House; American Heritage and Webster give both forms but indicate *crummy* predominates).

**cultured, cultivated.** *Cultured* for *cultivated,* in the sense of *educated, civilized,* has fallen under a shadow, somewhat like *refined* in the senses *educated* and *well-bred.* Fowler would like to see *cultured* retained in this sense, but speculates that the word has been tainted by association with *kultur* as it connotes militarism, race-arrogance and imperialism. He might have added that *culture* and *cultured* may have suffered by their association in recent years with the heavy-handed conceptions of culture exhibited by Communist countries.

**cum.** (Latin for *with.*) The use of this expression in English contexts (*the vagaries of want-cum-debt creation; education-cum-football*) is criticized by Copperud and Flesch as pretentious.

**cumulative.** See ACCUMULATIVE, CUMULATIVE.

**cupfuls, cupsful.** See -FUL.

**currently.** See PRESENTLY.

**cut in half.** There have been bitter protests against the phrase (and its analogues, *saw, break,* etc., *in half*) vs. *cut in halves* or *cut in two* but it is well established and standard (Bernstein, Copperud, Random House, Webster).

# D

**dame.** The title is analogous to *sir* (which see) and thus may not be properly used with the last name alone (*Dame Sybil Reagan* or *Dame Sybil;* never *Dame Reagan*).

**Dangling Modifiers.** This fault oftenest takes the form of a dangling participle, of which the following are examples: "Applying the brakes, the car skidded off the road"; "Born of a poor but proud Catholic family, few would have predicted greatness for young Konrad"; "Turning the corner, a church steeple appeared." With some exceptions, which will be noted, modern grammatical convention leads the reader to expect that participles like *applying, born,* and *turning* in the examples will modify the subject of the main clause. This makes it appear that the car applied its own brakes, that few (rather than Konrad) were born of that Catholic family, and that the steeple turned the corner. In honesty it must be said that readers are seldom actually misled by this error, unless the confusion is in the identity of people. Readers instead are usually brought up short, and caused to hesitate while they match the modifier with the modified, a job the writer should have done for them. Bernstein, Copperud, Follett, Fowler, Flesch, and American Heritage are critical of this construction when there is actual ambiguity. The best and most circumstantial discussion of the problem appears in Fowler under *Unattached Participles;* Follett also deals with it at length under *Danglers.* Bryant finds that the construction has been used for centuries in cultivated English, and adds that *when the meaning is unambiguous* (emphasis added) it is informal standard usage. Evans contains a discussion that is essentially an attack on critics of the dangling participle, but concludes with a restatement of the rule against it, restricted to ambiguous examples.

As pointed out by Bernstein, Bryant, Evans, American Heritage, and in most detail by Follett and Fowler, certain participles in this position have become prepositions or conjunctions and are not open to criticism. Some examples: *"Considering* the polls, voters are likely to turn out in force"; *"Speaking* of lions, this beast was a bad-tempered specimen"; *"Barring* objections, the measure should pass"; *"Granting* good faith, a contract will be signed." Some others: *failing, allowing for, generally speaking, provided, owing to, assuming.* It would be impossible to make up a complete list. The essential point is that participial constructions based on these words are felt as applying to the whole of the clause that follows, and not just to its subject. Whether the writer senses this depends on his discrimination.

Dangling participles are less obvious and less objectionable when the subject of the clause that follows is indefinite (like *there* or *it*): "Reading recent speeches of Albanian officials, it is clear they embrace the full Communist line." Nonetheless such sentences can be improved (Copperud). Evans in effect also covers this exception by citing unattached participles intended to apply generally.

Bernstein, Copperud, and Follett point out that appositives also are often danglers: "Until recently a resident of San Carlos, Peaches' real name is Mrs. Ralph Willson" (it is not her name that was the resident); "A devout, old-fashioned Moslem, his concubines are numbered by the hundreds" (it is not the concubines who are intended to be described as a devout, old-fashioned Moslem).

Adjectives may be similarly misplaced: "Tiny and slender, Yuomi's straight hair is clipped close in the trademark of a nurse" (her hair is not tiny and slender); "Now forty-four years old, his assignments have taken him around the world" (his assignments are not, it is to be hoped, forty-four years old). Gay and Skillin, in *Words Into Type*, offer a helpful test for a dangling modifier, namely, placing it after the subject, which makes its inappropriateness instantly evident: "His assignments, now forty-four years old, have . . ."

**Dangling Participle.** See DANGLING MODIFIERS.

**Dash.** Dashes serve usually to mark a sharp break in the train of thought in a sentence, or to set off a parenthetical element. Bernstein and Flesch cite examples of excessive use of dashes, or of dashes where commas would be preferable. These objections may be most simply summarized by advising that no more than a pair of related dashes (setting off either end of a phrase) be used in a single sentence, and that commas be considered before dashes are used.

Bernstein and Copperud point out that dashes tend to be misplaced: "This minister is giving too big—and too profitable a role—to private industry."—*and too profitable—a role* . . .

"Although Scranton is still a depressed area because of the continuing decline in anthracite coal mining—such projects have provided more than 100,-000 new jobs." The comma is better than the dash, which creates too sharp a break here.

A common error is to place a dash at one end of a parenthetical element and a comma at the other: "Then—with his appeal matured by further experience, he will be ready for the national prize." Either *Then, with . . . experience, he* or *Then—with . . . experience—he.*

Fowler says the comma or any other punctuation that would be required after a second dash if dashes were not present should be used. This may be British practice, but Bernstein, Copperud, Evans, and American Heritage point out that in the U.S. it is considered superfluous to combine any other punctuation with the dash.

The dash is properly formed on the typewriter by striking the hyphen twice, with spaces neither between the hyphens nor at either end of the dash. A floating hyphen (one with a space at either side) makes an ambiguous and unsatisfactory dash, and may be misunderstood by a typesetter. See also HYPHEN 9.

**dastardly.** Bernstein, Evans, Fowler, and American Heritage point out that the word means *cowardly* (which see), and is often misused to describe acts that require courage though they may be mean or vicious. Nevertheless, Random House gives "meanly base" and Webster gives "insidiously or despicably mean." Flesch considers the term, even though correctly used, old-fashioned for *cowardly,* and the comment seems valid.

**data, datum.** *Data* with a singular verb ("The data is

unreliable") is disapproved by Bernstein, Follett, and Fowler and considered acceptable by Bryant, Copperud, Evans, and Flesch. The American Heritage panel divided equally on this point. (Technically, *data* is a Latin plural of which *datum,* a rarely used term, is the singular.) Fowler, incidentally, recognizes that *data* is often considered a singular in the U.S. Three of four current desk dictionaries, as well as Random House and Webster, explicitly recognize *data* as a singular, and so the consensus is heavily on this side. *Data,* of course, is still also correct as a plural ("These data are unreliable").

**daylight saving, savings.** The first is correct; see SAVING, SAVINGS.

**de, du, la, le, van, von, zu, etc.** It is common practice to lowercase such particles when they occur within a name (*Charles de Gaulle*) but to capitalize them when they stand first (*De Gaulle, Von Hohenzollern*). This is a matter of mechanical style, however, in which consistency is what counts.

**dear.** Campaigns have been mounted against the use of *dear* in the salutations of letters, especially those addressed to people with whom the writer is not on familiar terms or may dislike. *Dear* in a salutation, however, is simply an impersonal formality. *My dear* (with a name) is more formal than *dear* (Copperud, Evans).

**debut.** As a verb, *debut* is regarded by some as slangy, but is considered standard by both Random House and Webster. "The automobile industry debuts its new models in the fall"; "Prohibition debuted last week south of the border." The American Heritage panel almost unanimously rejected it.

**Decimals.** The form *.24 of an inch* (of rain, for example) is preferable to *.24 inches* as less liable to both misinterpretation and typographical error. The form *24 hundredths of an inch* is even less so. See also FRACTIONS.

**decimate.** Although the term originally meant (in Latin) to strike down every tenth man by lot, it is widely used in the sense *destroy a large part of.* This modern meaning is considered acceptable by Bernstein, Copperud, Evans, and Fowler, and is recognized by all current dictionaries. All the commentators warn, however, of uses such as combining *decimate* with a fraction or a percentage (*decimated a third of the rats*), which is illogical, or of such contexts as "Some classrooms were nearly decimated by the student strike" when some other word (in this case *emptied*) is called for.

**declare.** Often used as a random variant for *say,* but it denotes more force (Bernstein, Copperud, Evans, Flesch).

**decline (or refuse) comment.** A journalese telescoping of *decline* (or *refuse*) *to comment. Decline* and *refuse* when not followed by an infinitive indicate rejection of something that has been offered. "The Negro declined use of his name" is incorrect; *refused to allow his name to be used.* Definitions in Random House and Webster support this view.

**deduction.** See INDUCTION, DEDUCTION.

**deem.** Criticized as pretentious for *think* by Evans, Flesch, and Fowler.

**defense, defence.** The first is the American, the second the British preference in spelling.

**Defining and Nondefining Clauses.** See RESTRICTIVE, NONRESTRICTIVE CLAUSES.

**definite, definitely.** *Definite* and *definitely* are overused for an often meaningless emphasis; *definitely* also displaces *certainly, decidedly,* etc.: "This car is definitely the best on the market" (Copperud, Follett, Fowler; American Heritage approves this usage). *Definitely* and *but definitely* are fads, now outworn, for *yes* or *of course* (Copperud, Follett, Fowler).

**definite, definitive.** The first means *precise, defined;* the second means *final, most complete* (Bernstein, Evans, Fowler, American Heritage).

**degree.** Fowler says the phrase *to a degree,* though illogical, is established beyond attack. Bernstein says *degree* and *extent* are often used in redundant constructions, for example *to a serious degree* for *seriously.*

**defy.** An absurd and misleading effect is created when *defy* is inadvertently followed by an infinitive, a construction common in journalism: "Negroes defied National Guard troops to stage a demonstration." It was not the National Guard, but the Negroes, who staged the demonstration: *defied National Guard troops by staging. Defy to* means *goad into.* See also INFINITIVES 2.

**Degrees** (honorary **and** earned). See DR.

**delectable.** Fowler says the word now is chiefly ironic, but this is not so in the U.S., as Evans points out. Flesch discourages it as arch for *charming, delightful,* etc.

**delusion, illusion.** A delusion is a mistaken belief; an illusion is a misleading appearance, or an idea based on one. An illusion is tentative, while a delusion is firmly fixed in the mind. The terms are sometimes interchangeable. A superstition is a delusion; the impression of reality created by a stage performance is an illusion, as is the impression of a mirage (Bernstein, Evans, Fowler, American Heritage). The most detailed differentiation is to be found in Fowler under *Delusion, Illusion.*

**demean.** Bernstein, Evans, and Fowler point out that this is two different words: to *behave, conduct,* or *comport oneself;* and to *debase* or *disparage.* This latter is an incorrect formation by confusion with the adjective *mean.* Follett and Fowler are leery of it; Bernstein and Evans defend it as standard. The main point here is that *demean* in the first sense is obsolescent, while in the second it is in wide and common use. All current dictionaries recognize both senses as standard.

**demise.** Evans, Flesch and Fowler object to *demise* as pretentious for *death* in ordinary contexts.

**Democrat, -ic.** *Democrat* for *Democratic* (*Democrat senators; a Democrat administration*) is a political mannerism fostered by certain Republican leaders with the irrational explanation that *Democratic* suggests a monopoly on democracy. It is apparently considered a disagreeable misuse even by most Republicans. Neither Webster nor Random House recognizes it.

The capitalized forms (*Democrat, -ic*) are usually reserved for references to the political party, the lowercase forms for references to democracy as a system or philosophy of government.

**denote.** See CONNOTE, DENOTE.

**dependant, dependent.** *Dependent* is customary for both noun and adjective; *dependant* is acceptable as the noun: (*a minor dependent, -ant; dependent on the weather* (Copperud, Evans, Fowler).

**depend(s)** Bernstein, Fowler, and American Heritage criticize *depends* as an intransitive verb not followed by *on* or *upon* in such constructions as "Whether the picnic will be held depends whether it rains" and "It all depends whether . . ." Random House and Webster bear out this judgment.

**deprecate, depreciate.** To *deprecate* is to *disapprove of* ("Dropping out of school is deprecated"); to *depreciate* is to *belittle, devalue, disparage* ("He depreciated his opponent's arguments"). *Deprecate* for *depreciate* (*a self-deprecating manner*) is given as standard by Random House and narrowly approved by American Heritage; the confusion is not recognized by Random House. The consensus heavily disapproves of it.

**derisive, derisory.** Fowler holds that *derisive* means *showing derision* and that *derisory* means *promoting derision* (*a derisory offer*). No such distinction is recognized in the U.S., however; the terms are given in dictionaries as synonyms, often in both senses, though the sense of *prompting derision* must be considered rare for either form.

**desalinate, desalt.** The second is the simple word for removing salt from seawater, but often *desalinate* or *desalinize* are used. A press association once used *desalinification,* but this is an invention with no standing.

**description.** Fowler criticizes the use of this word in fuzzy formulas like "automobiles of this description," where *kind* or *sort* would do. See also CHARACTER; NATURE.

**desegregation, integration.** By and large, the terms are used interchangeably. Efforts have been made, notably by the Southern Education Reporting Service, to establish a distinction to the effect that *desegregation* would apply to the abandonment of racial separation, for example in schools and the use of other public facilities, and *integration* to the disappearance of all discrimination based on race, in social situations and otherwise. Webster recognizes both the broad sense of *integrate* and the narrow one, in which it is equated with *desegregate.* Bernstein regrets that the newer sense of *integration,* having to do with race, as distinguished from that having to do with unifying in general, has made the word ambiguous. But, as he concedes, the context always indicates which sense is meant. Fowler says *integrate* has become a vogue word in its basic sense, but makes no mention of its racial meaning. In much the same vein, Evans says the word is overworked, but (probably because the book was published in 1957, before the civil rights movement gained momentum) does not refer to the word's racial sense.

**desert, dessert.** Sometimes confused. The first is dry, barren land, the second the sweet that ends the meal. *Deserts* are also what one deserves; the common phrase, *just deserts*, is redundant (Bernstein, Copperud). The error *just desserts* may be encouraged by the fact that these deserts are pronounced like the sweet, with the accent on the second syllable.

**designed.** Overworked, especially in the press, for *intended* or *planned:* "The rose bushes are designed to act as a net to catch cars hurtling off the road"; "The new fire engine is designed for protection of the entire county." Sometimes used superfluously: "Theater officials announced a new program [designed] to appeal to service clubs."

**desire, be desirous of.** Pretentious for *want to* (Copperud, Flesch, Fowler).

**despatch.** See DISPATCH.

**despite (in spite of) the fact that.** The long way around for *although.*

**destined to.** Criticized by Flesch and Fowler as worn out

as used in looks backward ("He was destined to succeed").

**develop.** Criticized by Flesch in the sense *become known, come to light,* but this meaning is described by Evans as standard, a judgment that is corroborated by the current dictionaries ("It developed that the venture was underfinanced"). In the sense *contract* in reference to disease ("The girl developed eczema"), specifically approved by American Heritage, considered standard by Webster, but not given by Random House.

**device, devise.** The first is the noun meaning a contrivance or mechanism, and the second ordinarily a verb meaning to contrive: *an ingenious device; devise a solution* (Copperud, Evans).

**devil's advocate.** Fowler says that the phrase is often misused in the sense of a tempter, or of one who espouses the cause of evil; whereas in fact the devil's advocate is the blackener of the good, not the whitewasher of the evil. This comes from the sense of the term in its native habitat, the proceedings for canonization. All current dictionaries recognize the extended sense of a person who upholds the wrong side, or argues perversely, and Evans too regards such senses as standard. This may be considered one of the numerous instances of popularization (and, inevitably, distortion) of a technical term.

**dexterous, dextrous.** Both forms are correct; the shorter is to be preferred (Evans, Fowler).

**Diacritical Marks.** The typesetting equipment of many publications, especially newspapers, does not ordinarily include such marks as the German umlaut, French accents, the cedilla, and others. This means that in such publications these marks are usually ignored, though sometimes the umlaut is indicated by spelling *(Luebeck* for *Lübeck).* Words that have been taken over from French into English, such as fiancé, protegé, and cliché, are tending to lose their accents. About the only English diacritical mark is the dieresis, which appears over the second *o* in *coöperate,* indicating that it begins another syllable. The usual form now, however, is *cooperate, coordinate,* etc., dispensing with both diereses and hyphens. Dictionaries retain the accents on fiancé, fiancée, cliché, protegé, and protegée. In a doubtful case, recourse to the dictionary is recommended (Copperud, Evans, Fowler).

**diagnose.** Bernstein points out that it is the ailment that is diagnosed, not the man, and thus it is wrong to say of a person that he was diagnosed as suffering from something. Definitions in Random House and Webster bear out this criticism.

**dichotomy.** Criticized by Flesch, Follett, and Fowler as an often pretentious displacement of *division, split, difference, cleavage,* etc.

**Dictionaries.** This entry is devoted mainly to some widespread misapprehensions about dictionaries, but some other comments are included.

To begin with, it is not true that preferred meanings are indicated by the order in which they are listed. No current dictionary follows any such plan. All senses, unless explicitly qualified (for example, as slang or substandard), are to be regarded as of equal standing. Some dictionaries (Webster, for example) list meanings in the order of historical development, while Random House and American Heritage place central or common meanings first and obsolete, archaic, and rare ones afterward.

If more than one spelling is given for a word, the one given first, or accompanying the definition, is the more prevalent, but both are correct.

Webster's Third New International, the largest current dictionary in America, aroused widespread criticism because it omitted many usage labels, and thus designated as standard many usages that are often considered questionable. For one thing, it dropped the label *colloquial* (which see). Among current desk editions, the American Heritage and the Standard College Dictionary are perhaps most discriminating about usage.

As explained in the preface, references to "current dictionaries" in this book mean Random House, Webster, the Standard College, Webster's New World, American Heritage, and the American College Dictionaries. See also MEANING.

**die, dice.** Evans says that *dice* (rather than *die*) is acceptable as the singular but only Webster's New World Dictionary recognizes this usage. The consensus thus is against it.

**die from.** Disapproved in favor of *die of* by Copperud and American Heritage.

**Dieresis.** See DIACRITICAL MARKS.

**different.** Often used unnecessarily: "We called on twelve different people." If *unlike* cannot be substituted for *different,* it is better omitted. *Various* is preferable to *different* to indicate diversity without emphasizing unlikeness: "*Various* (not *different*) actors have performed the role" (Bernstein, Copperud, Evans). Random House and Webster give *various* for *different,* but the consensus is with the objectors to this usage. Fowler adds disapproval of the term as used in advertising, particularly (but it is also common in conversation in the U.S.) when no indication is given of what is being compared; that is, describing something simply as "different." Random House and Webster recognize this sense (*unusual, not ordinary*), however.

**different from, than.** Bernstein refers at length to Evans to support the position that *different than* (rather than *different from*) is acceptable only in special circumstances, such as when it is part of an elliptical construction, after having scorned the argument in the same book (without identifying it) favoring a less restrictive position on this question. Evans quotes Walter Page's "See that you use no word in a different sense than it was used in a hundred years ago" as an example of such an elliptical construction, in which some such phrase as *that in which* has been omitted after *than.* Another example is Cardinal Newman's "It has possessed me in a different way than ever before" (*than that in which it had ever possessed me*). Fowler also agrees that *different than* is preferable to the long way around in such constructions. Random House reports the form is generally frowned upon. Copperud, Flesch, and Webster accept *different than* as a standard variant of *different from* in any context.

*Different than,* which Follett declares suspect and American Heritage rejects, though widespread, is most objectionable in simple comparisons: "Frogs are different than toads." Bryant finds that *different from* is more usual in such constructions, but adds that *different than* is also standard. The consensus is that *different than* is standard.

*Different to* is rarely seen in print in the U.S., but is common in Britain. Fowler defends it vigorously and Bryant also regards it as standard British usage.

**differ from, with.** *Differ from* indicates dissimilarity; ("Oranges differ from apples.") *Differ with* indicates disagreement ("They differed with me") though *differ from* is acceptable in this sense (Bernstein, Copperud, Fowler, Random House, Webster).

**dilapidated.** It is sometimes objected that the term properly applies only to what is made of stone, but like many another, it has parted from its Latin derivation. All dictionaries give the general sense of *decayed, in* *disrepair, deteriorated.* Sometimes misspelled *de-*.

**dilemma.** Strictly speaking, the term describes the choice between *undesirable* things; not merely a choice, nor a choice of some other combination. The retention of this sense, as against using the word as a loose synonym for *difficulty, predicament, problem,* etc., when no choice is present, is advocated by Bernstein, Copperud, Evans, Follett, Fowler, and American Heritage. Both Random House and Webster accept the extended sense, however. Flesch does not make this distinction but discourages *dilemma* as a pretentious displacement of the other terms.

**diphtheria, diphthong.** Often misspelled *diptheria, dipthong* (Copperud, Fowler).

**disassemble.** See DISSEMBLE.

**disassociate.** See DISSOCIATE.

**disaster proportions.** Accepted by American Heritage and disapproved by Copperud as an objectionable instance of making a noun serve as an adjective. See also HEALTH REASONS.

**disclose.** See ATTRIBUTION 2.

**discomfit, -ure.** Bernstein, Evans, and Fowler point out that the primary meaning of *discomfit* is *rout, overwhelm,* and that it tends to be used in too weak a sense, namely that of *make uneasy.* Copperud recognizes this, but adds that the weaker use is widely prevalent. The dictionaries, including American Heritage, agree that the weaker sense has established itself, for all give as synonyms in a separate sense such words as *disconcert, em-*

*barrass, confuse, make uneasy.* Opinion thus clearly favors the extended sense.

**discover, invent.** Often confused. To *discover* is to find what already exists; to *invent* is to *devise* or *create.* Natural laws (like that of gravity) are *discovered;* machines are *invented* (Bernstein, Copperud, Evans). See also ENGINEER, SCIENTIST.

**discreet, discrete.** The difficulty here generally arises out of the intention to use *discreet,* which means *circumspect. Discrete* means *separate.* "The information was discretely distributed to more than a thousand publishers." Separately? Unlikely. Circumspectly, i.e., *discreetly* (Copperud, Evans).

**disfranchise.** Preferable to *disenfranchise* (Evans, Fowler).

**disinterested, uninterested.** Bernstein, Copperud, Evans, Follett, Fowler, and American Heritage criticize the use of *disinterested* (strictly, *impartial*) for *uninterested* (*feeling no interest*). The umpire, ideally, would be *disinterested;* one who did not care about the game would be *uninterested.* A useful distinction is being blurred. Flesch concludes the battle is already lost, and Fowler wistfully wonders whether rescue is still possible. Some desk dictionaries regard *disinterested* for *indifferent* as loose or colloquial, but Random House and Webster accept *disinterested* for *uninterested* as standard though Random House points out the difference. Despite the critics, the battle does seem lost, and the writer who wants to be certain of being understood had better use *impartial* rather than *disinterested*.

**dispatch, despatch.** Fowler says that *dispatch* is preferable, but that *des-* occurs often. This may be true in Britain, but *des-* has almost disappeared from view in the U.S.

**disposal, disposition.** In general, *disposal* relates to getting rid of, *disposition* to arrangement (Evans, Fowler).

**dissemble, disassemble.** The first means to *pretend* or *misrepresent,* the second to *take apart.* Emotions may be *dissembled,* automobiles *disassembled* (Evans, Fowler). Follett considers *disassemble* unnecessary beside *take apart.*

**dissociate.** Both *dissociate* and *disassociate* are correct, but the first is encouraged on the principle that what is simpler is preferable (Copperud, Evans, Flesch, Follett, Fowler).

**distaff.** Discouraged by Copperud as journalese and by Flesch as pretentious for *female, women's.*

**distinctive, distinguished.** Sometimes confused; the first means *different, characteristic,* and the second means *eminent* or *outstanding* (Bernstein, Evans, Fowler).

**dived.** See DOVE.

**divulge.** Criticized by Copperud, Evans, and Flesch as a random variant for *say, tell, announce. Divulge,* like *disclose* and *reveal,* connotes previous concealment.

**dock.** Bernstein and Follett hold that only in loose, casual usage does *dock* mean *pier* or *wharf.* Copperud calls this restriction of *dock* to the water-way beside or between piers or wharves nautical cant, and he and Evans say it is interchangeable with *pier* or *wharf.* This view is borne out by all current dictionaries, which give *pier* or *wharf* or both as standard senses of *dock.* The consensus favors the extended sense.

**doctor.** See DR.

**doff.** *Doff* and *don* are regarded as affected by Evans and Flesch.

**dogs.** Few things are more tiresome than the habit, in newspaper pieces about dogs, of having recourse to expressions such as *a dog's life, going to the dogs,* and *doggoned* (Copperud, Evans). Except, perhaps, referring to dogs as *canines.*

**Dolley (Madison).** The usual form is *Dolly,* and this is how it is to be found in some reference works. *Dolley,* however, is the form Mrs. Madison used herself; the fact is amply documented.

**don.** See DOFF.

**donate.** Once often criticized as a back-formation, which of course it is, but it is recognized as standard by Copperud, Evans, and Fowler. All, in addition to Flesch, warn that it is formal or possibly pretentious for *give,* which is ordinarily preferable. Random House and Webster also consider the term standard.

**done.** For *through, completed* ("The book is nearly done"), narrowly approved by American Heritage; considered standard by Random House and Webster.

**dope.** Recognized as standard for *narcotic* by American Heritage, Random House, and Webster.

**double entendre.** Not French, as many assume, but English, established since the seventeenth century. The French phrase, which has a wider range of meanings, not limited to the sexual suggestion of the English, is *double entente* (Evans, Fowler, Follett).

**Double Genitive.** See POSSESSIVES 3.

**Double Negative.** The consensus on this subject is that the ordinary double negative is conspicuous and avoided by all except the unlettered ("It didn't do me no good"). The construction is more noticeable in short sentences than in longer ones, where the more sophisticated are often unwittingly guilty of it. The idea that the negatives cancel each other out and make the statement positive is a superstition fostered by old-fashioned grammar school teachers, except that such expressions as *not uncomfortable* do make a positive, albeit a weak one, and are standard (see NOT UN-). Double negatives ordinarily reinforce each other, and this is clearly felt by the reader. Double negatives with words other than *no* or *not* may be ambiguous, however, and some doubling slips by unnoticed: "Few will deny that the high temperatures of the last few days weren't pretty uncomfortable." The negatives are *deny* and *weren't;* strictly, *were pretty uncomfortable.* Few, however, would mistake the sense intended here. See also CAN

BUT, etc; HARDLY; MINIMIZE; UNDERESTIMATE; UNDUE; NOT . . . NOT; FAIL; NOT UN-.

**Double Passives.** Bernstein and Fowler warn against clumsy constructions like "The speaker was attempted to be contradicted," which any writer of sensitivity would avoid by instinct: "An attempt was made to contradict the speaker."

**Double Possessives.** See POSSESSIVES 3.

**Double Punctuation.** No longer considered meaningful, as in "Here, indeed, may be the real purpose of this bill,—to dull our awareness of taxation." Either the comma or the dash should be used. Here the dash is called for. See also DASH.

**doubt(ful).** Fowler says *that* should be used after these words only in negative statements. By this reasoning, *I do not doubt that* is right and *I doubt that* is wrong. Bernstein, Follett, and American Heritage say *that* may be used in a positive sense when unbelief rather than uncertainty is indicated. All prescribe *whether* or *if* to express uncertainty. Fowler's view on *doubt that* may describe British usage, but Bernstein's and Follett's surely describe American usage.

**doubtlessly.** Cumbrous for *doubtless* (Bernstein, Copperud)

**dove.** Bernstein, apparently following British practice, objects to *dove* as the past tense of *dive;* the American Heritage panel narrowly rejected it (51 per cent), but as in other examples where the editors seemingly did not agree with the panel, they chose to state the minority acceptance. Bryant,

Copperud, Flesch, and Follett consider it standard. Two of the current desk dictionaries consider it informal, two of them consider it standard; both Random House and Webster accept it. The consensus favors full acceptability for *dove*.

**downward revision.** See EU-PHEMISMS.

**Dr.** No question ordinarily arises over whether to bestow the title in print upon doctors of medicine and dentists. With respect to doctors of philosophy, veterinarians, optometrists, chiropractors, and osteopaths, it is another story. Ukases denying the title to some or all of these have appeared in the style books of the mightiest newspapers in the land, though the present trend is to use the title for all these professions. The decision with respect to doctors of philosophy and other academic doctors generally follows the preference of the holder. Around great universities, where such doctors abound, it may be considered sophomoric for the holder of the title to use it, though it is often applied by others as an honorific to the heads of departments and the like.

Those who use the title on the strength of an honorary degree are usually scorned if the fact becomes known. The commonest offenders in this respect are clergymen (usually D.D.'s).

If an academic doctor is identified as Dr., it is well to identify him further as an economist, or whatever, since the reader is likely to assume that he is a medical doctor in the absence of further information.

The commonest honorary degrees are D.C.L. (civil law), D.D. (divinity), D.Sc. (science), D.Litt., D.Lit., Litt.D. (literature), L.H.D. (humanities), LL.D. (laws). The commonest earned doctorates outside the medical fields are Ph.D. (technically philosophy, though awarded in many specialties of the humanities), S.T.D. and Th.D. (theology), and Ed.D. (education).

Curiously, to an American, physicians in Britain do not all hold the doctorate, but out of courtesy are addressed as *Dr.* regardless; surgeons, especially those who have made a reputation, are addressed as *Mr.*

Indications of the title *Dr.* should not be repeated: *Dr. George Anderson, M.D.* should be either *Dr. George Anderson* or *George Anderson, M.D.*

**drama critic, dramatic critic.** See -IC, -ICAL.

**dramatic, -ics.** See -IC, -ICS.

**dropout.** Overwhelmingly sanctioned by the American Heritage panel in the educational sense; considered standard by Random House and Webster.

**drug.** Although narcotics are generally drugs, and commonly thus referred to, many drugs are not narcotics, and for the sake of precision *narcotic(s)* is preferable when it applies. (Bernstein, Copperud).

**drunk, drunken.** The question is whether *drunk* is permissible as an attributive adjective, that is, standing before the noun: *drunk (drunken) driver.* Bernstein will not have it; Copperud says *drunken* is preferable but that *drunk* is winning acceptance; Evans that *drunken* sounds quaint; Fowler that *drunk* is increasingly used colloquially, as both attributive adjective and noun: *a common drunk* (which Bernstein will not have either). Fowler makes the perceptive point that *drunken* is always called for in the sense *given to drink (a drunken bum)* as against the sense *intoxicated,* and that it is idiomatic in some other contexts *(a drunken brawl).* Random House gives only examples showing *drunk* used predicatively, and Webster comments explicitly that the word is usually used this way, though it quotes Truman Capote in an attributive use. Both dictionaries accept *drunk* as a noun meaning both *a drunken person* and *a spree (a week's drunk).* The consensus, in which the American Heritage panel concurs, favors the adjective *drunk* in the predicate position, at least for the present; *drunk* as a noun is standard.

**due to.** The point of dispute is whether *due to* can be used in the sense of, and interchangeably with, *because of* or *owing to,* in such contexts as "Due to Asian flu, he missed school," as well as (correctly) "Asian flu is due to a virus." In the latter example, *due* may be smoothly replaced by *attributable;* this is the test of the difference in use. *Due to* has been objected to in the first construction because it modifies a verb *(missed);* or, to put it another way, because the phrase is used as a preposition. The distinction is hairsplitting, and cannot be defended on grammatical grounds. *Due to* is extremely popular in the criticized construction. Bryant, Copperud, Evans, and Flesch say it is now standard; Bernstein, Follett, and Fowler that the fight against it is being lost. The only adamant holdout is the American Heritage panel (83 per cent against); the editors imply lack of sympathy with this stand, saying the usage is widely employed informally. The consensus favors the criticized usage, which Webster too recognizes as standard. Random House gives only the sense *attributable.*

**due to the fact that.** Wordy for BECAUSE (Bernstein, Copperud).

**dump.** A stereotype of journalism in reference to rain and snow, which almost invariably are described as being dumped, and somehow cannot be allowed simply to fall.

**duo.** See TRIO.

**during the course of.** See COURSE, etc.

**dwell.** Unsuitable for *live* in everyday contexts (Flesch, Fowler).

**dyeing, dying.** The confusion is in using *dying (expiring)* for *dyeing (recoloring)* (Copperud, Fowler).

# E

**each.** When *each* stands as subject, it takes a singular verb: "Each *takes his* ration and *moves* along." Strictly, this is true also when *each* is followed by an *of*-phrase: "*Each* of the prisoners *takes his* ration and *moves* along." Bernstein, Follett, and Fowler hold to this strict construction. Copperud and Evans recognize that the second examples here would often be given "*Each* of the prisoners *take their* ration(s) and move along"; Evans adds that when *each* refers to both men and women, it may be referred to in the plural: "Each carried their own pack." Evans regards such usage as standard, and Copperud says it is verging into acceptance. American Heritage calls it informal. Bryant regards plural verbs and references with *each* as standard, but finds the singular twice as frequent. Random House says that careful speakers make certain that *each* is used with a singular verb; Webster allows the plural. Opinion is thus evenly divided. What is unquestionable is that plural verbs and references with *each* are extremely common in carefully edited material, and growing commoner. A similar problem occurs with other technically singular pronouns like ANYONE (which see).

When *each* is not the subject but modifies it, the number of the verb is governed by the subject: "We each are . . . ";
"The messengers each receive two assignments"; "John and Harry each are entitled to commendations" (Not *is* in any instance, though American Heritage accepts it).

Bernstein and Fowler agree that the number of a later noun or pronoun when a plural subject is followed by *each* depends on whether *each* comes before or after the verb. If it comes before, the reference to the subject is plural: "We each are accountable for our own families" (not *his own family*). If *each* comes after the verb, the reference will be singular: "We are each responsible for his own family" (not *our own families*). In the latter arrangement, there is more emphasis on distribution. See also ANYBODY, ANYONE; BETWEEN 3.

**each and every.** Criticized by Copperud and Evans as a pomposity and by Bryant and Follett as characteristic of officialese and redundant.

**each other.** The possessive is *each other's*, and is followed by a plural, not a singular: *each other's hats* (not *hat*). *Each others'* is wrong (Bernstein, Copperud, Evans, Follett, Fowler, American Heritage).

Bernstein, Bryant, Evans, Follett, Fowler, and American Heritage agree that *each other* and *one another* are interchangeable, and that there is no point in the efforts to restrict the first to two and the second to three or more. "All three hated each other" (or *one another*); "Mary and Sally admired one another" (or *each other*).

**eager.** See ANXIOUS, EAGER.

**early on.** A Briticism for *at an early stage* (Copperud, Random House, Webster) that is conspicuous and likely to sound affected in America.

**easy, easily.** *Easy* may not be used as an adverb except in such stock phrases as *take it easy, go easy:* "We accomplished it easily," not *easy* (Bernstein, Evans, Fowler).

**echelon.** Flesch deprecates the term in the sense of *rank* (*the upper echelons of the civil service*) as a fad, and Fowler as a distortion of the primary term, a military expression meaning a staggered formation. Follett calls it pretentious. Random House and Webster, however, both recognize the sense *rank* or *level of command*. In any event, it is now so popular that uprooting it would be a fearsome task.

**eclectic.** Means *selected from various sources,* not necessarily *the best;* thus it is not a synonym for *fastidious* or *discriminating* (Bernstein, Evans). The dictionaries concur.

**economic, -ical.** Although *economic* may mean either *pertaining to the science of economics* or *money-saving,* usage favors *economical* for *thrifty, money-saving:* "Economic, as well as social, factors were considered"; "The use of dried milk is economical." "The present system is an economical waste" contains an absurd contradiction; *economic* (Cop-

perud, Flesch, Fowler, Random House, Webster). See also -IC, -ICAL.

**economics, economies.** *Economics* is the science; dismal, they once called it. *Economies* is the plural of *economy,* in one ordinary sense a business and industrial system; in another, a saving. "The Common Market has boosted to unprecedented heights the economics of its members" is therefore wrong; *economies.* See also -IC, -ICS.

**ecstasy.** Sometimes given *ecstacy,* likely to be regarded as a misspelling; only Webster gives it as a variant.

**edifice.** Regarded as pompous by Evans, Flesch, and Fowler in ordinary contexts when *building* will do.

**editorial.** Often confused in relation to journalism. *Editorial,* the noun, is the name of the article in which the newspaper sets forth its own views and policy; readers often apply it to news articles or to contributed matter, such as columns, in which the writer's views are set forth. The confusion is encouraged by the fact that within the newspaper field, the adjective *editorial* relates to all the nonadvertising content of the paper, and *editorial department* to that department which produces and edits that content, without specific reference to editorials as such.

**Editorial (and Royal) We.** The use of *we* for *I* is out of place except in editorials, it is agreed by Copperud, Evans, Follett, Flesch, and Fowler, and this applies also to such expressions as *this writer, the* *present writer, this correspond-ent,* and the like as used in false modesty. By analogy with the royal *we,* the form used by kings and queens and popes, writers are led to such forms as *we ourself,* which sound absurd (Copperud, Evans, Flesch). The editorial *we* is particularly inappropriate under a by-line, which has already announced the writer's single identity. Copperud and Fowler warn that editorialists, who have a legitimate reason to use the editorial *we* as expressing the views of a group or organiza-tion, do not always guard against distinguishing between the editorial and the national we (referring to the people of the United States or its gov-ernment). Fowler cautions that *our* and *I* may be similarly ambiguous, though conceding that this confusion is rare. See also ONE.

**editress.** See FEMININE FORMS.

**educationist, educator.** *Edu-cator* is regarded with some suspicion among those to whom it is applied; Copperud, Evans, and Flesch agree that it is pom-pous. *Teacher* is better where it fits. *Educationist* is often derisory (Copperud, Flesch, American Heritage).

**-ee.** Bernstein, Copperud, and Fowler point out that for the most part the suffix *-ee* denotes the person to whom something is done, rather than the doer: *lessee, draftee, train-ee, addressee, appointee.* Bern-stein, Follett, and Fowler dis-courage the tendency to coin such designations, particularly when they designate the doer rather than the—well, doee.

Some exceptions are recognized as standard: *refugee, escapee, absentee,* and many others. For the standing of other terms (*quizzee, examinee,* etc.) the reader is referred to his favorite dictionary. Fowler will not ad-mit *escapee,* preferring *escaper,* as does Follett, but *-ee* is well established in the U.S., while *escaper* is rarely used. Both Random House and Webster recognize *escapee* as standard.

**effect.** See AFFECT.

**effete.** Bernstein and Evans point out that the term means *exhausted, spent,* or *unable to reproduce,* and protest that it is often misused in such senses as *effeminate, decadent,* or *weak.* Random House and Webster recognize *decadent,* and the Standard College Dic-tionary gives also "having lost strength or virility." Bernstein is surely right when he says the word is used a hundred times in the criticized sense for every time it is used in the primary one. The sense objected to may soon establish itself with the benefit of such towering odds of popularity. American Heritage, the newest of the desk dictionaries, gives *deca-dent* as one sense.

**efficacy, efficiency.** Some-times confused. *Efficacy* means *effectiveness; efficiency* has to do with economy of effort and productivity. "The panel dis-agreed on the relative efficacy of alcoholics and reformed al-coholics." *efficiency;* the refer-ence was to the way they did their jobs (Copperud, Random House, Webster).

**e.g., i.e.** Often carelessly in-terchanged. *E.g.* stands for

*exempli gratia: for example.*
*I. e.* stands for *id est: that is.*
Thus *e.g.* should be reserved
for the citing of an example,
*i.e.* for the citing of an equivalent (Copperud, Evans, Follett, Flesch, Fowler). In ordinary contexts, the abbreviations
should be avoided in favor of
words spelled out in English.

**egoist, egotist.** The distinction generally observed, Bernstein, Copperud, Evans, and
Fowler agree, is that the egoist
places his own interest first as
a principle of conduct; the
egotist is a braggart. There is
some blurring of the sense
owing to careless interchange.
Random House equates the
terms; Webster acknowledges
that *egotism* is sometimes used
for *egoism* but in general dif-
ferentiates the terms; the differentiation between *egoist* and
*egotist* is unqualified, which
indicates they are interchangeable.

**egregious.** Evans and Fowler
agree that the sense of the
word has been narrowed so
that it is now only derogatory;
Flesch discourages it as likely
not to be understood.

**either.** 1. In the sense *each
of two* or *both* ("There are
slums on either side of town"),
*either* is considered formal or
archaic by Bernstein, standard
in America but not in Britain by
Evans, and standard by Fowler,
Random House, and Webster.
2. *Either* with more than two
("Either of the three versions
is acceptable") is considered
abnormal usage by Bernstein,
rare but standard by Bryant
and Evans, questionable by
American Heritage, and loose
by Fowler.

3. *Either,* strictly speaking, is
singular when denoting one of
two, and thus takes a singular
verb: "Either of them is satisfactory." Copperud, Evans, and
Webster hold that the plural
verb ("Either of them *are . . .*")
is acceptable in the U.S. Bernstein, Fowler, American Heritage, and Random House say
the plural verb is wrong.
4. A singular verb is generally used with *either . . . or* (or
*neither . . . nor*), but if one of
the nouns joined is singular and
one is plural, the verb agrees
with the nearer: "Either food
or materials are required"
(Bernstein, Evans, American
Heritage).
5. *Either* is often misplaced,
as in "No date has been set
either for the election or independence." *for either the election.* "The fire either has
burned out or it has been put
out." *Either the fire has burned
. . .* (Bernstein, Copperud,
Fowler, American Heritage).
The point here is that *either
. . . or,* as correlative conjunctions, must be placed in grammatically parallel positions. In
the first example, *for* has as objects both *election* and *independence,* and *either* stands in
the same relation to *election*
that *or* does to *independence.*
This means that *either* must be
placed after *for* and before
*election.*
6. *Either* as an intensive
("I don't, either, water the
beer") is often unnecessarily
set off by commas as in the
example.
7. For *either* with *they, their,
them,* see ANYBODY, ANYONE.

**eke out.** Fowler, together
with Bernstein and Evans, insists that *eke out* can mean

only *add to,* and thus that *eke out one's income* is correct but *eke out a living* is impermissible. Five current dictionaries, however, including Random House and Webster, cite this expression specifically with the meaning *make a living with difficulty,* and so the objection to it must be dismissed as pedantry.

**elapse.** Now archaic or rare as a noun; thus *the elapse of time* is objectionable for *lapse* (Bernstein, Evans). Random House and Webster regard it as standard.

**elder, eldest, older, oldest.** Bernstein and Evans say that *elder, eldest* may be used only concerning people, whereas *older, oldest* may be used concerning either people or things. Neither Random House nor Webster recognizes this distinction, however.

**elderly.** Efforts by newspaper editors to fix a starting point, say at sixty or seventy years of age, for the application of the term constitute one of their more harmless follies. No dictionary attempts this. It is noticeable that, as the editors themselves grow older, their starting points tend to rise. Elderliness, like many other qualities, often resides in the eye of the beholder. Unless applied conspicuously too soon (to, say, middle age), *elderly* is a gentler term than *aged* or *old,* and as such has its uses. See also SENIOR CITIZEN.

**electric, electrical.** See -IC, -ICAL.

**electronic, -ics,** See -IC, -ICS.

**elegant.** Bernstein and Evans deplore the faddish or slangy use of the term for *pleasing* or *good.* This use is rare outside conversation, or writing that has a deliberately conversational tone.

**Elegant Variation.** This is Fowler's term for the unskillful and inadvisable use of synonyms to avoid repetition of a word, as in "About 76 per cent of Russia's doctors are women, while in the United States only 6 per cent are female." The change from *women* to *female* serves only to confuse the reader momentarily, making him wonder whether there is a reason for it. The analysis of this problem by Fowler has nowhere been equaled; it is treated in various aspects in his *Modern English Usage* under the headings *Elegant Variation, Repetition of Words or Sounds,* and *Sobriquets.* These discussions are commended to the reader. A treatment of the problem, including some aspects of it that appear to be peculiar to America, will be found in this book under the heading VARIATION. "Elegant variation," incidentally, is one of two of Fowler's invented names that have become more or less standard terms; the other is "fused participle."

**elemental, elementary.** Evans, Follett, and Fowler agree that *elemental* relates to the elements (i.e., the forces of nature) and *elementary* to what is simple, basic, or introductory. The distinction is borne out by Random House but Webster gives *elementary* in the sense of *elemental (elementary powers).*

**eliminate.** Often misused for *prevent;* what can be eliminated must already be present. "Use of this material will eliminate possible failure caused by brittleness." *prevent.* "The insulation eliminates rings caused by dishes." *prevents* (Copperud, Random House, Webster). Flesch says that *eliminate, elimination* too often displace simpler terms like *get rid of, do away with, cut out,* etc. See also AVERT.

**Ellipsis.** This is the grammarian's word for omission from a sentence of what the reader will readily understand or supply.

1. Copperud and Follett point out instances in which ellipsis would improve a sentence, making for both smoothness and economy: "McDonald said 189,344 members are on leave and 257,026 (members are) on part-time schedules"; "The plant is capable of handling 650 tons per hour, but is handling only 500 (tons per hour)"; "Jones was cited for driving without due caution, and Smith (was cited) for driving without a license." The dispensable elements are in parentheses. The principle here is that an element may well be omitted from the second of parallel constructions in which it would be repeated in the same position.

2. The first part of a compound verb may be omitted, Copperud and Fowler hold, even if its form changes on second occurrence: "One person was killed and seven injured in the accident" (for *were injured*). This principle is limited to forms of *be* and *have.* Bernstein and Follett express doubt about the propriety of such omission.

3. However, the *second* part of a compound verb may not

be omitted if there is a change in number or form: "The spokesman said another firm has or is about to file for a franchise." *has filed* (Copperud, Bernstein, Follett, Fowler). "The county is now or will develop a nature-study center on the tract." *is now developing.*

4. An improved style results from canceling the pronoun (*which, who, that*) plus companion forms of *to be* (*is, are, was, were*) in relative clauses: "Work is under way on an ice rink (*that is*) scheduled to open next month"; "The bridge would give access to an island (*which is*) now served by a ferry"; "Sibelius was stricken with a brain hemorrhage at the villa (*that*) he built near Helsinki fifty-three years before"; "Local issues were responsible for the clobbering (*which*) the Republicans took in the Maine election." Here again the dispensable words are in parentheses.

5. For the omission of THAT, see that entry; for ellipsis after *than,* see FALSE COMPARISON.

6. Extensive ellipsis, used usually to shorten quoted matter, is indicated by spaced periods, usually three: "The speaker said the book was 'ill-conceived, hastily written . . . and obviously the work of an ignoramus.'" The use of asterisks (* * *) for this purpose is old-fashioned and seldom seen (Copperud, Evans, Flesch). The use of three periods, with the addition of a fourth indicating the ending of a sentence within the ellipsis, may be considered standard practice, as indicated by Summey's *American Punctuation* and Perrin's

*Writer's Guide and Index to English*. But this is not universal. The University of Chicago Press specifies four plus a fifth as appropriate, and Random House says either three or four.

7. In such constructions as "Adjectives become nouns and nouns, verbs" the comma may be used between *nouns* and *verbs* to mark the place where *become* is understood, but is not necessary. "A sentence should contain no unnecessary words, a paragraph no unnecessary sentences." Likewise, the comma is optional after *paragraph*. Some aspects of ellipsis in which a negative is wrongly carried over from one part of a sentence to another are discussed by Follett under *Negatives, Trouble With,* and by Fowler under *Negative Mishandling*. An example of this fault, which can take various forms: "Then the conference would not be held at all and the students disappointed." Omission of part of the verb from the second clause suggests to the reader that he should carry over *would not be, making would not be disappointed* and reversing the intended sense. The correction is to supply the positive *would be*. As with DOUBLE NEGATIVES (which see), the reader is seldom actually misled by such constructions, but he may be momentarily put off, and they are what Fowler would call slovenly.

**elope.** Bernstein says that elopement means running off and does not necessarily involve marriage, but this latter sense is specifically recognized by both Random House and Web-ster and, indeed, is the one in commonest use.

**else, else's.** The question is whether one should say *everyone's else* or *everyone else's*. Bernstein, Copperud, Evans, Flesch, and Fowler agree that the second is now the idiomatic form. The first, which was once prescribed, remains correct, but is unusual and now sounds stilted. The principle holds for all combinations with *else: someone, nobody, who,* etc.

**elusive, illusive.** See ALLUSION, ELUSION, ILLUSION.

**emend(ation).** Now restricted to the correction of printed matter; *amend* means to improve or alter in general (Evans, Fowler).

**emigrate, immigrate.** The choice is a matter of viewpoint. One who leaves a country emigrates from it; one who comes in immigrates. Thus someone in the United States may speak of a person emigrating from another country, or immigrating into this one. The same principle holds for *emigrant* and *immigrant* (Copperud, Evans).

**eminent(ly), imminent(ly).** *Eminently* means *notably* or *conspicuously:* "The settlement was considered eminently fair." *Imminently* means *in a short time* or *very soon,* and is usually said of something that threatens: "The attack was expected *imminently*." Then there is *immanent,* which means *existing within:* "The god was believed to be *immanent* in the stone image." Only sheer ignorance accounts for the occasional confusion of these terms (Bernstein, Copperud, Evans, Fowler).

**emissary.** Once had a predominantly unfavorable sense, suggesting spying or similarly underhand activity. All dictionaries now give the neutral sense of *one sent on a mission,* as well as the other. The widespread use of the term in newspapers in the nonderogatory sense probably hastened its acceptance.

**emote.** A back-formation from *emotion;* it has a distinctly jocose connotation. It has generally been associated with meretricious acting, and thus suggests insincerity or superficiality (Bernstein, Copperud). Random House and Webster also give the neutral sense, however, of *show emotion.*

**Emphasis.** This consideration is the subject of numerous passing comments in this book. Among the books compared, it is discussed separately only by Follett, under that heading.

**employ.** Pretentious where *use* will do (Copperud, Flesch).

**employe, employee.** The difference is a matter of preference in spelling. Newspapers at one time tended to insist on *employe* (and on *cigaret*), but *employee* now predominates and most of them have reverted to it. The forms once made a distinction by sex but this is no longer so (Copperud, Evans, Fowler).

**endeavor.** Pretentious where *attempt* or *try* will do (Copperud, Evans, Flesch).

**ended, ending.** Bernstein, Copperud, Evans, and Fowler agree that *ended* is preferable for what is past, *ending* for what is to come: "The report covers the decade ended in 1950"; "He is enrolled in a course ending next year." *Ending* is permissible, however, for what is past.

**endemic, epidemic.** A disease is endemic that continuously prevails in a locality; one that breaks out and then subsides is epidemic (Copperud, Evans, Fowler). Bernstein, invoking derivation, an unreliable guide to usage, insists that *epidemic* may apply only to people, and that the term for a disease of animals is *epizootic.* Fowler calls this distinction pedantry, and Webster designates it as technical.

**endorse, indorse.** Fowler holds to the old view that *endorse* can only mean to sign (literally or figuratively). This rules out such uses as *endorsing products;* he acknowledges that this is American practice. Copperud and Evans say the terms are interchangeable in the U.S., except that *endorse* predominates in all senses. All current dictionaries recognize the forms as interchangeable.

**end result.** *End result* is redundant, unless there is occasion to differentiate between final and intermediate results (Bernstein, Copperud, Flesch). Flesch and Fowler criticize *end product* for the same reason.

**engine, motor.** Machines run by steam are always *engines;* those run by gasoline are indifferently *engines* or *motors;* those run by electricity are nearly always *motors.* In rocketry, *engine* is applied to rockets that use liquid fuels and *motor* to those that use solid fuels.

**engineer, scientist.** The general distinction is that a *scientist* is concerned with the creation of knowledge, an *engineer* with its application. Others who apply technical knowledge but do not originate it may be referred to as *technicians*. *Scientist* is so general, even when properly used, that it is hardly satisfactory these days. Some more explicit designation, such as *biologist, astronomer,* or *physicist,* is desirable. *Engineer* is often devalued, sometimes facetiously and sometimes seriously, by such terms as *sanitation engineer* for *garbage man* (Bernstein, Copperud).

**England, English.** See GREAT BRITAIN.

**enhance.** Fowler gives as an example of error a sentence in which Spain is said to be enhanced by neutrality, and adds that the term cannot apply to a person or people, but must apply to a quality or condition such as value, attractiveness, prosperity. Bernstein and Flesch concur in this; Bernstein adds that while *enhance* ordinarily connotes what is favorable, it is also correctly used in the sense of *augment* concerning what is unfavorable ("His bad reputation was enhanced by the disclosure"). These views are borne out by Random House and Webster.

**enigmatic.** Means *puzzling* or *mysterious,* but is often misused in the sense of *dubious* or *questionable.* "The success of the new system was enigmatic" was intended to mean not that the success was inscrutable but that it was in doubt (Copperud, Random House, Webster).

**enjoin.** Evans and Fowler point out that the legal and the ordinary senses of the word are opposites. To enjoin (with *from*) in a legal context is to forbid; to enjoin (with *upon,* or followed by an infinitive) in ordinary contexts is to command or urge.

**enormity.** Bernstein, Evans, Fowler, and American Heritage hold that the word may be properly used only in the sense of *outrage* or *wickedness* or *crime.* Copperud and Flesch note that it is now commonly used to mean *enormousness, hugeness, vast size: The enormity of the Merchandise Mart.* The difficulty is that a noun derived from *enormous* is needed, and, as Fowler concedes, *enormousness* is clumsy. Both Random House and Webster recognize the divergent sense of *immensity;* 93 per cent of the American Heritage panel rejects it. The Oxford English Dictionary defines *enormity* in the sense of *excess in magnitude* as an incorrect use, and notes that the error dates from 1846. The consensus rejects the extended sense.

**enough.** Fowler deprecates the displacement of *enough* as a noun by *sufficient:* "We have had sufficient." Webster recognizes *sufficient* as a noun but Random House does not. The use of *sufficient(ly)* where *enough* will do (*sufficient money; punished sufficiently*) is considered pretentious by Copperud, Evans, Flesch, and Fowler (who, however, offers some refinements of his judgment that in general *enough* is more vigorous).

**enquire, inquire.** The words are synonymous in the U.S.; Copperud and Evans agree that the second form predominates.

**ensure, insure.** Interchangeable in the sense *make certain*—"Hard work will ensure success"; "Careful workmanship insures quality"—but *insure* has a noticeable edge. *Insure* is the only form for *guarantee against loss* (Copperud, Evans, Follett, Fowler). Flesch says *ensure* means only *make certain,* and *insure* only to guarantee against loss, but this is an imaginary distinction recognized nowhere else, including the major dictionaries. See also ASSURE.

**entangling alliances.** George Washington is often misquoted as having used this phrase in his Farewell Address. The phrase comes, however, from Jefferson's First Inaugural Address: "Peace, commerce, and honest friendship with all nations—entangling alliances with none." Washington did say, toward the end of his Farewell Address: "Taking care always to keep ourselves on a respectable defensive posture, we may safely trust to temporary alliances for extraordinary emergencies." He also said: "The great rule of conduct for us in regard to foreign nations is, in extending our commercial relations, to have with them as little political connection as possible."

**enthuse.** A back-formation from *enthusiasm* that is disapproved for one reason or another by Bernstein, Copperud,

Flesch, Fowler, and American Heritage. It is noticeably shunned in careful writing. *Enthuse* is accepted as standard by Random House, which points out, however, that it is widely criticized, and by Webster.

**entomology, etymology.** Entomology is the study of insects, etymology the study of the derivations of words. The nouns for the practitioners are *entomologist, etymologist* (Copperud, Evans).

**enure.** See INURE, ENURE.

**envelop, envelope.** The verb for *wrap up* or *surround* is almost always *envelop,* though *envelope* is a variant; the noun for what encloses a letter is usually *envelope,* though *envelop* is acceptable (Copperud, Evans; Random House and Webster give the forms as interchangeable.)

**envisage, envision.** Evans makes the distinction that in the usual sense of *imagine, call up an image, envision* is more poetic and connotes less immediacy than *envisage,* which is considered closer to reality. All the current dictionaries but Webster corroborate this. Fowler protests that *envisage* is often pretentiously substituted for commoner words like *imagine, visualize.* The first meaning sometimes given for *envisage* is *to confront,* but this sense appears to have grown rare.

**epic.** Evans and Fowler protest that the word has been debased by loose application to movies (*an epic of the Panhandle*), in sports writing (*an* *epic home run*) and in gossip columns (displacing *fabulous*). The original is a narrative poem celebrating the exploits of a hero.

**epidemic.** See ENDEMIC, EPIDEMIC.

**epithet.** Bernstein, Copperud, and Evans all recognize that to many the connotation is derogatory; an *epithet* is a bad name. In its primary sense, *epithet* is neutral, and means simply a descriptive term, like William *the Conqueror.* American Heritage, Random House, and Webster recognize the derogatory sense; the Standard College Dictionary terms it "loose"; Fowler calls it a corruption. In the U.S., the neutral sense is generally found in literary contexts, particularly works on literature. The derogatory sense is in far more common use, and the writer should be aware of this so that he uses the term in a context that will not make it ambiguous.

**epitome.** A summary, condensation, abstract, or an ideal representation; not an acme, apex, high point, or climax. "His attire was the epitome [ideal representation] of fashion" is correct but "That triumph was the epitome of his career" is not; *high point, climax* (Bernstein, Copperud, Random House, Webster).

**epoch, epoch-making.** Bernstein points out that an epoch is the beginning of an era, but acknowledges that this distinction is little observed. Fowler protests that *epoch-making* is loosely used of circumstances that are far from marking a turning point. Random House

and Webster concur generally in the limited sense.

**equal.** As an absolute, see COMPARISON 3.

**equally as.** Criticized as redundant by Bernstein, Copperud, Evans, Flesch, Follett, Fowler, and American Heritage: "He remained equally as uncompromising on the other issues." *equally uncompromising.* When a comparison is expressed, rather than implied, *as* alone should be used: "He remained as uncompromising on the issue as his colleagues." Evans adds, however, that *equally as* is often used by people who are not illiterate. Bryant finds that *equally* is far more prevalent than *equally as,* which she traces to confusion with *just as.*

**equine.** An objectionable variant for *horse;* often journalese (Copperud, Flesch). See also VARIATION.

**equivocal.** See AMBIGUOUS, EQUIVOCAL.

**-er and -est, more and most.** See COMPARISON 4.

**era.** See EPOCH.

**ere.** See POESY.

**errant, arrant.** Sometimes confused. *Errant* means *wandering* or *straying; arrant* means *thoroughgoing* or *outstandingly bad.* "This is errant nonsense." *arrant* (Copperud, Evans).

**errata.** American Heritage rejects *errata* (strictly, the plural of *erratum*) with a singular verb (*the errata is on the first page*), as well as the bastardized plural *erratas;* Random House concurs, but Webster accepts both.

**erstwhile.** Criticized by Flesch and Fowler as archaic for *former* and unsuitable for ordinary contexts.

**escalate.** Criticized by Fowler as an unnecessary back-formation. He concedes, however, that it is likely to become established. Copperud considers it often inappropriately used and overworked. American Heritage and Random House recognize the new and widely popular sense of *increase in intensity, magnitude,* etc.: *to escalate a war.* Webster does not give this sense, probably because it gained its great vogue after publication of the Third Edition in 1961.

**escape.** Bernstein and American Heritage reject *escape* without *from* in connection with confinement: "They escaped from the stockade" (not *escaped the stockade*).

**escapee.** See -EE.

**especial, special; especially, specially.** Bernstein, Evans, and Fowler agree that *special* is driving *especial* out of business, and that *especially* means *to an outstanding extent; specially, for a particular purpose.* Thus "I like soft drinks, specially cream soda" should be *especially (outstandingly, particularly).* An example of the correct use of *specially:* "The troops were specially selected for the assignment" (that is, *specifically*). *Special* is over-used in journalism; it exemplifies the occupational disease of straining for effect. "A special invitation was extended to wives"; "The supervisor made a special presentation of an award." Usually the term is superfluously used to describe what is self-evidently out of the ordinary, as in these examples. See also JOURNALESE; RAMPAGE.

**espresso.** The correct term for the coffee; not, as often given, *expresso* (Copperud, Random House, Webster).

**-ess.** See FEMININE FORMS.

**essay.** See ASSAY, ESSAY.

**establishment.** The faddish use of the term to denote the ruling or influential members of any organization, particularly in government or politics, is decried by Fowler, who sees in it a sinister connotation, although this does not necessarily hold true in the U.S. The newly popular use is recognized as standard by American Heritage and Random House but is not given in Webster, probably because it had not yet become widespread when the Third Edition was published in 1961.

**estimate, estimation.** Evans and Fowler point out that *estimate* is the judgment, *estimation* the process of forming it. Thus usually the phrase *in my estimation* is wrong, when an opinion fully formed is given without reference to forming it. Evans concedes, however, that the interchange of the terms is so frequent as to be nevertheless standard; Random House and Webster both recognize it as such.

**et al.** *Et al.* is an abbreviation of the Latin *et alii* (*and others*); *others* refers here to people, not things. "He was interested in the discussion of bills having to do with education *et al.*" is an error, for the writer meant *and other* (presumably related) *subjects. Etc.* (which see), meaning *and other things, and so forth,* would have been preferable from the standpoint of exactness, but the use of such catchalls is slipshod at best, and they should be avoided unless the reader can be expected to have a clear idea what they are intended to suggest. In *et al., et,* as a complete word, does not take a period, but *al.,* for *alii,* does. This nicety is sometimes disregarded. Sometimes, too, the parts are erroneously run together: *etal.* The natural habitat of *et al.* is legal documents, where it is used to indicate persons whose names may not be known: *John Jones, Edward Thomas, George Swift, et al.* Perhaps the expression had best be left to such contexts (Copperud, Flesch). *Et al.* may also mean *et alibi* (*and elsewhere*).

etc. The common mistake is to misspell it *ect.* and thus advertise one's ignorance that it is the abbreviation for *et cetera* (Latin, *and so forth*). Partridge called it insulting when applied to people; Fowler says it is needless purism to restrict its sense to *and other things* as opposed to *and other persons.* A comma before *etc.* is unnecessary unless more than one term precedes it. *Etc.* is often lazily used as a bushel basket, as in "They form their own opinions about economics, etc." The reader should easily see what *etc.* is intended to suggest. Like ET AL. (which see), however, *etc.* is suited to technical contexts and not to ordinary prose. *And etc.* is

redundant (Bernstein, Copperud, Fowler).

-eth. The writer who finds it desirable to revert to Middle English for special effect should keep in mind that this termination indicates the third person singular (*he, she, it*): *He thinketh, she smileth, The Iceman Cometh, from whence cometh my help.* It invites derision to write things like *I cometh, you smileth.* The second-person ending is *-st,* and calls for *thou* as subject (*Thou doest*). (Quaker usage is specialized, and calls invariably for *thee.*) Flesch discourages use of the *-eth* ending as a phony device. See also THEE, THOU.

-ette. See FEMININE FORMS.

eulogy. Takes *a,* not *an.* See A, AN.

Euphemisms. Life is a hard business, as someone has said, and we often seek to soften its blows by giving them agreeable names. This device—for example, saying *passed away* instead of *died*—is known technically as *euphemism,* or pleasing talk. Euphemism is not something that can or should be done away with. In many instances, the bluntest names for things are intolerable in polite society and censurable in print. The so-called four-letter words are an example. On the rare occasions when they appear in print the effect on the reader may be one of shock, refreshment, amusement, or a mixture of all three, although this reaction too is changing as printed matter becomes more earthy.

We should at least be aware when we are using terms

that are at one or more removes from the most explicit versions. Euphemisms are distasteful when they indicate unnecessary squeamishness. The trend of our ordinary expression for many years has been away from the complex, the pretentious, the coy, and the flowery, and toward the simple, the unassuming, the frank, and the unadorned.

It is not long ago that *social disease* was as close as anyone but a doctor would come to saying *syphilis* or *gonorrhea*—and even the euphemism was used with reluctance. In fact, the medical campaign to curb syphilis was seriously impeded by the refusal, at first, of mass publications to even name the disease.

Here are some typical euphemisms. A cut or increase in wages or prices is often glossed over as a *downward revision* or an *upward revision* (or *adjustment*). In the jargon of business, especially, prices are unlikely to be raised, but more likely to be delicately *adjusted upward*. This may be all right for the public relations man, whose vocation is to gloss, but certainly such genteelisms should not be adopted by others with the idea that they possess some desirable elegance.

*Realistic* is a key euphemism in collective bargaining. *Realistic,* in this connection, is what the user's proposals are, in contrast to those of the other side, which are *unrealistic*. During World War II the public became familiar with *planned withdrawal*, the military's euphemism for *retreat* (usually *to prepared positions*). General Jonathan Wainwright was so outraged by this kind of mush that he described one reverse in these unequivocal terms: "We took a hell of a beating."

The name "Women's Christian Temperance Union," as nearly everyone must be aware, is a misnomer, for its members advocate abstinence, not temperance. *Belly* is all but indecent; the genteel speak of the *abdomen* or *stomach*. Edifying discussions of this subject, taking various approaches not dissimilar to this one, may be found in Bernstein, Evans, Follett (under *Genteelism*), and Fowler (under both *Euphemism* and *Genteelism*).

**evacuate.** Standard in the sense of removing people from a place, as well as in the sense of emptying the place itself, although in the past this use was much criticized (Copperud, Evans). The matter is settled by the presence of *evacuate* in this sense as well as *evacuee* (for the person removed) in all current dictionaries. See also -EE.

**even.** Problems of the placement of *even* in a sentence correspond to those of the placement of ONLY, which see. The matter warrants careful attention.

**event.** See IN THE EVENT THAT.

**eventuate, eventuality.** Criticized as pompous for *occur-(rence), develop(ment)* or *happen(ing)* by Evans, Flesch, and Fowler.

**ever.** As an intensive, see HOWEVER, HOW EVER; WHATEVER, WHAT EVER. Often unnecessarily joined to an adjective with a hyphen: *ever-increasing size.*

**ever so often, every so often.** The first means *very frequently,* the second *now and then* (Copperud, Evans, American Heritage).

**every.** Evans says it is used only as an adjective, a judgment in which the dictionaries concur. Yet Bryant points out that it occurs sometimes as an adverb in such phrases as *every so often, every now and then, every significantly new philosophy.* Whether *every* in these constructions, of which the dictionaries list the first two and analogous ones, is indeed an adverb may be a matter of opinion; American Heritage calls it an intensifier with idioms. At any rate, the phrases are idioms. For the number of the pronoun following *every* in such constructions as "Every one of the boys has (his, their) own canoe," see EACH.

**everybody, everyone, every one. 1.** Evans and Flesch say that though these pronouns take singular verbs, it is standard to refer to them by *they,* rather than *he.* Copperud and American Heritage say that, strictly speaking, the singular reference should be used—"Everybody shouldered his pack and moved on" (rather than *their packs*)—and adds that the plural reference (*they, their*) is permissible in conversation. Fowler tends to be equivocal on this question but on the whole recommends the singular reference. The question is discussed also under ANYBODY, ANYONE, and EACH. Evans points out that a singu-

lar pronoun in reference to *everybody, everyone* is impossible in a coordinate clause: "Everyone has gone home and it is about time he did." *they.*
**2.** The pronoun *everyone* must be distinguished from the adjective and pronoun *every one:* "He had something cheerful to say to everyone of his admirers" *every one* (Copperud, Fowler, American Heritage). Fowler adds that the test of the acceptability of *everyone* is whether *everybody* can be substituted.
**3.** *Everyone* and *everybody* are equally acceptable and interchangeable. See also ELSE'S.

**everyday, every day.** The adjective *everyday* (*an everyday occurrence*) and the adverbial phrase *every day* (*It happens every day*) should be distinguished. "Everyday the papers are full of his exploits." *Every day.*

**everyone.** See EVERYBODY, EVERYONE.

**everyone knows.** See OF COURSE.

**everyplace.** Recognized as standard by Bryant, Evans, Flesch, and Webster as a synonym for the adverb *everywhere;* American Heritage and Random House consider it informal. See also ANYPLACE.

**everytime, every time.** Flesch says the one-word form is often used, but Copperud prescribes two words. No current dictionary recognizes *everytime.*

**evidence.** Criticized as inexact or pretentious as a verb where *show* or *exhibit* will do by Copperud, Flesch, and Fowler.

**evince.** Copperud, Evans, and Flesch criticize it as pretentiously displacing *show;* Fowler says it is misused for *evoke.*

**ex-.** The question is whether the prefix must be attached to a noun (*ex-headwaiter*) or whether it may be attached to an adjective (*ex-Waldorf headwaiter*) without modifying only the adjective. Fowler will not permit attaching *ex-* to the adjective. But Bernstein and Copperud say this is permissible and, in fact, usually unavoidable: compare *ex-bathing beauty* with *bathing ex-beauty.* The deciding point seems to be that readers (in the U.S., at least) are well accustomed to interpreting *ex-* phrases in the senses intended, and thus Fowler's objection that a phrase like *ex-bathing beauty* would be understood as meaning the subject was formerly bathing but still a beauty sounds captious. The problem occurs mainly in composing newspaper headlines; when there is any danger of ambiguity it can easily be sidestepped in text by using *former.*

*Ex-* is hyphenated as a prefix meaning *former: ex-convict, ex-president, ex-queen,* etc. Otherwise, in the sense *out of,* it is solid: *excommunicate, expropriate, exterritorial,* etc.

**exact, exactly.** *Exact* may not be used as an adverb, as in this common construction: *the exact same policy. Exactly the same policy.* Neither Random House nor Webster admits *exact* as an adverb. The problem of

the placement of *exactly* is analogous to that of the placement of *only,* which see.

**exceedingly, excessively.** The first means *to a great extent,* the second means *too much.* Sometimes confused (Evans, Follett, Fowler).

**except, excepting.** Bernstein and Evans agree that, regardless of some differences among grammarians, *except* is a preposition and thus takes the objective case: *except me.* As prepositions, *excepted, excepting* are undesirable except in a negative statement: "Everything about the new cars is easier to handle excepting the payments." *except.* An example of correct use: "The movies were exciting, not excepting the American entry" (Bernstein, Copperud, Evans, Fowler, American Heritage).

**exception proves the rule.** The commonly accepted meaning of this is that the rule is strengthened or its validity is enhanced or certified by exceptions. Fowler devotes nearly two pages to the expression, setting forth five interpretations of it, and terming the generally understood one wrong. Evans makes essentially the same point in less space. It seems reasonable to suppose, however, that logical or not, an expression means what the overwhelming number of its users understand it to mean, regardless of its technical origins or the distortions it has undergone in arriving at its present popular sense. Webster's New World Dictionary says of the phrase, "the exception tests the rule; often used to mean 'the exception establishes the rule.'"

(Evans recognizes the *tests* interpretation as the most generally accepted explanation of the phrase; Fowler does not mention it.)

**exceptionable, exceptional.** That which is exceptional is outstanding or remarkable in some way; that which is exceptionable may be taken exception, or objected, to. What is unexceptionable is unobjectionable (Evans, Fowler). American Heritage rejects the use of *unexceptional* for *unexceptionable* as loose. Webster, however, gives it as standard.

**excess verbiage.** Redundant; *verbiage* denotes excess.

**excessively.** See EXCEEDINGLY.

**Exclamation Point.** Bernstein, Copperud, and Fowler agree that this mark is overused. But this is not the vice it once was, to judge from the criticisms that appeared in style manuals of a generation or two ago. Columnists (and others writing in a colloquial tone) often use the exclamation mark to call attention to a japery; perhaps they would be better advised to append (*joke*). At any rate, this punctuation adds no humor, and may, by reason of its obtrusiveness, subtract some.

Interjections in a single word (*Ouch! Indeed!*) generally take the exclamation mark. Fowler complains that it is often needlessly used with such statements as *You surprise me, How dare you?*, and *Don't tell such lies,* which are described as mere statement, question, and command. This seems, however, to overlook the fact that emphasis is conveyed by the

exclamation mark. *You surprise me* (period) is cool and tame; *You surprise me!* conveys excitement, if not indignation. *How dare you?* is much less indignant than *How dare you! Don't tell such lies* (period) is contemptuous; *Don't tell such lies!* is outraged. Whether such statements should be followed by exclamation points must be left to the judgment and intention of the writer; he is not open to critical quibbling over the suitability of his punctuation if he conveys what he intends, and does not falsify or misrepresent the tone. The end of Fowler's discussion of this subject seems to open a window that was earlier closed; that is, he says the mark may be used to convey a special tone. The present reader is referred to the heading *Exclamation* under the entry *Stops* so that he can make his own inferences. Flesch apparently would outlaw the mark altogether, a view that seems quixotic.

Exclamation points used after ordinary statements with the hope of giving them a transfusion are gushy; fortunately, this kind of thing is seldom found in print except for letters to the editor; more often it occurs in schoolgirls' letters. All this goes double for doubled (or otherwise multiplied) exclamation points ("I appeal to you for advice!!"; "Some of us are in a minority all the time!! Must we be content with perpetual inconsideration? I think not!!!")

F. Scott Fitzgerald, confronted with an example of such overexcited style, advised: "Cut out all those exclamation points. An exclamation point is

like laughing at your own joke"
(*Beloved Infidel*).

The exclamation point may
be formed on the typewriter
that does not have one by striking the apostrophe and period
while holding the space bar
down, or by striking the apostrophe, back-spacing, and striking the period. This latter
method, while more trouble,
brings the mark more neatly
up against the word preceding.

**ex-felon.** An absurdity often
encountered in the press. Once
a felon, always a felon. Users
probably have in mind *ex-convict.*

**exhaust.** As applied to people, a transitive verb, which
means it must take an object.
"She exhausted easily" thus
should be put "She became
exhausted easily" or "Things
easily exhausted her" (Copperud, Random House, Web-
ster).

**exhibit.** Bernstein says an
exhibit is an item or a collec-
tion of items in an exhibition,
and thus such an expression as
*art exhibit* is wrong. No such
limitation is recognized by any
current dictionary, however.

**exhilarate.** Often misspelled
*exhilirate.* See also ACCELERATE,
EXHILARATE.

**exist.** A superstition was at
one time fairly widespread that
only what is alive can exist. It
means *be* as well as *live,* and
is properly applied to inanimate
things and even insubstantial
ones, such as ideas. This view
is borne out by definitions in
both Random House and Webster.

**existence.** Sometimes misspelled *existance.*

**exorbitant.** Sometimes misspelled *exhorbitant.*

**exotic.** The word originally
meant only *of foreign origin,*
but Copperud and Evans point
out that it now is almost invariably understood in the senses
*strange, glamorous, unusual,
strikingly out of the ordinary.*
The American College Dictionary calls this more common use
colloquial; the three other desk
dictionaries recognize it as
standard, as do American Heritage, Random House, and
Webster.

**expatriot.** An occasional error
for *expatriate;* occurrences of it
in a headline and story in the
*New York Times* were complained of in the Winter 1966,
edition of the *Columbia Journalism Review. Expatriot,* to be
found in no dictionary, could
only mean a former patriot.

**expect.** In the sense of *suppose* or *believe* ("I expect it
will rain"; "I expect the chick-
ens have been fed"), described
by Evans as standard in the
U.S. but condemned in Britain.
Fowler, however, defends it
as firmly established in colloquial use. Bernstein and Copperud criticize this sense as
affected, local, or dialectal.
Among the dictionaries, Random House and Webster recognize the sense *suppose* as
standard, the Standard College
and American Heritage call it
informal, and the American
College and Webster's New
World call it colloquial. The
consensus is that this use is not

entirely out of the shadow of criticism. See also ANTICIPATE.

**expectorate.** Discouraged by Evans, Flesch, and Fowler as a euphemism for *spit*.

**expel.** Often misspelled *expell*, perhaps on the model of its past tense, *expelled*.

**expensive.** Means *high-priced*. Thus "The average man found the prices expensive" would better be *found the prices high*. Goods may be expensive, prices high (Copperud, Random House, Webster).

**expertise, expertize.** The first is a noun meaning *expertness;* it is in high fashion with pundits and those who aspire to being thought wise. *Expertize*, a comparatively odd fish, is a verb meaning *give expert judgment on.* They are unlikely to be confused in talking unless mispronounced, for *expertise* ends in *eez.* But writing is another matter: "He named a committee of conservative businessmen to expertise the foreign aid program." *expertize.* The confusion may arise from the fact, pointed out by Random House, that in British usage *expertize* is spelled *expertise.* This seems to be a rarity, however; neither the Oxford Universal Dictionary nor the Concise Oxford Dictionary gives it. Flesch criticizes *expertise* as a fad for *knowledge.*

**explain.** See ATTRIBUTION 2.

**explicit, express.** Evans and Fowler point out that while both terms (as adjectives) describe what is lucidly and completely set forth, *express* goes farther, indicating a commit-

ment or particular intention: *his express purpose.*

**explore every avenue.** Criticized by Evans, Flesch, and Fowler as a cliché.

**expose.** Often used in a mushmouthed way: "Entering freshmen are now so deficient they must be exposed to a remedial reading course before they can proceed." This would better be expressed exactly: *must take a remedial reading course. Exposure* suggests what is undesirable, ephemeral, or both; neither sense is appropriate to the example. "Children are being exposed to new exhibits in art, music, and science at the preschool level." *are being shown, are seeing* (Copperud, Random House, Webster).

**exposé.** Criticized by Evans and Fowler as a French word that is unnecessary beside the English *exposure* and *exposition. Exposé,* however, has become so popular in the sense of revealing what is blameworthy that it is unlikely to be dislodged.

**express.** Fowler criticizes the omission of *as* after *express,* as in "She expressed herself somewhat surprised" (*expressed herself as*). This is obviously unidiomatic though it is seen fairly often in the U.S. See also EXPLICIT.

**extended.** Inexact and pretentious when it displaces *long,* as in *an extended illness.* That which is extended has been given greater extent (Copperud, Flesch, Random House, Webster).

# F

**fabulous.** Criticized by Bernstein, Evans, and Fowler as a vogue word for *incredible, astounding, astonishing,* and the like. The original sense, it is pointed out, was *mythical, legendary;* that is to say, relating to a fable. The faddish use of the word is found mostly in advertisements, where it may be applied to anything from girls to typewriters. This sense is recognized as standard, however, by American Heritage, Random House, and Webster.

**face up to.** Bernstein spiritedly defends the phrase, as Copperud did in the magazine *Editor & Publisher* in 1960, as meaning something more than *face* and as serving a useful purpose. The expression was among Americanisms criticized at one time by Henry George Strauss, Baron Conesford, who found little good in the language he encountered on this side of the Atlantic. Fowler too concedes that *face up to* is not the same as *face.* American Heritage, Random House, and Webster explicitly recognize the expression as standard.

**facile.** Evans and Fowler point out that the word has a derogatory connotation; what is described as facile is understood to be not merely easy but too easy, and thus somehow lacking in virtue.

**facilitate.** Fowler holds that things may be facilitated, but not the doer of them; thus one may not say "The teacher was facilitated in his lecture by a complete set of notes." The *lecture* was facilitated. But both Random House and Webster say a person may be facilitated, in the sense *aided, helped.* Flesch criticizes the word when it displaces the simpler *ease, help.*

**facility, facilities.** Criticized by Flesch and Follett as displacing more precise terms such as *factory, center, establishment;* for example, *scientific facilities* for *laboratory.*

**fact, facts.** Bernstein, Copperud, and Evans say *the fact that* is often superfluous, as in "We admit the fact that an injustice has been done." *We admit that.* Bernstein and Copperud add that the phrase is sometimes used to describe what is not fact but supposition or assertion: "This could be just an expression of the fact that the Russians are unconcerned and content to play a waiting game." The context, however, made clear that this was merely speculation, and gave alternative explanations. Bernstein and Copperud say *true facts* is redundant, since what is fact must be true by definition. Flesch defends *true* (and *real*) *facts* as offering a distinction from false facts or lies. Flesch to the contrary, none of the current desk dictionaries defines *fact* in a way that allows *true facts;* reality and truth, or the assumption of them, are essential to *facts* in these definitions. Random House and Webster, however, allow the use of *facts* for what may be open to question, which seems to permit *true facts.*

**factious, factitious, fictitious.** Evans and Fowler warn against confusion, pointing out that *factious* pertains to politics, *factitious* means *artificial,* and *fictitious* means *fictional* or *invented. Fictitious* is often misspelled *ficticious,* and the term is often misapplied to checks written with intent to defraud. *Fraudulent* seems a better choice, for, as Webster notes, "fictitious applies to fabrication or contrivance, often artful, without necessary intent to deceive."

**factor.** Bernstein, Evans, Fowler, and Flesch agree that the word is properly used for a cause contributing to a result, and thus such phrases as *personal safety factor* (for *personal safety*) and *contributing factor* (for *factor*) are objectionable. *Factor* is often also used superfluously, and in any event is regarded by these authorities and by Follett as a counterword too often replacing more precise expressions such as *element, ingredient, component, constituent.*

**faculty.** Evans and Follett criticize the use of the term for *faculty members,* a popular locution, as Follett points out, around colleges: "Eight of the objectors were students and six were faculty." *faculty members, from the faculty.* The error is in treating *faculty* as other than a collective.

**Fad Words.** The term applies to words that have become too popular and thus tiresome. Many entries are so described in this dictionary. The subject is dealt with in general terms by Bernstein and Flesch under this heading, by Follett under *Vogue Words,* and by Fowler under the headings *Novelty Hunting* and *Vogue Words.* Examples of terms that have been so described: *image, status symbol, task force, charismatic, know-how, viable, crash program, rationale, angry young men, long hot summer.* These should be enough to show what the critics have in mind.

**faerie, faery, fairy.** Evans says that *fairy* as a slang term for *homosexual* is so widespread in the U.S. that it is almost impossible to use it in any other sense in public. This seems rather too sweeping; the context determines the sense; at any rate, *fairy* now seems less fashionable for *homosexual* than *fag,* or the adjective *gay.* Fowler (quoting the Oxford English Dictionary) had perhaps the same thing in mind in saying that *faerie* (of which *faery* is a variant) might be used "to exclude various unpoetical or undignified associations connected with the current form *fairy.*" But *faerie, faery,* are rarely used in the U.S. except in connection with Spenser, the inventor of *faerie.*

**fail.** Carries a strong implication of falling short in an attempt, but it is often misused, especially by newspapers, where there is no question of an attempt: "Buckingham Palace failed to confirm the story";

"The burning bed failed to disturb the sleeper." If there is any virtue in precise statement, *did not confirm* and *did not disturb* are preferable (Bernstein, Copperud, Flesch). Flesch adds that *failure* is often misused in the same way. Fowler points out that *fail* often figures in unconscious reversal of sense, as in "The decision can hardly fail to pass unnoticed," when the intention is *can hardly fail to be noticed.*

**fair-trade laws, agreements.** Political and commercial euphemisms. Such laws or agreements have nothing to do with fair trade from the consumer's viewpoint; their purpose is to force retailers to maintain a price structure fixed by the manufacturer, a stratagem that the bargain-hunter, at least, considers highly unfair, as does the cut-rate merchant. But it is called free enterprise. Some publications, unwilling to fall into the trap of misrepresentation set by this term, preface it by *so-called.*

**fall.** Fowler points out that this term for *autumn* is an Americanism and exceptionable in Britain. In the U.S., *autumn,* while still in service, is perhaps taking on a faintly literary tinge, as Evans notes; the ordinary word is *fall.*

**fallacy, fallacious.** Bernstein and Fowler point out that in logic, a fallacy is an error in reasoning, and that in the more common sense it denotes what is misleading, not merely wrong. Thus to describe a mistaken report as fallacious is objectionable; the word should be *false, mistaken, erroneous.* Dictionary definitions bear out this view.

**False Comparison.** Careless writers, apparently by carrying ellipsis too far, often stumble into false comparison. They write "Older houses are still selling here, unlike many cities" or "Like many patient folk, Russian violence can be brutal." The need is for "unlike *those in* many cities" and "like *that of* many patient folk." In the examples, *older houses* are actually though unintentionally compared with *many cities,* and *patient folk* with *Russian violence.* A variation of the same error: "Receipts from livestock sales were 7 per cent less than the corresponding period last year." *less than in* (Bernstein, Copperud, Follett, Fowler). Fowler notes, under *Ellipsis,* the variety of the error with *than,* and generally prescribes recasting (*than they were in the corresponding period*). See also COMPARISON 1.

**false illusions.** A common redundancy; falsity (i.e., unreality) is the essence of illusion.

**False Linkage.** See COMMA 5.

**False Possessive.** See POSSESSIVES 4.

**False Titles.** "*Griffelkin* is an opera for children by distinguished young California composer Lukas Foss." Piling up descriptives in this fashion is an idiosyncrasy of journalism, brought on by the urge to compress. The result, however, is hard to digest. For some reason, journalists are hostile to the appositive construction, which the false title displaces. Instead of *Renata Tebaldi, an Italian soprano,* they write *Italian soprano Renata Tebaldi;*

instead of *Eddie Crews, a carnival concessionaire,* they write *carnival concessionaire Eddie Crews;* instead of *Angelo Litrico, a Rome tailor,* they write *Rome tailor Angelo Litrico.* (Of course, the descriptive could as well stand before the name and still be in the appositive form: *a Rome tailor, Angelo Litrico.*) Sometimes journalists compound the error by using the comma but omitting the article: *Rome tailor, Angelo Litrico.* This mannerism is repeatedly deplored in newspaper stylebooks and critiques of journalistic writing, but there seems no hope of dislodging it. Follett calls this stylistic device offensive; Bernstein and Copperud identify it as one of the affectations invented by *Time* magazine. It is criticized also by Flesch.

**famed.** Criticized variously as journalese and as a peculiarity displacing *famous* by Bernstein, Copperud, and Flesch ("an internationally famed physicist"). Copperud adds that *famed* is more palatable as a predicate modifier than as an attributive (standing before the noun): "His deeds were famed in song and story" vs. "The world's most famed beer garden." Both unabridged dictionaries recognize the term as standard; the example in Random House gives it in the predicate position and that in Webster in the attributive. American Heritage too accepts it.

**fanatic, fanatical.** See -IC, -ICAL.

**fantasy, phantasy.** Evans points out that these are simply equivalent variants, and that the first is the predominant form, a judgment concurred in by both unabridged dictionaries. A distinction in sense set forth in the original Fowler has been omitted in Gowers' revision.

**far be it from me.** Criticized by Evans as a cliché and often deceptive, and by Flesch as stilted and old-fashioned. The latter descriptive seems curious in view of the current popularity of the phrase.

**farcical.** Sometimes given *farcial,* but there is no such word.

**farther, further.** The purist holds that *farther* applies to physical distance and *further* to anything else, e.g., *a farther journey, a further consideration.* This is the position of the American Heritage panel. Bernstein predicts that the distinction will be lost fifty years hence; Bryant, Copperud, Evans, and Fowler agree that it is already gone. To put it more explicitly, *farther* and *farthest* are used to refer only to distance, but *further* is used indiscriminately in both the physical and the figurative sense. *Farther* is never used in the abstract or figurative sense; no one says *a farther consideration, farther effort.* Those conclusions are borne out by the definitions in both unabridged dictionaries. Fowler speculated that *further* would drive out *farther,* and the prediction is repeated in the revised edition, but there is no sign of this in the U.S., at least, as Copperud and Evans point out.

**fartherest, furtherest.** Not standard forms.

**fatal, fateful.** Bernstein, Evans, and Fowler point out

that *fatal* means death-dealing, *fateful* productive of great consequences, for either good or evil.

**fault.** As a verb meaning *find fault with* or *blame* ("It's pretty hard to fault the tactics of Walter Reuther in his war with General Motors") the term is criticized as a fad by Copperud and Follett, and defended by Fowler as a useful revival to which exception should not be taken. Two current desk dictionaries recognize the sense as standard and two designate it "rare," showing that they are not as well up with the times as they might be. American Heritage (narrowly), Webster, and Random House also admit *fault* as a verb; the consensus is that it is standard.

**faze, phase.** *Faze* means *disconcert* or *daunt,* and is usually used with a negative: "We were not fazed by the setback." *Phase,* often wrongly used in that sense, is a noun meaning aspect: "The lecturer described the phases of the moon." (Copperud, Evans; Webster gives *phase* as a variant of *faze,* but neither Random House nor any desk dictionary recognizes this usage.) The consensus favors the distinction. With *in* or *out, phase* is a verb, usually found in military contexts, meaning *place in* (or *take out of*) *operation by stages:* "The program will be phased out by Christmas." Bernstein derogates this sense as a fad, but *phase in* and *phase out* are recognized as standard by both Random House and Webster. The current dictionaries, except for Webster, call *faze* colloquial or informal.

**feasible, possible.** Bernstein, Evans, and Fowler point out that *feasible* means *capable of being done,* and *possible* means *capable of happening.* They warn against misuse of *feasible* in such senses as "a storm seems feasible," where *possible* or *probable* is called for.

**feature.** Overworked, especially in advertising and journalism, in the sense *exhibit prominently:* "Yankee Stadium usually features bases 90 feet apart"; "Detergents are featured in this week's sale" (Bernstein, Copperud, Fowler). Evans, like Bernstein, defends the term against criticisms of it as an objectionable novelty that were made a generation ago; one such appeared in the original Fowler. Gowers, in the revised edition, speculates that the term is now worn out, at least in the world of entertainment.

**feel.** The use of the term in the sense *think, believe,* has been widely criticized. The argument usually runs that *feel* should not be used in this sense except to indicate emotion; Evans says strong emotion, or groping. Copperud dissents from this idea, and cites Shakespeare, Trollope, Thomas Hardy, and Abraham Lincoln as having used *feel* in contexts where it would have been interchangeable with *think* or *believe.* The Oxford English Dictionary gives one sense as "to apprehend or recognize the truth of something on grounds not distinctly perceived," and gives as an example "The proposed legislation was felt to be expedient." Fowler criticizes the term only as too weak for the announcement of official decisions, for which apparently it is often used in Britain. All current dictionaries give senses of *feel* that equate it with *think, believe, perceive, have a conviction of*. The consensus is overwhelmingly that *feel* is standard in these latter senses, divorced from either emotion or groping, a conclusion that is easily corroborated by observation of current educated usage.

**feel bad, badly.** Bernstein insists that *badly* can only be an adverb, so that *I feel badly* is wrong except when *badly* actually modifies *feel*. Webster, however, recognizes *badly* as an adjective in this construction, and Random House describes it as informal. The Standard College Dictionary says *feel badly* is in such common use it can no longer be considered substandard. Copperud says the forms are now standard and interchangeable; Follett says *feel badly* is established colloquially but that *feel bad* is strictly correct; American Heritage rejects *feel badly* in writing but accepts it for *be regretful* in speech. Flesch draws the distinction that *feel bad* should be used to describe physical discomfort or illness and *feel badly* to describe regret. Bryant finds usage almost evenly divided between the two forms. The consensus is that both *feel bad* and *feel badly* are standard and interchangeable with respect to regret and illness. Evans points out that with other than linking verbs like *feel, badly* is preferable: *It ached badly.*

**feline.** Journalese as a variant of *cat* (Copperud, Flesch).

**female, feminine.** Copperud says *female* is unsuitable or forcedly facetious in place of *girl, woman, lady;* Evans and Fowler say it is suitable for stressing the distinction of sex, and thus essentially technical or scientific; and Flesch would restrict its application to animals. The consensus is that the term is inappropriate, as either noun or adjective, when applied casually to girls or women, and particularly to describe qualities of the human female, for which the preferable term is *feminine. Female* is too clinical for ordinary use in reference to girls or women. Copperud and Flesch criticize *feminine* as a substitute for *woman:* "The problems of being Irish and feminine." *a woman.* "The accused said the suspect sometimes bought feminine clothes in London's West End." *women's clothes.* See also WOMAN, LADY.

**Feminine Forms.** Bernstein, Copperud, Flesch, and Fowler point out that many of these, such as *ancestress, aviatrix, authoress, poetess,* have fallen into disuse, perhaps proving that equality of the sexes is truly here. *Postmistress* is not recognized by the federal government, which designates all postmasters *postmasters.* Some such terms remain in common and undisputed use, however, such as *abbess, actress, governess, hostess, seamstress, stewardess, shepherdess, adventuress, waitress, usherette.* Fowler disparages *drum majorette,* but it has become indispensable in the U.S. Such designations as "lady physicist" are also often considered objectionable.

**fever.** See TEMPERATURE.

**fewer, less.** The general rule is that *fewer* applies to readily distinguishable units (*fewer people, ships, houses*) and *less* in other circumstances (*less sugar, time*) (Bernstein, Bryant, Copperud, Follett, Fowler, American Heritage). American Heritage, Bernstein, and Follett point out that *less* is used with plurals regarded as indicating a unit, such as distances (less than 150 miles), periods of time (less than 20 minutes), and sums of money (less than $200). Porter G. Perrin (*Writer's Guide and Index to English*) observes, "*Fewer* seems to be declining in use and *less* commonly takes its place," and cites *less hands* and *three less seats*. Bryant finds that although the preference follows the rule as stated, *less* is often found with plurals even in formal contexts, and Evans and Flesch consider this usage acceptable. Webster and Webster's New World give *fewer* as a synonym of *less;* Random House and the American College and Standard College dictionaries follow the rule. The consensus favors the rule, though strong forces are working against it.

**few (fewer) in number.** Belongs to a family of redundancies: *small* (or *large*) *in size; rectangular* (or *whatever*) *in shape*. Omit *in number, in size, in shape* (Bernstein, Copperud).

**Fiberglas, fiber glass.** The first is a trademark, and in deference to its owners should be capitalized, though there is no way such deference can be compelled. The generic term, which may be preferable for ordinary use, is *fiber glass* (sometimes *fibrous glass* or *spun glass*).

**fictitious,** See FACTIOUS, FACTITIOUS, FICTITIOUS.

**fiddle, violin.** Except as applied to what country performers play, *fiddle* is considered derogatory by the layman, who respectfully says *violin. Fiddle* is the common expression among musicians; nevertheless, they may resent its use by others (Copperud, Evans, Fowler).

**field.** In such constructions as *the field of telemetry,* Flesch and Follett say *the field of* can often be omitted; Follett disparages the term, in reference to branches of learning, as belonging to the jargon of education.

**fight with, against.** *Fight with* is ambiguous: "He fought with the Spaniards" fairly prompts the question "Which side was he on?" The context usually explains. Nevertheless, *fight against* or recasting is worth consideration.

**figuratively.** See LITERALLY.

**figure.** Disparaged by Bernstein and Evans for *suppose* or *think:* "I figure things will all work out." This usage is considered informal by Random House and standard by Webster. *Figure* is standard, however, in the sense *calculate* or *compute.* Evans points out that *figure* is the term for the numerical symbol (1, 2, 3) and that *number* can refer either to the symbol or the word expressing it (*one, two, three*). See also NUMBERS.

**figurehead.** Often misapplied to people. "The teacher is one of the figureheads if not the most important member of our community." A figurehead is a symbol, one with no real authority or responsibility, a leader in name only. Calling a person a figurehead thus is derogatory; the meaning intended in the example was *leading citizens.* "Bach is now recognized as the figurehead to whom all musical innovators have turned for inspiration in the twentieth century." Unintentionally demeaning: *lodestar, bellwether,* or something equivalent (Copperud, Random House, Webster).

**Figures.** See NUMBERS.

**final culmination.** "This club is the final culmination of the kind of intimate feeling we have been searching for." Redundant; *culmination.*

**finalize.** Criticized variously by Copperud, Flesch, Follett, Fowler, and American Heritage as gobbledygook or as an unnecessary neologism for *complete, finish, end.* The word has been widely derided, though on one occasion it was pointed out that President John F. Kennedy used it in a speech. Bernstein criticized it in an earlier work, but omitted the entry later, which could indicate that he had changed his mind or that he decided the fight was lost. The Standard College Dictionary points out that although frowned upon, the term has been in standard use for more than twenty years. The New World Dictionary calls it a neologism, Webster considers it standard, and the American

College does not list it. Random House extends the span of its standard use from twenty years to the last forty, and says it usually occurs in formal contexts. The weight of opinion is against it.

**financial.** Criticized by Flesch and Follett as often used pretentiously concerning small sums or in place of *money; financial matters* for *money matters.*

**fine.** Copperud calls it a superstition that the term may not be used as an adjective to denote superior quality, as in *a fine man, a fine day,* but must be reserved for the idea of physical fineness (*fine-grained*). This view is supported by all current dictionaries. Bryant points out that it has become a counterword and is overused in place of more specific descriptives. Bernstein, Bryant, Copperud, and Evans say it is colloquial as an adverb ("He is doing fine") and all dictionaries except Webster, which considers it standard, agree.

**finical, finicky.** Evans and Fowler agree that the second is the commoner form.

**finishing touch.** Sentences employing this and similar phrases including *touch* are often subjected to some painful twists. A finishing touch sounds like something that would be *given* a building, plan, or whatever. But frequently in print it is *made to, made on,* or *put to.* "He put a personal touch to the story" is a gaucherie for "He gave the story a personal touch."

**fire.** Slang for *dismiss, discharge* (Bernstein, Fowler, Evans); Random House and Webster consider it standard; American Heritage labels it informal.

**firm.** The technical meaning is a partnership of two or more persons not recognized as a legal person distinct from the members composing it. Thus Bernstein says it is unacceptable as a synonym for *corporation,* a distinction that all current dictionaries but Webster concur in.

**first and foremost.** Criticized as bombast by Copperud and Evans.

**first come, first served.** The form of the expression. It is often heedlessly bobtailed to *first come, first serve,* which changes its sense, and thus it is the victim of the same kind of inattention that affects AS (SO) FAR AS . . . and COULDN'T CARE LESS, which see.

**firstly, secondly, etc.** Evans and Fowler say the long-continued arguments over these forms vs. *first, second,* and especially the criticism of *firstly,* etc., are pedantry; Bernstein, Copperud, and Flesch recommend *first, second,* which Bernstein points out are also adverbs as much as *firstly,* etc. To this it may be added that at least the user should be consistent: either *first, second,* etc., or *firstly, secondly,* etc., *not firstly, second,* etc. All current dictionaries recognize *firstly* without qualification.

**first name.** See CHRISTIAN NAME.

**fish, fishes.** Both forms are standard as the plural (Evans, Fowler, Random House, Webster).

**fit, fitted.** Bryant and Evans say *fit* is preferable for the past tense when the verb is used intransitively, as in reference to clothing: "The suit fit perfectly." Evans adds that *fitted* is invariable when the verb takes an object ("The key fitted the lock," "The work fitted his temperament"). Bernstein and Follett insist on *fitted* without distinction. Random House has *the dress fitted her perfectly* and Webster gives examples with both *fit* and *fitted* used transitively (*fitted his job, fit him to perfection*). Thus the distinctions given by the authorities on usage are ignored, and the forms are used interchangeably. There is no consensus, only a diversity of opinion.

**fix.** The word has many senses as both noun and verb in the U.S.; Bernstein, Evans, and Fowler criticize it as a word-of-all-work, especially in the sense *repair,* that often would better be replaced by something more precise.

**flagrant.** See BLATANT, FLAGRANT.

**flagship.** "The *President Jackson* was the first American flagship to enter the canal." Unhappy compression is at the root of this trouble, which is recurrent. The writer meant "the first ship flying an American flag," but by condensing it, presumably to "the first American-flag ship," set the stage for "the first American flagship." This is confusing and erroneous, for a flagship is a naval vessel carrying the commander of a force, or, occasionally, a merchantman designated as foremost in a fleet.

**flair, flare.** *Flair* in the primary sense means *a keen scent;* Bernstein approves the extension to *discernment, instinctive feeling for,* but disapproves the senses *flourish, talent,* or *aptitude;* in a somewhat cryptic entry, Fowler apparently would allow none except a figurative extension of *keen scent for,* and cites an example where *flaire* [sic] is apparently given for *eagerness* or *enthusiasm.* Evans allows *talent, aptitude, perception,* and in some contexts *fondness.* Copperud and Evans both warn against confusion with *flare* (usually a flame, but sometimes a widening, a sense in which *flair* may also be used). All current dictionaries give such meanings as *natural aptitude, bent* for *flair,* and the American College also gives *fondness.* The consensus is that *aptitude, bent, knack* are acceptable senses; *fondness* is questionable.

**flamboyant.** Fowler says the term should be held to its original sense of *flamelike;* Evans approves *showy,* and so do all current dictionaries. This, in fact, is the most popular sense of the term, and it is doubtful that the ordinary user is even conscious of the sense *flamelike* or of the technical architectural applications of the term.

**flaming inferno.** Redundant; both words denote fire.

**flammable, inflammable.** Fire underwriters and others interested in safety have promoted the use of *flammable* in preference to *inflammable* on the assumption that *inflammable* may be misunderstood to mean *noncombustible.* The terms are synonyms and equally reputable (Bernstein, Copperud, Evans, Follett, American Heritage). Fowler objects to *flammable* and calls it rare. This may be so in Britain but not in the United States.

**flaunt, flout.** *Flaunt* is incessantly confused with *flout.* *Flaunt* means to display in an ostentatious or boastful manner: "The faction flaunted its superior strength." *Flout* means *mock* or *scoff at:* "A speeding motorist flouts the law" (Bernstein, Copperud, Evans, Fowler, American Heritage).

**flautist, flutist.** Copperud, Evans, and Fowler point out that the second form is the older and regard it as preferable. Fowler says *flautist* has displaced *flutist,* but in the United States it is in fact something of an affectation, only occasionally met.

**flay.** Few perhaps are now aware that the original sense was *strip the skin off.* It is now primarily a headline word meaning *criticize harshly, excoriate.* Bernstein apparently considers it misused in any but the primary sense; Evans and Flesch discourage it as overwrought for *criticize.* The secondary (and commonest) meaning is recognized as standard by all dictionaries, though it is true that it is probably unsuitable for ordinary contexts. Owing to the advantage of its shortness, however, no discouragement probably will ever drive it from headlines, but there readers have come to understand it as usually used in a much weakened sense, ranging from mild reproof to sterner criticism, as Evans points out.

**floor.** See CEILING.

**flotsam, jetsam.** Since these terms are often paired, they are assumed to be the same or similar things. Flotsam is goods lost by shipwreck and found floating in the sea; jetsam is goods thrown overboard during a storm to lighten a vessel. The relation to *float* and *jettison* can serve as a reminder of the difference (Copperud, Evans, Fowler).

**flounder, founder.** Often confused. To flounder is to struggle or thrash about; a fish out of water flounders. To founder is to go down, in the case of a ship to fill with water and sink. Ships are sometimes described as floundering, as well they may in a stormy sea, but the intended meaning usually is *founder*. "This attitude misses the whole point on which the policy of the United States has floundered." Conceivably; but more likely *foundered* (failed). "In public favor, the governor is foundering even worse." *floundering* (Copperud, Random House, Webster).

**flout.** See FLAUNT, FLOUT.

**flu.** Except by Webster, the term is regarded by current dictionaries as informal or colloquial for *influenza*, though the long form is so seldom seen that the clipped version may soon become standard. There is no occasion for *'flu*.

**fluorine, fluorescent, etc.** Often misspelled *flourine, flourescent.*

**flush, flushed.** *Flush* is the term for *fully supplied, well filled;* a man who had just received his pay check might describe himself as flush. *Flushed* is the term for *excited, thrilled,* as in *flushed with victory* (a cliché).

**fob, foist.** The idiomatic forms of the phrases are *fob off on* and *foist on; foist off* is wrong (Evans, Fowler).

**folks.** *Folks* for *people* or *relatives* is considered colloquial or informal—"You folks are all right" (Bernstein, Bryant, Copperud, Evans, Follett). Fowler recognizes the locution without disparagement; it is described as primarily American. Random House considers only the application to members of one's family informal; Webster gives both applications as standard.

**follow(s).** See AS FOLLOWS.

**following.** Criticized where it displaces a simple *after* ("Following the movie, we had some ice cream") by Copperud, Flesch, and Fowler. Fowler considers it permissible as a preposition when the idea of consequence or result is present: "Following the war, terms of occupation were agreed on."

**for.** The word must be used with care in connection with criticisms or accusations: to say that a man was criticized for committing perjury is to assume that the perjury was committed. Recasting to attribute the criticism to whoever made it is required so that the writer does not unintentionally leave the impression he concurs in it (Bernstein, Copperud). Starting sentences with *for* and *thus* is an affectation of some writers, particularly columnists. This is warranted only when the sentence draws a conclusion based on what has gone before; the words in such constructions are the equivalent of *consequently*. "But will the prisoners again read into the president's words a promise such as they thought they had in April 1961? For they risked their lives then." The second sentence does not draw a conclusion from the first; it merely carries the argument forward: "They risked their lives then."

**force, -d.** Often used inappropriately, so that it conveys a stronger sense of compulsion than is warranted. "Pupils through the third grade at the Roosevelt School will be forced to attend half-day sessions this term." This conjures up an image of the wretched kids manacled together and marching to their half-day sessions in lockstep. It would be more in key with the circumstances to say "Half-day sessions will be necessary" or that the pupils will have to attend half-day sessions. "Some of the sixteen squad cars were forced to go bouncing over bumpy roads to catch the elusive hotrods." *had to go.* *Force* seems the wrong word in these examples because it connotes overcoming resistance, which in these instances is not evident. This view corresponds with definitions and examples in Random House and Webster.

**forceful, forcible.** Both words mean possessing, or using, force, but *forcible* is generally preferred for physical contexts: *a forcible entry* (the police broke down the door). Instinct serves us here; we would be unlikely to describe these circumstances by *a forceful entry*. *Forceful* is generally the word for abstract contexts: "It brought a forceful reminder of another truth" (Copperud, Evans). Fowler says the distinction turns on the amount of force suggested, and regards *forceful* as the stronger. He considers *forcible* the ordinary word, which may be true in Britain but not in the United States. Fowler's examples, however, bear out the distinction set forth by Evans and Copperud. To recapitulate, *forceful* is preferable except to denote physical or exceptional force. *Forceful* often also has a favorable connotation, relating to force used admirably; *forcible* is either neutral or pejorative.

**forecast, forecasted.** Both forms are acceptable as the past tense, but *forecast* is preferable (Copperud, Evans, Follett, Fowler).

**Foreign Terms.** Copperud, Evans, Fowler, Flesch, and Follett all warn against the dangers of misspelling and misusing foreign terms; the consensus is that such terms are best avoided if there is an English equivalent. The danger of misapprehending them is one reason. There is also the likelihood of confusing the reader, or of giving the impression of showing off. Lists of foreign terms misused in various ways are to be found in Evans under the heading *Foreign Plurals*, in Flesch under *Foreign Words, French Words, German Words*, in Follett under *French Words and*

*Phrases,* and in Fowler under *Foreign Danger, French Words,* and *Gallicisms.*

**foremost.** American Heritage allows the term to apply to more than one: *one of the foremost musicians.* Neither Random House nor Webster is explicit on this point, and no dictionary of usage takes it up.

**foreseeable future.** The phrase is sometimes criticized as foolish on the ground that not even the next second is foreseeable.

**foreword, introduction, preface.** In reference to the front matter of a book, the words are now synonyms, Evans, Follett, Fowler, and Random House agree. Copperud, Follett, Random House, and Webster say *preface* applies more properly, however, to a statement by the author, and other current dictionaries except Webster's New World confirm this distinction. *Introduction* is the term usually applied to a statement contributed by someone other than the author, but all three may be applied to a statement by the author. *Foreword* is often misspelled *foreward,* under the influence, perhaps, of *forward.*

**for free.** Objectionable for *free* or *free of charge:* "the pennants will be distributed for free" (Bernstein). The objection seems well taken since *free* is not a noun and thus cannot be the object of a preposition. Nevertheless, Webster recognizes the expression as standard and quotes four reputable writers in its use.

**Formal.** See COLLOQUIALISMS.

**former, latter.** Bernstein, Fowler, American Heritage, and Random House say both terms should be used to refer only to one of two things, not to one of three or more: "He spotted a man and a woman and two children, all obviously hurt, the former more seriously." This is a misuse; the right words here would be *the first* or *the man.* This view represents the consensus. Evans, however, approves of *the latter three,* and Copperud and Webster allow *latter* to refer to the last of more than two. Fowler adds that *former* and *latter* may not be used to refer to pairs of dissimilar things, such as people and objects. Bernstein, Copperud, and Flesch point out that *former* and *latter* are objectionable in that they often make the reader look back and figure out which is which. Fowler says too that *latter* should refer to a noun (*Jones; the dog*), not a pronoun (*he, it*). Boswell said of Dr. Johnson: "He never used the phrases the former and the latter, having observed, that they often occasioned obscurity; he therefore contrived to construct his sentences so as not to have occasion for them, and would even rather repeat the same words, in order to avoid them." See also WAS A FORMER.

**formulate.** Criticized by Bernstein and Evans as pretentious for *form,* as in *formulate an opinion.*

**for the purpose of.** Verbiage in place of an infinitive construction. *For the purpose of circumventing* equals *to circumvent* (Bernstein, Copperud, Flesch).

**for the (simple) reason that.** Excessive for *because;* beyond this, *simple* insults the reader's intelligence.

**for . . . to.** Such constructions as "I want for him to be elected," in which the *for-*phrase is the object of a verb (in this case *want*), are described as objectionable by Bernstein. Evans says their acceptability depends on whether the infinitive is replacing a *that-*clause, as in "The lawyer said for him to file suit immediately," which is described as standard. Bryant and Evans also say the *for* before the infinitive, as in "He hoped for to sell the farm," is substandard. This is the consensus.

**fortuitous.** Means simply *chance* or *accidental,* as in *a fortuitous encounter.* It is often incorrectly used in the sense of *fortunate,* as in *a fortuitous deal.* "A time of transition may be fortuitous after all, went the argument." *favorable, advantageous* (Bernstein, Copperud, Evans, Flesch, Fowler, American Heritage). Random House, oddly enough, considering its generally conservative bent, allows *lucky, fortunate;* Webster does not. Random House's example, however, is ambiguous: *a series of fortuitous circumstances that advanced her career; fortuitous* here could just as easily mean *accidental.*

**forward.** Criticized by Evans and Flesch when it displaces *send,* rather than *send on.* Webster, however, gives *transmit.*

**founder.** See FLOUNDER, FOUNDER.

**fraction.** Criticized by Bernstein in the sense *a small part* (rather than simply *a part,* large or small). Evans reports, however, that this usage is more than three hundred years old, and Fowler concludes that the sense has established itself. Random House regards it as standard, but Webster does not give this sense. The consensus narrowly favors it.

**Fractions.** It is well to defer to consistency by shunning such mixtures as *one and ½ feet, two and ¼ miles,* in favor of *1½ feet, 2¼ miles,* or *one and one-half feet, two and one-quarter miles.* And *.13 of an acre* is preferable to *.13 acres* as less likely to lend itself to error. Technical publications often place a zero in front of a decimal point: *0.13 of an acre.* When fractions must be constructed, it is better to separate the numerator and the denominator with the virgule than with the hyphen: *6 7/8* (not *6 7-8*).

The hyphen is used as indicated in writing fractions in the form *one-fourth, six thirty-seconds* (Copperud, Evans).

**Frankenstein.** Often as not applied to a monster. Frankenstein was not the monster, however, but the scientist who created it, as set forth in the novel of that name by Mary Shelley. Bernstein regards the shift in sense as an error, though he admits it is prevalent. Copperud points out that it is recognized by all current dictionaries except Random House; Evans regards it as established and derides Fowler's description of it as "almost but not quite sanctioned by custom" (which appeared in the original of 1926 and was retained in the revision of 1965); Follett defends it as following a natural process. The consensus is overwhelmingly in favor of *Frankenstein* in the sense of both a monster and of anything that destroys its creator.

**free, freely.** *Freely* means *liberally, without stint,* and may be ambiguous for *free of charge.* The person who wrote of a *freely distributed paper* did not mean it was distributed widely or without restraint, but rather that it was a throwaway, distributed at no cost to the recipients. *Distributed free of charge* would have been unambiguous. "They charge for the groceries, but Della distributes freely her cures for what ails you." *free, free of charge.* The confusion probably arises out of a feeling that *free* is an adjective, not an adverb, and needs *-ly* to make it an adverb; in fact, *free* is both adjective and adverb in the sense *without cost. Freely* means without restraint. This view is corroborated by the definitions in Random House and Webster. See also FOR FREE.

**free gift, pass.** Common redundancies; both passes and gifts are by definition free.

**frenetic, phrenetic.** The word means *frantic,* and the variants are equally acceptable, though the first predominates (Copperud, Random House, Webster).

**friendlily, friendly.** *Friendlily* is standard but seldom used because of its awkward form. *Friendly,* however, may also be

used as an adverb: "A few were not very friendly disposed toward him" (Random House, Webster).

**frightened of.** Should not be used in place of *afraid of:* "The child is frightened of dogs" (Bernstein, Evans). Random House and Webster specifically sanction *frightened of,* however.

**from . . . to.** A redundant construction in such contexts as "The Chinese still hold from 12,000 to 14,000 square miles of Indian territory." *hold 12,000 to 14,000.* See also OF BETWEEN, etc.

**from hence, whence.** *From* is redundant with *whence,* which means *from which* (Bernstein, Fowler, Copperud, American Heritage). Copperud and Evans comment that *whence* is bookish; Flesch flatly calls it obsolete, recommending *from where.* Evans allows *from whence. Hence* is also somewhat stilted; *from hence* is considered archaic. Copperud says that *from where* is questionable even though *where* can be a pronoun and thus the object of a preposition. *From where* is acceptable when the word order is inverted: "Where did the cake come from?" (though Fowler considers this construction clumsy and recommends *whence*). *From here* and *from there* are well established, and it seems likely that *from where* will also establish itself. It might be kept in mind, too, that the Bible says "I will lift up mine eyes unto the hills; *from whence* cometh my help" (Psalms CXXI:1), though Fowler disparages this as an archaic and thus inapplicable example. See also SEE WHERE.

**front runner.** Originally meant only an entrant in a race who does best when ahead, but now the sense nearly always intended is *leader* (as in a race). Criticism of the change is probably futile, since the general sense is recognized by both Random House and Webster.

**fruition.** Bernstein, Flesch, Follett, and Fowler insist that the term can mean only *enjoyment*, not *bearing fruit*. The fact is, however, that the sense *enjoyment* is unknown in ordinary discourse. All current dictionaries give without qualification such meanings as *attainment of anything desired, a state of bearing fruit, realization*. The insistence on the rare sense of the word, flying as it does in the face of overwhelming usage, can only be regarded as a striking example of pedantry.

**-ful.** Plurals of words ending in *-ful* are normally formed by adding *s: handfuls, teaspoonfuls, cupfuls;* not *handsful, teaspoonsful, cupsful* (Copperud, Evans, Fowler, Random House; Webster gives both forms).

**fulsome.** Means *excessive* or *disgusting*, not *ample* or *abundant*. "There are fulsome and informative chapters on what to pack, what to buy." *Fulsome praise* is objectionable, not lavish, praise; the word connotes insincerity and baseness of motive (Bernstein, Copperud, Flesch, Follett, American Heritage, Random House, Webster).

**fun.** As an adjective (*a fun party*), deplored by Follett, considered informal by Copperud, American Heritage, and Random House and standard by Webster.

**function.** As a noun in one sense, *function* means a ceremony or meeting of some importance, and is misapplied to lesser events, such as tea parties (Bernstein, Fowler, Evans, Random House, Webster). As a verb, it is pretentious for more specific words such as *work, operate, act*—"The machine is functioning properly" (Flesch, Fowler). Saying that something is *a function of* something else, as in mathematics, is often pretentious for saying it *depends on* (Fowler).

**fundamental.** Flesch recommends *basic* or *real* as preferable, and Fowler concedes with regret that *basic*, a new interloper, is displacing *fundamental*.

**funds, funding.** Criticized by Evans and Follett as pretentious when *money* or *raising money* will do ("I was completely out of funds").

**funny.** Bernstein considers the word under a shadow in the sense *strange* or *peculiar* ("That's funny; it was here a minute ago"; "He gave them a funny look"). Evans calls the usage "widespread and not without charm." All the current dictionaries but Webster and American Heritage, which give it as standard, consider the usage informal or colloquial.

**furlough.** No longer current in military connections; all branches of the armed services now use the term *leave*.

**furnish, furnishings.** *Furnish* is sometimes criticized as a verb in the sense *supply* (*furnish refreshments*), but this sense is recognized by all current dictionaries without qualification. Similarly, it is sometimes said that furniture is what one puts in a house, and furnishings is what a haberdasher sells. *Furnishings* is correct in both senses.

**further.** See FARTHER, FURTHER.

**fuse, fuze.** The common term for the device used to ignite explosives and also for the electrical circuit breaker is *fuse*. *Fuze* is generally preferred in connection with ordnance, especially in technical contexts.

**Fused Participle.** This is the name Fowler invented for a gerund with a subject that is in the objective rather than the possessive case. "I object to him being appointed" is an example, and the correct form would be "I object to *his* being appointed." The reasoning is that *him* cannot modify *being appointed*, and so the adjective *his* is necessary. The principle applies to nouns as well: "She resented John('s) ringing the doorbell." The possessive is far from invariable in this construction, however. Curme, who went into the subject more exhaustively than Fowler, cites numerous examples from good writers to show that the possessive is most likely to be used when the subject of the gerund is a pronoun. But he then adds: "We regularly use the accusative [that is, objective]

when the subject is emphatic: 'She was proud of *him* doing it.' The emphasis often comes from contrasting the subjects: 'We seem to think nothing of *a boy smoking*, but resent *a girl smoking*.'" All other current authorities but American Heritage, which stands with him, take exception to Fowler's flat prohibition of anything but the possessive (or genitive) in this construction. Gowers, in revising *Modern English Usage*, was constrained to qualify Fowler's dictum with a long addendum. Gowers points out that Jespersen challenged Fowler on this point, and that it continues to be a subject of controversy. Gowers concludes that the fused participle is objectionable with a proper name or personal pronoun: "We approved of John going" (*John's*); "Nobody noticed us arguing" (*our*). Bernstein, Bryant, Copperud, Flesch, and Follett all generally concur in this qualification of Fowler's original view, with some special variations. Follett follows Curme in allowing the fused participle for emphasis on the subject of the gerund, and points out that some words are incapable of possessive forms, for example *that* ("I doubt the likelihood of that [hardly *that's*] happening"). He also exempts phrases that form cumbersome possessives ("Constitution of the United States") and abstractions, on which possessives cannot logically be formed ("philosophy becoming a major issue"). Bernstein recommends the possessive form whenever it is possible, and recasting when it is not. Flesch says the possessive is used now only with personal pronouns, obviously a faulty conclusion. Evans allows a free choice between the possessive and other forms with either nouns or pronouns. Gowers' conclusion is perhaps the closest to a consensus on this problem, together with Bernstein's advice to use the possessive when possible (and, it might be added, when it makes for a smooth and idiomatic construction).

**futilely.** Often misspelled *futiley.*

**future.** The key word in two fuzzy expressions: *in the near future,* which means *soon;* and *in the not-too-distant future,* which may mean *before long, eventually, finally, next year, sometime,* or *sooner or later* (Bernstein, Copperud, Flesch).

**future plans.** Redundant, as is *advance plans,* since plans, unless otherwise qualified, are inevitably for the future. See also REDUNDANCY.

# G

**gabardine, gaberdine.** Technically interchangeable, but the first version is so predominant for the fabric that *gaberdine* is likely to be taken for an error. *Gaberdine,* furthermore, has a distinct sense as the name of a medieval garment or, by extension, any cloak (Copperud, Random House, Webster).

**gag, gagged.** See QUIP, QUIPPED.

**gag it up.** A tiresome descriptive in the legends beneath pictures showing people, usually from show business, engaged in horseplay.

**gainsay.** Considered old-fashioned by Flesch and literary by Fowler for *deny.*

**galore.** The term, which comes from the Irish or Gaelic, calls down upon itself the disapproval of Bernstein, Evans, Flesch, and Fowler as humorous or colloquial. It is given as standard in all current dictionaries, however.

**gambit.** The basic sense, which comes from chess, is an opening move made at a deliberate sacrifice of some piece. Thus Bernstein, Follett, and Fowler object to the extended use of the term to mean simply any opening, as, for example, for a conversation, without the idea of an attendant sacrifice. Fowler cites the use of *gambit* for *opportunity,* but this is not observable in the U.S. American Heritage, Webster, and the Standard College Dictionary recognize as standard the general sense of *opening;* Random House gives the precise extended sense; the American College and Webster's New World dictionaries recognize only the application to chess. The consensus is that the extension should preserve the idea of sacrifice for an advantage.

**Gandhi.** Often misspelled *Ghandi.*

**gantlet.** See GAUNTLET, GANT-LET.

**garb.** Regarded as an affectation for *clothing* by Evans and Flesch.

**gas.** Unexceptionable for *gasoline,* as Evans points out, except that ambiguity and possible confusion with cooking gas is possible in some contexts, particularly in journalism.

**gauge, gage.** The first gives so much difficulty, often being misspelled *guage,* that the simpler version might have been expected to displace it. *Gage* is preferred in technical writing, perhaps for this reason.

**gauntlet, gantlet.** The first was originally a glove, the second a form of military punishment in which the victim runs along a lane formed by men who strike him (hence, *run the gantlet,* which is often used in figurative extensions). Bernstein and Evans say *gauntlet* is preferred for the glove and *gantlet* for what is run or endured. The usual form, however, is *run the gauntlet.* American Heritage, Random House, and Webster give *gauntlet* as the predominant form for both senses, with *gantlet* as a variant. Thus opinion is divided on this point.

**gendarme.** A *gendarme* is not the counterpart of an American *policeman,* but rather of a *sheriff's officer* or *state policeman.* French cities have *policemen;* villages and other small communities have what we would call *constables.* *Gendarme,* then, in indiscriminate reference to any French police officer is inaccurate, and in reference to an American po-liceman is worn-out humor (Bernstein, Copperud). Both Random House and Webster, however, give *a French policeman* as a general sense.

**gender.** *Gender* for *sex* is felt as a facetious extension; the term strictly applies to grammatical classifications, which do not consistently correspond with sex. "Two performers of the feminine gender" would better be "Two women performers" (Bernstein, Copperud, Fowler).

**general.** When the term forms part of a title like *attorney general* it is an adjective in the unusual predicate position; the meaning is *general attorney,* and the parts are not hyphenated. This applies to similar terms like *postmaster general, secretary general.* All current dictionaries except American Heritage sanction either *attorney generals* or *attorneys general* for the plural, but Random House inconsistently recognizes only *postmasters general* for that office. The consensus is that forming the plural on *general* rather than on the noun is predominant, though either form is acceptable (Copperud, Fowler). See also COURT-MARTIAL. British titles on this pattern are discussed by Fowler under the heading *Plural Anomalies.*

**general consensus.** Redundant; *consensus* implies generality. See also CONSENSUS OF OPINION.

**general public.** Says nothing that *public* alone does not, when there is no contrast with some segment of the public.

**Genitive.** See POSSESSIVES 3.

**gentle art.** The *gentle art* of whatever the writer names is ridiculed by Fowler as a battered ornament.

**gentleman.** For ordinary use, or when there is a choice, *man* is preferable (Bernstein, Evans, Fowler). The relation of *gentleman* to *man* is analogous to that of *lady* to *woman;* see WOMAN, LADY.

**genuine.** See AUTHENTIC, GENUINE.

**geometrical (progression).** See ARITHMETICAL, GEOMETRICAL.

**Gerunds.** A maladroit construction often comes of putting a gerund between *the* and *of,* on the model of *The Taming of the Shrew* and *The Shooting of Dan McGrew.* In these instances, of course, it accomplishes what is intended, namely, setting the gerunds (*taming* and *shooting*) in the forefront. But consider "Stevens repeated that the responsibility for the filing of the charges was his." It is recommended here that *the* and *of* be omitted, making the succeeding element the object of the gerund: *the responsibility for filing the charges.* As Perrin notes in *Writer's Guide and Index to English,* "This emphasizes the verbal phase of the word and makes for economy and force." Other examples: "Improvement in (the) gathering (of) and reporting on such data is needed"; "The proposals call for (the) setting up (of) a joint staff."

Fowler points out that a possessive pronoun modifying a gerund, as in "He was disappointed at his missing the show," is superfluous when the pronoun refers to the subject of the sentences: "He was disappointed at missing the show" (omitting *his*). See also FUSED PARTICIPLE.

**gesticulation, gesture.** A gesture is the motion (in the literal sense) of head, hand, etc.; gesticulation is the act of making a gesture or gestures (Evans, Fowler, Random House, Webster).

**get.** Evans and Flesch criticize the substitution of *become* for *get* in attempts at elegance in such idiomatic phrases as *get sick, get lost,* though Evans describes this usage as more characteristic of speech than of writing. Bernstein considers *get* weak for *obtain;* Copperud regards the substitution of *obtain* for *get,* when *get* comes naturally, as an affectation. Evans says *get* implies coming into possession of by any means, while *obtain* implies effort, and cites *get* (vs. *obtain*) the measles. See GOT, GOTTEN; OBTAIN.

**get under way.** See UNDER WAY.

**Ghanaian, Ghanian.** Though Random House and Webster give both forms, *Ghanaian* is the preference of the government of Ghana, and on the principle that their owners are the final judges of the spelling of names, it is correct.

**gibe, jibe.** *Gibe* means *taunt, jeer at:* "The hazing went no farther than gibing at the freshmen." *Jibe,* in its commonest sense, means *match* or *correspond with:* "His performance did not *jibe* with his campaign promises." Confusion is encouraged by the fact that the words are pronounced identically (Copperud, Fowler, Random House; Webster regards the forms as interchangeable).

**GI.** The term is applied ordinarily to enlisted men, not to officers (Copperud, Random House, Webster).

**gift.** Disapproved by Copperud and Follett as a verb in the sense *give* or *make a gift of,* though it is recognized without qualification by all current dictionaries except Webster's New World, which does not list it, and American Heritage, which roundly rejects it.

**gimmick.** Flesch reports that the term is listed in the dictionaries as slang (which is true, except for Webster) and protests that it has long since graduated into standard English. Fowler identifies the word as an Americanism that came to Britain after World War II and "passed in record time through the slang and colloquial stages to the dignity of use without inverted commas in leading articles and reviews in *The Times.*" This judgment is followed by a long list of examples. Despite Flesch and Fowler, in the U.S., at least, *gimmick* retains a slangy tone, for all its usefulness and prevalence.

**give(s) (furiously) to think.** Disparaged by both Evans and Fowler, whether used facetiously or seriously.

**given.** See WAS GIVEN.

**given name.** See CHRISTIAN NAME.

**give way.** The idiom (not *give away*) for *yield to* or *be displaced by.* "Radio gave way [not away] to network television" (Copperud, Random House, Webster).

**glamour.** Bernstein, Follett, and Evans protest that the term is applied indiscriminately. Bernstein says the tendency is to forget its basic suggestion of magic and to use it for any kind of attraction or impressiveness. Evans singles out its use as a synonym for *beautiful* or *lovely* in reference to women as a misapplication. Both Random House and Webster, however, give a combination of beauty and charm as constituting a sense applicable to a person. All, in addition to Copperud and Fowler, give the spelling *glamour* as preferable to *glamor,* and agree also that the adjective is preferably *glamorous,* not *glamourous.*

**glance, glimpse.** A glance is a quick look, a glimpse what is seen by it (Evans, Fowler).

**glean.** Bernstein and Evans point out that the word means to gather laboriously, little by little (the term comes, of course, from the work of those who follow the harvesters in a field of grain and gather what has been left on the ground). Bernstein particularly criticizes its figurative use in the sense of *learn, understand, discover,* etc., though both Random House and Webster give this meaning as standard.

**glittering.** A journalese counterword, too often automatically applied to anything that is new, elegant, or impressive in any way: "a glittering new shopping center"; "John Steinbeck accepted the Nobel Prize for Literature at glittering ceremonies"; "the appointee has a glittering name." Literally, that which glitters shines or sparkles. Some dictionaries give the sense *showy*, which would fit some of these examples but not all. Even so, overwork has made *glittering* a tiresome descriptive. Moreover, Webster gives as one sense of *glitter* "to be brilliantly attractive in a superficial way," which means that careless users of *glittering* risk being thought derogatory when they intend to be complimentary.

**Gobbledygook.** The use of the term in its present sense (the turgid language characteristic of bureaucracy) was established by Maury Maverick in an article that appeared May 21, 1944, in *The New York Times Magazine*. *Governmentese, federalese, officialese,* and in England, *pudder, barnacular,* and *gargantuan* are sometimes used in this sense, but *gobbledygook* predominates, at least in the United States. William and Mary Morris, in their *Dictionary of Word and Phrase Origins,* present claims that Rep. Maverick did not originate the term, but there is no question that his article, protesting the diction used in reports of the Smaller War Plants Corporation, of which he was then chairman, popularized it. The word is sometimes spelled *gobbledegook;* this is the way it appears in Evans and Random House, and Webster recognizes this form as a variant. The version with *y* is much commoner, however, and in any event is the one Rep. Maverick used. *Gobble-de-gook* and *gobbledygock* are errors. A good illus-

tration of gobbledygook and its cure developed in a wartime press conference at which President Franklin D. Roosevelt read an order concerning blackouts that had been prepared by the director of civilian defense:

"Such preparations shall be made as will completely obscure all federal buildings and nonfederal buildings occupied by the federal government during an air raid for any period of time from visibility by reason of internal or external illumination. Such obscuration may be obtained either by blackout construction or by terminating the illumination. This will of course require that in building areas in which production must continue during a blackout, construction must be provided that internal illumination may continue. Other areas, whether or not occupied by personnel, may be obscured by terminating the illumination." After the reading of this order had been interrupted several times by laughter, President Roosevelt directed that it be reworded.

"Tell them that in buildings that will have to keep their work going, put something across the windows. In buildings that can afford it, so that work can be stopped for a while, turn out the lights."

The difference between gobbledygook and plain English is the difference between *terminate the illumination* and *turn out the lights.*

Another splendid example of gobbledygook appeared in the *Federal Register* in Washington as an attempt to define the term *ultimate consumer* in connection with eggs:

"Ultimate consumer means a

person or group of persons, generally constituting a domestic household, who purchase eggs generally at the stores of retailers or purchase and receive deliveries of eggs at the place of abode of the individual or domestic household from producers or retail route sellers and who use such eggs for consumption as food."

This was indignantly translated as "Ultimate consumers are people who buy eggs to eat them."

Other discussions of gobbledygook are to be found in Evans under that heading, and in Fowler among other terms discussed under the heading *Jargon*. A related problem is dealt with in this book under the heading POMPOSITY.

**goes without saying.** The critic may object that if it goes without saying, why not leave it unsaid (Copperud); Flesch says that *naturally, of course,* or omission is preferable. Fowler points out that the expression is a translation from the French, but describes it as nearly naturalized and unobjectionable; he does not challenge it on logical grounds. See also NEEDLESS TO SAY; OF COURSE.

**good.** Evans and Flesch call *good* as an adjective an error ("He doesn't see good"), a judgment so obvious that other commentators have not even troubled to make it. Yet Bryant and American Heritage somewhat surprisingly conclude that *good* is becoming increasingly common in standard usage in reference to inanimate things; Bryant cites as an example of this. "The car runs good."

Otherwise, Bryant says, except after *feel,* as in "He doesn't feel good," the usage is substandard. Webster's New World and the American College dictionaries say *good* for *well* is variously regarded as substandard, dialectal, or colloquial; Webster III says "not often in formal use." Random House describes this usage as uncommon in educated expression and disagrees with Bryant by saying *well,* rather than *good,* is proper after *feel.* American Heritage rejects it out of hand. There seems little question that *good* for *well* is avoided in writing.

**(a) good few.** Considered an old-fashioned expression by Evans; sometimes criticized as a regionalism.

**goodwill, good will.** Copperud says these forms are preferable as both noun and modifier to *good-will,* and this is the consensus of current dictionaries. Fowler, while preferring these forms in general, recommends *good-will* as an attributive modifier: *a good-will offering.* American usage, however, holds predominantly to the unhyphenated forms: *a goodwill offering, the good will* (or *goodwill*) *of the community.*

**go on a rampage.** Journalese, as applied to rivers that overflow.

**got, gotten.** *Have gotten* has passed out of use in England and has been supplanted by *have got. Have gotten* (for *have acquired, obtained:* "We have gotten the provisions") is recognized as American idiom by Bernstein, Bryant, Copperud, Evans, Flesch, and Fowler, though Bernstein considers *have gotten* and *have got* more appropriate to speech than to writing, and recommends a more precise verb when one is available. Follett expresses a preference for *have got* over *have gotten*, but fails to point out the clear distinction noted by Marckwardt (as quoted by Bernstein) that *have got* conveys the idea of *being in possession of*, whereas *have gotten* means *have obtained* (e.g., "We have got the money"—*have, possess*—vs. "We have gotten the money"—*have obtained*). Random House gives *have got* as standard. Fowler explains that *have got* is colloquial in Britain for *possess;* this expression is not usual in America, where *have* alone is more likely to be used. Bryant, however, cites examples from such sources as *Harper's,* and calls the usage characteristic of speech or informal English. The consensus on *have got* for *possess* is that it is standard. Bernstein and Evans point out that *got married* may be necessary to distinguish the act from the state, since *were married* may be ambiguous. Bryant cites this usage as frequent. *Have* (or *has*) *got to* for *must* ("I've got to go") is regarded by Fowler as no better than "good colloquial," but Evans calls it thoroughly acceptable in the U.S. and Bernstein says it is likely to gain literary acceptance. Bryant cites it from the *American Scholar.* Webster calls it unliterary and more common in speech; to Random House it is standard, and this is the consensus.

**gourmand, gourmet.** It has been aptly said that the first lives to eat, the second eats to live. *Gourmand* generally implies *glutton; gourmet, a connoisseur of food* (Copperud, Evans, Fowler). Random House unaccountably gives *gourmand* as a synonym of *gourmet;* Webster's *epicure* (for *gourmet*) is appropriate to the distinction recognized by the consensus.

**graduate.** The passive form (*was graduated,* declared requisite by purists) is described variously as old-fashioned, no longer standard, and inferior to *graduated* by Bernstein, Bryant, Copperud, Evans, and Flesch. American Heritage, Random House, and Webster give *graduated* as standard. They agree also that such forms as "He graduated college" are wrong; *from college* is required, though Random House accepts *graduated college.*

**graffiti.** This newly popular term for writings on walls is a plural; the singular is *graffito,* dictionaries agree. Thus the newsmagazine picture caption "Prague graffiti mocks Soviets" was wrong; it should have been *mock,* or *graffito.*

**grammar.** Often misspelled *grammer,* especially when advice on the subject is being given. This may only illustrate the natural perversity man must contend with, like the probability that a slice of bread will fall buttered side down. Fowler points out that grammar as a science includes inflection (changes in the form of words) and phonology (pronunciation), as well as syntax (the arrangement of words in sentences).

**grammatical error.** Follett calls the objection to the expression, on the grounds that it is a contradiction in terms, pedantry. This is borne out by definitions in Random House and Webster, which define *grammatical* as *of or relating to grammar*.

**gratuitous.** Has nothing to do with gratitude, though the words are related in origin. *Gratuitous* means *granted freely, uncalled for, unwarranted:* "a gratuitous insult" (Copperud, Random House, Webster).

**gray, grey.** The first is the American, the second the British, preference (Copperud, Evans, Fowler). Fowler adds the interesting note that *grey* has predominated in Britain despite the recommendation of Dr. Johnson and subsequent lexicographers.

**Great Britain, British, English.** *Great Britain* is an island comprising England, Scotland, and Wales. The *United Kingdom* is Great Britain plus Northern Ireland. *The British Isles* applies properly to the United Kingdom and the islands around it—Scilly to the southwest, the Isle of Man to the west, the Channel Islands to the east, and the Orkneys and the Shetlands to the north of Scotland. For all this, *Britain, United Kingdom,* and *England* (as well as *British* and *English*) are often used interchangeably. It is well to bear the distinctions in mind, however, for those occasions when they are useful (Copperud, Evans).

Fowler concurs in general, and offers some special considerations limiting the terms from the viewpoint of the Englishman.

**Grecian, Greek.** The first now is usually limited to the ancient Greeks and their works and *Greek* is used in other connections (Evans, Fowler).

**grievous, -ly.** Often misspelled *grievious -ly,* as a result, perhaps, of mispronunciation (Copperud, Fowler).

**grill, grille.** The cooking grate is *grill;* other gratings are *grill* or *grille,* though *grille* is somewhat pretentious. The verb for *interrogate* (always *grill*) is regarded by Evans as slang, but this is a severer judgment than is to be found in the current dictionaries. Webster considers it standard and Random House calls it informal.

**grisly, grizzly.** *Grisly,* which means *horrible, gruesome,* is often misspelled *grizzly,* which means *gray* or *grizzled* (Copperud, Evans, Random House; Webster gives the terms as variants, but indicates that the distinction made here predominates).

**groom.** Bernstein questions *groom* for *bridegroom,* though concedes it is common usage. Copperud and Evans regard it as standard, and so do all current dictionaries. Sometimes it is said in objection to this sense that a groom can only be a man who cares for a horse, but this only dates the thinking of the critic.

**ground, grounds.** Regarded by Bryant, Copperud, and Evans as interchangeable in the sense of *basis: ground(s) for* *objection. Grounds* is usual in legal connections: *grounds for a lawsuit.* Random House and Webster concur. Flesch recommends *because* in place of *on the grounds that.*

**group, bracket.** Fowler derides the use of these terms in such contexts as *upper-income group, high-income bracket.*

**Group Names, Words.** See COLLECTIVE NOUNS.

**guarantee, guaranty.** Both are correct as noun and verb in the sense *ensure, warrant,* but *guarantee* is by far the more commonly used (Copperud, Evans, Fowler). Fowler says *guaranty* may be preferred in reference to the act rather than the security given, but this distinction is not observed in the U.S., where *guaranty* is mainly to be seen in the names of long-established firms dealing in insurance and finance.

**guarded.** The term has recently come to be used by doctors to describe the conditions of patients, and apparently means *serious* or possibly *critical.* It has been taken up uncritically by the press, which is always as eager to jump overboard with new terminology, especially if it is technical, as it is negligent in explaining it. No dictionary yet gives any such definition of *guarded.*

**guerilla, guerrilla.** Fowler prescribes the first spelling, and Evans accepts either, but *guerrilla* is overwhelmingly predominant in the U.S.; this preference is indicated by Random House and Webster.

**guest.** Vain efforts have been made to restrict the term to recipients of hospitality, as distinguished from those who pay for their food, lodging, etc. It applies equally now to the paying and the nonpaying, although one often sees the qualified *paying guests,* when it is necessary to distinguish the two varieties. But Random House and Webster both recognize the application of the term to one who pays for what he gets.

**guest speaker.** Usually redundant for *speaker* in announcements of meetings and the like.

**guilt (feelings, etc.).** Although nouns steadily become adjectives, this is a matter of general acceptance and the consensus of usage. No dictionary yet recognizes *guilt* as anything but a noun, and consequently such expressions as *his guilt feelings,* which offend the fastidious ear, must be considered unacceptable in careful writing. Preferable: *his guilty feelings, his feelings of guilt.* See also HEALTH REASONS.

**guts.** Described by Evans as coarse for *courage, fortitude,* or *impudence;* Flesch says its current wide use in these senses counteracts its designation in dictionaries as slang (Webster is the only exception). Flesch is right about its prevalence, although it cannot be denied that the word is always used with the deliberate intent to shock or to be rough-hewn.

**gypsy, gipsy.** Evans reports that the first is the American, the second the British preference in spelling, though Fowler argues for *gypsy* on the basis of derivation. Both Random House and Webster give *gypsy* as the predominant form.

# H

**habitual.** See A, AN.

**had.** Criticisms of such sentences as "The motorist had his driver's license revoked," on the grounds that it suggests the man instigated the revocation himself, are dismissed by Bernstein and Copperud as pedantry. Webster gives one meaning of *have* as "to experience, esp. by submitting to, undergoing, being affected by, enjoying, or suffering," and an older edition cited as an example "he had his back broken." A related idiom is illustrated by "The woman broke her back in a bobsled accident." This is sometimes criticized on the same grounds as the foregoing. But anyone who objects to it would also have to object to *I broke my leg* or *He stubbed his toe* or *She cut her finger.* See also BREAK, BROKE; SUSTAIN. Evans, however, calls such constructions as "I had my ankle broken" and "I had my house broken into" ambiguous, and recommends that they be avoided in writing. Follett also disapproves of them and recommends recasting to avoid them.

**had (have) reference to.** Often wordy for *meant* or *mean:* "That was the property I had reference to." *meant.*

**had better.** See BETTER.

**hadn't ought.** See OUGHT.

**had (would) rather.** See RATHER.

**hail, hale.** *Hale,* in the sense concerned here, means *haul;* people are *haled* (not *hailed*) into court. *Hail* means *call, shout a greeting,* or *acclaim:* "We hailed a taxi"; "The new king was hailed by the crowd." Often confused, especially *hail* for *hale.* The accolade is *hail* (not *hale*) *fellow well met* (Bernstein, Copperud, Evans).

**hairbrained.** See HAREBRAINED.

**half.** See CUT IN HALF.

**hamstringed, hamstrung.** Both forms are in use; Fowler recommends the former, and Bernstein and Evans the latter, which predominates in the U.S. Follett devotes a column to the subject without being able to arrive at a recommendation. Current dictionaries unanimously give the preference to *hamstrung.*

**handfuls, handsful.** See -FUL.

**hang, hanged.** See HUNG.

**happening.** The use of the term as a noun for *event* or *occurrence* is denounced as an affectation by Fowler, defended as standard by Evans. Current dictionaries recognize the usage without qualification. The term has gained a new vogue in the lexicon of hippiedom.

**hara-kiri.** The correct form for the Japanese ceremonial act of suicide; mistakenly given *hara-kari* and *hari-kari* (Bernstein, Fowler; Random House and Webster give *hari-kari* as a variant.

**hard, hardly.** The adverbial form of the adjective *hard* (in the sense *severely*) is preferably also *hard*, not *hardly*, Evans and Fowler point out. Fowler adds that *hardly* in this sense may be ambiguous as well as unidiomatic, as in "The company was hardly hit by the Depression," when *hardly* may be understood in the sense *scarcely*, though the intention was *severely*, which would have been conveyed unmistakably by *hard*. *Hardly* for *severely* and in similar senses is designated a Briticism by Random House; Webster gives several examples but they all seem to be from British writers.

**hardly.** A negative, and thus it should not be used with another negative as in *could not hardly, hardly without, can't hardly* (Bernstein, Bryant, Copperud, Evans, American Heritage). This also applies to *barely* and *scarcely*.

**hardly . . . than, when.** *Hardly than* ("Hardly had the pot begun to boil than the telephone rang") is regarded by Bernstein, Bryant, Evans, Follett, Fowler, and American Heritage as an error for *hardly when*. The same reasoning applies to *barely . . . than, scarcely . . . than*.

**hard put, hard put to it.** Bernstein calls the forms equally acceptable; Follett discourages the first as an unidiomatic clipped form. Both are considered standard by Random House and Webster.

**harebrained, hairbrained.** Although the reference originally was to the brain of a hare, both Random House and Webster recognize *hairbrained* as a variant.

**have.** See HAD.

**have got, have gotten.** See GOT, GOTTEN.

**he, she; his, her; him, her; himself, herself.** 1. "The employee can appeal to the state if he or she feels that he or she is being exploited." *He or she* (and, in other circumstances, the other pairs) is not only clumsy but unnecessary. It is a well-established convention that the masculine form alone is taken as applying to both sexes (Bernstein, Bryant, Copperud, Evans, Follett). The plural pronoun is commonly used in speech but is questionable in writing: "Every boy and girl had *their* own cup." Copperud says *his* is preferable here, but Evans calls the plural form more natural English. See also THEY (THEIR, THEM); EACH.

2. *He (Smith),* or whatever. "The county manager noted that the assessor's requests would add up to $2 million more than he (the manager) was willing to recommend." The writer has decided that *he* alone may be ambiguous, so he (the writer? yes) has placed *the manager* in parentheses beside it. Constructions like this constitute editing that has been obtruded on the reader. There is no more reason to write *he (the manager)* than to let any other lapse, together with its correction, stand in print. The example should have read *more than the manager was willing to recommend* (striking out *he*). This applies also to proper names following the pronoun: *he (Smith); she (Mrs. Jones).* If there is danger of ambiguity, let the name stand alone. Often

the *he (Smith)* construction is the worse because there is no ambiguity to begin with. "The governor decided to resign in favor of the secretary of state, so that he (the governor) could be appointed to the Senate." *He* can logically be taken as referring only to the governor, but if the writer was doubtful he should simply have repeated *the governor.* "Lundberg asked which of his colleagues had told the mayor that he (Lundberg) had made the criticism." *He* can reasonably refer only to Lundberg, but if there is doubt, *Lundberg* alone will resolve it. The *he (Smith)* construction is called for only in a direct quotation when it is necessary to prevent ambiguity and at the same time preserve the exact form of the words quoted: "The observer reported, 'Some believe that he (Alexander) is only waiting for the right moment.'" Technically, the parentheses here should be brackets, indicating an editorial insertion (Bernstein, Copperud, Follett).

3. *His, her.* The pronouns should not be used if the antecedent is not exact: "It was the second time that tragedy struck the John Doe family. His two-year-old son suffocated two years ago." Whose son? Doe's, apparently, but the visible antecedent is *family. Doe's two-year-old son* is preferable. The society columns often refer to a couple (Mr. and Mrs. Roe) and then proceed with something like "He is a sanitary engineer. She first met him on a European trip." This irks the fastidious, who would prefer "Mr. Doe is a sanitary engineer; his wife (or *Mrs. Doe*) first met him on a European trip." "Things at first looked

good for the Jones family. The Travelers Aid Society placed them in a hotel suite for the weekend, and he promptly got a job." *Jones,* not *he.*

4. Evans and Flesch consider the objective form acceptable in such sentences as "I thought it was him," in which *him* is not in the normal position for the subjective, or nominative, form *(he);* Fowler says such forms have won standing as idiomatic spoken English, but by implication disapproves of them in writing.

For the use of *himself, herself* see MYSELF. See also PRONOUNS; IT'S ME, etc.

**head over heels.** Often criticized by the literal-minded as illogical since the usual place for the head is over the heels. Webster reasonably gives one sense as suggesting the motion of a somersault. Alfred H. Holt, in *Phrase and Word Origins,* concedes to the critics that when one stops to think, it should be *heels over head,* and goes on to speculate that it may originally have been *over head and heels,* a translation of *per caputque pedesque* (Catullus). But it is no good trying to force language into the strait-jacket of logic, least of all a sprightly idiom like this. Or is it now a cliché? (Copperud, Evans.)

**headquarter.** As a verb ("The company is headquartered at Toledo"; "The expedition will headquarter in the valley"), rejected by American Heritage, but accepted as standard, in both transitive and intransitive use, by Random House and Webster. Other desk dictionaries do not give it, which appears to indicate that it is a neologism.

**headquarters.** May take either a singular or a plural verb, but the plural is usual: "The company's headquarters is (are) in New York" (Bernstein, Evans, Random House, Webster).

**head up.** Journalese for *head, direct, lead:* "A doctor was chosen to head up the study." *direct* (Copperud, Fowler). *Head up* is also aspersed by American Heritage.

**healthful, healthy.** Bernstein, Copperud, and Fowler agree that although *healthful* means conducive to health and *healthy* means possessing it, *healthy* has established itself in both senses: "Eating apples is healthy." Random House and Webster concur. Bernstein disapproves *healthy* as an intensive, as in "a healthy raise in pay," but Webster gives as one sense "large in quantity."

**health reasons.** This instance of making a noun (*health*) serve as an adjective is rejected by Copperud, and by the American Heritage panel as an "uncouth construction." See also GUILT FEELINGS.

**heap, heaps.** Evans describes the terms as not standard in the sense *large amount (heaps of self-confidence; a heap of living);* Webster recognizes them as standard and other current dictionaries designate them informal or colloquial. Fowler calls *heaps* colloquial and specifies that it takes a singular verb (heaps *is*, not *are*). The consensus is that *heap* and *heaps* are good colloquial usage.

**heart attack.** The idea that the expression suggests an attack upon, or by, the heart, and thus cannot be used to describe a seizure, is absurd. The term is standard (Copperud, Random House, Webster) and is preferable to the newly prevalent *coronary* in reference to heart attacks. Technical language is best left to those equipped to use it precisely.

**heart condition.** Sometimes regarded as a euphemism or as an inexact term for *heart ailment,* on the ground that every heart has some condition, good or less so. Both unabridged dictionaries give *heart disease* but neither gives *heart condition.* See also EUPHEMISMS.

**heave.** Evans and Fowler agree that *heaved* and *hove* are both correct for the past tense, but Evans (corroborated by Random House) notes that *hove* is usually preferred in nautical connections (*hove into sight; hove to*).

**Hebrew.** In modern usage, the name of a language; not usually applicable to people except as the equivalent of *Israelite,* though sometimes it is resorted to as a genteelism in mistaken avoidance of *Jew, Jewish,* which see (Copperud, Evans, Fowler). *Jew* as an adjective (in place of *Jewish*) is derogatory (Copperud, American Heritage, Random House, Webster).

**hectic.** Fowler disapproves of the expression in the sense *excited, filled with activity* as a vogue word. The judgment on this point, implying that *feverish* is the only acceptable sense, is picked up almost verbatim from the original (1926) edition, and cites the Concise Oxford Dictionary's labeling of it as slang. The basis for this critical opinion is the Greek from which the word derives. In this instance, it appears, as in some others, Fowler neglected to take his own advice (given under the entry *True and False Etymology*) that "What concerns a writer is much less a word's history than its present meaning and idiomatic habits." Bernstein and Evans defend it as standard, a judgment concurred in by all current dictionaries, including American Heritage.

**hegira.** Fowler asserts that the pronunciation with the accent on the long *i* is wrong, but this must represent British practice, since that version is recognized by all current American dictionaries that list the word. Flesch frowns on casual use of the term as a synonym for *flight*.

**height.** Sometimes misspelled *heighth*, perhaps as a result of the prevalent mispronunciation (Copperud, Evans).

**helicopter.** Often mispronounced *helio-* and consequently sometimes misspelled (Copperud, Webster).

**help.** The use of the term in such expressions as "Don't eat more than you can help" is described by Follett as idiomatic, but at the same time it is pointed out that recasting is available to anyone who considers this construction illogical. Fowler's advice is much the same; the construction is designated a "sturdy indefensible," even though Winston Churchill is quoted as having used it. Random House and Webster give "refrain from, avoid" thus recognizing this usage as standard. The idiom is so well established that objections to it sound like pedantry. For *cannot help but*, see CAN BUT, CANNOT BUT, etc.

**helpmate, helpmeet.** Evans, Follett, and Fowler agree that *helpmeet* is an erroneous form derived from a misinterpretation of Genesis 2:18, and that the correct form is *helpmate*. Both forms are considered standard by Random House and Webster.

**hemorrhage.** Pretentious in nontechnical contexts for *bleed*. "The victims were hemorrhaging profusely." *bleeding*.

**hence.** Bookish for *thus, therefore, consequently* (Copperud, Flesch). See also FROM WHENCE, etc.

**hep.** See HIP.

**her.** See IT'S ME; HE, SHE, etc.

**here at, we at.** These expressions, as they occur in "We at Nutzan Boltz, Inc." and "Here at Lefthand Monkeywrench," have come to be staple, slightly patronizing pomposities of the public-relations operators. Highly skilled practitioners sometimes manage to combine them: "We here at Lefthand Monkeywrench."

**heroic.** Takes *a*, not *an*: "A heroic deed." See A, AN.

**hers.** *Her's* is an incorrect form (Copperud, Evans).

**herself.** See MYSELF; REFLEXIVES.

**hiccup, hiccough.** *Hiccough* is declared erroneous by both Evans and Fowler, but is given as a variant by both Random House and Webster; *hiccup*, however, predominates.

**high, highly.** *High* may be an adverb ("The plane circled high above the city"); the choice between the forms is governed by idiom. Usually *high* is preferred in the literal sense, indicating distance above something; *highly* in the figurative sense, as an intensive, means *to a high degree* ("We were highly amused by his chatter"). On this principle, *highly paid executive* is preferable to *high-paid*, though there are exceptions: *highly priced* is unacceptable for *high-priced*. *High-strung* and *high-toned* are also idiomatic. The correct forms for most such combinations are to be found in dictionaries (Copperud, Evans, Fowler). American Heritage, however, inexplicably omits to recognize *high* as an adverb. Fowler adds that *highly* in the figurative sense may sound patronizing when praise is being given *(highly entertaining)*, but that must be a British reaction, since this connotation is unknown in the United States.

**high, wide, and handsome.** The correct form of the expression. "The new satellite rode high, wide, and handsomely around the earth this week." *Handsome; handsomely* results from an undiscriminating overcorrectness.

**hijack.** Bernstein argues for the utility of the word in its newest sense, to seize, or commandeer, a vehicle illegally while in transit, and while describing this usage as casual, predicts that it will become standard. It is considered slang by the New Standard Dictionary, colloquial by Webster's New World, and standard by American Heritage, Random House, and Webster. The usage is unhesitating and widespread in the press to describe the seizure of airplanes, ocean liners, and other forms of transport. At the time such seizures began, *hijack* was known chiefly in the sense in which it had been used during the Prohibition era, *to steal while in transit*, relating to the theft of bootleg liquor being carried in trucks.

**hike.** Disapproved by Bernstein in the sense of *increase*. American Heritage, Random House, and Webster regard it as standard, but two current desk dictionaries designate it as colloquial.

**hilarious.** The word relates not merely to amusement, but loud mirth. It is often used in a way that hopelessly exaggerates, especially in advertisements of plays and movies (Bernstein, Copperud).

**him.** See IT'S ME, etc.

**himself.** See MYSELF.

**hip, hep.** Copperud and American Heritage recognize that *hep* is passé, having been displaced by *hip* (in the sense *au courant, up with the times, knowing*). Count Basie, the orchestra leader, was said to have been pestered by an insistent drummer who begged to be permitted to sit in with Basie's musicians. Basie politely explained that it wouldn't work, because the orchestra's music was scored, and his men labored through hours of rehearsal to produce the correct balance. The outsider remained insistent. "But, Count, man, I'm hep," he said. At this Basie suavely responded, "I'm hip you're hep, man, and that's why you can't sit in."

**hippie.** The preferable form (rather than *hippy,* which had a previous meaning, *large-hipped*) for the nonconformist (Copperud, American Heritage).

**hippopotamuses, hippopotami.** Copperud and Fowler express preference for the first form; Evans considers them equally acceptable. The form given as predominant by Random House and Webster is *-muses.*

**his, her.** See HE, SHE, etc.

**historic, historical.** The first means *memorable, important,* or *figuring in history (a historic expedition).* A historical novel is one based on, or dealing with, history; a historic novel is a literary landmark, one that makes history. "The historical ranch changed hands recently" is wrong; *historic* (Bernstein, Copperud, Evans, Flesch, Fowler, Follett, American Heritage; Random House and Webster generally recognize the distinction set forth here, while at the same time permitting interchange of the forms). Copperud says *history, historian, historic, historical* take *a,* not *an* (see A, AN); Fowler says the use of *an* with these terms lingers curiously.

**hither.** Described by Evans and Fowler as archaic or obsolescent for *here;* Fowler adds, however, that the phrase *hither and thither* remains current. Random House and Webster consider *hither* current for *here, to this place,* but Fowler's view that the term tends to be literary or pretentious seems valid.

**hitherto.** Bernstein points out that the word means *until now,* but sometimes displaces *previously,* as in "The economy then sank to a point hitherto not experienced." Random House and Webster concur. Flesch discourages use of the expression at all as old-fashioned.

**Hobson's choice.** Bernstein points out that this is no choice at all, not merely a choice, as in a dilemma, between things that are undesirable; Random House and Webster corroborate this; Evans agrees on the meaning, and while finding no misuse of the expression calls it a cliché.

**hodgepodge, hotchpotch.** Fowler reports that *hotchpotch* (in the sense *mixture, jumble*) prevails in Britain, and Evans that *hodgepodge* prevails in America, a sound judgment in which Random House and Webster concur, though *hotchpotch* is occasionally seen here.

**hoi polloi.** Evans and Fowler point out that *hoi* is *the* in Greek, so that English references to *the hoi polloi* contain an ignorant repetition. Random House and Webster, however, allow *the hoi polloi.* (The term means *the masses, the ordinary people,* and is usually used in a patronizing way.) Both commentators recommend avoidance of the expression.

**hold.** Widely though inexplicably aspersed, especially in journalism, in the sense *conduct* (*hold court, hold a meeting*). This is perhaps as good an example as can be found of what Fowler would call a superstition. No dictionary, new or old, British or American, gives any indication that the word is not thoroughly standard in this sense.

**hold steady.** The idiomatic form; not *hold steadily.*

**holdup.** See BURGLARY.

**holocaust.** Bernstein argues that by derivation, the term can properly relate only to destruction by fire (and loss of life). All current dictionaries, however, recognize it as denoting destruction in general, not necessarily by fire, and sometimes not necessarily entailing loss of life; Evans concurs in this but adds the distinction that a holocaust, unlike some kinds of disasters, may be the result of human intention. No current dictionary suggests this.

**home, house.** Objections are often raised, as by Follett, that an unoccupied dwelling cannot properly be referred to as a *home;* such a place, it is insisted, is a *house.* This is sentimental; no dictionary specifies occupancy as a requisite for applying the term *home.* Polly Adler, the ineffable madam, held that "a house is not a home," but then she was talking about a special kind of house, one that nobody would equate with a home. In general, the terms are interchangeable, except for some idiomatic phrases like *house and lot* (Bernstein, Copperud, Evans).

Bryant, Evans, and Fowler agree that *home* for *at home,* that is, using *home* as an adverb ("He was home all the time"), is good American usage, but not British; Evans and Fowler agree that *home* for *to home* ("We went home") is standard in both countries. Fowler prescribes *homy* in preference to *homey,* but

*homey* predominates in the United States.

**homosexual.** Despite widespread misuse as applying only to men, the term denotes one who feels sexual attraction for the same sex, and thus may be applied to either a man or a woman. The opposite of *homosexual* is *heterosexual.* The misapprehension probably grows out of an assumption that *homo-* here is the Latin for *man;* it comes from the Greek *homo-,* meaning *same* (Evans, Fowler, Random House, Webster). There is a strong tendency to use *lesbian* in contradistinction to *homosexual.*

**honeymoon.** Unexplainably proscribed in some newspaper stylebooks in favor of *wedding trip. Honeymoon* is the usual term, however, and it is considered standard by all dictionaries.

**honor, honorable.** To honor is to pay tribute to; the word is unsuitable in the sense *mark* or *observe,* as in "The community will honor Public Schools Week." *observe. Honor* is not an adjective; therefore, not *honor guests* but *honored guests* (Copperud, Random House, Webster).

*Honour* is British spelling, used in America mainly on invitations, where, as in other contexts, it is an affectation.

*Honorable* is a courtesy as a title in the United States; it has no official standing. It is never used with the last name alone unless followed by *Mr.:* either *the Honorable James Jones* or *the Honorable* (often abbreviated *Hon.) Mr. Jones* (Copperud, Evans). The usage of

131                                    HOWEVER

*honorable* parallels that of REV-
EREND, which see.

**Honorary Degrees.** See DR.

**hoof.** The predominant plural
is now *hoofs; hooves* has become literary (Bryant, Evans,
Fowler).

**hooky.** The predominant
spelling (*Play hooky from
school*); not *hookey* (Copperud, Random House, Web-
ster).

**hopefully.** Until about 1960,
the word was used only in the
sense *in a hopeful way* or *feeling hope:* "The sailors looked
hopefully at the sky for a break
in the clouds." Since that time,
however, it has been more and
more widely used in the sense
*it is hoped,* as in "A new session will meet late in the spring
to vote new credits, hopefully
at a reduced figure"; and "The
report will serve, hopefully, to
keep Congress to the $4 billion
mark." This misuse is protested
by Bernstein, Copperud, Flesch
Follett, and American Heritage.
Considering how popular it has
become, however, the protests
are probably in vain. The
Standard College Dictionary
(1963) and Random House
have already recognized it as
standard, in function like an
adverbial clause modifying a
whole sentence: *"Hopefully,* I'll
finish next week."

**horn.** As strictly used among
musicians, the term refers to
the French horn. Loosely, however, among both musicians
and others, it may be applied
to any brass instrument (especially trumpets and trombones),
and sometimes even to any
wind instrument, including
such woodwinds as the clarinet.

This is especially true in the
world of jazz.

**host.** As a verb ("The East
Side Club will host the gathering"), considered journalese by
Copperud and Flesch and unacceptable by American Heritage.
Both Random House and Webster recognize the usage, which
is endemic in the press.

**hotel.** Takes *a,* not *an* (Copperud, Fowler). See A, AN.

**hot-water heater.** A redundancy, but the term may be
solidly enough established to
have passed beyond criticism.

**house.** See HOME, HOUSE.

**how.** *How* for *that* ("He told
us how he had watched the
sun rise that morning") is
aspersed by Bernstein as substandard. It is described as
standard by Evans, however,
and so given by Webster.

**how come.** In the sense of
*why* ("How come the pencils
are missing?"), regarded as
idiom by Flesch but as unsuitable for writing by Bernstein
and Evans. Random House
considers it informal; Webster
and American Heritage give it
as standard.

**however, how ever.** *However,* as both an adverb meaning *in whatever manner* and as
a connective meaning *nevertheless,* should be distinguished
from the adverbial phrase *how
ever,* an emphatic form of *how:*
"It was a mystery, however he
carried it off" (*in whatever
manner*); "We noticed, however, that the money was not
refunded" (*nevertheless*); "The
neighbors wondered how they
ever managed to pay off the
mortgage"; "How ever did he

get promoted?" *how*. In this latter sense, *how* and *ever* are two words (Bernstein, Copperud, Evans, Fowler, American Heritage).

The main question about *however* as a connective concerns its placement. Its function is to indicate a contrast, and it should not break a sentence except for that purpose. In "We noticed, however . . . " the stress of contrast is laid against *we noticed*. If the arrangement were "We, however, noticed . . ." the stress would be against *we*, contrasted with others. If *however* comes first, it contrasts what follows with what has gone before. It modifies the whole sentence when placed at the end, but late placement is usually discouraged. The user must decide which element of his sentence is to be contrasted and place *however* accordingly. When *however* begins a second clause, it is preceded by a semicolon: "Several topics of interest will be discussed; however, election of officers will be the main business of the evening." *However* as a connective is always set off by commas or otherwise. Flesch, however, reports a growing trend to dispense with the commas and says this speeds reading. It is questionable whether the examples he quotes represent deliberate omission of the commas or carelessness. *But however* is redundant; use one or the other (Bernstein, Copperud, Fowler, American Heritage).

**huh-uh.** See UH-HUH.

**human.** The use of the word as a noun and not only as an adjective ("Humans are sen-

tient beings") has been the object of severe criticism. Bernstein, Evans, Flesch, and American Heritage regard this usage as standard. Copperud says it is acceptable but may sound technical or quaint in ordinary contexts, and adds that *person* or *people* are the natural words to distinguish, for example, between the human and the nonhuman ("The cast consists of nineteen humans and one goat"). *people*. This is essentially also the conclusion of Bryant, who finds the use of *human* as a noun more frequent in speech than in writing. Follett says that while *human* as a noun can be defended, its use in this way is a stylistic fault. Among the dictionaries, Random House, Webster, and the Standard College Dictionary accept *human* as a noun; the American College Dictionary designates it colloquial or humorous; and the New World Dictionary says "a person; usually *human being*." The conclusion is that while *human* is acceptable as a noun, there is still substantial objection to it.

**humanist, humanitarian, etc.** A humanist is a classical scholar whose subject is the humanities; a humanitarian is concerned about human welfare. The terms are sometimes confused; particularly, the scholar is called a humanitarian. *Humanity, humaneness,* and *humanitarianism* are approximate equivalents as nouns, not to be confused with *humanism* (Copperud, Follett).

**humble.** Takes *a*, not *an*. See A, AN.

**humblebee.** *Bumblebee* predominates (Evans, Fowler,

Webster); *humblebee* is described by Random House as chiefly British.

**humble opinion.** An obsequious expression. The truly humble, in any event, probably do not have opinions but instead humbly adopt the views of their betters.

**hung.** Copperud and Evans say that *hung* is now standard in the sense *executed,* though at one time only *hanged* was considered proper. The distinction was usually illustrated by the dictum that pictures are hung, people are hanged. American Heritage accepts only *hanged* for execution, but other current dictionaries do not asperse *hung,* though they indicate that *hanged* is the usual form. Bryant says *hung* is used but *hanged* is more common (this, incidentally, is the only sense in which *hanked* is now used). *Hung,* of course, has the rough-and-ready flavor of the Old West. Fowler insists on *hanged.* The consensus is that *hung* is standard, but more informal and less frequent.

**hurl.** Often an excited variant of *make* or *throw,* especially in *hurl a charge* (for *make an accusation*), a conspicuous concretion in the news columns. Epithets, too, are invariably hurled, together with insults and imprecations. The great advances in rocketry have given *hurl* another outlet; satellites, it seems, must always be *hurled into orbit. Hurl* is conspicuously journalese; its overuse and misuse grow out of straining for dramatic effect, a practice that defeats its own end. *Hurl* connotes great force, which makes "The people were hurling flowers and confetti at the distinguished visitor" inept.

**hurricane, typhoon.** See TYPHOON, HURRICANE.

**hurt.** Bernstein cites the Oxford English Dictionary to disapprove as "now only colloq." the use of *hurt* in such constructions as "The states are hurting from inadequate federal aid." Webster quotes *Newsweek* without qualification: "Atomic-energy programs are hurting from lack of enough scientific help." Random House gives "to cause injury, damage, or harm," which covers the same ground. American Heritage gives "The tax bill hurts." The consensus is that this sense (*cause or feel hardship or damage*) is standard.

**Hyphens. 1.** The authorities generally agree that the use of hyphens tends to defy rules. Perhaps the best general advice that can be given is to consult the dictionary, especially for the forms of compounds and to determine whether a given prefix is joined solid or hyphenated. The tendency is for the hyphen to be used in a compound when it is new, but for it to be dropped after the expression becomes familiar. Bernstein points out that in the interval between Webster II and Webster III, *pin-up* became *pinup, nimbo-stratus* became *nimbostratus,* and *saw-tooth* became *sawtooth.* It should be remembered, too, that the hyphen joins, in contrast to the dash, whose job is to separate.

**2.** Compound Modifiers. These should be joined by a hyphen as necessary to assist understanding: *snow covered hills, an odd looking man, dark* *brown cloth, and power driven saw* do not require the hyphen, though its use would be strictly correct. Such combinations as *strong-navy agitation, small-animal hospital,* and *old-time clock* require the hyphen for clarity. The desirability of the hyphen in such instances must be decided by the writer (Copperud, Evans). Nevertheless, it is worse to leave out the hyphen where it is desirable than to use it where it is not essential. Judicious hyphening unquestionably aids comprehension and speeds the reader on his way. A dictionary will indicate the style for compound nouns as well as for some compound adjectives, but many compound adjectives are formed for the occasion and thus are at the mercy of the writer's judgment. One test of the desirability of the hyphen in such combinations is to apply the adjectives separately to the noun. If they are ambiguous unless taken together, they should be joined by a hyphen. Compound modifiers formed by several paired expressions, as in "a coalition of Southern white-big city-big labor-ethnic minority votes," are confusing and should be avoided. This idea would be more clearly expressed in the form "a coalition of votes representing Southern white, big-city, big-labor and ethnic-minority elements."

Compound modifiers do not require the hyphen when they occur in the predicate position (that is, standing after the element modified), as Bernstein, Evans, and Fowler point out. These often are combinations with *well: A well-educated man;* but *The man was well educated.*

Flesch advocates imaginative compound modifiers, giving *early-business-letter English* as an example, but protests against such examples, common in journalism, as *Chinese-dominated town, Red-leaning Cambodia,* and *health-enforced retirement.* Fowler also deplores such constructions, which exemplify the compression characteristic of journalese, and come about from avoiding prepositional phrases: *a town dominated by the Chinese, a retirement enforced by health.*

3. Hyphens with Numbers. The hyphen should be retained throughout compounds containing numbers: not *a 25-mile an hour speed* but *a 25-mile-an-hour speed;* not *a 50-foot long relief map* but *a 50-foot-long relief map.* Numbers preceding nouns as simple modifiers, however, should not be hyphenated: *$400 million was raised,* not *$400-million;* the hyphen is required only when the number forms a compound with another modifier: *a $5-million building; a ten-foot pole.* Indications of quantity standing after the noun are not hyphenated: "The boy was 10 years old" (not *10-years-old,* as it often appears in print). When the hyphen joins two figures, it means *through,* and it is generally used this way with dates: *July 15-19.* Otherwise, it is preferable to use *to* in indicating a span: "40 to 50 per cent of the cost" (not "40-50 per cent"). Hyphens are sometimes omitted from, but more commonly used in, compound numbers (like *sixty-eight*) and

fractions (*three-fourths*) (Copperud, Evans).

**4. Hyphens with Phrasal Verbs.** Verbs that are formed by a combination of verb and adverb, such as *cash in, hole up, put out, pay off,* do not take the hyphen, but modifiers formed from them do, and nouns formed from them may. Examples: "The Communists *stepped up* infiltration" (phrasal verb, no hyphen); "A *stepped-up* campaign is planned for spring" (compound adjective modifying *campaign,* hyphen required); *a big flare-up* (noun) (Copperud, Evans).

**5. Prefixes and Suffixes.** In accordance with the principle stated earlier, hyphens are no longer used with many prefixes and suffixes that once were regarded as requiring them. Such prefixes as *mid-, non-, pre-* and *super-,* and such suffixes as *-down, -fold, -less,* and *-wise* are usually joined solid. Such questions may most easily be settled by consulting the dictionary. For ready reference, here are the commonly used prefixes usually set solid: *a-, ante-, anti-, bi-, by-, circum-, co-, counter-, dis-, down-, electro-, extra-, fore-, hydro-, hyper-, hypo-, in-, infra-, inter-, mal- micro-, mid-, multi-, non-, on-, out-, over-, pan-, post-, pre-, re-, semi-, sesqui-, sub-, super-, supra-, trans-, tri-, ultra-, un-, under-, uni-, up-.*

Prefixes usually hyphenated: *all-, ex-, no-, self-, vice-, wide-.*

Suffixes usually set solid: *-down, -fold, -goer, -less, -like, -over, -wise.*

Suffixes usually hyphenated: *-designate, -elect, -odd, -off, -on, -to, -up, -wide.*

There are some inconsistent exceptions to these generalizations. A prefix or suffix otherwise set solid is usually but not invariably hyphenated to avoid doubling a vowel, and always to avoid tripling a consonant, or when joined to a word that is capitalized: *anti-intellectual, bill-like, non-Asiatic.*

**6. Hyphens in Titles.** Hyphens are often used confusingly in corporate titles indicating combined positions: "He was chief engineer-general manager." Not *engineer-general,* as might appear, but chief engineer *and* general manager. The dash would be better than the hyphen in such instances, if the use of *and* is too much to ask. The same objection holds for such forms as *vice president-sales* and *vice president—sales.* Fowler cites similar examples involving place names and prescribes the same remedy. Sometimes the virgule, or slant ( / ), is used instead of the hyphen in such instances, and sometimes an odd beast known as the en-dash, a hybrid of the hyphen and the dash. The en-dash, however, is likely to be mistaken for the hyphen and it is often unavailable except in the typesetting equipment used for books.

**7. Hyphen with *-ly.*** As Fowler points out, an adverb that is the first word of a compound should not be joined to the next unless it may be mistaken for an adjective: *little-used car* (vs. *little used car*). Words ending in *-ly* are almost invariably adverbs, and this is the signal that the hyphen is superfluous: *an easily grasped concept, a beautifully executed painting,* not *easily-grasped, beautifully-executed* (Bernstein,

Copperud, Evans). See also ALMOST.

**8. Hyphen in Definitions.** The dots used to separate syllables in entries in the dictionary should not be mistaken for hyphens, as they sometimes are. Hyphens are indicated in their usual form in such entries or sometimes by a double hyphen (=).

**9. Hyphen vs. Dash.** The hyphen joins, the dash separates—a principle that, when fully grasped, will help prevent many errors in dealing with these marks. The dash is formed on the typewriter by striking the hyphen twice (- -); when this rule is observed, confusion is prevented when typescript is set into type. See also DASH.

**10. Superfluous Hyphens.** Hyphens are often used to join phrases when there is no reason for them: *profiles-in-depth, a pat-on-the-back, once-a-week, point-of-view, minute-by-minute*. The hyphens are all unnecessary except when the phrases are used as modifiers (*a minute-by-minute account*).

# I

**I, we.** Columnists and others using an informal style sometimes self-consciously avoid *I* by omitting it and starting sentences endlessly with verbs, leaving the subject to be supplied by the reader: "Appeared on a television program last week, and . . . "; "Was embarrassed by some criticism . . . " This avoidance is even more conspicuous than the use of *I*.

Fowler cites a number of literary precedents for *between you and I* and similar constructions in which *I* is the second of two objects ("criticized Charles and I," etc.). He concludes that despite its frequency, it is not approved, even colloquially, unlike *it's me* and *that's him*. American Heritage calls it nonstandard though common in speech.

A somewhat similar lapse is exemplified by "This is repugnant to we, the people." *We, the people* is a set phrase of some dignity, but when it is an object, *we* must become *us*. See also EDITORIAL WE; IT IS I WHO (IS, AM); IT'S ME, etc.

**-ic, -ical.** The authorities in general warn that some pairs of words having these endings (*politic, political*) have clearly differentiated meanings, while others (*electric, electrical*) are for practical purposes interchangeable. *Economic* and *economical* are fairly well differentiated, but not entirely so; the first is generally used to mean *pertaining to economics,* and the second *money-saving,* though occasionally the first is used in this latter sense. These comments generally summarize the views of Copperud, Evans, and Fowler. Fowler adds that when the forms are synonymous as adjectives, and the *-ic* form is also in use as a noun, it would be well to differentiate their use. Although *fanatic* and *fanatical* may both be adjectives meaning the same thing, he advocates that *fanatic* be reserved for the noun and that *fanatical* be used exclusively as the adjective form. *Musical critic* is not the idiomatic form in the U.S., since *musical* now suggests the production of music, rather than discord, which is often the critic's output. True, George Bernard Shaw wrote a book entitled *How to Become a Musical Critic*. This may mean either that *musical* where we now use *music* as an adjective is a Briticism or that it is old-fashioned. Similarly, *drama critic* is displacing *dramatic critic,* but here the difference is not so evident. Follett says both forms are in use but that the shorter is favored.

**-ic, -ics.** Confusion may arise in the use of certain words with these endings when the writer does not have clearly in mind whether he requires the noun form as a modifier (usually ending in *-ics*) or the adjective form. An example is *dramatic, -ics.* A *dramatic instructor* might be one who used histrionic techniques in putting his lessons (in whatever field) across; a *dramatics instructor* could only be a teacher of drama. The difference between an *athletic director* and an *athletics director* corresponds to that between a *musical critic* and a *music critic.* Some other words with which the distinction should be observed are *narcotic(s), cosmetic(s), statistic(s),* and *economic(s).* A *narcotics agent,* for example, is

one concerned with narcotics; a *narcotic agent* would be an agent that stupefied.

Names of studies or activities ending in *-ics* are usually singular: *mathematics is, athletics is, politics is* (not *are*). *Accoustics* may be either singular or plural; as a science it is singular, as an attribute plural: "the acoustics are good" (Bernstein, Copperud, Evans, Fowler).

**icecap.** Follett protests that the term is widely misapplied to the *polar pack* (the floes covering the North Pole). An icecap is a vast field of glacial ice, sloping from a high central point, over northern land areas. The dictionaries unanimously bear out the distinction.

**identical.** Bernstein and Follett insist that *identical* takes *with;* Webster says usually *with,* sometimes *to.* Although *with* is favored, observable educated usage indicates that *to* is firmly established.

**identify, -fied with.** Pretentious for *belongs to, member of, works for, associated with, takes part in* (Copperud, Evans, Fowler). Follett criticizes *identify* for *find, name,* or *define* (for example, problems), and adds that the drama critic should be careful to say he *identifies himself with* rather than *identifies with* the characters; from this latter point American Heritage dissents. See also AFFILIATED WITH.

**ideology.** Bernstein, Evans, and Fowler all come to the defense of the word in its relatively new extension to politico-social systems from the original sense of a system of ideas. All current dictionaries concur. Bernstein cautions against applying it to lesser matters than communism, fascism, and the like. Flesch objects to it as a pretentious synonym for *idea* or *ideas*. Fowler warns that the spelling *idea-* is wrong on the basis of derivation, but Webster recognizes it as a variant.

**Idiom.** In this, as in any book on usage, there is frequent appeal to idiom as justifying some usage or other. Idiom, in the sense at hand, is defined by Webster as "an expression established in the usage of a language that is peculiar to itself either in grammatical construction (as *no, it wasn't me*) or in having a meaning that cannot be derived as a whole from the conjoined meanings of its elements (as *Monday week* for 'the Monday a week after next Monday'; *many a* for 'many taken distributively'; *how are you* for 'what is the state of your health or feelings?')." To this it may be added that idiomatic expressions are considered standard though they may defy grammatical analysis. The subject is discussed under the heading *Idiom* by Fowler and under *Lo, the Poor Idiom* by Bernstein.

**idiosyncrasy.** Often misspelled *-cracy* (Copperud, Fowler).

**idle.** Approved in its new sense as a transitive verb ("The strike idled thousands of workmen") by American Heritage, Random House, and Webster.

**i. e.** See E.G.

**if, whether.** Two principles, now generally regarded as superstitions, may raise doubts about the choice between *if* and *whether*. The first is that only *whether* may be used to introduce a noun clause (usually after *see, doubt, ask, learn, wonder, know*): "I do not know whether he will come." Bernstein, Bryant, Copperud, and Evans agree, however, that *if* and *whether* are interchangeable in this construction, though Bernstein calls *whether* the "normal" word. Bryant finds usage divided. The second principle is that *whether* is required when an alternative is stated: "We shall go whether it rains or clears." Copperud says that this rule too is a superstition; Evans implies it is outmoded; Bryant says *whether* is commoner in such constructions in formal written English but that *if* occurs in conversation. Fowler says that *if* should be restricted to introducing a condition, and that *whether* should be used where an alternative is either stated or implied. Fowler and Flesch also object to *if* for *though:* "The fruit was delicious, if a trifle overripe." The consensus is that *if* and *whether* are interchangeable where they make sense and are not ambiguous. *Whether* enjoys some preference where an alternative is stated or implied, but *if* is acceptable.

**if and when.** Castigated by Bernstein, Copperud, Flesch, Follett, and Fowler as verbiage; they prescribe one or the other, as appropriate to the context. See also UNLESS AND UNTIL.

**if I was, were.** See SUBJUNCTIVE.

**if. . . then.** The use of *then*

to begin the conclusion that follows a conditional clause starting with *if* is described by Copperud as usually making for unnecessary emphasis and perhaps indicating an immature style; Evans says that *then* usually detracts force: "If he can't be a bullfighter right away then he'd like to be a steeplejack"; "If one Democrat deserts to a united opposition, then the vice president can cast the deciding vote." Omit the *thens*.

**ignoramus.** The plural is *ignoramuses*, not *ignorami* (Evans, Fowler).

**ilk.** The basic objection is that *ilk* is a Scots term meaning *same name or place,* and thus may not properly be used to mean, as it incessantly is, *kind* or *breed* or *class* or *stripe*. Webster has two entries, one for the Scots denotation, which usually relates a personal name to a clan or place—"Scott of that ilk"—and the other giving the ordinary use. Bernstein and Fowler deplore the use of *ilk* in any but its pristine, Scots sense, though Fowler concedes that *ilk* for *kind* (*an educator of that ilk*) is often used facetiously. Copperud says the second sense is established, though often facetious; Evans says this sense is now not only standard but primary, which is probably so. Bernstein thinks it is a mistake to consider *of that ilk* disparaging, but Flesch considers it nothing else. The truth appears to be, as Webster points out, that it *is* often disparaging; the context shows the discerning reader whether this is so. Current dictionaries, including American Heritage but

excepting Webster's New World (which designates it colloquial), recognize *ilk* for *kind* as standard; this is the consensus.

**ill.** See SICK.

**illegible, unreadable.** Evans and Fowler point out that the first means *undecipherable* (for example, bad handwriting) and the second means *dull* or *badly constructed* (for example, poor composition). Both Random House and Webster, however, give *undecipherable* as one sense of *unreadable*. If *unreadable* were saved for *dull*, etc., a useful distinction would be preserved.

**illuminate, illume, illumine.** The second and third are discouraged by Evans and Fowler as poetic, literary, or obsolescent.

**illusion, illusive.** See ALLUSION, etc.; DELUSION.

**illy.** Since *ill* is both adverb and adjective, *illy* (though recognized) is superfluous (Copperud, Follett). Many are likely to regard it as an outright error; in any event, it is comparatively rare.

**image.** In the sense of public impression (*improving the image of the business world; the actor's image*), deplored as a fad by Bernstein and Fowler. The newness of this sense is indicated by the fact that, among conventional dictionaries, only American Heritage explicitly recognizes it. Its popularity is such, however, that it seems likely to become standard. Flesch says it seems to fill a need.

**imaginary, imaginative.** *Imaginary* relates to what exists in the imagination in contrast to what is real: "Pink elephants are likely to be imaginary." *Imaginative* means *characterized by,* or *showing use of, the imagination:* "The plans for the Civic Center are imaginative." Disregard of this distinction causes trouble: "A variety of imaginative space people have long thrived in the pages of science fiction." Did the writer intend to say that these people possess imagination, or that they are figments? He meant the latter, as the context showed, and thus the word should have been *imaginary* or *imagined* (Copperud, Evans, Fowler). Another possible interpretation of the example, one not admitted by its context, is that the writers showed imagination in creating the space people; this would make it correct.

**Immaculate Conception.** Evans points out that the Catholic dogma refers to the conception of the Virgin Mary, not that of Jesus Christ, as is often erroneously assumed. The confusion is with *Virgin Birth,* which refers to the birth of Christ. This is corroborated by Random House and Webster.

**immanent(ly), imminent(ly).** See EMINENT(LY), etc.

**immediately.** Disapproved by Evans for *immediately after:* "Immediately the law was passed, a great howl was set up." *immediately after, as soon as.* The usage seems British rather than American.

**immigrate.** See EMIGRATE, IMMIGRATE.

**imminent(ly).** See EMINENT(LY), IMMINENT(LY).

**immoral, amoral.** Evans and Fowler point out that the first means contrary to moral standards, and the second means having no relevance to them; *unmoral* is synonymous with *amoral.* Dictionary definitions support this distinction.

**immunity, impunity.** Evans and Fowler profess that the terms are sometimes confused. *Immunity* means *exemption,* and is often used of diseases: *immunity from smallpox. Impunity* means *freedom from punishment;* Gilbert's pirates saw in the nieces of the Major General an opportunity to get married with impunity.

**impact.** *Impact* for *effect* or *influence* ("For years scientists have recognized the impact of the immense Greenland icecap on the North Atlantic climate") is criticized as a fad by Bernstein, Copperud, Follett, and Fowler. This view, however, is contradicted by the fact that American Heritage, Webster, the Standard College Dictionary, and Random House all recognize this sense. The probability is that it is well on the way to universal recognition as standard.

**impeccable.** A counterword of music-reviewing. Somehow considered preferable, in critical contexts, to *flawless* or *perfect.* See also CONSUMMATE.

**impecunious.** Pretentious for *poor* (Evans, Flesch).

**impel.** Often misspelled *impell.*

**implement.** Criticized by Bernstein, Fowler, Flesch, and Follett as a verb meaning *accomplish, fulfill, complete, carry out:* "The farm program will

be implemented in the fall."
Copperud says it is standard
but so characteristic of gobbledygook that the fastidious
shun it; Evans recognizes the
criticisms of it but defends it
as standard. The complaint that
this usage is a novelty is de-
molished by the fact that it
was aspersed by Fowler in the
original (1926). All dictionaries now admit the usage as
standard. Perhaps the only criticism that remains valid is the
one by Bernstein, Evans, and
Fowler that it is overworked.

**imply, infer.** To imply is to
hint at, or suggest; to infer is
to draw a conclusion. Only the
speaker can imply, and only
the hearer can infer. *Infer* is
often used where *imply* is
called for: "The remark inferred that he was not to be
trusted." Only a person can
infer, and he may do so (that
is, draw an inference) without
saying anything. The confusion
is denounced by Bernstein,
Copperud, Evans, Follett, and
American Heritage, though
Evans is tolerant of it, saying
*infer* has been used for *imply*
for centuries. The confusion is
abetted by the fact that dictionaries tend to give *infer* as
a synonym for *imply*. Random
House is firm on the distinction; Webster quotes two examples of *infer* as standard that
are actually misuses. The confusion does not occur except
in writing that shows other evi-
dences of unsureness. The distinction is a useful one, and
worth preserving.

**important.** See MORE IM-
PORTANT(LY).

**impracticable, impractical.**
For the distinction see PRAC-
TICABLE, PRACTICAL, to which
the same principles apply.

**impresario.** Often misspelled
*impressario*. The word has no
relation to *impress. Impresario*
comes from the Italian *im-
presa,* meaning *enterprise; impress* comes from the Latin for
*press upon.*

**in, at.** See AT, IN; IN LENGTH,
etc.

**in, into.** Bernstein and Flesch
insist that *in* may not be used
with verbs of motion; that is
to say, one may not jump *in,*
but must jump *into,* the lake.
Copperud calls this view pedantry, and American Heritage
and Evans say *into* suggests
motion more emphatically but
that either may be used. Webster gives *broke in pieces,
called in council, threw it in
the fire, wouldn't let her in
the house.* Random House
gives as one sense of *in* "used
to indicate motion or direction
from outside to a point within,"
and cites as an example "Let's
go in the house." All current
dictionaries except the Standard College equate *in* with *into.*
The Concise Oxford Dictionary
says *in* may be used with verbs
of motion or change, and cites
these examples: *put it in your
pocket, throw it in the fire.*
The consensus overwhelmingly
approves *in* in the sense of
*into.* See also INTO, IN TO.

**in, on.** It is British practice
to speak of a house or an
address as being *in* a street;
American idiom calls for *on*
(Copperud, Evans).

**in addition to.** Often wordy
for *besides* (Copperud, Flesch).
See also WITH.

**in all probability.** Excessive for *probably.*

**in a manner similar to.** See LIKE, etc.

**inapt, inept.** See UNAPT, etc.

**inasmuch (insofar) as.** *Inasmuch as* is the correct form; not *in as much as* or *inasmuchas.* Even so, it is a clumsy expression whose meaning can usually be expressed more neatly by *because, since,* or *for.* "Double sessions were instituted inasmuch as the school was overcrowded." *because* (Copperud, Evans, Follett). Flesch discourages the expression as formal and stilted; Fowler calls it pompous for *since.* Follett says *so far as* is preferable to *insofar as,* and Fowler counsels avoidance of *in so far as* (which he gives as four words), citing a variety of objectionable examples.

**inaugurate.** Journalese for *open, begin, start* (Copperud, Evans, Flesch). See also LAUNCH.

**in back of.** See BACK OF, IN BACK OF.

**in behalf.** See BEHALF.

**in charge of.** Equally correct meaning *in the charge of* (*the program is in charge of Smith*) and *responsible for* (*Jones is in charge of entertainment*). Sometimes it is protested that constructions like "the children are in charge of the nurse" are ambiguous, but this is surely wrongheaded. Evans and Fowler suggest *in the charge of* when there is genuine danger of ambiguity. *Charge* takes *with,* not *of: charged with a crime* (Bernstein, Fowler).

**inchoate.** Fowler says the word means *just begun, unde-veloped,* and Flesch adds that writers constantly confuse it with *chaotic.* This is evidently a case of emergence of a new sense; Webster gives also *disordered, incoherent, unorganized;* the Standard College gives *lacking order, form, coherence,* etc.; and Random House gives *not organized, lacking order.*

**incident.** Copperud and Fowler note that the word has become a euphemism for *attack, violence, blow,* etc.: "The Negro pupils attempting to board the bus were surrounded and headed off by the police, but there were no incidents." The statement is contradictory, in the light of the established meaning of *incident,* that is, an occurrence of no great importance, since what was described was itself at least an incident. No dictionary recognizes the extended meaning of *incident;* the consensus is that it is objectionable because it blurs the intended sense.

**incidentally, incidently.** Evans calls *incidently* a once correct form that now is "simply an error"; Copperud points out that Webster recognizes it though no other dictionary does. The consensus is that the form is likely to be considered wrong, though it is fairly common.

**in close proximity.** See CLOSE PROXIMITY.

**include.** Often inexactly used in the senses *belong to, comprise, consist of,* or *be composed of.* That which includes is not all-inclusive, careless use to the contrary. One should not say "The group includes

. . ." unless he intends to omit some members of the group. *Are* or *comprises* is preferable to introduce the all-inclusive (Bernstein, Copperud, Evans, Flesch, Follett, Fowler, Random House, Webster).

**incomparable.** See UNCOMPARABLE.

**incompetence, -cy.** The usual form is *-ce,* though both are standard (Copperud, Fowler).

**in connection with.** Generally regarded as verbiage when the phrase displaces prepositions like *by, from, about, at:* "He expressed his disapproval in connection with the exhibit." *of* (Bernstein, Copperud, Flesch, Fowler).

**incredible, incredulous.** *Incredulous* applies only to people, and means *skeptical* or *disbelieving:* "The testimony was given with conviction, but the jury was obviously incredulous." *Incredible* may apply to people, but is used oftenest of things, and means *unbelievable:* "The alibi was incredible" (Bernstein, Copperud, Evans). See also CREDULOUS, etc.

**inculcate.** Idiomatically takes *in* or *into,* or sometimes *on* or *upon;* a philosophy may be inculcated *in* a person, he is not inculcated *with* it (Bernstein, Evans, Follett, Fowler). Webster and Random House, however, both make the distinction that these prepositions are used with the word in the sense *teach* or *impress upon,* and that *with* is used in the sense of influencing someone to accept an idea, as in "inculcate students with love of knowledge." The dictionaries' view seems more consonant with current usage than that of the commentators.

**incumbent.** See PRESENT INCUMBENT.

**independent.** Sometimes misspelled *independant.* There is a choice, however, between *dependent* and *dependant* (which see) as either noun or adjective.

**indexes, indices.** The first is the Anglicized form, the second the Latin form. *Indexes* is recommended for ordinary use by Copperud and Fowler; Evans expresses no preference.

**indicate.** Criticized by Flesch and Follett as an overworked and imprecise variant for *say.* Follett and Flesch also object to the medical sense of *indicate* (and *contraindicate*) in nonmedical contexts: "A large grant of money is indicated to keep the program going." Evans calls this usage a vogue.

**indict, indite.** *Indict* is pronounced as if it were spelled *indite,* which is now quaint for *write* (Copperud, Evans).

**Indirect Questions.** See QUESTIONS.

**indiscriminate.** Not *un-,* though either *un-* or *indiscriminating* is correct. *Undiscriminating* is more usual (Copperud). Fowler calls *indiscriminating* incorrect, but this may reflect British preference; most American dictionaries give it.

**indispensable.** Sometimes misspelled *indispensible.*

**individual.** While *individual* for *person* is recognized by the dictionaries as standard ("Give the ticket to the individual in the green hat"), this usage is discouraged by Bernstein, Copperud, Evans, Fowler, and

American Heritage except when single identity is being contrasted: "Individuals and organizations have different rights." Use of the term in facetious or disparaging senses is now quaint.

**indorse.** See ENDORSE, INDORSE.

**induction, deduction.** Evans and Fowler point out that the first is deriving a general principle from specific instances; the second is applying a general principle to a specific instance.

**inedible.** See UNEATABLE, INEDIBLE.

**ineffable.** Flesch says the sense *indescribable* is a misuse, and Evans likewise gives only *unutterable,* but every current dictionary except the New World gives *indescribable.*

**in effect.** Should not be set off by commas: "The former president of the Ford Motor Company, in effect, told his congressional critics to put up or shut up." Usually the commas are merely superfluous, but in this instance they may be misleading, suggesting that the person referred to was only in effect the former president of Ford.

**inept.** See UNAPT, etc.

**inequity, iniquity.** Sometimes ignorantly confused; inequity is inequality, iniquity is evil. "Punishment is visited upon the sons for the inequity of their fathers." Possible, but more likely *iniquity.*

**inevitable.** Fowler criticizes the term as overworked by critics of works of art, and as often inappropriately applied to what does not qualify as inevitable (that is, in perfect proportion or harmony, so that any change or omission would be damaging to the whole). He may be overlooking another sense of *inevitable,* however: *certain to come* or *occur,* which is what some critics may have in mind. All dictionaries give this sense, which may be regarded as predominant. For other overworked critics' terms, see CONSUMMATE; IMPECCABLE; ADEQUATE.

**in excess of.** The long way around for *more than, over* (which see). "In excess of a thousand delegates will attend the convention." *more than, over* (Copperud, Flesch).

**infer.** See IMPLY, INFER.

**inferno.** See FLAMING INFERNO.

**infinite(ly).** Evans and Fowler caution, the latter somewhat equivocally, against careless use of the word for exaggeration when *great(ly)* or *far* will do.

**Infinitives. 1.** Split Infinitive. The arbitrary rule against splitting an infinitive was once and may still be one of the most solidly established of superstitions affecting grammar. (An infinitive is said to be split when an adverb comes between *to* and the main verb: *to quickly go.*) The consensus of Bernstein, Bryant, Copperud, Flesch, Follett, and Fowler is that infinitives may be split when splitting makes the sentence read more smoothly and does not cause awkwardness. Some examples of awkwardness, in which the adverb would go more smoothly at the end of the sentence: "I want to consistently enforce discipline"; "His purpose was to effortlessly be promoted"; "Jones was ordered to immediately embark." On the other hand, there is good reason not to change the following: "Production of food fats is expected to moderately exceed domestic use and commercial imports" and "This will permit the nation to quietly drop her violent opposition to the treaty." See also COMPOUND VERBS.

2. Infinitives of Purpose. These indicate intention, as in "He went to the store to get some ice cream," but the construction is often awkwardly used when there is no reason to indicate intention, as in "He made the trek in four days to arrive here exhausted" and "Increased sales are announced by many companies to confound the pessimists." These examples would be better put with a participial phrase that would avoid ambiguity: "He made the trek in four days, arriving here exhausted"; "Increased sales are announced by many companies, confounding the pessimists."

3. Infinitive for the Future. The infinitive is occasionally used to indicate the future: "He is to leave in the morning." Curme points out that this construction has some modal force, conveying the idea of necessity or compulsion, and Evans concurs. Very often, however, writers who use the infinitive in this way intend a simple future. They say, "I am to meet the 5:15" when they mean simply "I will (or shall) meet the 5:15." The use

of *am to, is to,* and *are to* for *shall* or *will* should be discouraged. This usage is possibly fostered by newspaper headlines, in which it is the convention to indicate the future with the infinitive: "Statesmen to Meet in London."

4. Misleading Infinitives. Some other misuses of the infinitive also create ambiguity: "It was the largest maneuver ever to be held in the South." The intended meaning was *that has ever been held,* but the reader might easily have understood *that will ever be held. Largest maneuver ever held* would have been unambiguous. "This is one of nineteen communities to have such a program." *That has,* or *that will have?* The intention was *that has,* and this form should have been used.

5. Infinitives With and Without *to.* Bernstein, quoting Evans, cautions against omitting *to* where idiom calls for it, as in "An enriched instructional program is planned to assist pupils having deprived backgrounds qualify for college." *to qualify.* Evans offers a list of verbs and describes the circumstances under which *to* need not be used with them, but mastering them is a little like learning rules for English spelling—it is easier to learn to spell than it is to learn the rules. The infinitive with *to* predominates in English, however, and *to* should be supplied if the construction sounds the least bit maladroit. There is little danger of using *to* where it is not required: "We were expected to help him [to] change the tire."

**6.** Infinitive Displacing Gerund. Bernstein and Fowler warn against unidiomatic infinitives: "She always enjoyed to look for an apartment." *enjoyed looking.* This is a matter primarily of having an ear for the preferable construction. Fowler deals with this lapse exhaustively, giving specimens (under the entry *Gerund*) after nouns, adjectives, and verbs.

**infinitude.** Described by Evans and Fowler as an unnecessary variant of *infinity.*

**inflammable.** See FLAMMABLE.

**inflict, afflict.** Evans and Fowler warn against confusion of these terms. *Afflict* takes *with, inflict* does not: "They were afflicted (not *inflicted*) with hives." The object of *afflict* must be or imply some living thing: "Sorrow afflicted (not *inflicted*) him"; "A crop failure afflicted (not *inflicted*) the country" (in which *country* implies the people inhabiting it); *inflict* takes an inanimate object: "He inflicted (not *afflicted*) punishment."

**informal, informally.** Excessively used, especially in journalism, to describe what cannot be anything but informal: "perched informally on top of a desk"; "seen chatting informally"; "makes some of his most informal cracks while posing for pictures." The descriptives are foolishly superfluous under the circumstances, which could hardly be regarded as formal. See also COLLOQUIALISMS for *informal* as a status label.

**informant, informer.** Evans says that the first is neutral, and that the second strongly connotes the stoolpigeon. Both major dictionaries, however, give *informant* as a synonym of *informer,* and it seems likely that the context will be decisive as to the sense intended.

**infringe.** Fowler holds that *trespass* or *encroach* is preferable to *infringe upon* (or *on*), and that *infringe* should be used only when it can stand alone, as in *infringe patents, infringe sovereignty.* Both major American dictionaries, however, give examples with *on.*

**in future.** A Briticism; American idiom calls for *in the future.*

**-ing.** See GERUNDS; FUSED PARTICIPLE ("*him* vs. *his* seeing the light"); DANGLING MODIFIERS.

**ingenious, ingenuous.** Evans and Fowler warn against confusing the terms. The first means *clever* (*an ingenious solution*) and the second either *frank and open,* or often *naive: an ingenuous maiden.*

**in (his, her) own right.** The expression indicates individual possession of something that might otherwise be held in common. If a man is a poet, it is correct to refer to his wife as a poet in her own right. But if he is a religious leader, it is meaningless to refer to her as following some other endeavor in her own right: "Each morning, the mystic's fourth wife, a poet in her own right, massaged him with oil for two hours in accordance with Hindu practice" (Copperud, Follett).

**iniquity.** See INEQUITY, INIQUITY.

**Initials.** The use of a single initial (*R. Roe, J. Doe*) is considered inadequate identification by most publications, which insist on a full first name (*Richard Roe*), at least two initials (*R. W. Roe*), or a combination of given name and initial. Preferably, the form should be that used by the owner of the name. See also NAMES OF PEOPLE.

**in length, in number, in size, etc.** The phrases are often used redundantly, as in the following examples: *shorter in length; large (small, many, few) in number; rectangular* (etc.) *in shape; small, large* (etc.) *in size* (Bernstein, Copperud, Flesch).

**in line.** See ON LINE.

**innocent.** See PLEAD INNOCENT.

**innocent of.** Fowler says the phrase in the sense *lacking in* ("His head was innocent of hair") is worn-out humor.

**innovation.** See NEW INNOVATION.

**in number.** See IN LENGTH, etc.

**inoculate, vaccinate.** These terms for immunizing by vaccine are interchangeable (Copperud, Random House, Webster). *Vaccinate,* however, has been firmly established by custom for immunization against smallpox. *Inoculate* is favored for immunization against diphtheria and other diseases. *Inoculate* is often misspelled *innoculate.* The example of *innocuous* may have something to do with this.

**in order to, that.** Bernstein, Copperud, and Flesch say *in order to* is usually superfluous for the infinitive alone: "He bought the suit [in order] to impress his girl." Follett says objections to the phrase are pedantic, but he appears to strain for an example in which *in order* serves some purpose. Copperud says *in order that* can usually be replaced, for the better, by *so, so that.* Fowler has no objection to the expression, but gives a list of examples in which it is used unidiomatically, saying that it should be followed by *may* and *might,* or sometimes *shall.* These distinctions do not appear meaningful in American eyes.

**in question.** Bernstein points out that the phrase is superfluous except to designate one of two or more subjects that have been mentioned; Flesch objects to it as "ugly."

**inquire.** See ENQUIRE, INQUIRE.

**in receipt of.** Commercial jargon in such sentences as "We are in receipt of the shipment." *have received.*

**in regard(s), relation to.** See REGARD.

**in respect to (of), with respect to.** The idiomatic form of the phrase meaning *about* or *concerning* is *with respect to.* "Firm action was advised in respect to the Soviet Union." *with respect to; in respect to* may be understood to mean *having respect for,* and thus makes the statement ambiguous. "Requirements for lighting are stringent, particularly in respect of allowable brightness levels." Fusty; *particularly in allowable brightness levels;*

or, perhaps preferably, *particularly in allowable levels of brightness*. Copperud and Fowler agree that *about* is preferable to *with respect to*.

**in routine fashion.** An inflation of *routinely*.

**insanitary.** See UNSANITARY, INSANITARY.

**in shape, in size.** See IN LENGTH, etc.

**inside of.** Bryant says *inside of* is a standard variant of *inside;* Copperud and American Heritage say *of* is unnecessary, and no example by either of the major dictionaries uses *of*. The consensus is that *of,* if not wrong, is at least dispensable.

**insigne, insignia.** Copperud and Follett point out that technically, on the basis of the Latin derivation, *insigne* is the singular and *insignia* the plural. Evans cites literary examples of *insignia* as a singular ("The insignia was tarnished") and reports that in the U.S. Army, it is officially singular, with a plural *insignias* (a form Follett deplores as "manufactured"). Both major dictionaries, as well as American Heritage, recognize *insignia* as the singular and *insignias* as a plural; this may be regarded as the consensus.

**insist.** Often used in newspapers as a random displacement of *said* in ATTRIBUTION (which see). *Insist* should be used only when there is insistence. *Contend* is similarly misused; it is appropriate only when there is disagreement or contention.

**in size.** See IN LENGTH, etc.

**insofar as.** See INASMUCH AS.

**inspirational.** As applied to speeches and writings, particularly, this descriptive should be used with care, for the knowing tend to associate it, through hard experience, with pap.

**in spite of (or despite) the fact that.** Usually excessive for *although* (Copperud, Evans, Fowler).

**install.** In such constructions as "He was installed president," idiom calls for *as* with *install:* "He was installed *as* president." (Copperud, Webster).

**instance.** Occurs in redundancies like *in the instance of; instance* is sometimes substituted for *case,* which see. "Obscenity was charged in the instance of this movie." Recasting is advised: "This movie was described as obscene." See also REDUNDANCY.

**instinctual.** Bernstein and Fowler attribute the form to psychologists, and regard it as an unnecessary duplication of *instinctive*.

**insufficient.** Fowler regards *insufficient* where *not enough* is called for as worse than *sufficient* for *enough* (which see). Examples: "There was insufficient rainfall"; "We have had insufficient to eat" (*We have not had enough . . .*).

**insure.** See ENSURE.

**integration, desegregation.** See DESEGREGATION, INTEGRATION.

**intensive.** Evans and Fowler complain that *intensive* tends to displace *intense* in such sentences as "He put in a period of intensive study." The implied principle: don't use the longer word when the shorter will do. Flesch says *intensive* is overused for *steady, hard, strong, thorough,* a criticism that parallels the others. As Fowler recommends, it is best to leave *intensive* for technical contexts where it has a precise and well-understood denotation.

**interesting.** Copperud says it is simpleminded of a writer to inform the reader that a fact being related is interesting, for interest is a subjective consideration and the reader will make his own judgment about it. Evans says the descriptive often is lazily substituted for something more specific and meaningful.

**interfered.** Often misspelled *interferred,* perhaps by the influence of *inferred.*

**interment, internment.** *Interment,* a favorite in obituaries, means *burial.* ("The good is oft interred with their bones.") *Internment* is a form of imprisonment and the term is generally used to describe what happens to aliens living in an enemy nation during wartime (Copperud, Evans).

**intermittent.** See CONTINUAL.

**in terms of.** Bernstein, Copperud, and Follett castigate the phrase as often an inflation of simple prepositions such as *at, in, for, by.* "The Chinese Army is well equipped in terms of infantry weapons." *with.* "One limitation of this method is that it is relatively slow in terms of production rates." *slow;* what comes afterward is surplus. Follett comments that *in terms of* supplies "a loose coupling

of ideas whose exact connection had not been thought out by the author." Bernstein and Follett point out that, properly used, the phrase signifies translation from one kind of expression to another; both describe its inexact use as pretentious.

**internecine.** The word has acquired a generally accepted meaning that departs from its original and derived sense. Basically, *internecine* means simply *destructive.* Fowler explains this, and goes on to argue that the idea of mutuality (that is, *destructive of one another*) "is what gives the word its only value, since there are plenty of substitutes for it in its true sense—*destructive, slaughterous, murderous, bloody, sanguinary, mortal,* and so forth." Dictionaries now not only admit the idea of mutuality, but recognize a further refinement, the idea of conflict within a group; this, in fact, is now the predominant sense. The tendency of popular usage is usually to broaden the meanings of words; in this curious instance, the meaning has been narrowed (Copperud). Bernstein concurs that the sense *mutually destructive* is both necessary and well established. American Heritage approves the new sense, and regards the question of usage as hinging primarily on whether the conflict must be fatal or mutually destructive; the panel's decision is, not necessarily.

**interpersonal.** Excessively and meaninglessly used in pedagese. Professors seem unable to refer to any relation between people without calling it interpersonal; a glaring example is *interper-*

*sonal friendship.*

**interpretative, interpretive.**
The words are exact synonyms,
but Bernstein, Evans, and
Fowler describe *-ative* as the
preferred form; Fowler says this
is a matter of derivation from
the Latin. But as between *preventative* and *preventive*, he
curtly says the short form is
better, and refers the reader to
a lecture on the undesirability
of long variants. Random House
and Webster both give *-ative*
as the predominant form.
American Heritage approves it.
(Copperud believes that *interpretive*, as the simpler form, is
preferable, and points out that
usages based on knowledge of
Latin have been steadily cast
aside. Nevertheless, the consensus favors *-ative*.

**in the altogether.** The expression for *naked* ("We used to
swim in the altogether"); *in
the all together* is erroneous
(Copperud, Random House,
Webster).

**in the circumstances.** See
CIRCUMSTANCES.

**in the course of.** See COURSE,
etc.

**in the event that.** The long
way around for *if* (Copperud,
Flesch). Fowler, usually critical
of redundancy, describes the
phrase merely as an Americanism, and gives as the British
version *in the event of* followed
by a present participle, such as
(something's) *happening.*

**in the final analysis.** See
ANALYSIS.

**in the midst of.** Often wordy
for *amid* (Bernstein).

**in the (immediate) vicinity of.**
Roundabout for *near* (Bernstein, Flesch, Copperud).

**in the (near, not too distant)
future.** See FUTURE.

**in the neighborhood of.** See
NEIGHBORHOOD.

**into, in to.** The preposition
*into* should be distinguished
from *in to* (the adverb *in* followed by the preposition *to*):
"We went into the city"; "We
dropped in to coffee with the
Smiths." An absurd confusion
of these forms is illustrated by
"A man wanted as an Army
deserter for fifteen years turned
himself into the police last
night" (Copperud, Evans, Follett, American Heritage). For
*in* vs. *into*, see IN, INTO.

**in toto.** Often misspelled:
"She said the story was ridiculous and denied it en toto."
The phrase (for *totally, entirely*)
is Latin, not French, and the
preposition is *in*, not *en*. It is
questionable whether any foreign phrase is suitable to most
informal contexts; the consensus of authorities on this subject
is to avoid them and use English. Fowler criticizes the misuse of *in toto* in the sense *on
the whole.*

**intrigue.** Fowler in the original denounced *intrigue* in the
senses *arouse interest, desire,
curiosity,* or *beguile* or *fasci-
nate* ("The handsome stranger
intrigued her"), and Bernstein,
following this lead, says the
word is erroneously taken from
the French, in which its meaning is *puzzle.* Long lists could
be compiled of words taken
into English from other languages and given different
meanings, however. In the revision of Fowler, Gowers (citing the Oxford English Dictionary's 1933 Supplement) gives

up on the objection to these senses, and contents himself with saying that sometimes *intrigue* displaces simpler words. Copperud, Evans, and Flesch agree that the newer senses are standard and established; the major dictionaries have long recognized them; American Heritage accepts them narrowly, commenting that they sometimes displace more precise expressions. Evans adds, however, that *intrigue* is overworked.

**introduction.** See FOREWORD.

**inure, enure.** The words are simply variants, of which the first is to be preferred (Evans, Fowler, Random House, Webster). The word means, in its usual sense, not just to become accustomed, but to become accustomed to something disagreeable: "For one inured to the singer's style, the transition is unsettling." *accustomed.* Bernstein warns that *immure* (*wall in*) is sometimes given where *inure* is called for. Flesch regards *inured to* as bookish for *used to*.

**invective.** Coupled with HURL (which see), a stock expression of journalese.

**invent.** See DISCOVER, INVENT.

**Inversion.** The term refers to placing elements of a sentence in something other than their natural or ordinary sequence. Fowler deals with the subject exhaustively, classifying inversion under eight headings, describing some of the varieties as permissible, most of them as not. This analysis covers seven pages and is to be found, as may be expected, under the heading *Inversion.* The treat-

ment in this book deals mainly with the conspicuous, objectionable kinds of inversion, resorted to chiefly by journalists desperate to vary the structure of their sentences, as criticized by Bernstein, Copperud, and Flesch. Inversion in attribution is dealt with under the general heading ATTRIBUTION, and one aspect of it is also taken up in the entry AS IS, AS ARE, etc. See also SUBJECT-VERB AGREEMENT 5.

Bernstein, Copperud, and Fowler all trace the journalistic variety of inversion to *Time* magazine, where it was a conspicuous mannerism in *Time's* early years. Copperud quotes Wollcott Gibbs' satire on *Time:* "Backward ran sentences until reeled the mind." Fowler quotes P. G. Wodehouse: "Where it will all end knows God, as *Time* magazine would say."

Like the atmospheric inversion that is blamed for smog, the inversion of sentences creates a kind of linguistic smog that puts the reader to work sorting out the disarranged elements, causes his eyes to smart, and perhaps makes him wish he were reading something else. As has been said, straining for variety in sentence structure is usually the cause. Tired of starting with the subject and adding the predicate, some writers make a mighty effort and jump out of the frying pan into the smog.

Sometimes they grab a hapless auxiliary verb by the ears, yank it out of the protective shadow of its principal, and plop it down at the beginning of the sentence: "Encouraging the United States were Britain and France." The natural way to say this is "Britain and France were encouraging the United States"; or, passively, "The United States was being encouraged by Britain and France." The usual word order has been varied by moving *encouraging* forward, but the variety has been gained at too high a price. Americans, unlike Germans and ancient Romans, are not used to holding some element of a sentence in suspension until the other pieces of the puzzle come along. Inversion, of course, is not grammatically wrong; it is an irritant and the mark of a faulty style because it is overdone, or because it misplaces emphasis. Versifiers have an excuse for this kind of thing when they find it necessary to place the word with the rhyme at the end of the line. They can plead poetic license.

"Hiring the men will be ranchers in the vicinity" should be recast to "Ranchers in the vicinity will hire the men." Examples like "Damaged were the cars of two motorists"; "Suffering minor injuries in the crash was his wife, Viola"; and "Caught in the school during the explosion were twenty girls" are gawky and inexcusable.

Sometimes writers start sentences with auxiliary verbs only because they think there is no other way out when introducing a series of names: "Passing their intermediate tests were George Sims, Ernest Worth, Alben Smith, Nelson Raddle, and Alex Jones." But there *is* another way out: "Those who passed their intermediate tests were . . . " ("Intermediate tests were passed by . . . " is possible, but would be a clumsy use of the passive.)

It should be kept in mind that emphasis is given a word that is taken out of its normal position. When a sentence is disarranged for no other reason than to give variety to its structure, the effect may be awkward. The reader gets an impression of emphasis where emphasis makes no sense. Better methods are available for structural variety, such as beginning with subordinate elements (e.g., clauses introduced by *when, although,* or *nevertheless*), prepositional phrases, infinitives, or participial phrases.

The uprooted word is sometimes an adjective: "Responsible for all cultural questions is a key member of the city administration." There is no good reason for standing this sentence on its head. Fowler calls the abuse of inversion one of the most repellent vices of modern writing, and adds that by betraying his anxiety over boring the reader, the writer only bores the worse. See also ATTRIBUTION 1.

**in view of the fact that.** The long way around for *since, because,* or *considering that.*

**invite.** As a noun ("The invites went only to the contributors"), considered humorous by Bryant, a barbarism by Copperud, an unrespectable colloquialism by Fowler, dialectal by Random House and Webster; American Heritage gives it the most reputable label, *informal.* Evans says that it has "remained impudently in use for 300 years" despite criticism, but warns that in some quarters it is condemned. The consensus is overwhelming that it is nonstandard.

**invited guest.** Often criticized, especially in journalism, as redundant, on the ground that being invited is essential to guesthood.

**involve.** Described by Copperud, Evans, Flesch, and Fowler as too freely and imprecisely used for *cause, result in, mean, have to do with, use,* and many other more appropriate verbs. "This involved a complete change of plans." *caused.* The meaning of *involve* is *enfold, envelop, engage*: "The realtor became deeply involved in the litigation."

**inwardness.** Described by Flesch and Fowler as literary and as often pretentiously used for *true meaning, reality,* or as superfluous.

**in which.** Often dispensable, and when it is then dispensed with, expression is improved: "Everybody is aware of the disorganized way [in which] the Senate and the House carry on their work." See also REDUNDANCY.

**iron out.** Both Evans and Fowler recognize this, in its figurative sense (*settle, remove difficulties*), as an Americanism in good standing, and Fowler welcomes its introduction to Britain. Both warn, however, of its use in incongruous contexts (*iron out bottlenecks*). American Heritage and Webster consider it standard; Random House labels it informal.

**irony, irony of fate.** Irony denotes a double meaning and a double audience, one part of which gains a meaning that the other does not. Thus, in dramatic irony, the audience comprehends a part of the meaning of a statement uttered by an actor that the other actors do not. Or irony may be described as the contradiction between the literal and implied meanings of a statement. *Irony of fate* should be reserved for a contradiction of some kind; Follett cites as an example, you have a chance to cruise around the world—you should be happy, but you are ill and condemned to bed for six months. *Ironic, irony,* and *irony of fate* should not be applied to any oddity, disappointment, or defeat; Fowler regards the phrase, in any event, as a cliché. These comments summarize the views of Evans, Flesch, Follett, and Fowler.

**irregardless.** Criticized by Bernstein as illiterate, by Copperud and Evans as a redundancy, by Follett as a barbarism, and by American Heritage, Random House, and Webster as nonstandard.

**irrelevant.** Often carelessly mispronounced *irrevelant* and consequently thus (or otherwise) misspelled.

**irreligious.** See UNRELIGIOUS, IRRELIGIOUS.

**is, are.** See SUBJECT-VERB AGREEMENT.

**-ise, -ize.** See -IZE, -ISE.

**Israeli.** See JEW, JEWISH.

**issue.** See NONCONTROVERSIAL ISSUE.

**issue with.** Described by Evans as redundant for *issue* and by Fowler as recognized and here to stay ("Every pupil was issued with a pencil and paper"). No current dictionary in this country gives an example containing *issue with,* and so it may be assumed that the form is uncommon in the U.S.

**is to, am to, are to.** See INFINITIVES 3.

**it.** Use of *it* as the anticipatory subject ("It was a raw, windy night") is not wrong, but can easily be overdone, and this makes for a muffled (Flesch says pompous) style. Sometimes such expressions as *it is believed* are used to avoid personal pronouns: "I believe." This is undesirable unless there is an overriding reason to keep the statement impersonal; personal ones have more interest and immediacy. The use of *it* as a subject, and sometimes as an object, has been classified under various headings; Fowler has a two-page discussion of it. Bryant takes up five classifications (anticipatory, formal, indefinite, general, and emphatic *it*) at some length. The conclusions are not reviewed here because all except the emphatic use are described as standard. The emphatic sense ("This is *it*") is described as appearing only in spoken English, a conclusion that seems questionable. See also IT IS I WHO; IT'S ME.

**Italics.** Used generally in carefully edited material for the titles of books, musical compositions, paintings, and other works of art, for foreign words, and to convey emphasis or sharp contrast. Fowler gives the foregoing, and adds names of newspapers, on which practice is divided in the U.S. Fowler also gives several classifications of the use of italics for emphasis, and warns against setting whole passages in italics to attract attention. Flesch advocates sparing use of italics for emphasis.

One should be certain that italics are available in the typesetting equipment to be used before indicating them (which is generally done in typescript and longhand by underlining). Most newspapers are not able to set italics in body type conveniently. When italics are not available, titles are often enclosed instead in quotation marks, although the growing tendency is to set them without any distinctive mark. Boldface type is suitable in place of italics to denote emphasis of single words, but not for foreign words or titles. When something that would ordinarily be set in italics occurs in what is already italicized, the desired differentiation is indicated by reverting to Roman.

**it goes without saying.** See OF COURSE; NEEDLESS TO SAY.

**it is I who (is, am).** In constructions like "It is I who am the nominee," strictly speaking the verb *am* agrees with its subject, *I.* But there is a strong tendency to use *is,* since *am* sounds artificial. Fowler cites a similar construction, *it . . . that,* and says the verb following *that* agrees with the word *that* represents "It is trees like these that bear [not *bears*] the best fruit."

**its, it's.** *Its* means *belonging to it:* "The cat is washing its fur." *It's* is the contraction for *it is:* "It's one o'clock." None of the possessive pronouns takes an apostrophe: *its, hers, theirs, ours* (Copperud, Evans, Fowler).

**itself.** See MYSELF; REFLEXIVES.

**it's me (her, him, us, them).** Bryant says the objective forms (as given here) are frequently found in conversation and in fiction, and calls them appropriate in spoken English; the nominative forms (*I, she, he, we, they*) are described as generally, but not always, found in expository writing. Copperud, Evans, and Flesch regard the objective forms as standard usage, and make no distinction between speech and writing in this respect. Fowler finds *it's me* colloquially acceptable, and so does Perrin, who comments: "All the large grammars of English regard *it's me* as acceptable colloquial usage—and since the expression is not likely to occur except in speech, that gives it full standing." Perrin approves of the objective forms generally "in their natural settings." Follett too finds *it's me* not only acceptable but preferable, though he prescribes *I* when it is followed by a relative clause: "It is I who am the nominee." Probably the use of the contraction *it's,* setting a tone of informality, would tend to encourage *me* even in such constructions, however; this is a distinction Follett neglected to make. A construction like

"It is I/me whom they nominated" would, by strict grammar, also require *I* on the principle that the case of a pronoun is determined by its function in its own clause. Bernstein and American Heritage would permit *It is me* only in speech, not in writing.

**-ize, -ise.** With familiar exceptions (*advertise, advise, apprise,* and some others), *-ise* is the characteristically British termination, *-ize* the American: *apologise, apologize.* This is so even though Fowler, quoting the Oxford English Dictionary, holds that the *-ise* termination (on words other than the exceptions mentioned) is wrong. Americans who use *-ise* on such words are likely to be considered affected or precious in this respect. See also -OR, -OUR.

Tacking on *-ize* is a convenient method of making a needed verb from a noun, and sometimes from an adjective: *concertize, hospitalize, burglarize.* There are numerous such established verbs, but Bernstein, Copperud, Follett, and Fowler discourage the invention of new ones, such as *concretize, martyrize, secretize, decimalize, capsulize, comprehensiveize, therapize.* The consensus is that such words tend to be ungainly and are often unnecessary. Nevertheless, what counts in the end is wide enough acceptance of a new verb in *-ize.* Words of this kind that have been the subject of individual criticism, like *finalize,* will be found in their alphabetical places in this book.

# J

**Jap, Japanese.** *Jap* was freely used during World War II, with malicious satisfaction in the fact that it is derogatory. Since then, *Japanese* is carefully chosen nearly everywhere as both noun and adjective: *four Japanese; Japanese ships.* The pejorative implication of *Jap* is so clear that it is avoided even in newspaper headlines, despite the pressure of small space. *Nip,* as a clipped form of *Nipponese,* is considered equally offensive (Copperud, Evans, American Heritage, Random House, Webster).

**jargon.** See ARGOT, JARGON.

**jetsam.** See FLOTSAM, JETSAM.

**Jew, Jewish.** The terms are sometimes carelessly used in connection with Israel. Although that nation is closely identified with Jews and Judaism, the expressions *Jew* and *Israeli* are not interchangeable. Israel, like other nations, is composed of peoples of many races and religions, including a substantial number of Arabs and Mohammedans, and Christians of various races too. *Jew* and *Jewish,* then, in reference to the nationals of Israel, are called for only in circumstances where those terms would be applied to the nationals of any other country. *Jewish* is not the name of a language; usually *Hebrew* or *Yiddish* is intended. *Jew* as an adjective is now derogatory, whatever it

may have been a generation ago when Frank Harris referred to "the handsome Jew journalist Catulle Mendes . . . " The inoffensive way to say this today would be *Jewish journalist.* See also HEBREW.

**Jewess.** Like *Negress,* often considered derogatory (Copperud, Evans, American Heritage, Random House; Webster unaccountably does not label it).

**jibe.** See GIBE, JIBE.

**Jingles.** Writers are cautioned by Evans, Flesch, Fowler, and Follett to avoid unintended repetitions of the same word or of similar sounds, such as "The *object* of the *project,* "No *evidence* of *negligence,*" "He looked *backward* on his experiences with *backward* peoples." See also REPETITION.

**job, position.** Neither observable usage nor the definitions in Random House and Webster substantiate the idea sometimes advanced that *job* necessarily connotes manual labor or low rank. It is the homelier word of the two, and *position* would probably not be applied to ditch-digging. *Job,* sometimes qualified by *big,* is applied casually to employment at all levels. *Position* is sometimes suspect because it may be used to confer a spurious dignity. See also WAGE; RAISE, REAR, RISE.

**jobless.** Once derided as an unnecessary invention, *jobless* long since has won its spurs; both Random House and Webster recognize it. The inventor undoubtedly was a frustrated headline-writer confronted with fitting *unemployed* into half the space during the Great Depression.

**join together.** Bernstein and Copperud agree that despite the example of the Bible, this redundancy may well be put asunder; Evans considers it established and acceptable.

**journalese, journalism, journalistic.** Before 1954, when pressure was successfully brought to bear against the G. & C. Merriam Co. by Sigma Delta Chi, the professional journalistic society, the definition of *journalistic* in the Merriam-Webster dictionaries was similar to the definition of *journalese;* it was as if the words were really *journalese* and *journalese-tic.*

*Journalese* is what linguists describe as a pejorative; that is to say, a word that depreciates. It applies to all that is bad in journalistic writing. *Journalistic,* on the other hand, properly means *pertaining to journalism,* and ought not to have any derogatory connotation. Nor does it, ordinarily. The old Webster definition of *journalistic* was "Characteristic of journalism or journalists; hence, of style characterized by evidence of haste, superficiality of thought, inaccuracies of detail, colloquialisms, and sensationalism; journalese." In the revised definition, the derogatory aspects were replaced by "appropriate to the immediate present and phrased to stimulate and satisfy the interest and curiosity of a wide reading public—often in distinction from *literary.*" The definition of *journalistic* in the Third Edition of Webster has been further revised, but the effect is the same and it remains neutral.

The Third Edition defines *journalese* first as a style of writing held to be characteristic of newspapers, and goes on with "writing marked by simple, informal, and usu. loose sentence structure, the frequent use of clichés, sensationalism in the presentation of material, and superficiality of thought and reasoning."

The Dictionary of Contemporary American Usage remarks that "As a term for all newspaper writing, journalese is a snob term. There is just as good and effective writing in the best newspapers as in the best books, and the faults that are commonly classed as journalese are to be found in all writing." This is a fair judgment, but something more may be said on the subject of snobbery. *Journalese* is seldom applied to all newspaper writing, and when it is, the tone is so bitter that there is little hope of bringing the critic to reason. The truly snob term is *journalism,* applied, as Webster put it, in distinction to *literature.*

Often, when used in this way, *journalism* is preceded by *mere: mere journalism,* says the reviewer, and thus consigns the subject of his comment to perdition. Such judgments are often stupid, and amount to depreciating folk music by comparing it with classical music. Journalism and literature nurture each other, as do folk and classical music. Much that is unpretentiously journalism is superb, as for example the kind of writing found in *The New Yorker;* much that aims at being literary is atrocious.

Now and then *journalese* is mistaken for a neutral descriptive of newspaper style. The author of a book on English usage and the compiler of a college newspaper stylebook misapplied it as the term for the cant, or technical terminology, of journalism.

Most inferior writing is cliché-ridden, but newspapering has developed its own clichés. In journalese, a thing is not *kept secret,* but *a lid of secrecy is clamped* on it; rain and snow do not *fall,* but *are dumped;* a river does not *overflow* or *flood,* but *goes on a rampage;* honors are not *won* or *earned* but *captured;* divisions are too often *crack;* a reverse does not *threaten,* but *looms;* an occurrence is not *unprecedented,* but *precedent-shattering* (as if precedents were glass, when everyone knows they are rubber); large buildings are not *extensive,* but *sprawling,* which has less life left in it than *extensive,* for all its colorlessness.

All such expressions have something in common besides extreme fatigue. If the reader can shake off, for a moment, the anesthesia they produce, he will see that originally they were dramatic. Even if they were too dramatic to suit the occasion—another characteristic of journalism, not necessarily related to clichés—the first few times they were used they piqued the reader's attention. But that was long ago. How,

then, do they continue to be used so much? The obvious explanation is laziness. These expressions and many equally tired ones have become fixed in the minds of the lethargic and unimaginative as the only ones that are suitably descriptive.

When reporters are taxed with the stereotyped flavor of newspaper writing, they sometimes offer as an excuse that much of their work must be done in haste, to meet a deadline. This does not happen to be a good excuse, however, for it would be easier and faster to use the plain language the clichés conceal. Thus if the lazy were even lazier, the results would be happier.

Plain language—the words the cliché expert uses himself when he is talking instead of writing—often looks surprisingly fresh in print. It will never wear out, as the clichés have, because it is the natural and inevitable currency of expression.

Fairly extensive entries under the heading *Journalese* appear in Evans and Follett. Evans deprecates blanket application of the term to newspaper writing, as noted; they both criticize journalese for sensationalism, overdramatization, pomposity, and overuse of superlatives. See also CLICHÉS; ELEGANT VARIATION; VARIATION.

**Jr., Sr.** It is a growing practice to omit the comma once generally used before *Jr.* and *Sr.: Joseph Williams Jr.* The omission has grammar on its side, for such designations, like *II, III* in *William II, George III,* are after all restrictive modifiers. The words are capitalized when spelled out and appended to a name: *Joseph Williams Junior*. A young woman should not be described as junior though her name is the same as her mother's. The use of *Jr.* is considered unnecessary with the name of a man who has a title, such as *Dr.*, that is not possessed by the father (Copperud, Evans).

**judgement, judgment.** The first is the British preference, the second the American (Copperud, Fowler).

**judicial, judicious.** Evans, Follett, and Fowler warn against confusing the terms; ordinarily the first relates to legal proceedings (*judicial chambers*), the second to wisdom or judgment (*a judicious choice*). In places where either term will fit it is well to use a nonambiguous synonym or to recast to make the meaning inescapable.

**juncture.** Evans and Fowler say the phrase *at this juncture* should refer to a convergence of events, and should not merely displace *at this moment* or *now*. Flesch calls the phrase pompous.

**junior, senior.** See JR., SR.

**junket.** Not a neutral equivalent of *trip, journey,* or *excursion,* for the word has a derogatory connotation in that sense. One kind of junket is a

trip taken by a politician at public expense, ostensibly on public business but really for his own enjoyment. Because of this connotation, the Foreign Press Association in 1960 banned the use of the term in its bulletin and ordered the substitution of *facility trip* for travel provided to journalists. *Junket* is generally applied by newspapermen to joyrides provided not to facilitate news coverage, but to create goodwill. There is a hazy line between these and travel provided at someone else's expense, for example the military services or a corporation, with legitimate news coverage in view (Copperud, Evans, Random House, Webster).

**jurist.** Bernstein and Flesch hold that, common newspaper use to the contrary, a jurist is merely one versed in the law; the word is not an exact synonym for *judge.* Copperud speculates that identity of meaning is becoming established, and Random House and Webster both give *judge* for *jurist.* Among four current desk dictionaries, only Webster's Collegiate recognizes the terms as synonyms. The consensus is against using the term *jurist* for *judge.*

**just exactly.** Criticized by Bernstein and Fowler as a redundancy.

# K

**keep pace with.** The form of the phrase; not *keep in pace with.*

**kerosene.** Called coal oil in some parts of the U.S. and paraffin in Britain. Sometimes spelled *kerosine* (Copperud, Evans, Fowler).

**ketchup.** See CATCHUP, etc.

**kick off.** Either as a verb (*kick off the campaign*) or as an adjective (*a kick-off dinner*), this is a frayed figure from the football field. Not given as a verb by American Heritage, but considered standard as a noun; labeled slang by Random House; given as standard in both uses by Webster.

**kid, kids.** A generation ago, teachers busily instructed their pupils that kids could only be young goats, but the real goats were the kids who swallowed this pedantry; *kids* for *children* is well established colloquially. Flesch calls *kid* on its way to acceptance as standard English. Random House calls it informal, the American College Dictionary slang, Webster's New World colloquial, and the Standard College and American Heritage dictionaries informal. Webster considers it standard. The consensus is that it is informal, which means well suited to most contexts.

**kilt, kilts.** Bernstein and Follett hold that a kilt is a single garment, and thus "the man was wearing kilts" is an error for "a kilt." Random House gives *kilt* as a singular, but Webster cites an example like the one given. The consensus favors *kilt* as a singular. Thus the corrected example would be "The man was wearing a kilt." American Heritage adds another distinction, that *kilts* is an acceptable singular in reference to a woman's skirt imitating the Scotch garment.

**kin.** The term has given rise

to some interesting and contradictory comment. Bernstein and Evans insist that it cannot be singular, but must refer to relatives collectively, a judgment that neither Random House nor Webster supports. Opinion thus is evenly divided. Flesch criticizes the term as to be found only in headlines and pompous literary prose, a view that is patently mistaken.

**kind.** There are three constructions based on *kind* (and *sort*) that cause trouble. The first is *these, those kind* ("Those kind of flowers"). Since *those* is plural and *kind* is singular, strictly speaking the correct forms are *that, this kind* or *these, those kinds.* Bernstein, like Copperud, disapproves of *those kind* followed by a singular (*of flower*) but is indulgent toward it followed by a plural (*of flowers*). He quotes an unspecified but well-educated President as having said "Those kind of tests." Bryant calls *these kind* followed by a plural colloquial, but Fowler is receptive to it and quotes Shakespeare: "These kind of knaves." American Heritage roundly rejects *those kind.* Evans calls this construction standard. The consensus is that while *kind* preceded and followed by a plural is irregular, it is easily forgivable.

The next difficulty arises with *kind of a, an* ("What kind of a notion is that?"). Bernstein, Copperud, and Follett disapprove of the use of *a, an* (correctly, "What kind of notion is that?"); Bryant calls it colloquial; Evans defends it, citing Henry James; Fowler calls it the least excusable of faults with *kind*. The consensus is negative. (Similar constructions follow *sort, species, manner, type*.)

The third troublesome construction is *kind of* in the sense *somewhat* or *rather:* "It's kind of cold out." Bernstein and Copperud discourage this usage; Bryant, without making an explicit judgment, finds *kind of* standard in many parts of the country; Evans describes it as widely heard at all levels, though universally condemned; Flesch condones it; Random House considers it objectionable but Webster gives it as standard. The consensus is negative.

**kindly.** Evans and Flesch disapprove of *kindly* for *please: Kindly remit;* but Random House and Webster explicitly recognize this usage. Fowler disapproves of such constructions as *you are kindly requested,* in which the requester seems to impute kindness to himself.

**kith and kin.** Called a cliché by Evans and an archaism by Fowler. Both explain that *kith* means acquaintances and *kin* means relations.

**kneeled, knelt.** Both forms are declared acceptable by Bryant and Evans, though *knelt* is described as predominant for the past tense. Random House and Webster concur. Fowler admits only *knelt,* apparently a British usage.

**knit, knitted.** Bryant, Evans, and Fowler find that the forms are equally acceptable, and that *knit* as a modifier (*a knit scarf*) is too. Webster recognizes this latter use but Random House does not. The consensus is that it is standard.

**knock(ed) up.** The difference in meaning of this slang expression in Britain and America has yielded much merriment. The British senses of *knock up* are *wake up* or *tire out;* the American sense is *make pregnant.* The latter is illustrated in Webster by "no girls get married around here till they're knocked up." There are other senses, but they are not confused (Copperud, Evans, American Heritage, Random House).

**knot.** Often, incorrectly, *knots per hour;* a knot is a measure of speed, not distance, and it is a nautical mile per hour. *Knots* is also wrong as a measure of distance (*eighteen knots up the coast*) in place of *nautical miles* (Bernstein, Copperud, Evans, Follett, Fowler, American Heritage). Fowler, however, while pointing out the misapprehension, condones *knots per hour,* and Random House, American Heritage, and Webster admit *knot* as a loose usage for *nautical mile,* which permits *knots per hour.* The consensus is against this usage.

**know as.** Rejected by Nicholson and American Heritage as a displacement of *know that* or *whether:* "I don't know as he's coming." *whether.* The absence of this point from other books on usage probably is explained by the strong dialectal flavor of the expression, leading to the conclusion that disapproval would be unnecessary.

**know-how.** Described as standard English by Bryant, Evans, Random House, Webster, and even by Fowler, who concedes it has made its way in England, after having originated in America. This is a considerable tribute; the mere fact of American origin or American popularity is usually enough by itself to damn an expression in the eyes of British critics. Bernstein, however, classifies it with fad words, by which he means it is overused.

**kudos.** Not a plural any more than *pathos;* thus one can no more speak of a *kudo* than of a *patho.* The term means *fame,* *glory.* Some sample misapprehensions: "The correspondent deserves a Congo kudo"; "Kudos are in order for Edmund Wilson." Sometimes *kudos* is even misused as a verb: *"Life* Kudos Capitol's Cast Albums" (Bernstein, Copperud, Fowler, American Heritage, Random House, Webster). Bernstein adds the view that even used correctly *kudos* is pseudo-literary, and Evans, without noting the confusion in number, calls it an academic affectation. Webster, however, gives as a verb *kudize.*

# L

**la, le.** In proper names, see DE, DU, etc.

**lack for.** Where *lack* alone will do ("The program lacks for public interest"), rejected by American Heritage. Random House and Webster confirm this by implication; none of their examples uses *lack for.*

**lady.** See WOMAN, LADY.

**lama, llama.** The first is the name of the priest in Tibet and Mongolia; the second that of the South American beast of burden and source of fleece (Evans, Fowler).

**(a) large portion, number, of.** Verbiage for *much of, most of, many.* "A large portion of his popularity is due to habit." *Much of.* "A large number of flamingos were crowding to the gate." *Many.*

**largely.** Fowler points out that after *loom* and *bulk,* idiom calls for *large,* not *largely;* examples in Webster corroborate this. See also WRIT LARGE.

**last, latest.** Copperud, Evans, Follett, and Fowler agree that *last* and *latest* are often interchangeable, in spite of the occasional insistence that *last* can only mean *final.* Thus, as Follett points out, one may speak of an author's last book and be correctly understood as meaning his most recent, not his final one. *Latest* is desirable in other references to mean *immediately preceding* where *last* could be misunderstood: "The *latest* issue is dated Dec. 15; the one to be published in January will be the *last.*" See also PASS, PAST.

**late.** Redundant in *widow of the late;* correctly, *widow of* (Bernstein, Copperud).

**latter.** See FORMER, LATTER.

**laudable, laudatory.** Sometimes confused; what is laudable deserves praise, what is laudatory confers it (Copperud, Evans, Fowler).

**launch.** Standard but overused in journalism for *start, open, initiate, begin.* See also INAUGURATE.

**law business, concern.** Bernstein frowns on *law business* for *law profession,* and Copperud on *law concern* as unidiomatic for *law firm.*

**lawman.** Bernstein calls the term unnecessary in the popular sense *law enforcement officer;* Copperud approves of that usage, but warns that *lawman* should not be used for *lawyer.* Both Random House and Webster give *lawman* (as *law enforcement officer*) without deprecation, so the consensus is that the term is standard. Its growing popularity seems to be ascribable to Westerns on television, where the sheriff and his aides are often referred to as lawmen.

**lawyer.** See ATTORNEY, LAWYER.

**lay, laid.** See LIE, LAY.

**layman.** The primary meaning is "of or pertaining to the laity, as distinct from the clergy." It is well established, however, and recognized by both Random House and Webster, as also designating one outside some other profession or field of endeavor. Thus *layman* may be used in contradistinction to *doctor, lawyer, engineer, teacher,* etc., as well as *clergyman,* despite criticism of this usage.

**lb., lbs.** The use of these abbreviations (which derive from *libra,* the ancient Roman pound) for *pound(s) sterling* and similar monetary units is confusing and undesirable. These forms should be used only for units of weight. When the symbol for pound sterling, £, is not available, it is preferable to spell the designation out. A workable substitute for the symbol can be made on the typewriter by striking the hyphen over the *L.*

*Lbs.* is often used for the plural of the unit of weight, but the plural form is unnecessary. This applies to any abbreviation: *in.* (not *ins.*); *sec.* (not *secs.*).

**lead, led.** The past tense and participle of the verb meaning *to head, direct* is *led:* "They led us to the mouth of the tunnel." Sometimes it is erroneously given as *lead,* perhaps from confusion with the name of the metal, whose pronunciation is the same (Copperud, Evans). In the cant of printing, *lead* is a verb (as well as a noun) pronounced *led,* meaning to space out lines by inserting strips of metal. In an effort to prevent confusion, the *Linotype News* invented the spellings *ledd* and *ledding* for this use, but they have not been generally adopted (Copperud, Fowler).

**leading question.** The term derives from the courts, and there it means a question that suggests or elicits (that is, leads to) its answer, not necessarily a significant or critical or unfair question. This distinction is explained by Copperud, Evans, and Fowler, and the legal definition is the only one given by Random House and

Webster. The casual use in the sense *pointed, important,* or *embarrassing question* is, therefore, mistaken.

**leak.** In the sense *disclose information, become known* ("word of the appointment was leaked to the press"), recognized as standard by Follett, Fowler, Random House, and Webster.

**leap, leaped, leapt.** *Leaped* is preferred in the United States for the past tense and participle; *leapt* (pronounced *lept*) is chiefly British (Copperud, Evans).

**learn, teach.** To learn is to acquire knowledge, to teach is to impart it; *learn* for *teach* ("She learned us arithmetic") is described variously as rustic, uneducated, vulgar, jocular, or dialectal by Bryant, Copperud, and Fowler. Evans justifies it as acceptable, citing examples from literature. This seems wrongheaded, for the examples are at least a century old, and usage changes. American Heritage, Random House, and Webster label *learn* for *teach* substandard.

**leastways, leastwise.** Evans and Fowler agree that *leastways* is nonstandard. American Heritage, Random House, and Webster call it dialectal. American Heritage and Random House designate *leastwise* informal; Evans and Webster consider it standard.

**leave, let.** Although *leave* (for *let*) *me alone* is widely seen and heard, a useful distinction is lost by neglect of *let. Leave,* in its primary sense, means *go away from,* and *let* means *permit* or *allow. Leave me alone* strictly means *leave me by myself; let me alone,* which is usually intended, means *don't bother me. Leave* has become popular, with a whimsical tinge, in the imperative where *let* is called for: *Leave us go.* This is in fact a revival of an archaic usage. "This publisher leaves his editors alone, while he concentrates on business matters." Ambiguous as it stands; the editors are not left in solitude, but are spared interference. *lets.* These comments reflect the views of Bernstein and Copperud; American Heritage, Bryant, and Evans defend *leave* (with *alone*) for *let* as standard English, but call other uses of *leave* for *let* substandard. Random House admits *leave alone* in the sense *let alone* but does not recognize other substitutions. Webster too admits *leave alone* but calls such constructions as *leave him be* substandard. The consensus is that *leave* for *let* is acceptable only with *alone.* See also FURLOUGH.

**lectern.** See PODIUM.

**legible, readable.** See ILLEGIBLE, UNREADABLE.

**lend, loan.** See LOAN, LEND.

**lengthways, lengthwise.** Evans and Fowler call both forms standard, and so do Random House and Webster.

**lengthy.** The word seems to have displaced *long* in much writing, Copperud observes, especially in newspapers. Fowler describes it as a jocular or stylish synonym for *long,* but says it also appears more usefully to suggest tedium, a judgment in which Evans concurs. The sense *tedious* is given by both Random House and Webster. Bernstein says the word is often used vaguely, and recommends something more precise, such as *tedious* itself. The consensus is that *lengthy* is best used to suggest tedium, and not merely as a variant of *long*.

-less. Solid as a suffix: *childless, conscienceless,* etc., except after *ll: bell-less* (Copperud, Fowler). Flesch discourages the fabrication of new words by appending *-less: sceneryless, moneyless.* Fowler, however, says that there is no reason why any noun may not be compounded with *-less,* but objects to such compounds with verbs, except for those already established, like *tireless*.

less, fewer. See FEWER, LESS. For *less* as an adverb wrongly joined to an adjective with a hyphen, see ALMOST.

let, let's. Fowler and American Heritage warn against the wrong case in constructions like "Let you and me settle the matter," where the nominative is often erroneously used ("let you and *I*"). Evans considers the nominative wrong only when a third person is being addressed, as in "Let John and I settle the matter." Bryant considers *let us* formal, *let's* informal, and *let's us* colloquial. Evans considers *let's you and I, let's you and me,* and *let's us* all acceptable. Bryant describes *let's not* as standard and *don't let's* and *let's don't* as colloquial.

let, leave. See LEAVE, LET.

level. As a verb, in such constructions as *level a charge,*

described by Copperud as excessive for *charge,* and by Flesch as stuffy.

The popular use of *level* as a noun in such expressions as *on the local level* (for *locally*), *at a record low level* (for *at a record low*), *at the junior high school level* (for *in junior high schools*), and others where it is automatic, vague, and avoidable, is criticized by Flesch, Follett, and Fowler.

liable. See APT, LIABLE, LIKELY.

liaison. Evans holds that the term should be reserved for the military, cooking, and sexual senses, and not used indiscriminately for any kind of association. Random House and Webster allow extensions to other associations. The word is often misspelled; *liason,* among other ways.

libation. Evans and Flesch both disapprove of the term as a humorous variant for *drink*.

libel, slander. Bernstein, Evans, Follett, and Fowler point out that in common parlance, the terms are used interchangeably for defamation, but that in the eyes of the law, libel is defamation by graphic means, recording, or broadcast, and slander is defamation by other spoken utterance or by gesture.

liberal. It may be misleading to capitalize the term in the general political sense; this should be done only in reference to a Liberal Party (as in New York or Britain). See also CONSERVATIVE.

lie, lay. The chief difficulty here is remembering that the

past tense of *lie* is *lay*, not *laid*—"After dinner I lay down"; "The book lay on the table"—and that the participle is *lain*, not *laid:* "The tools have lain in the grass since Sunday." *Laid* is the past tense and participle of *lay* (meaning *place down*): "She has laid the silver in the closet." *Lay* and *lie* are often erroneously interchanged: "Let us lay down in the shade." *lie.* These general principles, which represent strictly correct usage, are concurred in by Bernstein, Bryant, Copperud, Evans, Follett, and Fowler. Evans, however, regards "lay down for a nap," "the book is laying on the table," and "he has lain it down" as also correct; Bryant finds such uses common in well-educated speech, though not in writing; Follett calls the distinctions more trouble than they are worth; and Fowler, in an indulgent tone, says the confusions are common in talk. The consensus is that forms of *lay* for *lie* are verging into standard usage. Evans calls for *lay low* (not *laid*) as the past of *lie low*.

**light.** *Lighted* and *lit* are both standard for the past and participle (Bryant, Evans, Fowler). Evans adds that this is true also of *light* in the sense *land* (*the ball lit in the water*) and *alight;* Random House and Webster concur except for *alight.*

**lightening, lightning.** The first is the act of making less dark or heavy, the second the flash in the heavens (Copperud, Evans).

**-like.** Solid as a suffix: *childlike, lamblike,* etc. But hyphenated after *ll: bill-like* (Copperud, Evans, Fowler).

**like, as, as if. 1.** Copperud, Evans, Fowler, and Flesch all consider *like* standard as a conjunction; that is, in introducing a clause: "He said the movies are not going to stand still *like* they have for twenty-five years." All warn, however, that there is widespread prejudice against *like* instead of *as* in such constructions. Bryant finds *like* for *as* common in informal expression, but says *as* is preferred in formal English; Bernstein concedes that the preference for *as* is not logical, but advises against the use of *like* as a conjunction; American Heritage and Follett are adamantly against it. Random House recognizes *like* as a conjunction but warns that it is "universally condemned by teachers and editors, notwithstanding its wide currency"; Webster accepts it without qualification. The consensus is that while *like* as a conjunction is defensible, the user should be prepared for criticism.

The disapproval of *like* for *as* has generated in some writers an undiscriminating fear of *like* in any context. Thus they shun it even when it is required in its legitimate role as a preposition, and out of overcorrectness commit error. They write things like "He ate as a beast," "She trembled as a leaf," and "Editors, as inventors, are creative people." In all three instances, *like* is not only right but inescapable, and *as* is wrong (Bernstein, Bryant, Copperud, Flesch, Follett, Fowler, American Heritage).

2. *Like* for *as if, as though. Like* is often used in place of *as if, as though,* as in "The Kremlin has been making noises like it wants such a meeting." The acceptance of this usage by the authorities parallels that of *like* for *as,* and the same consensus applies. For those who want to avoid all criticism of these usages, a rule propounded by Frank O. Colby (*Practical Handbook of Better English*) is useful: "If *as, as if, as though* make sense in a sentence, *like* is incorrect. If they do not make sense, *like* is the right word." But this rule will not help anyone whose ear is so bad he is capable of writing "He ate as a beast."

3. Some who strain to avoid *like* use *as with* or go the long way around with *in a manner similar to:* "The offense was relatively trivial, as with going barefoot to a black-tie affair"; "The unique plane stands on the ground in a manner similar to a camera tripod." In both instances, *like* is called for. *As with* is suitable when neither *like* nor *as* will do: "The best course, as with so many things, lies somewhere in between" (Copperud, Follett). Such expressions as "He ran like mad" and "They cheered like crazy" are considered acceptable by Bernstein, Bryant, and Evans.

For the error illustrated by "Like many patient folk, Russian violence can be brutal," in which *like that of* is required, see FALSE COMPARISON. For *should, would like,* see SHALL, WILL, SHOULD, WOULD. See also SUCH AS.

like for. As in "We would like for it to rain," called a Southern locution by both Bryant and Evans, and considered acceptable at least in speech. American Heritage rejects it.

likely. As used for *probably* ("The concert will likely be a benefit"), approved by Copperud and Flesch, oddly regarded as acceptable but quaint by Evans, and approved as an American usage by Fowler. Bernstein, Follett, and American Heritage hold that it must be preceded by *very, quite,* or *most* to be correct in this sense; Evans regards this as the standard usage. Both Random House and Webster consider *likely* for *probably* standard. The consensus is that it is correct. To people unaccustomed to it, however, it sounds unnatural. See also APT, LIABLE, LIKELY.

likes of. Bernstein and American Heritage disapprove of *likes of* for *like of* (*the likes of Scott Fitzgerald*), but both Random House and Webster regard *like of* and *likes of* as standard.

limited. Bernstein, Evans, Follett, and Fowler criticize the use of the word for *small, inadequate, few, rare* (*limited funds, limited interests, limited ideas,* etc.) in contrast to applying it where a limit has actually been set. The definitions in Random House and Webster appear to confirm this judgment.

linage, lineage. Copperud, Evans, Follett, and Fowler advocate restricting *linage* to printed lines (as most often used concerning advertising) and *lineage* to considerations of descent. Dictionaries give the forms as synonymous for *printed lines*.

**line.** Regarded as slangy for *occupation* by Bernstein and Evans, as in the title of the television show, *What's My Line?* Evans concedes, however, that it is now all but standard. Fowler gives *what's my line* without aspersion (as a near-synonym of *field*), and both Random House and Webster also recognize this sense as standard. See also ON LINE.

**lion's share.** In one of two fables from which the expression derives, the lion's share was not the greater part, but all or nearly all. Bernstein insists on this sense. The currently predominant *greater part* is accepted by Copperud, Evans, American Heritage, Random House, and Webster. However used, it is, as Evans says, a cliché.

**lit.** See LIGHT.

**litany, liturgy.** Bernstein objects to *litany* in such contexts as "The lecture was a litany of complaints about the high cost of living," arguing that the term is misused except in reference to a religious ceremony. Random House, however, gives "a prolonged or monotonous account," and Webster gives "a recital or chant having the resonant or repetitive qualities associated with a litany (the author recites his litany of the great mysteries)." Evans and Fowler are concerned about the confusion of *litany* (a form of responsive prayer) with *liturgy*

(a form of public worship or a particular arrangement of services).

**literally.** Unliterally used to mean (a) *figuratively*, (b) *almost* or *virtually*, or (c) nothing much at all. Seldom is the word employed in its exact sense, which is *to the letter, precisely as stated*. Some examples: "The actor was literally floating on applause." The word wanted was *figuratively*, unless levitation occurred. "Flowing through the buttes and deep washes of South Dakota, the Missouri River literally cuts the state in half." *Literally* here is excess baggage, for the sentence is more forceful without it. So also in "A marble bust of Tom Paine may soon leave Philadelphia, where it literally has been a controversial object for seventy-eight years." It has become a habit of heedless writers to use *literally* for a usually unnecessary emphasis, without reference to its meaning (Copperud, Bernstein, Evans, Follett, Fowler). Webster, however, gives as one sense *in effect*, which would legitimize the misuses cited. The consensus, however, is heavily against this sense; Random House does not recognize it.

**Literary Allusion.** A discussion of the device usually thus referred to appears in Fowler under the heading *Generic Names and Other Allusive Commonplaces*; its essence is that the writer should temper his choice of such allusions to the comprehension of his audience, and that, like foreign terms, they must be accurately used. Bernstein concurs. See also ALLUSION; MISQUOTATION.

literature. Evans defends application of the term to the body of writing on a subject ("the literature on taxation") but regards its use for sales brochures and other promotional material as not standard. Copperud, however, calls this an established and useful sense; Fowler considers it colloquial and adds it is on the verge of becoming standard. Both Random House and Webster recognize the application to handbills, etc. The consensus is that this usage is standard.

little man, people. In an author's note in *McSorley's Wonderful Saloon,* Joseph Mitchell wrote: "The people in a number of these stories are of the kind that many writers have recently got into the habit of referring to as 'the little people.' I regard this phrase as patronizing and repulsive. There are no little people in this book. They are as big as you are, whoever you are." *The little man* has incurred the distaste of the Canadian Press, whose stylebook enjoins: "Do not use the term *little man* in referring to the population generally or any segment of it. The term has no precise or defensible meaning in that connection and has long since become objectionable."

littler, littlest. Bernstein objects to the forms as dialectal or juvenile and recommends *smaller, smallest, less, least.* Evans, however, points out that *littler* and *littlest* fill needs that the other words do not; Random House and Webster give both forms without aspersion. The consensus is that they are standard.

littoral. Described by Fowler as pretentious in ordinary (that is, nontechnical) contexts where *coast* will do.

liturgy. See LITANY, LITURGY.

live. The word is often enclosed in quotation marks when used in reference to broadcasts ("The show was televised 'live' "), presumably to warn the reader that this is the term that rhymes with *hive* and not the one that rhymes with *give*. But the chance of confusion seems remote, since the association of *live* with television is now abundantly familiar. Copperud, Evans, Webster, and Random House regard the expression as standard. Bernstein warns that *live* and *alive* are not interchangeable: "Frank Buck brought them back alive" (not *live*). He adds that *live* almost invariably precedes the noun it modifies: *live oysters, a live issue.*

lives with his wife at . . . The phrase, a favorite of journalists in biographical sketches, has an unhappy ring, because it seems to suggest the alternative of separate maintenance. Something like "He and his wife live at . . ." or "The Tannenbaums make their home at . . ." sounds more suitable.

livid. Bernstein holds that the term means either black and blue or the color of lead (grayish). These hues are included in Webster's definition, which adds that *livid* can qualify any color (*livid pink*), and that it can also mean *pallid, ghastly, gray,* or *lurid;* Random House also gives *bluish, deathly pale, ashen.*

**llama, lama.** See LAMA, LLAMA.

**Lloyd's.** The correct form in reference to the place in London where underwriting is done; not *Lloyds* or *Lloyds'* (Evans, Fowler).

**loan, lend.** The idea that *loan* is not good form as a verb is a superstition ("Loan me your pencil"; "The bank was ready to loan the money"). It is recognized as standard by both Random House and Webster; Flesch calls it a common idiom; Bernstein recognizes its legitimacy but recommends *lend;* Fowler calls it a needless variant; Evans describes it as thoroughly respectable, especially in connection with money; Bryant regards it as standard; American Heritage rejects it. The consensus is overwhelmingly that it is beyond reproach, though still the object of occasional criticism. *Loan* perhaps is encouraged by the curious avoidance of the past tense of *lend,* that is, *lent,* in favor of *loaned.*

**loath, loathe.** *Loath* is the adjective meaning reluctant ("I am loath to criticize him"); *loathe* is the verb meaning *detest* ("I loathe spinach"). "Officers have been loathe to make arrests in such cases." *loath.* It's *loathsome,* not *loathesome* (Copperud, Fowler).

**locate.** Properly, the word is not simply a synonym for *find,* but means *discover, fix the position of.* Thus one would *find,* not *locate,* a lost child, but might either *find* or *locate* a lighthouse (Bernstein, Evans, Flesch, Fowler). Copperud and Evans allow *located* (the pas-

sive form) to designate position ("the barn is located near the creek"). They also approve *locate* for *settle, become situated,* etc. ("They located in Boston"), but Flesch recommends *settle.* Copperud, Flesch, and Follett point out that *located* is often superfluous: "The house is [located] on the wrong side of the tracks." Random House and Webster corroborate all these views except Flesch's objection to *locate* for *settle.*

**lone.** See POESY.

**loom.** Journalese in the sense *threaten, be expected* (Copperud); pompous (Flesch). See also LARGELY.

**loot.** The slang use of the term to mean a large sum of money or valuables in general is unsettling because of the conflict with the standard denotation of ill-gotten gains. Thus the result may be ambiguity, as in "He will pay roughly a million and a quarter for the mansion, which contains that much loot in the form of tapestries and paintings." The writer meant simply *value;* the owner of the place would be justified in taking offense at the implication, though unintended, that the tapestries and paintings were stolen goods. The use of *loot* for objects of value, with no suggestion of being ill-gotten, is considered informal by Random House and standard by Webster.

**lose, loose.** *Loose* is often misused (or mistaken) for *lose:* "Don't loose your money." *Loose,* though principally an adverb (*the gown hung loose*) or an adjective (*loose change*), is occasionally a verb, but then it is the equivalent of *let go*, or sometimes of *loosen: loose the animals*.

**lot, lots.** The sense *a great deal* is described by Copperud as informal, but as suitable to nearly any context; Bryant calls it informal; Fowler points out that although the Concise Oxford Dictionary says it is informal, Winston Churchill did not hesitate to employ it, nor did an unnamed author on style who is quoted. The first edition of Fowler called it colloquial. Random House says this usage is informal; Webster gives the definition *a great deal* as standard. The consensus is that the usage, if not now standard, is so nearly so that to call it into question is quibbling. Bryant and Random House approve *a lot, lots* as informal adverbs ("He sees her a lot"; "He eats here lots"); Evans and Webster consider them standard but Evans says *a lot* is oftener used.

**loud.** Defended as an adverb by Evans without qualification ("They sang too loud"); Bryant says *loudly* is more frequent in formal writing and *loud* commoner in speech. But there is no question that *loud* as an adverb is standard; both Random House and Webster recognize it.

**lunch, luncheon.** Evans, Flesch, and Fowler agree that *luncheon* is more formal.

**luxuriant, luxurious.** The first means *lush, thick, flourishing;* the second means *rich, lavish, choice, costly*. A head of hair or tropical vegetation can be luxuriant but not luxurious; a dwelling or a meal can be luxurious but not luxuriant (Copperud, Evans, Fowler).

**-ly.** Fowler and Flesch caution against the disagreeable effect caused by adverbs ending in *-ly* modifying each other: "It was nearly certainly a failure." *almost certainly*. Copperud and Flesch say there is no need to add *-ly* to ordinals (*firstly, secondly,* etc.) but adds that if it is done it should be done consistently in a sequence. Fowler says insistence on *first* is pedantry.

The hyphen is wrong after adverbs ending in *-ly*. An adverb can only modify the adjective following: *an equally-good choice*. Omit the hyphen.

**lyric(s).** Evans describes the term as slang in reference to the words of a song ("The tune is good but the lyrics are poor"), but Fowler, Random House, and Webster recognize this usage as standard.

# M

**mad.** The idea that *mad* should not be used to mean *angry* is described by Cop-

perud as a nearly forgotten pedantry; Evans says the sense has been long and universally in use, but warns that it may bring on criticism, and describes *angry* as the formal word; Flesch flatly calls *mad* standard. Random House and Webster concur that it is standard, and this is the consensus. (Perhaps it should be explained that the purist traditionally insisted *mad* can mean only *insane,* a sense that remains in use; it is somewhat literary.)

**madam, madame.** *Madam* is the term for the keeper of a whorehouse, not *madame.* The polite term of address is also *madam; Madame* (often *Mme.,* plural *Mmes.*) is the form for a title prefixed to a name: *Mme. Lafond* (Bernstein, Copperud, Evans, Fowler).

**made possible.** The phrase has grown tiresome, and is often probably an overstatement, in acknowledgments of assistance in literary and other endeavors. All hail, then, the author who said of such assistance that it had made his book less impossible than it might otherwise have been. See also POSSIBLE.

**Magna Charta, Magna Carta.** Although *Charta* is neither Latin nor English, Evans points out that the form has become well established in America, a judgment borne out by the fact that Random House and Webster both give it as the predominant form. Fowler asserts there is unimpeachable authority for *Carta.* The consensus favors *Charta,* at least in the United States.

**magnitude.** Evans discourages the figurative use of the astronomical term *of the first*

*magnitude* as a cliché; Flesch objects to *magnitude* as pretentious when *size* will do.

**Mahomet.** See MOHAMMED, MOHAMMEDAN.

**maintain.** Often questionably used in attribution in newspapers; what is maintained should have been previously asserted. See also ATTRIBUTION.

**major.** Bernstein, Evans, Follett, and Fowler agree that *major* as an adjective is correctly used only in the sense of *greater,* with comparison in mind, and that it is misused for *important, chief, principal, weighty, fundamental,* etc. Thus a major work would be one that stands out by comparison with others, not a great one in absolute terms. Webster's New World Dictionary concurs. The authorities named also agree that whether correctly used or not, *major* is overworked as a modifier. Random House, however, gives "great, as in rank or importance: *a major question; a major artist*"; Webster gives "notable or conspicuous in effect or scope"; the Standard College Dictionary gives "having a primary or greater importance, excellence, rank, etc." The consensus is that the comparative sense is preferable, but that the positive sense ( *important,* etc.) is perhaps well on the way to becoming standard. Copperud calls *major portion* excessive for *most;* Evans says it is pretentious and vague for *greater part.*

**majority, plurality.** A majority is more than half, and the term is best reserved for elections and other circumstances when numbers are involved. *Majority* should be distinguished from *plurality,* which refers to the largest number of votes received by any of three or more candidates (Copperud, Evans, Fowler). Copperud, Evans, Follett, Flesch, and Fowler disapprove *majority* where *most, the greater part, many* will serve, and where numbers are not concerned: "The majority of the land was sold." *Most.* Fowler approves *great majority,* but calls *greater* and *greatest majority* illiterate as forms of intensification; American Heritage concurs.

**male.** The term (like *female,* which see) is too technical or clinical for ordinary contexts where *man* will do (Flesch, Fowler).

**mania, phobia.** Why *mania* should be confused with *phobia* is inexplicable, but it often happens. A *mania* is a craze, as *a mania for cards;* a *phobia* is an exaggerated or irrational fear, as *a phobia of snakes* (Copperud, Random House, Webster). Fowler considers *phobia* a popularized technicality (borrowed from the literature of Freud).

**manner.** Circumlocutions are often formed on the word in place of using an adverb: *in a patient manner (patiently), in a laughable manner (laughably).*

**(to the) manner born.** The correct version, as it appears in *Hamlet* (Act I, sc. iii); not *to the manor born.* The phrase refers to familiarity with local customs, not breeding or inheritance (Copperud, Evans).

**manner, shape, or form.** "He would not accept the honor in any manner, shape, or form." A pomposity.

**marginal.** Bernstein and Fowler object to the loose use of the word in the sense *small* or *narrow* or *slight,* and recommend that it be saved to describe what may easily fall on either side of a borderline, or for its use in economics. By this reasoning, one might speak of a marginal return on an investment (barely over the line from loss), but not of a marginal effort to accomplish something. This corresponds with the definitions in Random House and Webster. For the smallest possible amount, Fowler prescribes *minimal* when *small* is unsatisfactory.

**marital, martial.** The easy transposition of letters that makes the one the other is the bane of proofreaders and editors, and the source of some unintentional humor, especially when what is intended to be *marital* comes out *martial. Marital* relates to marriage, *martial* to arms and war.

**marry, married.** There is a delicate and fairly widespread conviction that the man *marries,* but the woman *is married to,* or, rarely, *by.* The idea behind it is that the man is, or is supposed to be, the aggressor in marriage. In these days of equality of the sexes, however, there seems no warrant for preserving this polite fiction, and it appears to be disappearing, except perhaps from society pages. It attracts no notice now, usually, to say a woman *married* a man, instead of saying she *was married* to him. Random House gives an example in which the woman marries the man. The phrases *married his wife, married her husband* are open to the objection that the wife and husband acquire their status by the act of marriage; the expressions cited suggest they already had it. See also GOT, GOTTEN, for *get, got married*.

**marshal.** The spelling *marshall,* as either noun or verb (*parade marshal; marshal the forces*), is likely to be considered a misspelling; only Webster gives it.

**massive.** Fowler complains with justice that the word has become a fad in the senses *large, sweeping, vigorous,* etc.: *a massive program to combat illiteracy.* No other commentator has noticed this overuse.

**masterful, masterly.** Bernstein, Copperud, Flesch, Follett, and Fowler agree that *masterful* means *domineering* ("she wanted a masterful husband") and that *masterly* means *skillful, expert: a masterly work of art. Masterful* is often misused in the latter sense, and, as Bernstein, Follett, and Fowler concede, the error is probably encouraged by the lack of an adverbial form of *masterly,* leading to the use of *masterfully* ("He played the violin masterfully"). When the adverbial form is required, they prescribe recasting the sentence to preserve the distinction. Both Random House and Webster equate *masterful* and *masterly* without aspersion, however, and Flesch adds in an afterthought that perhaps the fight to keep the distinction is lost. The consensus still favors it.

**material, materiel.** The second is a military term for supplies and equipment as distinguished from personnel; the terms are not interchangeable (Copperud, Fowler).

**materialize.** Bernstein, Copperud, Evans, Flesch, Fowler, and American Heritage criticize use of the term for *develop, occur, happen, appear,* etc., instead of *take material form.* Thus "The clear skies predicted for the weekend failed to materialize" would be objectionable, but "Marley's ghost materialized for Scrooge" would be correct. Random House and Webster, however, both recognize the senses *appear, become fact* as standard. The consensus is against this usage, but it unquestionably is on the way to becoming standard.

**mathematics.** See -IC, -ICS.

**matutinal.** Objected to by Flesch and Fowler as pretentious for *morning:* "The matutinal song of the birds."

**maunder, meander.** Evans and Fowler warn against confusing these terms. The first means to whine, grumble, or complain; the second, to follow a winding course (*the stream meandering through the valley*).

**may.** See CAN, MAY.

**may, might.** *May* is sometimes misused for *might* to describe hypothetical conditions, or when the past tense is required: "The Bible ought to be banned; then it may be read instead of gathering dust on shelves" (*might*); "If property owners had not seen the new sign erected during the night they may not know they

are officially in the county"
(*might*); "If the committee had
had all the facts, it may have
changed its mind" (*might*)
(Copperud, Follett).

**maybe.** The term was questioned in the original Fowler
as not normal for *perhaps;*
Evans accurately spots this as
a British view, and the revised
Fowler not only concedes that
it is the ordinary word in
America but finds it is making
headway in Britain.

**me.** See IT'S ME, etc.

**mean.** See AVERAGE, MEDIAN,
MEAN.

**Meaning.** It is a delusion that
any but the primary or basic
meaning of a word is suspect
if not actually erroneous. The
significations of some of the
simplest and commonest words
run on for columns in unabridged dictionaries. The most
that can be said with any
validity is that some meanings
are older than others; in many
instances, the form from which
a word developed is traced
back in the dictionary to an
original in another or a predecessor language (Latin, Greek,
Middle English, French, etc.).
Those who hold the primary-
meaning delusion would likely
say that the most reputable
sense is that which most closely
approximates that of the root.
But in many instances that
meaning is obsolete. Usage and
acceptance are what establish
meaning, and any sense given
in a dictionary without a quali-
fier, such as *dialectal, substandard,* or *slang,* is regarded
as standard. Perrin points out
that no one can tell whether
*check,* by itself, is noun or

verb or adjective, much less
which of its forty senses is
intended. Fowler in the original
(under *Spiritism*) derided an
"extravagant theory that no
word should have two meanings—a theory that would require us . . . to manufacture
thousands of new words."
Fowler also points out (under
*True and False Etymology*) the
obvious fact, of which authorities on usage sometimes seem
to be oblivious, that the derivation of a word is not a reliable
guide to its current meaning.
The word *set* has been shown
to have 286 different meanings.
Ninety per cent of all words
have one meaning; the average
is three meanings each. This
means that the relatively small
number of common words have
large numbers of meanings. It
is also sometimes wrongly assumed that the order in which
definitions are entered in a
dictionary indicates preferen-
tial standing. There is no basis
for this idea. See also DIC-
TIONARIES.

**means.** In relation to money,
the term is always plural ("His
means were inadequate for his
tastes"); otherwise, in the
sense of an agency, it may be
either singular or plural ("The
means is, are, justified by the
end") (Bernstein, Evans, Fowler, American Heritage, Random House, Webster). Follett
says either singular or plural is
correct, and he does not except
money, though this may be an
oversight.

**Mecca.** Figurative use of the
term (literally, the holy city of
Islam) should be reserved,
Evans says, to describe a place
to which people are attracted

by some deep purpose, not merely a place to which people go for lesser reasons; Bernstein objects to its figurative use as a cliché, a view that seems better based. Both caution against using the term in reference to members of other religions, such as Judaism or Catholicism, which may result in a ludicrous inconsistency.

**Medal of Honor.** The correct form; not *Congressional Medal of Honor.*

**media, medium.** *Media* is the plural of *medium:* "The media used were newspapers, magazines, and television." Thus *medias* is incorrect, and so is *media* used as singular: "In the debate over toll TV the mathematics peculiar to a mass media have tended to run away with common sense" (Bernstein, Copperud, Follett, American Heritage). Evans, however, finds *medias* acceptable. Flesch and Webster recognize *media* as a singular but Random House does not; none recognizes *medias.* The consensus is that *media* is the standard plural, and that *medias* and *media* as a singular are incorrect. Copperud, Evans, and Fowler point out that *mediums* is a standard alternative plural form. Usually, however, *media* is preferred for agencies of communication.

**median.** See AVERAGE, MEDIAN, MEAN.

**mediate.** See ARBITRATE, MEDIATE.

**medic, medico.** Bernstein and Flesch deprecate the terms as not standard; Random House calls them slang, though Webster considers them standard

and American Heritage informal (for *doctor*). The consensus is that they are not standard.

**mediocre.** Most dictionary definitions are *of average quality, medium, commonplace, neither very good nor very bad.* Copperud says, however, that the word is commonly used to mean not *average* but *poor* or *inferior,* and warns that this is so common that the writer who uses the word in the dictionary sense may be misunderstood. Evans also recognizes this, and speculates that the pejorative use of *mediocre* may become standard. That time appears to have arrived; Random House gives *rather poor* or *inferior,* and American Heritage acknowledges, "Usually used disparagingly." That sense of *mediocre* perhaps is encouraged by the senses *poor worth* or *inferiority* that Webster gives for *mediocrity.*

**medium.** See MEDIA, MEDIUM.

**meet.** There is an unreasoning prejudice, especially on newspapers, against the term as a noun in the sense *meeting* (of which, no doubt, it is a clipped form). *Track meet* and *swimming meet* are of course established, even in the press. *Meet* in the general sense is unqualifiedly recognized by dictionaries, and no authority on usage has anything to say against it.

**meet, pass.** Though the terms are carelessly interchanged with respect, for example, to trains on parallel tracks or to automobiles on the same highway, a distinction is worth encouraging, especially to make accounts of accidents clearer. *Pass,* in these connections, at least, might be reserved to mean *overtake,* or better, be abandoned in favor of *overtake* (Copperud, American Heritage).

**memorandum, memorandums, memoranda.** The plural is either the Latin form *memoranda* or the Englished *memorandums,* Evans and Fowler say. Evans adds that *memorandas* is acceptable, but neither unabridged dictionary recognizes it. The consensus is that it is nonstandard.

**menial.** Though the term was once neutral, designating a class of servant, it is now derogatory and should not be used unless aspersion is intended (Bernstein, Copperud, Evans).

**mental attitude.** Although an attitude may be mental or physical, the context always makes clear which is intended, and so the phrase may be set down as redundant.

**mentality.** Evans, Flesch, and Fowler object to the term as overused in the sense *mental attitude* ("The mentality of the prisoners"); Fowler adds that it is also often disparaging, which adds to its appeal.

**mental telepathy.** Since telepathy is thought transference, *mental* is redundant.

**merchandise, merchandize.** The second is a correct but uncommon variant.

**message.** Recognized as a verb ("They messaged headquarters") by Webster but not by American Heritage or Random House.

**Metaphors.** The usual difficulty here is mixing metaphors, the figures of speech in which a comparison or identity is implied for rhetorical effect ("The sun cut a flaming swath through the sky"). The writer who loses sight of the images he is creating, or is carried away by his eagerness for drama, is likely to mix his metaphors, that is, to juxtapose them incongruously, as in an example cited by Flesch: "A clash of wills between the White House and the Southerners jelled after Rep. Smith postponed the hearings." A clash, of course, cannot jell. Extended discussions of this rhetorical fault, with a profusion of examples, are to be found under this heading in Bernstein, Evans, Flesch, Follett, and Fowler.

**methodology.** Evans and Follett object to the term as a pretentious displacement of *method:* "The methodology of early-day logging operations was extremely wasteful." Evans gives as the proper sense of *methodology* a branch of logic seeking to show how abstract principles of a science may be used to gain knowledge. There are other technical senses, none of which is synonymous with *method,* as indicated by the definitions in both Random House and Webster. The conclusion is that *methodology* should not be used when *method* will serve.

**meticulous.** Bernstein insists that the word may not be used to mean *careful* or *very careful,* but must be restricted to its etymological sense, which is that of care prompted by timidity or fear. This was the view of Fowler in the original, but the revised version recognizes the new and universally accepted sense of *careful, exact, punctilious, precise,* etc., adding that "it would be idle to try to put it back into an etymological straitjacket." Copperud says that *meticulous* may mean *overcareful* or *fussy,* but that it also has a positive sense: *commendably thorough or precise.* Webster designates the connotation of timidity obsolete, and Random House omits this sense in defining the term. Evans too recognizes the shift in sense from the original. Follett says the term has lost its overtone of fear and has come to seem just the right word for *exceedingly careful.* The consensus is overwhelming that the word now means *painstaking, fussy,* and may have a positive as well as a faintly disparaging sense.

**Mexican, Spanish.** *Spanish* is often a euphemism for *Puerto Rican* in the East and for *Mexican* or *Mexican-American* in the Southwest. Use of the precise terms is advisable to avoid ambiguity; evading them implies there is something wrong with being Mexican or Puerto Rican.

**midnight.** Bernstein points out that midnight of a given day is the end of that day, and warns against mistakenly referring to it in connection with the next day.

**might, may.** See MAY, MIGHT.

**mighty.** As an adverb (*a mighty fine day*) considered informal by Bryant, quaint by Evans, colloquial by Fowler, informal by Random House,

and standard by Webster. American Heritage rejects it in writing, accepts it in speech. The consensus is that it is informal.

**militate.** See MITIGATE, MILITATE.

**minimal.** The adjective comes from *minimum.* Fowler says it may mean only *least possible,* but Random House and Webster give also *very small, extremely minute.* Flesch considers it pretentious in these latter senses.

**minimize.** Bernstein, Evans, Flesch, and Fowler are corroborated by Random House and Webster in insisting that the word means only *reduce to the smallest possible amount* or *estimate in the least possible terms,* and cannot properly be used to mean *diminish, belittle, brush off, underrate,* etc.; American Heritage, however, gives *depreciate.* Nor, American Heritage agrees, since it denotes an absolute idea, can it rightly be qualified by *greatly, as far as possible, somewhat,* or any other adverb. It is often unintentionally used in a way that reverses the intended sense: "Its influence on modern American architecture cannot be minimized." The writer meant that the influence cannot be overstated or overestimated, not that it is so small nothing can diminish it, which is what he said.

**minister.** See REVEREND.

**minus.** Criticized as facetious by Bernstein and Copperud in the sense of *lacking* or *having lost* (*minus a tire; minus three teeth*). Both unabridged dictionaries recognize this sense as standard, however.

**minuscule.** Often misspelled *miniscule* (Bernstein, Copperud).

**mis-.** Solid as a prefix: *misadventure, misinform, mispronounce,* etc. (Copperud, Fowler).

**mishap.** See ACCIDENT, MISHAP.

**mislead, misled.** Confusion about the form of the past tense is often evident, as in "The voters were mislead on this issue." The problem is analogous to that of LEAD, LED, which see.

**Misquotation.** This is the subject of articles in Bernstein, Copperud, and Fowler. Bernstein and Fowler, incidentally, differ on whether well-established misquotations are open to criticism, e.g., "In the sweat of thy face" (not *brow*) and "noiseless (not *even*) tenor of their way." Bernstein insists on the exact form; Fowler is inclined to be lenient about variations. There are, of course, several dictionaries of quotations in which exactness can be checked. The best-known of these are Bartlett's *Familiar Quotations, The Oxford Dictionary of Quotations,* and Stevenson's *Home Book of Quotations* (by far the most comprehensive).

**Misrelated Modifiers.** See DANGLING MODIFIERS.

**miss.** A curious lapse from chivalry is shown sometimes in omitting the title when publishing the names of unmarried women who are in trouble with the law. Such references are in the form *the Smith woman* instead of *Miss Smith.* This seems to be an unnecessary aspersion, since the form used is usually considered derogatory. *Miss* is properly applied to women, married or not, when they are named in connection with their careers, and whether or not, as is often true of actresses, they have professional names that differ from their given ones.

**missile.** Often misspelled *missle.* And, curiously, *missive* (a message) and *missile* (a projectile) are sometimes confused.

**misspell.** Often, with ultimate perversity, misspelled *mispell.*

**mistake.** Evans derides *mistake* as an intransitive verb, in such constructions as "She mistook because her name was left off the list," but Random House and Webster both recognize this use as standard.

**mitigate, militate.** To mitigate is to soften ("His apology mitigated the insult"); to militate (with *against*) is to have an adverse effect on ("The rumor militated against her success"). *Mitigate* is sometimes used where *militate* is required (Bernstein, Copperud, Evans, Follett, Fowler).

**Mixed Metaphors.** See METAPHORS.

**modernistic.** The word is often misused for *modern* in reference to painting and design, Copperud, Evans, and Follett agree. *Modernistic* in this connection refers to Cubism or, in general, to a school of angular, jagged design that lived and died in the twenties and thirties. Random House, however, gives a derogatory sense, *falsely modern*. Other dictionaries do not recognize a distinction, and it may be that only people versed in art and design are sensitive to it.

**Modifiers. 1.** Participial Modifiers. One-word participial modifiers beginning a sentence are a peculiarity of journalese: "Shortlived, the committee was a thorn in the growers' flesh"; "Married, he is the father of a young son." Better, because less clipped and telegraphic: "Although the committee was shortlived, it was a thorn in the growers' flesh"; "He is married and the father of a young son."

Appositives are used similarly, but perhaps are less objectionable: "A salesman, he spent a lot of time away from home." But the pattern is overdone in newswriting.

The participial modifier should form a logical sequence with the rest of the sentence. This principle is often disregarded in biographical sketches: "Born in Illinois, he was admitted to a partnership in the firm at the age of 24." Better: "Mr. Smith, who was born in Illinois, was admitted . . ." (Bernstein, Copperud, Follett). Fowler objects to opening a sentence with a participle modifying the subject as a device that is overworked in newspapers. This is patently so in the United States as well as Britain.

**2.** Position of Modifiers. It is preferable that modifying phrases and clauses should stand next to what they modify: "He has been executive vice president since 1952, an office that will not be filled immediately." But the clause after

the comma does not modify *1952*. Better: "Since 1952, he has been vice president, an office that . . ."

**3.** Elision of Modifiers. "This self-effacing, dedicated woman in her mid-40s bears one of the most delicate yet little-known responsibilities of anyone around the president." Adverbs that modify adjectives in parallel constructions should not be carelessly elided; the reader does not readily apply *most* to *little-known*, as the writer intended, because *most little-known* is not idiomatic. *most delicate and yet least known . . .*

**4.** Piled-Up Adjectives. This is a mannerism primarily of the news columns; it reflects the urge to condense, and hasty work. Some examples: "He was arrested on conspiracy and concealing stolen property charges" *(on charges of conspiracy and receiving stolen property);* "A 15-cent per $100 assessed valuation road tax increase was proposed" *(A road tax increase of 15 cents per $100 assessed valuation . . .)* The cure here is to limit the number of adjectives before the noun for the sake of readability.

**5.** Limiting Adjectives. These are often used in a way that has ambiguous effect: "His labor turnover is nominal, and he is proud of the loyalty of his nonunion employees." This sounds as if the subject may have had two kinds of employees, union and nonunion, and as if only the nonunion ones were loyal. In fact, however, all the employees were nonunion, and this might have been expressed by "He is proud of the loyalty of his employees, who are nonunion." "The speaker cited Professor A. M. Low, Britain's inventive version of Thomas A. Edison." The effect is to suggest that Edison was not inventive. Unambiguous: "Professor A. M. Low, Britain's counterpart of Thomas A. Edison."

6. Misplaced Modifiers. Misplaced adverbial modifiers in the pattern of "Details are slipping out of plans for the first Soviet-bloc beauty contest" are criticized by Bernstein, Copperud, and Follett. Emended, the example should read "Details of plans for the first Soviet-bloc beauty contest are slipping out." Another example, whose correction requires a different approach: "The Israelis were accused of firing on the Egyptian post of Deir el Balat for ten minutes without causing casualties." This may sound like a reproach for poor marksmanship. *for ten minutes; there were no casualties.* See ADJECTIVES; ADVERBS; DANGLING MODIFIERS; WORD ORDER.

**modus vivendi.** Flesch agrees with Fowler that the phrase (from the Latin) means a temporary arrangement that enables people to carry on pending settlement of a dispute, but both Random House and Webster recognize *manner of living, way of life,* and it is hardly arguable that this sense is by far the more usual.

**Mohammed, Mohammedan.** Copperud quotes John Gunther to the effect that there are at least a dozen ways to spell *Mohammed,* the form American usage calls for. Random House gives *Mohammed* as the primary form, but Webster surprisingly gives *Muhammed.* Fowler grudgingly concedes that *Mohammed* has established itself, displacing *Mahomet.* The consensus is that *Mohammed(an)* is the prevalent form, and that *Mahomet(an)* and *Muhammed(an)* are comparatively unusual variants. Fowler calls *Muhammed(an)* pedantic.

Moslems are said to object to the term *Mohammed(an)* and its variants as implying that Mohammed is the object of worship, that is to say, a deity, but the term is so firmly established without any derogatory intention that this quibble is not likely to make any headway. *Moslem* means "those who submit to the will of God." Although Random House and Webster regard *Muslim* as the predominant form, this is plainly wrongheaded as far as America is concerned; as American Heritage points out, *Moslem* is the preferred form in journalism and popular usage. *Muslim* is gaining on *Moslem* in Britain, Fowler reports. It is curious that the American Black Muslims should have adopted the spelling they did. *Mussulman* is a variant of *Moslem.*

**moisturize.** Used to mean *impart moisture to;* apparently invented by the writers of cosmetics ads, since it is seldom seen elsewhere. Recognized only by Random House among current dictionaries.

**molten.** Evans and Fowler point out that usually *molten* (rather than *melted*) is used for what requires great heat to liquefy (metals, lava), and this distinction appears to be borne out by usage. Webster cites *molten Parmesan cheese,* but there may be some question whether this is not figurative language.

**momentarily, momently.** Follett and Fowler hold that *momentarily* means *for a moment (momentarily out of breath)* and *momently* means *from one moment to the next (momently expecting a telegram).* Copperud says the distinction is now dead, an opinion borne out by both Random House and Webster, which give both senses for both words. The consensus is that the terms are interchangeable.

**moment of truth.** Flesch refuses to recognize any application of the term except the original, that is, the point in a bullfight at which the matador is about to make the kill. It is hardly arguable, however, that the other sense given by Random House, the moment of an extreme test or a critical moment, is the one in widest use and thus is unexceptionable.

**Money.** See SUMS OF MONEY.

**monster.** Copperud points out that the term has often been criticized as an adjective (*a monster celebration*) but adds that what counts is the sense conveyed, and that this usage is acceptable. This view is concurred in by both Random House and Webster, which give *monster* as an adjective without qualification.

**moot.** As an adjective in ordinary contexts, the term means *debatable, open to question,* as in "It is a moot question whether the issue has been settled" (Copperud, Evans). Bernstein adds that the word is sometimes misused in the sense *hypothetical* or *academic.* This is a technical sense and out of place except in legal contexts (*a moot court*), as the examples in Webster show. Both senses are correct in their proper habitats (American Heritage, Random House, Webster).

**more, most vs. -er, -est.** For comparison of adjectives (e.g., *more beautiful* vs. *beautifuler,* etc.), see COMPARISON 4. For comparison of absolutes see COMPARISON 3.

**more important(ly).** The American Heritage panel divided evenly on the acceptability of these forms; no dictionary of usage deals with them.

**more preferable.** Redundant for *preferable,* which alone is a comparative (Copperud, Follett).

**more than one.** Takes a singular verb ("More than one of the legislators was embarrassed by the disclosure"), Bernstein, Bryant, Evans, Fowler, and Flesch agree.

**mortician.** Mencken described the term as "a lovely euphemism" invented by undertakers to dignify their macabre trade; Fowler calls it an American genteelism. Random House and Webster both give the term straightfacedly, however, and it is likely that it is now so common that it has lost the derisory or pretentious overtones it once had.

**Moslem.** See MOHAMMED, MOHAMMEDAN, etc.

**most.** *Most* for *almost* is called colloquial by Bryant and

Fowler, folksy by Bernstein, schoolgirlish by Copperud, and dialectal by Follett ("Most anyone can participate"). Flesch, however, calls it idiomatic usage, and Evans sees no objection to it. Random House considers it informal, and Webster gives *most* as a standard shortened form of *almost*. American Heritage rejects it. Webster's New World and the Standard College Dictionary consider the usage informal or colloquial. The consensus is that it is good informal usage. See also ALMOST for misuse of the hyphen with *most*.

**motivate, motivation.** Criticized by Flesch, Follett, and Fowler as pretentious when *cause* (as verb or noun) or *reason* will do: "His motivations for declining the part were obscure." *reasons*.

**motor.** See ENGINE, MOTOR.

**Mr., Mrs.** Flesch and Fowler agree that it is an impropriety for a woman to refer to her husband or for a man to refer to his wife by using the title. Most newspapers that ordinarily dispense with *Mr.* use it as a mark of respect in obituaries, and in subsequent references (after the first full identification with REVEREND, which see) to Protestant ministers. *Mrs.*, strictly speaking, should not ordinarily be used with a woman's given name (*Mrs. Ethel Adams*) but only with her husband's given name (*Mrs. Anthony Adams*). This rule may now be passé, however, and in any event is little observed. Copperud and Evans agree that *Mrs.* should not be used with other titles, such as *Dr. (Mrs. Dr. Smith)*, whether the title is the woman's own or her husband's, nor with the indication of an academic degree (*Mrs. John Smith, Ph. D.*).

**much.** For *much* as an adverb wrongly joined to an adjective with a hyphen, see ALMOST.

**muchly.** The form is described by Bernstein, Evans, Follett, and Fowler as superfluous; *much*. The judgment is more or less substantiated by the fact that American Heritage and Random House do not include the term and Webster describes it as now not often in formal use, indicating that, as Fowler says, it is usually facetious.

**mucous, mucus.** The first is the adjective, the second the noun: *a secretion of mucus; the mucous membranes* (Copperud, Fowler, Random House, Webster).

**munch.** A journalistic stereotype that regularly displaces *eat, chew,* etc. *Munch,* the dictionaries agree, means to eat with a crunching sound, and its overuse in news publications can be traced to the journalistic straining for graphic expression, regardless of appropriateness. The ultimate may have been reached by the newsmagazine that described someone as munching soup.

**music, musical.** See -IC, -ICAL.

**music critic, musical critic.** See -IC, -ICAL.

**Muslim.** See MOHAMMED, MOHAMMEDAN, etc.

**must.** Copperud and Flesch describe *must* as standard as both noun and adjective: "Aid to education is a must on the administration's legislative program"; "The lawmakers have their own idea of must legislation." Fowler regards the term as colloquial, and says that it sometimes should still be enclosed in apologetic quotation marks; Copperud and Flesch consider this unnecessary. Random House does not give this sense. Webster considers it standard; this is the consensus. American Heritage considers the noun standard, the adjective informal.

**must needs.** See NEED(s) MUST.

**mutual.** The term has provided the occasion for much hairsplitting. Precisians insist (or used to) that it must be restricted to the idea of reciprocity; that is, to the relation of two or more persons *to each other*. Thus they may have a mutual admiration, but not a mutual friend. *Mutual friend* is considered correct by Bernstein, Copperud, and Evans; no doubt the title of Dickens' novel had much to do with encouraging its acceptance. The reason given is that *common*, which ordinarily would be the precise word here, is capable of being misunderstood in the sense *commonplace, ordinary*. Bernstein, Evans, and American Heritage insist, however, that in describing such things as a shared interest, the expression should be *common*, not *mutual*. Copperud, Fowler, and Follett accept *mutual* where *common* would be regarded as strictly correct. Random House says *mutual* is open to criticism though commonly used to describe what does not involve an exchange but rather a rela-

tion to a third person or thing; Webster recognizes *a mutual hobby* and similar uses. The consensus thinly accepts *mutual* where *common* (*mutual interest*) would formerly have been insisted on.

*Mutual* is often used redundantly with words like *exchange, cooperation, each other, both, friendship* (Copperud, Evans, Fowler).

**my dear.** In salutations, see DEAR.

**my, mine.** Evans and Fowler contradict each other about the correct form in such constructions as "my and her cars"; Evans says it should be *mine*, Fowler that it should be *my*. Since this construction is now quaint and little used, the point is more or less academic. Logic and consistency favor Fowler's opinion, however.

**myself.** The disagreements over the use of this form revolve around whether it is acceptable when *I* or *me* will serve. (The same reasoning applies to other reflexives, *himself, herself, yourself, yourselves, itself, ourselves, themselves*.) There is no argument about the strictly reflexive use, when *myself* refers to *I* as subject: "I did it myself"; "I hurt myself"; "I myself take the responsibility." In general, Bernstein, Copperud, Fowler, and American Heritage object to *myself* in a compound subject in place of *I* ("Myself and my wife will be present"); Bryant and Evans and Webster approve (Evans calls this usage old-fashioned and describes it as criticized; Random House does not specifically deal with it). There is no consensus here but rather a 4–3 split. As part of a compound object of a verb or as the object of a preposition ("My income supports my wife and myself"; "The honor was accorded to the mayor and myself"), Bryant, Evans, Copperud, and Webster approve, but Fowler, American Heritage, and Random House disapprove. The consensus favors this usage. Random House disapproves of *myself* where *me* is normally called for, as when *myself* occurs as a single direct object: "He gave it to myself." Evans also criticizes this by implication. Evans and Webster specifically approve of *myself* in comparisons after *than* or *as:* "He is as tall as myself." The conclusion is that, in general, opinion is narrowly divided on what have formerly been regarded as wrong uses of *myself*. In instances like this it is safe to assume that the criticized uses are substandard or will soon be so.

# N

**naïf, naïve, naïveté, naivety.** Copperud, Evans, and Fowler favor *naive* over the French original *naïf*, with the difference that Fowler prefers *naïve*, though recognizing that the word is often written without the dieresis. Random House and Webster both indicate that the form with the dieresis predominates. As for the noun, all three of the commentators on usage agree that naïveté (retaining both dieresis and acute accent) predominates over the Anglicized *naivety*, a conclusion in which both dictionaries concur.

**naked.** See NUDE, NAKED.

**Names of People.** Most publications consider identification with one initial (*J. Smith*) unacceptable, and require two initials, given name, or initial and given name. Designations like *II, III* are restrictive modifiers and not to be set off from a name with commas.

Flesch objects to the use of commonplace names like *Smith* or *Jones* when it is desired to conceal identity; more interest is aroused, he says, by using "natural-sounding fictitious names" like *Agnes Gentry,* or first names with the initials of the last names, or first names alone, while explaining that they are fictitious (*a man whom we will call George Pferd*).

Names of people should be given in the form in which they are most familiar, or, if there is any doubt about this, in the form that they use themselves: Richard Harding Davis (not, for example, *Richard H. Davis*); John D. Rockefeller (not *John Davison Rockefeller*); Norman Vincent Peale (not *N. V. Peale*). Departing from the familiar and established form is inexcusable and only causes confusion (Copperud, Follett). See also ABBREVIATIONS; HE, SHE, 2; INITIALS.

**narcotic, -ics.** See -IC, -ICS.

**native.** Copperud points out that though it is often insisted that *native* in reference to a person can only describe one born in the place indicated, it may also be used in the sense *local* or *original inhabitant,* as distinguished from visitors or strangers, a sense that is recognized by both Random House and Webster. Flesch inexplicably says the term carries an overtone of contempt, a view borne out nowhere but perhaps traceable to confusion with the wholly different sense of *native* as applied to uncivilized aborigines.

**nature.** Criticized as roundabout and superfluous by Copperud, Evans, Flesch, Follett, and Fowler as used in constructions like *comment of an adverse nature* (*adverse comment*); *a mixture of a cloudy nature* (*a cloudy mixture*); *the neighborhood is of a restricted nature* (*is restricted*). See also CASE; CHARACTER.

**naught.** Regarded as quaint or bookish for *nothing* or *zero* by Copperud, Evans, Flesch, and Fowler.

**nauseated, nauseous.** Bernstein, Copperud, Follett, and American Heritage hold that the original difference in meaning should be maintained, i.e., that *nauseated* means *suffering from nausea,* and that *nauseous* means *causing nausea.* Thus sufferers from seasickness are *nauseated;* the illness itself is *nauseous.* Random House, however, allows *nauseous* in the sense of *nauseated* as informal, and Webster gives *affected with* or *inclined to nausea* for

*nauseous.* The consensus is narrowly in favor of keeping the distinction, but it may be that the cause is already lost.

**naval, navel.** Often confused; *naval* pertains to *navy; navel* is the name of the depression in the belly where the umbilical cord was attached. The orange is *navel,* owing to its having a similar depression (Copperud, Evans).

**near.** *Near* is an adjective as well as an adverb, as illustrated by the familiar though fuzzy expression *near future,* and others like *near relative, near thing,* and even the now happily faded *near beer.* Expressions like *near-riot, near-holocaust, near-disaster* were probably encouraged by the practice in World War II of referring to a *near-miss* in a bombing attack. There is no consistency among the authorities in hyphening these expressions, and it seems useless to discuss this point, though Fowler attempts a distinction which leads him to the opposite of what is general practice in America. For the form in a specific case, the reader is referred to a dictionary. Bernstein, Copperud, and the two unabridged dictionaries give such expressions as standard.

**near future.** See FUTURE.

**nearly.** See ALMOST; -LY.

**nee.** Bernstein, Copperud, and Follett insist on the sense corresponding to the derivation: *born,* and applicable only to a married woman to indicate her maiden name: *Susan Warfield, nee Smith.* American Heritage and Random House too give only this use. (There is a specifically masculine form, *ne,* but it is rarely employed.) Webster, however, gives four examples of *nee* followed by a given name instead of a surname alone, which is regarded as the strictly correct traditional use, including a curious instance, "nee Miss Carol Milford," quoted from Sinclair Lewis. It goes farther, giving *formerly* as an extended meaning and describing *nee* as applicable to "a group (the Milwaukee Braves, nee the Boston Braves), place (Kernville, nee Whiskey Flat—Roy Milholland), or thing (sonata for flute, oboe, and basso continuo nee sonata for violin and harpsichord— P. H. Lang)." Some may feel these extensions to be facetious, but Webster attaches no label to them, which means they are considered standard. And there can be no doubt that *nee* is often used in these ways. Nonetheless, the consensus overwhelmingly favors the narrow application given at the beginning of this entry.

**needless to say.** Flesch says the phrase should usually be omitted; Copperud says that like *goes without saying* and OF COURSE (which see), it is a conventional device for conceding that the reader may have drawn the conclusion or acquired the information that follows, and calls it an escape hatch from giving an impression of pomposity or didacticism. There is no consensus here, but there is an indication that the writer would do well to think twice before using the phrase.

**need(s) must, must needs.** Regarded as archaic constructions by Evans and Flesch ("He must needs find himself"). Fowler says they are now restricted to ironical or contemptuous expression.

**negative.** See AFFIRMATIVE, NEGATIVE.

**Negatives.** Reversal of sense often occurs as the result of inattention by the writer. Two examples once appeared in a single issue of *The New Yorker* in the quotations of lapses from newspapers that it uses to fill out columns: "And quite suddenly this young pianist of tired mien is immersed in the business of producing sounds of such high-voltage individuality as to quickly dispel any notions that the evening would be anything but routine." The writer apparently was carried away by his determination to produce an effect. Perhaps haste prevented a critical second reading before the words were committed to print. Obviously, he meant "dispel any notions that the evening would be routine." The other example: "Not even a blizzard prevented friends of the former ambassador and his wife from missing their cocktail party yesterday in honor of a former Washingtonian here from London on a holiday visit." *prevented . . . from attending* or *was enough to make friends . . . miss.* Involved construction probably helped to lead the writers astray in both instances. Similar mischances are dealt with by Follett under *Negatives, Trouble with* and by Fowler under *Negative Mishandling.* See also DOUBLE NEGATIVE.

**negotiate.** Narrowly rejected by American Heritage in the sense *get over* or *through* (*negotiated the heavy traffic*); considered standard by Random House and Webster.

**Negress.** Usually considered derogatory (Copperud, Evans, Random House, Webster).

**Negro.** Copperud, Evans, Random House, and Webster agree that the term is capitalized in ordinary use in reference to race.

**neighborhood.** *In the neighborhood of* for *about* is considered objectionable (as pretentious and redundant) by Copperud, Flesch, and Fowler. Evans notes that Horwill and Partridge also object to it; Evans considers it standard in the U.S. but "awkward, vague, and unnecessary."

**neither.** 1. Copperud and Webster agree that as a pronoun, *neither* may take a plural verb if a prepositional phrase intervenes, as in "Neither of them (come, comes) regularly." Fowler calls the plural here an error, though he acknowledges that it is often seen, and Random House gives only an example with a singular verb. Follett and American Heritage also consider the plural wrong. Opinion on this usage thus favors the singular.

Evans and Bryant hold that *neither* as a pronoun may refer to more than one: "Hope, faith, charity, neither were evident," and thus, as here, may take a plural verb. Follett, Fowler, and American Heritage say that *neither* may refer only to one of two alternatives. Webster cites *neither of three,* and thus opinion is divided.

2. Copperud, Random House,

and Webster say that *neither* may be followed by *or* and not necessarily by *nor;* Follett favors *nor;* Bernstein, Fowler, and American Heritage consider *or* wrong; and Evans curiously regards *neither . . . or* as archaic. The consensus narrowly favors *neither . . . nor* over *neither . . . or.* See also EITHER. For *neither* with *they, their, them,* see ANYBODY, ANYONE; EVERYBODY, EVERYONE.

**neither . . . nor.** See NEITHER; EITHER 3.

**neophyte.** Discouraged by Evans and Flesch where *beginner* (or, as an adjective, *new* or *novice*) will do.

**nerve-racking (wracking).** See RACK, WRACK.

**new innovation.** Redundant for *innovation* (Bernstein, Copperud).

**new record.** See RECORD.

**newsman.** Though sometimes criticized as illegitimate, the term is given as standard by Copperud, Random House, and Webster.

**nice.** The puristic injunction, now less heard than a generation ago, is that *nice* should be reserved for the senses *exacting, precise* (*a nice sense of balance*) or *decorous* (*a nice girl*) and should be avoided in the greatly predominant sense *agreeable* (*a nice day; a nice compliment*). The Concise Oxford Dictionary labels the sense *agreeable* colloquial, and Fowler, in a complaint reproduced from the original edition of 1926, counsels avoidance of it. The indications are, however, that these are British scruples, which have no meaning in America. Bernstein, Bryant, Flesch, and Follett omit any mention of *nice,* which may be taken as indicating they consider the issue settled; Copperud and Evans recognize that the term is used overwhelmingly in the sense *agreeable,* which they recognize as standard; the context indicates whether some other sense is intended. Both Random House and Webster also give the sense *agreeable* as standard; this is the unanimous consensus of American authorities.

**nicely.** For *satisfactorily* (*the suit fits nicely*), approved by American Heritage and considered standard by Webster; Random House does not give a specific definition.

**nickel.** The form *nickle,* which originated as a misspelling and became common, is recognized by Webster for the coin but not for the metal (for which the coin was named). American Heritage and Random House do not recognize it; Copperud considers *nickle* a misspelling, which is the consensus.

**Nicknames.** The prevalent practice today is to introduce a nickname in parentheses, rather than enclose it in quotation marks: *Meyer (Mike) Berger.* The use of nicknames in print to refer to people who are not widely and publicly known by them may be regarded as patronizing or unduly familiar; it is avoided by carefully edited publications.

**Nigra.** Though, as Webster says, the term is often taken to be offensive, there is evidence that it is not so intended,

but is merely an attempt to represent the Southern pronunciation of *Negro,* intended respectfully, or at least neutrally. Joe Holt Anderson of the Washington *Post* has pointed out that people are sometimes quoted, by reporters with ears unpracticed in Southern inflections, as having said *nigger* when what they really said was *Nigra.* A persuasive case for this viewpoint is made by Sarah Patton Boyle in *The Desegregated Heart.*

**Nip.** See JAP, JAPANESE.

**nobody, no one.** For the agreement of verbs with these and other pronouns, see ANYBODY, ANYONE; EVERYBODY, EVERY ONE.

**nohow.** Copperud, Evans, and Webster say the word has a standard sense, *not, in no way: could nohow start the car.* Evans warns against its use in a double negative as ungrammatical (*couldn't nohow*) and Random House calls the term dialectal but gives only a sentence with a double negative as an example of use. The consensus is that *nohow* has a standard use. But it so often occurs in a double negative that it is likely to be regarded as substandard by most readers in any context.

**noisome.** Sometimes confused with *noisy; noisome* means *disgusting, foul-smelling,* etc. (Bernstein, Copperud, Evans, Follett, Random House, Webster).

**non-.** Fowler objects to the random creation of negative forms by affixing *non-* to positives, as in *nonessential,* when *inessential* is already available;

and Flesch objects to *non-* forms on principle as "ugly," a judgment that seems quixotic.

**noncontroversial issue.** A pertinent observation for this age of controversy was made by Robert M. Hutchins in *Look:* "An issue is a point on which the parties take different positions. A noncontroversial issue, therefore, is as impossible as a round square. All issues are controversial; if they were not, they would not be issues." By the same token, the frequent *controversial issue* is redundant. See also CONTROVERSIAL.

**noncooperative.** See COOPERATE, etc.

**none.** It is a superstition to suppose that *none* must take a singular verb (e.g., that *none is* is correct and *none are* is incorrect); *none* may take either a singular or a plural depending on the writer's intention and the context, but the plural is by far the commoner. On this Bernstein, Bryant, Copperud, Evans, Follett, and the dictionaries, including the American Heritage Usage Panel, agree. There is no easy rule to govern the choice; the best advice the writer can be given is to use what makes for the smoothest sentence.

**Nonrestrictive Modifiers.** See RESTRICTIVE AND NONRESTRICTIVE CLAUSES.

**Nonstandard.** See STANDARD.

**noon luncheon.** Redundant to the extent that luncheons are usually held at midday.

**no one.** With *they, their, them,* see ANYBODY, ANYONE.

**noplace.** Considered standard for *nowhere* by Evans and Webster, and colloquial by Bryant; Random House labels it informal (*We argued but got noplace*). Follett gives only *no place,* and calls it a barbarism. The consensus is that it is standard.

**nor.** See NEITHER 2; OR, NOR.

**normalcy.** Authorities agree that President Warren G. Harding has been unjustly derided as having invented this expression. Copperud, Evans, and Flesch agree that *normalcy* is (and was, long before Harding) a standard equivalent of *normality,* i.e., *the state of being normal.* Though Fowler looks down his nose at the word and the Concise Oxford Dictionary calls it irregularly formed, both Random House and Webster consider it standard, making for a solid consensus. The American Heritage panel rejects it, however, by 59 per cent, although the editors describe it as widely employed in standard usage.

**no sooner.** Followed by *than,* not *when:* "No sooner had the whistle blown *than* the workmen thronged out of the factory" (Bernstein, Copperud, Follett).

**nostalgia, nostalgic.** While *nostalgia* originally meant *severe homesickness,* Bernstein and Fowler are willing to accept the popular and extended senses of longing or yearning for the past or a return to some place. Evans is suspicious of these newer meanings. They are extremely popular, however—much more so than the original sense—and

Random House and Webster accept them without question. The consensus thus solidly favors them.

**no such.** See SUCH.

**not about to.** An odd colloquialism with the sense *not going to.* It should be avoided in writing, for it also has the literal sense *not on the verge of:* "The secretary said he isn't about to make another trip to press for an agreement." Ambiguous; the desired meaning was *does not intend to,* but the statement might have been understood as saying the secretary would not make a trip soon. The American Heritage panel is reported in an introductory essay as rejecting the expression, but the judgment was not included in the lexicon.

**not all, all . . . not.** Sentences on the pattern "All is not gold that glitters" are often criticized on the basis that they do not say what is intended, but rather its opposite. Analyzed grammatically, the example seems to say that anything that glitters is not gold, which would include gold itself, whereas the intention is to say that not everything that glitters is gold. Another example: "Every story with an unusual feature does not call for a humorous headline." The fact is, however, that like double negatives, such constructions are never misunderstood, and are very common. Bernstein, Bryant, Copperud, Evans, and Fowler agree that they are acceptable and perfectly clear despite their apparent illogicality. The authorities leave the door open, how-

ever, for more precision in word order for those who prefer it: "Not all that glitters . . ." and "Not every story . . ." Follett prescribes precise placement in these instances.

**not all that.** See ALL THAT.

**not . . . but.** This construction, meaning *only* and followed by a number, as in "I did not notice but three umbrellas," is described by Bryant as standard but occurring mainly in speech, and by Webster as often considered substandard.

**not.** Bernstein, Copperud, and Fowler point out that *not* is sometimes inadvertently introduced into sentences whose meaning is then reversed: "Current discussions cannot be oversimplified merely by referring to the administration as antibusiness." The intended meaning was *can be oversimplified.* For similar errors, see UNDERESTIMATE; MINIMIZE; DOUBLE NEGATIVE; NEGATIVES.

**not only . . . but also,** See ONLY.

**not so . . . as.** See AS . . . AS, etc.

**not so (as) much . . . as.** The correct form; incorrectly, *not so (as) much . . . but:* "Not so much sinning as sinned against" (Bernstein, Copperud).

**not that.** See ALL THAT.

**not too.** In the popular and literal sense *not very* ("She testified that her husband was restless and did not like to stay put too long"), disapproved by Bernstein, Copperud, Follett, and American Heritage because it is imprecise and open to misconstruction as

meaning *not more than enough.*
For example, the statement
"Elsewhere, there was not too
much resistance to the price-
support program" may be understood as meaning that the
resistance was inconsiderable
(as intended) or that it was not
excessive. Fowler calls this construction illogical but is nevertheless indulgent of it, an attitude perhaps explained by the
reasonable suspicion that *not
too,* like *not that,* originated in
Britain. Fowler is its only de-
fender.

**notorious.** Means *well known
for unfavorable reasons* ( *a notorious prostitute; a notorious
deadbeat* ). Not to be confused,
as it sometimes is, with *famous, noted,* or *notable* (Copperud, Evans). Similarly, *notoriety* should not displace
*notability, celebrity,* or *notice.*
A publication for college professors once described one of
their number as a modest fellow who did not seek notoriety.
The adverse implication of
*notorious,* it should be remembered, applies only to people;
Webster gives *well* or *commonly known* as one sense,
but the examples are impersonal: *Iron is a notorious conductor of heat; a notorious fact.*
Other dictionaries concur in
this distinction.

**not un-.** The deliberate creation of a positive, albeit a
weak one, by an intentional
double negative on this pattern
("We were not unaccustomed
to doing this"; "The pleasure
was not unexpected") is
grudgingly accepted by Evans
and Fowler only in what they
consider appropriate contexts,
i.e., those in which understate-

ment is called for. Both regard
it as overworked and recommend avoiding it in general;
Flesch calls the construction
pompous. To this might be
added that it creates a mo-
mentary puzzle for the reader,
who is then put to the task
of deducing the intended meaning. A similar effect is created
by a sentence like "I would
not be annoyed if they did not
agree with me," which must
be untangled to "I would not
be annoyed if they disagreed
with me." American Heritage
considers the construction generally accepted. See also DOU-
BLE NEGATIVE; NEGATIVES.

**Nouns of Address.** See
COMMA 7.

**Novelty Hunting.** See FAD
WORDS.

**now.** The word has become
popular as an adjective in
hippie and teenage argot ( *the
now generation, a now fashion* ).
Neither Random House nor
American Heritage, the newest
of the dictionaries, recognizes
this usage but Webster does;
its examples, however, seem to
come from an earlier time:
*the now judge; the now king.*
It appears from this that the
current vogue for *now* is a
revival and modification of an
older usage.

**nowheres.** Considered standard by Random House, peculiar
to speech by Evans, and dialectal by Copperud and Webster. The consensus is that it
is not standard in writing.

**nth.** Fowler is very positive
in asserting that the term, as
used in such expressions as *to
the nth degree,* indicates only
an unknown quantity of any

size, and he denounces its use in the sense *to the utmost* or *infinitely.* Copperud and Evans, however, hold that these senses have been established by popular usage, and Random House and Webster both recognize them without qualification. The consensus overwhelmingly favors the extended sense.

**nubile.** Originally the term meant only *suitable for marriage,* but the sense that now predominates is that given by Webster as "physically suited for or desirous of sexual relationship." Random House does not recognize that sense, but American Heritage reports a suggestion of sexuality.

**nude, naked.** As applied to people, *nude* is at the same time something of a euphemism and, paradoxically, more suggestive than *naked.* The connotation of suggestiveness may arise from the reader's sensing that *nude* has been chosen to sidestep the honest starkness of *naked.* In a poem entitled "The Naked and the Nude," which appeared Feb. 27, 1957, in *The New Yorker,* Robert Graves wrote: "For me, the naked and the nude . . . stand as wide apart / As love from lies, or truth from art."

**number.** Evans regards the term as applied to a song (*She performed a couple of numbers*) as substandard, but it is recognized as standard by both Random House and Webster.

With rare exceptions, when preceded by *a, number* is plural: *a number were waiting.* Preceded by *the,* it is singular: *the number of voters was diminishing* (Bernstein, Copperud, Evans, Fowler, American Heritage).

For *number* in the grammatical sense, see SUBJECT-VERB AGREEMENT; PLURAL AND SINGULAR.

**Number in Addition.** Bryant and Evans find that singular and plural verbs are equally frequent in such constructions as "Two and two is four" and "Two and two are four."

**Numbers. 1.** Figures vs. Words. Whether numbers should be spelled out or given in figures is a matter primarily of style, that is to say, of arbitrary choice between two practices that are equally correct. Newspapers generally follow the rule of ten, under which the numbers one through nine are spelled out and those larger are given in figures. Exceptions are usually specified, however, such as time of day, ages, vote totals, and most units of measurement, among others. Evans, following a style used in editing books, recommends that figures be used for any number that cannot be expressed in two words (*sixty-eight;* but *101*); Flesch considers it pompous to spell out numbers at all.

**2.** Figure at Beginning of a Sentence. Copperud, Evans, and Flesch agree that it is not the usual practice to begin a sentence with a figure ("2,000 troops were surrounded"). Either the number should be spelled out or the sentence should be recast.

**3.** Consistency. Even though strict observance of the rules may require it, Evans and Flesch agree that both a figure and a spelled-out number should not appear in the same sentence: "Six of the statues were damaged, but the other 12 were intact." *other twelve.* This principle is generally followed in editing for newspapers. Newspaper practice also usually calls for handling large figures in such forms as *22 million, $9 billion* to enhance readability.

4. Separation. Figures standing next to each other should be separated: "The students totaled 2,456, 900 of which were freshmen." *2,456, of which 900* (to improve readability and prevent confusion).

5. Hyphenation. Hyphens are uniformly used for compound numbers (*sixty-eight*) and for fractions (*nine-tenths*).

See also COLLECTIVE NOUNS; PREPOSITIONS 1; A, AN (with *hundred, thousand,* etc.); ROMAN NUMERALS; FIGURE.

**numerous.** Copperud and Fowler say the word is an adjective and may not be used as a pronoun: "Numerous errors defaced the typescript" but not "Numerous of the errors were misspellings." This judgment is borne out by Random House and Webster, neither of which gives *numerous* as a pronoun. In constructions like the second example the word should be *many.*

# O

**O, oh.** Bernstein, Copperud, Evans, Fowler, and American Heritage make the distinction that *O* is used in invocations (*O Lord, we beg Thy forgiveness*) and *oh* otherwise, as in ordinary exclamations (*Oh, you forgot the dessert!*). Neither Random House nor Webster recognizes this distinction, however. Fowler cites a volume in which *O* is used uniformly, and Copperud finds that the distinction is not uniformly observed. Indications are that the forms are becoming interchangeable.

**objective.** The displacement of *object* by *objective* is protested as pretentious by Copperud and Fowler; Flesch prefers *aim.* In general, the *object* is the *purpose,* the *objective*

(as in military connections) is the *goal.* "The objective was to tell the people about the record of Congress." *object.* The simplest advice is to use *object* when it will fit.

**objet d'art.** Often erroneously given *object d'art.*

**obligate, oblige.** *Obligate* should not be used to acknowledge a favor; the term should be *oblige* ("I am obliged to him for his help"). *Obligated* is a narrower term, often found in legal contexts, and indicating the imposition of a duty: "The decision obligated him to remove the fence." On these points Bernstein, Evans, Fowler, and American Heritage agree. Random House and Webster, however, regard the terms as synonyms; the consensus narrowly favors the distinction.

**obliqueness, obliquity.** Evans and Fowler hold that the first usually applies to the physical ("the obliqueness of the angle") and the second to the abstract ("We were surprised by the obliquity of his viewpoint"), or divergence from moral conduct, etc. In general, Random House and Webster corroborate this view, though it seems to be contradicted by the term *obliquity of the ecliptic,* in which the sense is clearly physical.

**oblivious.** Fowler and Follett insist that the term should be restricted to its original sense, *forgetful;* Bernstein, Evans, and American Heritage are willing to accept the extended (and popular) senses of *unaware, heedless, unconscious,* or whatever. Bernstein and Fowler agree, however, that it is best to use the word precisely suited to the occasion: *forgetful, unaware, unconscious,* etc. Both Random House and Webster recognize the extended senses, which means the consensus heavily favors them. In the sense *forgetful, oblivious* takes *of;* in other senses, it may take either *of* or *to.*

**observance, observation.** The first is the word for following, conforming to, or marking a religious rite, holiday, etc.: "The bank was closed for observance (not observation) of Veterans Day." *Observation* is *looking, watching, noticing:* "The candidates were under observation" (Bernstein, Copperud, Fowler). Random House follows this principle; Webster allows *observation* for *observance.* The consensus favors the distinction.

**obtain.** Considered pretentious by Copperud, Evans, Flesch, and Fowler when *get* will do. See also GET.

**obtrusive, -ly.** Sometimes misspelled *obstrusive, -ly.*

**obviate.** Bernstein and Follett point out that the word means *make unnecessary* ("His resignation obviated his dismissal"), but it is often misused in the sense *remove* ("The difficulties were obviated"). The definitions in Random House and Webster support this distinction.

**Occupational Titles.** See FALSE TITLES.

**occur, take place.** Bernstein, Copperud, and American Heritage agree, though other dictionaries do not make the distinction, that what occurs is accidental and unforeseen ("The accident occurred in the rain") and that what takes place is planned or arranged ("The coronation will take place May 12"). *Occurrence* is sometimes misspelled *occurrance.*

**octopus, octopi.** Fowler, whose decisions are often based on derivation from the Latin or Greek, flatly considers *octopi* a wrong form for the plural; Copperud and Evans, however, say it is nevertheless established and standard, and it is recognized as such by both Random House and Webster. *Octopuses* is also correct.

**oculist, etc.** Although the word is technically equivalent, as Evans says, to *ophthalmologist* as designating an M.D.

whose specialty is the eye, a shadow, apparently acquired through misuse at one time, hangs over it, and it is avoided by the medical profession. Copperud, Evans, and American Heritage call attention to the distinctions between these terms and *optometrist,* for one who is licensed to prescribe glasses but is not an M.D.; and *optician,* the term for the technician who makes glasses.

**-odd.** Hyphenated as a suffix: *thirty-odd,* etc. Redundant with *some:* "Some thirty-odd soldiers." Use one or the other. See also SOME, ODD.

**oe, e.** See AE, E; OE, E.

**of.** See PREPOSITIONS; COMMA; ALL OF; OFF OF; POSSESSIVES 3.

**of any, of anyone.** See THAN ANY, THAN ANYONE; COMPARISON 1.

**of between, of from, etc.** Prepositions are often doubled with numbers indicating a range: "An appropriation of from six to eight million dollars." *of six to eight.* "A rise in temperature of between three and five degrees." *of three to five* (Bernstein, Copperud).

**of course.** It is sometimes advisable to concede that the reader may already know what he is being told, lest the writer sound didactic; at the same time, the writer may not be able to risk omitting what he qualifies by *of course,* if it is essential to comprehension by those who do not know. Overly cautious writers tend to slip in *of course* by reflex action, as a kind of running apology. Sometimes it is attached to curious facts that only the rare reader could be expected to have at his fingertips; this is obsequious. Every *of course* should be weighed critically with a view to striking it out. This applies also to *as is well known, needless to say, as everyone knows,* and *it goes without saying;* the critic may object that if it goes without saying, why not let it go unsaid? (Bernstein, Copperud, Evans, Flesch, Fowler).

**off.** See OFF OF.

**offhand, offhanded, offhandedly.** The first, as both adjective and adverb, will do neatly for the other two, which are cumbersome forms, though correct.

**officer.** Bernstein objects to the application of this term to ordinary policemen (as distinguished from those holding a rank above patrolman); Evans and Copperud point out that any policeman is an officer of the law. Evans adds, however, that there is a tendency to reserve the term for those holding higher rank. American Heritage, Random House, and Webster do not recognize the distinction. Thus opinion is divided. There seems little doubt, however, that application of the term to a policeman, especially in addressing him, is intended as a courtesy. See also COP.

**official, -ly.** Overused in contexts where there is no occasion to think the action described could be unofficial, as for example the conduct of business by public bodies.

**Officialese.** See GOBBLEDYGOOK.

off of. *Of* is superflous with *off:* "He jumped off of the bridge." *off the bridge* (Bernstein, Copperud, Evans, Flesch, American Heritage). Bryant considers the usage informal.

of from. See OF BETWEEN, etc.

offspring. Evans considers the word a plural, adding that its use as a singular is now considered standard. The word has been recognized as both singular and plural as long ago as the turn of the century, however, as evidenced by the Century Dictionary. What *is* often considered a misuse is forming the plural by adding *s: offsprings.* This form is seldom seen. Evans does not recognize this problem, but *offsprings* is accepted as standard by both Random House and Webster.

of the order of. See ORDER.

of which. See WHOSE VS. OF WHICH.

oh. See O, OH.

O.K. Copperud, Evans, Follett, and Fowler all have sizable entries on this expression, much of the space being taken up with various speculations on its origin, to which no attention will be given here. There are various forms: *O.K., okay, oke, okeh, okey,* among others. Although only one commentator expresses an opinion, it is easy to deduce from both books on usage and dictionaries that the form *O.K.* greatly predominates, though there is no basis for considering the others wrong. The consensus is that the expression is informal or colloquial, though Webster regards it as standard. The Amer-

ican Heritage panel accepts *O.K.* only as a noun ("His O.K. was necessary") and rejects it as a verb, adjective, or adverb.

old adage. Redundant for *adage* (Bernstein, Copperud).

older. See COMPARISON 2.

older, elder. See ELDER, etc.

old-fashioned. The form of the modifier (*an old-fashioned girl*); not, as sometimes given, *old-fashion* (Copperud, Random House, Webster). Webster gives *old-fashion* as archaic; the current use of it appears to be merely careless.

oldster. The term, which looks as if it might have been invented by *Time* magazine, is considered objectionable or derogatory by Evans and Flesch, but there is no hint of this in either Random House or Webster, which give it as standard; American Heritage considers it informal. Nor is it new; it appears (labeled *colloquial*) in the Century Dictionary, published in 1897.

-ology, -ologies. Flesch and Follett discourage the loose use (and coinage) of terms with these endings; Follett explains that they are often erroneous, since the endings indicate a theory or system or science, and not the thing itself. Thus, for example, *methodology* is used when *method* is meant.

Olympian, Olympic. Evans and Fowler hold that the first relates to Olympus, including the sense *majestic* (or sometimes *pompous*), and the second relates to the games. The definitions in Random House accord with this, but Webster gives both *Olympic Games* and

*Olympian Games*. It is evident, however, that the form *Olympic Games* is all but invariable. Opinion is unanimous that only *olympian* is used in the senses *majestic, lofty,* etc.

**Omission.** See ELLIPSIS.

**on.** Bernstein and Copperud protest against the displacement of other and more precise prepositions by *on*, as in the following examples: "He can be reassured on one thing" (*about* or *of*); "The mayor was dismayed on the denial of the permit" (*at* or *by*); "We were waiting on him" (*for*); "Developments on Middle East problems dominated the session" (*in*); "Apathy marks the public's attitude on government" (*toward*); "The aim is to educate the populace on the proper use of English" (*in*). Bernstein traces such misuses to the all-purpose use of *on* in newspaper headlines, but it seems likely that other stimuli are also at work here, considering their prevalence.

**on, in.** See IN, ON.

**on, upon.** The consensus of Bryant, Copperud, Flesch, Follett, and Fowler on the choice between these words, which have no clearly defined difference in meaning, is to use *on* whenever possible. American Heritage says they are often interchangeable. Idiom, however, occasionally calls for *upon: put upon* (in the sense *imposed on*).

**on account of.** For *because,* a regional spoken colloquialism, not found in writing except that representing speech (Bryant).

**on behalf.** See BEHALF.

**once.** See ALMOST.

**one.** A coy displacement of *I,* as used by a music critic in "This program brought confirmation of the conviction that Mozart is one's favorite composer"; considered objectionable by Copperud, Flesch, Follett, and Fowler. Another example: "This performer is, one suspects, headed for international recognition." The suspicion was the writer's and *one suspects* should have been *I suspect.* This use of *one,* however, should be distinguished from the truly impersonal *one,* in which the word is used not in false modesty to sidestep *I,* but to represent *a person:* "One does one's duty." Fowler logically enough points out that the impersonal *one* takes *one's* and the *one* used in place of *I* takes *his:* "One saw his hat on the table." This usage is uncommon in America. *One* as a noun takes *a,* not *an:* "Such *a* (not *an*) one is readily available." *An* here is archaic. See also EDITORIAL WE; YOU.

**-one.** A distinction should be made between the pronouns *anyone, everyone, someone* and the adjective-pronoun phrases *any one, every one, some one:* "Anyone can do that": "Take any one of the pieces"; "Everyone knew the story"; "They walked off with every one of the awards"; "Someone is on the phone"; "Some one of the books will have the answer." Usually the indefinite pronouns refer to people, the phrases to things, but not invariably.

**one another.** See EACH OTHER.

**one of the (only, etc.) . . . if not.** The sentence "California is one of the few, if not the only, states subsidizing its college students" illustrates a common snare; *states* does not go with *the only*. Rearrangement to the pattern "California is one of the few states subsidizing its college students, if not the only one" (moving *if not* to the end) is recommended by Bernstein, Copperud, and Fowler.

**one of (those who, etc.) is, are.** Doubt about the correct number of the verb often arises with such sentences as *I am one of those who hope (hopes?) for a peaceful settlement.* Bernstein, Follett, Fowler, and 58 per cent of the American Heritage panel holds that the verb should be plural (*hope*) to agree with *those*. Bryant, Copperud, Evans, and Flesch say that although the plural is strictly correct, the singular is often used and is unexceptionable. Opinion is thus divided.

**on line.** *On line* for *in line* is a regionalism peculiar to New York City and the Hudson River Valley: "They stood on line for hours" (Bryant, Copperud). American Heritage give it as standard; neither Random House nor Webster includes it.

**only.** The problem here is placement, and it may be illustrated by the sentence "He only arrived a week ago." This arrangement is often criticized on the ground that *only* belongs before *a week ago* to convey the meaning intended, and that as it stands the sentence will be interpreted as "None but he arrived . . . " or "He did nothing but arrive . . . " Fowler, and Follett, who follows his lead, are vehement in

insisting that the supposed misplacement of *only* represents the usual form of expression, and that it is fussy to insist that it be placed before the element it modifies. Bernstein and Copperud cite a sentence from the publication *Word Study,* "I hit him in the eye yesterday," illustrating that different meanings result from placing *only* in the eight positions possible. Both would allow *only* in some position other than before the element it modifies when misunderstanding is unlikely, but in general encourage precise placement. Bryant reports that a study of magazines shows *only* to be precisely placed 86 per cent of the time, and regards the inexact placement as characteristic of speech rather than writing. Evans devotes much space to justifying the loose placement of *only* except when there is good reason to place it elsewhere, which seems somewhat ambiguous. American Heritage favors precise placement. About the best that can be said on this subject is that opinion is divided. There is general agreement, however, that precise placement of *only* should be made if there is good reason for it (that is, avoidance of ambiguity), and there is no reason why anyone who chooses to be precise in this respect should not do so, especially in writing.

Ambiguity seems more likely with loose placement of *not only . . . but also:* "The strike has not only created problems for the company in maintaining the goodwill of its customers but also of the general public." *Customers* should be balanced against *general public,* and the only way to do it is by writing "not only of its customers but also of the general public" (Copperud, Follett). See NOT ALL . . . ALL NOT, which presents a similar problem.

*Only* for *except that* ("He would have bought the suit, only it cost too much") is rejected by American Heritage but considered standard by Random House and Webster.

**only too.** Discouraged by Evans and Fowler as imprecise and overworked in such expressions as "only too glad," "only too willing," etc. See also NOT TOO.

**onset.** Evans holds that only in medical connections may the word be used to describe the beginning, but this runs contrary to both observable usage and the dictionaries. Random House and Webster both give as examples *the onset of winter*.

**on the basis of.** Criticized by Flesch and Follett as a cumbersome and overused expression that can often be replaced by *on, by, after, because of.* "The change was made on the basis of expediency." *for. Based on* is often similarly open to criticism. Fowler points out that such expressions as *on a permanent basis* are overblown for *permanently.*

**on the grounds that.** See GROUND, GROUNDS.

**on the order of.** See ORDER.

**on the part of.** Usually excessive for *by, among*: "There is less studying on the part of high school students these days." *by* (Bernstein, Copperud, Flesch).

**on to, onto.** Bryant, Evans, Fowler, and American Heritage call attention to the distinction between *onto* in the sense *to a position on* ("He climbed onto the table") and *on to* in such constructions as "We traveled on to San Francisco," in which *on* becomes part of a phrasal verb (*traveled on*).

**onward, onwards.** Only *onward* can serve as an adjective: *the onward thrust* (never *onwards* in this construction). *Onward* may also be an adverb (*we pressed onward*), but where there is a choice between the forms *onward* is preferred by both Evans and Fowler. Random House mistakenly gives *onwards* as an adjective, but Webster observes the distinction, which is also favored by the consensus.

**operation.** Copperud and Follett criticize the fad of giving projects names like "Operation Breakthrough," which had its origin in World War II. At that time, military operations were so designated but with code names carefully chosen to give no inkling of what they referred to. "Operation Overlord," for example, was the designation for the Allied invasion of France. Since the war, military and other undertakings have been widely designated "Operation This" and "Operation That," usually with names intended to indicate their nature. The practice has grown tiresome, especially when writers resort to it casually: "The Legislature began Operation Adjournment this week."

**ophthalmologist, optician, optometrist.** See OCULIST, ETC.

**opine.** Considered quaint or facetious by Copperud, Flesch, and Fowler. This is the consensus; although the two unabridged dictionaries regard it as standard, three of four current desk dictionaries designate it humorous.

**optician.** See OCULIST, ETC.

**optimism, -ist(ic).** Bernstein, Copperud, Evans, and Fowler agree that the terms denote a hopeful outlook, and that *optimism* or *optimistic* should not displace *hope* or *hopeful* in reference to specific instances, as in "She was optimistic about being admitted to college"; nor should *optimistic* displace *favorable* as in "He cited several optimistic factors." Random House and Webster in general appear to support these views, though the first gives *an optimistic plan* and the second gives *an optimistic view.* The consensus favors the distinction. See also PESSIMISM, etc.

**optimum.** Evans, Flesch, and Fowler protest against the loose use of the term as a synonym for *best;* it properly means *most favorable,* or *best under the circumstances.* Definitions in both unabridged dictionaries support this distinction. Thus "The optimum readability of a line of type is contingent upon the size of the type and the length of the line."

**optometrist.** See OCULIST, ETC.

**or, nor.** Either *or* or *nor* may be used after a negative in such sentences as "They will not fish (or, nor) cut bait," Bernstein, Evans, Fowler, and American Heritage agree. But they point out that *nor* must be used if the negative in the introductory statement does not

affect what follows the conjunction: "They refused to fish, nor would they cut bait." The difference here is that the negative (*refused*) does not affect the part of the sentence following *nor.* See also NEITHER 2; EITHER; BETWEEN; SUBJECT-VERB AGREEMENT.

*Or* (like *and, but, nor*) may be used to begin a sentence. When this is done, the conjunction ordinarily should not be followed by a comma: "Or the tables may be turned" (Bryant, Copperud). See also AND.

**-or, -our.** When there is a choice between these endings, *-or* is American practice and *-our* British: *honor, honour.* Fowler points out that even in British usage there is no consistency since it calls for *horror, pallor, tremor,* not *horrour, pallour, tremour,* and concludes in general that there is no real basis for the British *-our.*

**oral, verbal.** Bernstein, Copperud, Evans, Follett, Fowler, and American Heritage encourage observance of the distinction that *oral* means *by mouth* and *verbal* means *in words,* either spoken or written. *Verbal* is often used ambiguously: "He verbally assaulted the committee." This does not indicate whether the assault was spoken or in writing. *Verbal,* however, as Copperud, Evans, and Fowler agree, is often used to mean *oral,* particularly in *verbal contract, verbal agreement,* where the intention is *spoken* as against *written.* Both Random House and Webster give *oral, spoken* as synonyms for *verbal,* however, and Flesch concurs. The consensus favors the use of *verbal* to mean *in words* and not specifically *oral* or *spoken.*

**orate.** The word (a back-formation from *oration*) usually has a derisory or humorous connotation, Evans, Fowler, and dictionary definitions agree.

**orchestra, band.** The basic distinction, as applied to groups playing classical or light classical music, is that an orchestra contains stringed instruments and a band does not, being made up entirely of woodwinds and brasses. Thus the term *wind orchestra,* as applied by one university to its concert band, is a misnomer. As applied to jazz ensembles, however, the term *band* does not necessarily imply the absence of strings. These distinctions are supported by the definitions in Random House and Webster.

**order.** *On* (sometimes *in*) *the order* and *of the order,* followed by quantities, are inflations of the technical writer. They sound to the uninitiated as if they have some deep and precise connotation, but they are merely ostentatious displacements of *about* or *approximately.* Apparently *on the order* and *of the order* are offshoots of the concept *order of magnitude,* which does have a precise technical meaning: "A range of magnitude extending from some value to ten times that value (two quantities are of the same order of magnitude if one is no larger than ten times the other, but if one is one hundred times the other it is larger by two orders of magnitude)."—Webster. Some examples of the pretentious use of *order:* "The number of troops is

estimated to have increased sharply, to something on the order of 10,000." *something like* (*approximately, about*) *10,000.* "The budgetary deficit is still on the order of $150 million." *about* (Copperud, Flesch, Fowler). See also IN ORDER TO, THAT.

**ordinance, ordnance.** Often confused; an ordinance is a law, usually local (*a curfew ordinance* was adopted): ordnance is military weaponry, primarily cannon or artillery (Copperud, Evans).

**orient, orientate.** Copperud and Evans regard the shorter form as preferable in all senses; Fowler regards the longer as likely to predominate in figurative use, which apparently reflects British usage. The unabridged dictionaries indicate that *orient* is the basic form.

**oscillate, osculate.** Absurdly though not uncommonly confused. Oscillate means *flutter* or *move to and fro;* a pendulum oscillates. *Osculate* means *kiss,* and the word is now heavy humor. Readers are amused by occasional references to *osculating fans.*

**ostensible, -bly, ostentatious, -ly.** Evans and Fowler consider it necessary to distinguish these terms, the first of which means *apparent(ly),* and the second *showy, demonstrative.* The confusion is extremely rare, if it is not a species of nonce-error that happened to catch the eye of these commentators.

**other, any other.** For comment on such constructions as "He has more readers than any other financial writer on a New

York newspaper" see COMPAR-
ISON 1.

**other than.** In general, without going into hairsplitting distinctions, it may be said that
Bernstein, Evans, Flesch, Fowler, and American Heritage discourage the use of this construction when *otherwise,
otherwise than,* or *except* will
fit. "The door was kept locked
other than when the neighbors
were at home." *except.*

**otherwise.** *Otherwise* used as
an adjective in such sentences
as "She did not like any of the
hats, fashionable or otherwise"
and "The museum contains a
miscellany of oriental vases,
authentic and otherwise" is
roundly denounced by Follett
and Fowler, though both admit
that this construction is widely
prevalent and all but idiomatic.
The objections to it are based
on the reasoning that one could
not say *otherwise hats* or *otherwise vases* (placing *otherwise*
in the attributive position).
Evans defends the construction, citing *few and far between* as an example of what
is ordinarily an adverb (*far between*) modifying a noun. Random House and Webster,
however, both explicitly list
*otherwise* as an adjective. Both
give examples placing it in the
attributive position: *their otherwise friends.* American Heritage
not only recognizes *otherwise*
as an adjective but gives an
example using it in the predicate position: "The evidence
is otherwise." The objections to
*otherwise* as an adjective appear to be pedantry.

Fowler protests against *otherwise* as a noun: "His competence or otherwise was not in
question." This seems better
based, since neither dictionary
recognizes *otherwise* as a noun.

**ought.** Bryant describes
*hadn't ought* as not used in
present-day writing, and American Heritage calls it and *had
ought* wrong; Fowler deprecates the similar form *didn't
ought,* apparently common in
Britain but seldom heard in the
U.S., as a colloquial vulgarism.
The consensus is that *ought*
with auxiliaries (in this case,
*had* and *did*) is not standard
in written expression; this includes *had ought,* which should
be simply *ought.* Follett deplores the omission of *to* after
*ought,* as in "He thought he
ought not go" and "We ought
not think of it" and Evans regards the retention of *to* as
preferable. The unabridged dictionaries bear this out by implication, since none of their
examples omit *to.*

**-our, -or.** See -OR, -OUR.

**ours.** The form *our's* is
wrong (Copperud, Evans).

**ourself, ourselves.** See EDI-
TORIAL (AND ROYAL) WE for
the first, and MYSELF and RE-
FLEXIVES for the second.

**outside.** *Of* is superfluous
with *outside* as a preposition
("They stood outside of the
door") according to Copperud,
Evans, and American Heritage,
though Bernstein considers *of*
acceptable, as does Webster.
Thus opinion is divided, and
the writer may exercise his
preference between the forms.
Bernstein disapproves *outside
of* for *except for* ("Outside of
the climate, the place has no
advantages"). Evans and Webster consider this usage stand-

ard; Random House labels it informal, and Bryant considers it colloquial. The reasonable deduction is that it lies somewhere between colloquial and formal.

over. It is a superstition endemic to newspapers that there is something wrong with *over* in the sense *more than.* Curiously enough, in view of how widely this idea is held, only one of the current dictionaries of usage takes up the point. The prejudice against *over* for *more than* apparently stemmed from Ambrose Bierce's *Write It Right,* an extremely idiosyncratic guide published in 1909, whose opinions now fly in the face of standard usage, if in fact they ever represented anything but the author's crotchets. At any rate, *over* for *more than* ("It cost over five dollars") is recognized without cavil by all dictionaries.

Bierce also aspersed *over* for *down upon from above,* as "he was hit over the head," but this expression is given to illustrate one sense of *over* as a preposition in both unabridged dictionaries.

Bernstein, Copperud, and American Heritage warn of the misuse of *over* in such constructions as "Considerable reductions over single-performance prices are again being offered," when *from* or *under* is called for.

overall. Evans, Flesch, and Fowler object to the loose and sometimes superfluous use of the word in the senses *absolute, complete, comprehensive, general, inclusive, total, whole,* etc. Often it appears to be used

simply as an intensive—"The overall result of the discussion was confusion"—when it might as well be omitted. In the sense under discussion, Random House gives the definition *covering or including everything* and Webster gives *of or relating to something as a whole,* with *viewed as a whole,* general, comprehensive as synonyms. Perhaps the best advice in this case is to make certain that the word is used in those senses, and that it cannot be dispensed with.

overestimate. See UNDERESTIMATE.

overlay, overlie. The same principle governs the forms of these verbs as governs LAY and LIE, which see.

overlook, oversee. Although Copperud and Fowler criticize the use of *overlook* in the sense *supervise* ("The foreman overlooks the construction"), holding that *oversee* should be reserved for this use, American Heritage, Random House, and Webster all give *supervise* or its equivalent as one sense of *overlook,* and so do desk dictionaries. The context must be depended on to prevent ambiguity caused by understanding *overlook* in its sense of *ignore, fail to notice.*

overly. Bernstein and Follett severely criticize the use of this word, holding that *over-* as a solid prefix is preferable: *overgenerous* rather than *overly generous, overenthusiastic* rather than *overly enthusiastic.* But Evans defends it as acceptable in the U.S., and both major dictionaries give it without qualification. The American Heritage panel accepts it. The fact that a word duplicates a sense already available seems like a thin reason to object to it, since English is full of such examples.

**Overwriting.** See JOURNALESE.

**owing to.** See DUE TO.

**owing (or due to) the fact that.** Redundant for *because, since* (Copperud, Fowler). See also DUE TO.

# P

**pachyderm, pachydermatous.** Criticized as a synonym for *elephant, elephantine* by Copperud, Flesch, and Fowler. *Pachyderm* was at one time the fond variant for *elephant* among newspaper writers, and elsewhere was often intended to be humorous.

**package.** The fondness for *package* in such expressions as *a package deal* and *package rates* is deplored by Bernstein, Flesch, and Follett. American Heritage, Random House, and Webster, however, give *package deal* as a separate entry, and Webster offers so many examples of *package* in these senses that the usage seems to be established beyond any quibble. Obviously, though it once was a fad, it serves too useful a purpose to be aspersed. Flesch confesses a suspicion that it is here to stay. Bernstein, too, concedes that it serves a purpose, though it is overused. Fowler examines the new uses of *package* as a verb and noun (*package a TV show; a package plan*), and not only refrains from disparaging them but concedes their utility. The consensus favors these extended meanings, overused or not.

**packing.** Journalese as used in weather stories: "A hurricane packing 90-mile-an-hour winds."

**pair, pairs.** Either form may be used as a plural (*six pair of trousers; six pairs of scissors*), though *pairs* is the newer form and is predominant. *Pair* in relation to people should take a plural verb: "The pair of comedians were next on the program" (Copperud, Evans, American Heritage; Random House and Webster concur on the plural forms). See also COUPLE.

**pajamas, pyjamas.** The first is the American spelling, the second the British (Copperud, Fowler, Random House, Webster).

**palpable.** Evans and Fowler point out that the word means *capable of being touched* or *perceptible by any means;* Evans criticizes *palpable lie* as a cliché; to Flesch the word sounds bookish and is to be avoided. The consensus seems to be that this is a term whose misuse or overuse has raised the hackles of the commentators, and thus it should be handled with care.

**pan-.** Solid as a prefix: *panatrophy, pangenesis, pansophism.* But most combinations with *pan-* are proper names, with the result that the hyphen is used and both elements are capitalized: *Pan-Arabic, Pan-American, Pan-Pacific.* Exception: *Panhellenic, -ism.*

**panacea.** Bernstein and Evans point out that a panacea is a cure-all, and whether the term is used literally, in reference to ailments, or figuratively (*a panacea for economic woes*) it is not properly applied to a single affliction. Thus one could not well speak of a *panacea for debt.* The definitions in Webster and Random House support this conclusion.

**paradise.** The preferred adjectival form among the several available (*paradisaic, paradisaical, paradisal, paradisiacal, paradisial, paradisian, paradisic, paradisean, paradisiac, paradisical*) is, Evans and Fowler agree, *paradisal.* But Random House gives *paradisiacal* as primary, and Webster accords that form and *paradisal* equal standing.

**paraffin.** See KEROSENE.

**Paragraphs.** Bernstein, Evans, Flesch, and Fowler all discuss the uses and structure of paragraphs; they agree on warning against excessive length.

**Parallelism.** The name for following the same pattern with constructions that naturally fall into it. It makes for ease in reading and therefore is to be encouraged. Most offenses against parallelism consist in switching verb forms: "It is a matter of letting tavern owners know their rights and to avoid confusion." *Of letting* should be matched by *of avoiding.* Some other examples, with corrections: "Vladimir Petrov was reported as having asked for and was granted asylum in Australia." *having asked for and having obtained,* or *having been granted.* "The state suspended sixteen driver permits, and one was revoked for vehicle violations" is not incorrect, but it does violate the principle of parallelism by changing from active to passive. *suspended sixteen . . . and revoked one.* Various aspects of parallelism are discussed by Copperud under that heading, by Flesch under *Lists,* by Follett under *Linking* and *Matching Parts,* and by Fowler under *Enumeration Forms.*

**paramount.** Evans and Flesch warn against loosely using the term for *first, important;* it means *preeminent, chief in rank.* Random House and Webster corroborate this view.

**parliamentarian.** Bernstein objects to the use of this term to mean *a member of parliament* (as distinct from *an expert in rules of procedure*) but this sense is recognized by both Webster and Random House; the latter, however, designates it as British.

**parlous.** Evans and Fowler both discourage this term as affected or heavily humorous. (It is a variant of *perilous.*)

**parson.** Bernstein and Evans describe the term as somewhat rustic, or as used humorously for the most part in the United States. This judgment is obviously correct, though neither Webster nor Random House gives any indication of this shade of meaning.

**partake of.** Criticized by Bernstein, Evans, and Flesch variously as a cliché or as stilted.

**part and parcel.** The phrase is discouraged by Bernstein and Evans as a cliché.

**partially, partly.** Where there is a choice, as in "The words were partly unintelligible" and "The grass was partly mowed," *partly* is recommended over *partially* by Copperud, Evans, Flesch, and Fowler. Although the words are recognized as synonyms in this sense by dictionaries, *partially* also has the meaning *showing favoritism* (i.e., *being partial*) and thus there is danger of ambiguity in some contexts when *partially* is used in the sense of *partly*. American Heritage gives a distinction no other book does; that *partly* applies in physical connections and lays stress on the part, *partially* refers to conditions or states and stresses the whole.

**Participles.** See DANGLING MODIFIERS; FUSED PARTICIPLE; GERUNDS; MODIFIERS.

**particular.** Described by Copperud and Fowler as often used for an unnecessary emphasis when there is no need to particularize. The test of its usefulness is to strike *particular* out and decide whether anything has been lost, or whether the word has just been put in by reflex action.

**parting of the ways.** Regarded as a cliché by Evans and Fowler.

**party.** *Party* when *person* is called for is considered inappropriate or humorous by Copperud and Evans. "Firemen helped remove the injured parties from the car." *people.*

**pass, past.** *Passed* is the past tense of *pass* ("We passed a tree on the hill"); *past* may be an adverb, adjective, noun, or preposition, but not a verb ("My era has past" is wrong; *passed*), Copperud and Fowler agree. Evans curiously approves of such usages as "They past the crossroad," but neither Webster nor Random House recognizes *past* as a verb. The consensus is that *past* may not be used in this way. See also MEET, PASS.

**pass away, pass on.** Objectionable euphemisms for *die* (Copperud, Evans, Flesch).

**Passive Voice.** The use of the passive, in which the subject is acted on by the verb ("The ball was thrown by the boy" vs. "The boy threw the ball"), has a long history of discouragement as a weak form of expression. All the works on usage surveyed for this book deal with the question. Flesch and Follett content themselves with repeating the general discouragement; the others present more discriminating analyses, including concessions that the passive has its uses. Follett, however, discusses other aspects of the problem under the heading *voice*. Bryant and Evans find that the passive is on the increase, discouragement or no, and they agree with Bernstein that its use is much commoner among the well educated and sophisticated than among those less favored. There is a general agreement that the passive is permissible, and perhaps desirable, when the performer of an act is not known or of no importance, so that he may be omitted ("The door was closed quietly"; and that the active voice is preferable to the passive in narration and description. Evans and Fowler criticize the use of the passive to evade responsibility, as is sometimes done in bureaucratic correspondence—"It is felt that your request must be denied" in place of "We (or I) must deny your request." Though the passive has its uses, and is gaining in popularity, the active is far more common because of its naturalness and vigor. The writer who wants his prose to be direct and lively will be aware when he is using the passive and will do so only when he has a good reason for it. Use of the passive simply to vary sentence structure, in such sentences as "Further education was gained in Europe" (in a biographical sketch) and "France and Germany were visited next" (in a travel account), is objectionable. See also DOUBLE PASSIVES.

**past.** Redundant with *history,* since history is inevitably of the past (Copperud, Evans). This is true also of *past* with *experience, records, precedent, achievements, accomplishments,* despite the frequency of such expressions, except when there is reason to differentiate those that are past from others. See also LAST, LATEST, PAST.

**patron.** Bernstein, Evans, and Fowler criticize the use of the term in the sense of *customer* as pretentious. Webster and Random House, however, both give this meaning as standard. The Concise Oxford Dictionary does not recognize it, which, together with Fowler's disapproval, may indicate that *patron* for *customer* is an Americanism. This is unquestionably true of *patronize,* as Evans points out, and as is corroborated by Fowler's disapproval of it in the sense *trade at.*

**peacenik.** *Tips and Slips,* the critique of its own content put out by the *Cleveland Press,* commented that this is "a manufactured word with a built-in sneer. Forget it. There is nothing wrong with being in favor of peace." The expression is too new to be in any dictionary. It is the successor to *peacemonger,* and apparently was generated by the hawks-doves division on the Vietnam War.

**peacock.** The use of this form instead of *peahen* in reference to laying eggs and other female functions is regularly criticized, often scornfully. Strictly speaking, the peacock is the male of the peafowl. But *peacock* as a general term of reference to members of this species is sanctioned as standard by both Random House and Webster, as well as most desk dictionaries.

**peculiarly.** Evans says the word cannot properly be used in the senses *especially* or *particularly,* but may mean only *highly individually.* This judgment, like most that are based on derivation (in this case, from Latin), is erroneous; it is supported by neither Webster nor the Concise Oxford Dictionary. (Random House does not give a separate definition.)

**Pedantry.** See POMPOSITY.

**pedigreed.** See THOROUGH-BRED.

**peer, peer group.** *Peer* is often mistakenly thought to mean *superior;* in fact, it means *equal.* The misuse is illustrated by "He regarded all men as his equals, but none as his peers" (Copperud, Evans). *Peerless* thus means *without an equal,* not *without a superior.* The confused usage in this respect probably arises from another sense of *peer: nobleman.* *Peer group* is described by Copperud and Flesch as sociological and educational jargon that is often used in inappropriate (i.e., nontechnical) contexts.

**Peking, Peiping.** The name of the capital of China was Peiping ("Northern Peace") from 1928 to 1949; in 1949 it was renamed Peking ("Northern Capital") by the Communists. There is much confusion on this subject, though it is explained by both Random House and Webster. The current version, then, is Peking.

**penny.** The term is sometimes criticized as used in reference to the U.S. cent, but Copperud and Evans describe it as established, a judgment borne out by dictionary definitions.

**people, persons.** Follett holds to the traditional view that the terms are not interchangeable, and that *people* correctly designates a large and indefinite group, as in *the British people* or *We, the people.* The corollary, observed in newspaper offices, particularly, is that a figure must always be followed by *persons,* never by *people: sixteen persons.* Copperud, Evans, and Flesch, however, opt for *people* in preference to *persons,* which they believe now often sounds stiff. Bernstein and Copperud warn against following the traditional rule out the window, as is often done in newspaper writing, on the assumption *people* is to be avoided, leading to such absurdities as "The job of the comedian is to make persons laugh." Bernstein, nevertheless, favors *persons* with an exact number, and the definitions in both Random House and Webster follow the traditional rule of using *people* only in the indefinite sense. American Heritage considers the forms interchangeable for small numbers. Opinion thus is divided on this usage, with a slight edge favoring the traditional rule.

**per.** Copperud, Follett, and Fowler frown on the indiscriminate use of *per* for *a* (*the mailman used to come twice per day*); Bernstein and Fowler object to *per* for *by* (*he traveled per automobile*) and, with Follett, to *as per* for *in accordance with* as used in business correspondence; Flesch and Fowler prefer *a year* to *per annum.* The consensus is heavily against *per* where *a* or some other native expression will do.

**peradventure.** Described by Fowler (who calls it archaic) and Flesch (who considers it pompous) as often inappropriately used; the usual phrase is *beyond the peradventure of a doubt.*

**per capita.** Fowler protests that this is a legal term, incorrectly used in the sense of *per person, per head,* but he is outnumbered by American Heritage, Random House, Webster, the Standard College, and the New World dictionaries, which give this sense as standard.

**percentage.** Not necessarily a small part; a percentage may be any fraction of the whole (Bernstein, Fowler, American Heritage). See also FRACTION.

**perfect.** The idea, approved by Bernstein, that *perfect* as an adjective is an absolute and thus incapable of being qualified (*more perfect, most perfect*) is said to be without substance by Bryant, Evans, Follett, and Fowler, and the same conclusion is indicated by examples in Webster, which quotes, among other things, the Constitution: "We, the people of the United States, in order to form a more perfect union . . ." Random House cites *nearly perfect;* American Heritage allows comparison. Thus the consensus is that *perfect* may be freely compared. See also COMPARISON 3.

**permit.** *Of* with *permit* in the sense *admit* or *allow* ("The document permits of two interpretations") is described by Copperud as unnecessary, but this form is recognized as standard by American Heritage, Random House, and Webster.

**pernickety, persnickety.** The consensus of the dictionaries is that the first is the original form, but most of them give both versions, and so they must be considered equally correct.

**perpetrate, perpetuate.** Misuse of the first for the second is warned against by Copperud and Flesch. *Perpetrate* means *commit, perform, do* (usually something objectionable); *perpetuate* means *continue, make endure.* Examples of misuse: "He is the worthy perpetrator of an illustrious tradition." *perpetuator.* "This outmoded theory is still perpetrated in many schools." *perpetuated.*

**persecute, prosecute.** Sometimes confused. To *persecute* is to *afflict, harass,* or *annoy:* "The Nazis persecuted the Jews." To *prosecute* is to *carry out the legal procedure against one accused of a crime:* "Trespassers will be prosecuted" (Copperud, Evans).

**persnickety.** See PERNICKETY.

**person.** See PEOPLE, PERSONS.

**personal, personally.** *Personal* in the phrase *personal friend* is described by Bernstein, Copperud, Evans, and Follett as usually redundant, unless there is reason to distinguish between, say, a business and a personal friendship. *Personally* is described by Copperud, Evans, and Fowler as often used for a meaningless emphasis or as redundant in such examples as *an employer who was personally popular with his workers* and *Personally, I believe . . .*

**personality.** American Heritage and Follett object strenuously to the widespread use of the term for *celebrity, notable,* or what would formerly have been called a *personage.* Fowler, however, considers this sense unexceptionable, and so do Webster and Random House.

**personnel.** Evans and Fowler think the term, introduced into English from French, still needs defending against criticisms that it is an objectionable neologism. Bernstein, Evans, and American Heritage disapprove of its use with a figure (*three personnel were fired*), but Copperud considers this usage standard, and so does Webster, which gives *34,000 personnel*. Random House, however, favors use of the term only to indicate a large or indefinite group: *the personnel of the factory; military personnel.*

**persons.** See PEOPLE, PERSONS.

**perspicacious, perspicuous.** Copperud, Evans, and Fowler warn against confusing these words (and their related nouns, *perspicacity* and *perspicuity*). Briefly, *perspicacious* means *shrewd* or *discerning*, and describes an attribute of people; *perspicuous* means *clear, easily understood*, and is ordinarily applied to things, such as arguments. Evans says that *perspicuous* has long been misused as a synonym of *perspicacious* (*a perspicuous*—i.e., *shrewd—bidder*). Fowler agrees that the common error is to use *perspicuity* for *perspicacity*: "Stock traders showed perspicuity in buying up the issue." Both Random House and Webster give *perspicacious* as a synonym of *perspicuous*, which means that one might speak of a *perspicuous* (meaning *shrewd*) *person*, and thus they approve of what Evans and Fowler criticize. Webster calls *perspicacious* substandard

when used in the sense *perspicuous*: *a perspicacious line of argument*. Fowler's advice is no doubt the best: avoid both words in favor of *shrewd* (for *perspicacious*) and *clear* (for *perspicuous*) or choose other short synonyms.

**persuade.** See CONVINCE.

**persuasion.** Phrases on the model "of the Republican persuasion" are discouraged as outmoded by Flesch and Fowler.

**peruse.** Evans and Flesch criticize the loose substitution of the word (which means *read with great care or attention*) where *read* is called for.

**pessimism.** See OPTIMISM; the views on use of the term are analogous, except that there is no dissent in the dictionaries from the principle that *pessimistic* relates to an outlook and properly is applicable to a person, as distinguished from a factor, etc.

**phantasy.** See FANTASY, PHANTASY.

**phase, faze.** See FAZE, PHASE.

**phenomenal.** Evans and Fowler agree that the sense *prodigious, extraordinary, remarkable*, although originally a corruption, can no longer be argued against. The original meaning applied to that which was apprehended by the senses, as contrasted with that which was not. Dictionaries give the newer meaning as standard, and most people will be surprised to learn it was ever under a shadow.

**phenomenon, phenomena.** Copperud, Fowler and Follett hold that the first is the proper form for the singular (*this phenomenon*) and the second for the plural (*these phenomena*); Bryant recognizes *phenomenons;* Evans considers *phenomenons* or *phenomenas* acceptable plurals; Random House and Webster also accept *phenomenons* but do not give *phenomenas,* and so the consensus is that it is nonstandard, and that *phenomenons* (as well as *phenomena*) is correct.

**Philippines.** Often misspelled *Phillipines, Phillippines.*

**phobia.** See MANIA, PHOBIA.

**phony.** Considered slang by Bernstein and Copperud, informal by Random House, and standard by Webster. Fowler discusses theories of its origin but does not indicate any disparagement. Its progress to standard seems to be beyond doubt. The dictionaries and Fowler recognize the variant spelling *phoney.*

**Phrasal Verbs.** See HYPHEN 4.

**phrenetic.** See FRENETIC, PHRENETIC.

**pier.** See DOCK.

**pinch hitter.** Bernstein, Copperud, and Evans agree that the original meaning, which comes from baseball, is a replacement sent to bat with the expectation he will do better than the man he is substituting for, and that the expression is often misused in other connections simply to describe a substitute, with no suggestion of superior performance. The sense *substitute* is recognized by American Heritage (as informal), Webster, and Random House, however, and is in such

wide use that its acceptance as standard seems beyond doubt.

**place.** The adverbial use of *place,* as in *some place nearby* and *going places,* is considered questionable by Fowler but approved as idiomatic by Bernstein and Evans. The dictionaries are not explicit on this point, though Random House calls *go places* in the sense *succeed* slang.

**plan.** The fulcrum for a number of redundancies. Planning must relate to the future unless otherwise qualified; thus *plan ahead, advance plans,* and *future plans* are technically redundant, though they occur often in educated prose.

**plead innocent.** There is no such plea in jurisprudence; the correct form is *plead not guilty.* Bernstein and Copperud point out, however, that the form *plead innocent* is often prescribed in newspaper journalism to avoid the error caused by inadvertently omitting the *not* in *not guilty;* American Heritage considers the form well established in nonlegal contexts.

**pleasantry.** The word now means not something pleasant, or amiable conversation, but a joke or banter. "They exchanged pleasantries about the rigors of campaigning" (Copperud, Follett, Random House, Webster).

**pled.** Recognized as a standard form of the past tense of *plead,* as acceptable as *pleaded,* by Bryant, Copperud, Evans, and Fowler; to Follett, it is "unsavory." Recognition of *pled* as standard by American Heritage, Random House, and

Webster makes the approval nearly unanimous, however.

**plenty.** Bernstein, Copperud, Evans (somewhat ambiguously), and Fowler disapprove of *plenty* as an attributive adjective in such expressions as *plenty brains, plenty money* (correct: *plenty of . . .*), and American Heritage calls it informal. Random House, however, gives *plenty helpers,* and Webster gives *plenty men.* The consensus is against the usage.

**Plural and Singular. 1.** Bernstein, Copperud, and Fowler point out that the plurals of proper names ending in *s* are formed by adding *es: Jones,* (*the*) *Joneses; Adams,* (*the*) *Adamses.* Such plurals are often erroneously formed by adding an apostrophe, which properly indicates possession: *the Adams'.*

**2.** Copperud, Evans, Fowler, and American Heritage agree that the plurals of figures and letters may be formed by adding *s: the 1920s, GIs, MPs.* (This is a relatively new usage that appears already well entrenched; older practice called for adding *'s: the 1920's.*)

**3.** Miscellaneous problems affecting the formation of plurals are dealt with under that entry in Bernstein, Copperud, Evans, and Fowler.

**4.** The singular, rather than the plural, is used in such constructions as *six-mile race, three-month investigation* (not *miles, months*) (Copperud, Evans).

**5.** Bernstein and Copperud agree that plural forms are sometimes used pretentiously. "Charges of vagrancy were lodged against the transient."

*a charge was.* "The dedication ceremonies were canceled." *ceremony was.* "He has ambitions to be a bank president." *an ambition.*

See also COLLECTIVE NOUNS; COURT-MARTIAL; GENERAL; -IC, -ICS; IT IS I, etc.; SUBJECT-VERB AGREEMENT; ANYBODY, ANYONE; EACH; EVERYBODY, EVERYONE; LB., LBS.

**plurality.** See MAJORITY, PLURALITY.

**plus.** Not the equivalent of *and,* Bernstein and American Heritage agree, and Bernstein says it may take only a singular verb: "Three plus two is (not *are*) five." American Heritage concurs in such instances; Bryant and Evans say the verb may be either singular or plural. American Heritage points out that a plural verb is required when the subject is plural: "His talents plus his ambition were irresistible." *Plus* for *besides* ("The liquor was expensive, plus it was of poor quality") is a disagreeable vogue.

**p.m.** See A.M., P.M.

**podium.** Copperud has pointed out the widespread confusion of this term, for the platform a speaker or orchestra conductor stands on, with *lectern,* the stand on which a speaker places his manuscript. One critic, after reading in a newspaper that a speaker had pressed both hands down hard on the edges of the podium to emphasize his words, commented derisively that the speaker must have been on his hands and knees. The confusion has been dignified by the recognition of *podium* in the sense of *lectern* by Webster; no other dictionary accepts this meaning. The consensus is that the usage is at least questionable.

**Poesy.** The gentlemen of the press are sometimes eager to show that the often humdrum task of reporting the news has not entirely numbed them to the finer things in life. They do this with random poetical touches, like *'twas, 'tis, 'twere,* and *'twill. Lone* is a commoner example; it has all but supplanted the homely *only* or *sole:* "He cast the lone dissenting vote." Fowler cited *save* (in the sense of *except*) and *ere* as examples of words abandoned to the journalists, who, he said, had not yet ceased to find them beautiful. The fault of using words inappropriate to the context is discussed in various aspects by Copperud under *Poesy* and by Fowler under *Archaism, Battered Ornaments, Incongruous Vocabulary, Poeticisms, Vulgarization,* and *Wardour Street.*

**poetess.** See FEMININE FORMS.

**pointed out.** See ATTRIBUTION 2.

**point of view.** Use of the phrase in pompous constructions like the examples is criticized by Evans and Fowler: "His point of view was that the program was unnecessary." *view, opinion.* "From the point of view of legibility, typing is preferable to writing." *Typing is more legible than writing.* See also VIEWPOINT.

**politic, political.** See -IC, -ICAL.

**politics.** See -IC, -ICS.

**Pomposity.** All agree that the use of unnecessarily long words, complicated constructions, or technical language is a serious fault. Discussions of it may be found in Bernstein under the heading *Windyfoggery,* in Evans under *Pedantry,* in Copperud under *Pomposity,* in Follett under *Educationese* and *Pedantry,* and in Fowler under *Love of the Long Word, Pride of Knowledge,* and *Pedantry.* Throughout these books there is persistent discouragement of pretentiousness. See also SCIENTIFIC ENGLISH.

**Popularized Technicalities.** The term was invented by Fowler in the original; both the revision and Follett contain long entries under this heading listing the expressions the authors regard as having been objectionably popularized. Judgments on this matter, of course, are even more idiosyncratic than judgments on usage in general, since technical terms are constantly being placed in general use, often with more or less distorted meanings.

**pore, pour.** The second is often given when the first is intended, e.g., *pour over a book. Pore* means *read studiously; pour* means *tip out of a container* (Copperud, Evans).

**position.** See JOB, POSITION.

**Possessive Pronouns.** The possessive pronouns ending in *s* (*yours, his, hers, its, ours, theirs*) do not take apostrophes: *Its fur was mangy; The purse was hers.* The commonest error here is confusing the contraction *it's* (*it is*) with *its* (*belong-*

*ing to it*). (This represents modern usage. Two centuries ago, the forms *their's, our's, her's* were considered correct.) See also POSSESSIVES.

**Possessives. 1.** Such possessive forms as *the water's temperature, the sky's color* (rather than *the temperature of the water, the color of the sky*) are described as standard by Bryant and criticized as sometimes unfelicitous by Bernstein and Copperud; Flesch and Follett disapprove of them altogether. (The question here is whether the possessive form may be used for inanimate things; no such question ordinarily arises concerning such expressions as *the dog's collar* and *the cat's pajamas*, and even some referring to inanimate things, such as *today's newspaper*.) The consensus disapproves such possessives.

**2.** Apostrophe vs. Apostrophe-s. There is no disagreement with the universal principle that the possessive of words ending in any letter but *s* or *z* is formed by adding *'s*: *boy, boy's; men, men's; George, George's; paper, paper's*. Uncertainty arises, however, over forming the possessive of singulars that end with *s* or *z* (or an *s*- or *z*- sound): *Jesus, Jones, Keats*. These are mainly proper names, but some common expressions, like *conscience' sake, innocence' evidence*, come under this heading. Bernstein, Copperud, and Evans agree that the apostrophe alone is used to avoid producing a triple sibilant in pronouncing the possessive form: *Moses'* rather than *Moses's* (which would be pronounced *Moseses*),

*Jesus'* rather than *Jesus's*. Fowler seems ambiguous on this point. Bernstein, Flesch, and Fowler prescribe *'s* to form the possessives of proper nouns ending in *s*: *Keats's, Charles's;* Copperud and Evans say *Keats'* and *Charles'* are equally acceptable. (Copperud offers the principle that pronunciation should be allowed to govern the choice in forming all possessives on *s* or *z* sounds, and Flesch allows exceptions when physical possession is not indicated, as in *Holmes' London*.) Bernstein and Evans favor *conscience' sake;* Fowler approves both that form and *conscience sake*.

**3.** Double Genitive (Possessive). The term refers to constructions like *a property of Smith's, a friend of my uncle's, an opinion of the teacher's*. Technically, the possessive forms *Smith's, uncle's*, and *teacher's* are redundant because possession has already been indicated by *of*. Two points are worth noting: the object of the phrase is always animate (usually a person or an animal), and identical constructions in which the object is a pronoun raise no question: *a friend of mine, some books of yours*. Double genitives, though avoided by some writers as excessive constructions, are described as idiomatic by Bernstein, Bryant, Copperud, Evans, and American Heritage. Fowler does not discuss the subject, but appears to give tacit approval of it by citing an example, in another connection (under *Double Case*), that contains a double genitive. The double genitive often appears in constructions like "Their idea is the same as that of the tariff commission's"; "The footprint is fully as long as that of a large gorilla's"; "Her Christmas wish was no longer that of a child's." These are sometimes considered more objectionable than other double genitives. They may be avoided by dispensing with either *that of* or the possessive form of the noun that follows: "Her Christmas wish was no longer a child's" or "that of a child." Users of the double genitive, several of the authorities point out, must be on guard against ambiguity, especially in speaking. Thus *an opinion of the teacher's,* spoken, might be taken to mean either *an opinion held by the teacher* or *an opinion concerning the teachers.*

4. False Possessive. Modifiers ending in *s* are often wrongly construed as possessives and given apostrophes they should not have: *General Motors scholarship* (not *Motors'*); *United States* (not *States'*) *citizen.* The use of the apostrophe in such phrases as *five months' probation, six weeks' vacation* is considered necessary by Bernstein but described as optional by Copperud and Fowler.

For a discussion of constructions like *him going* vs. *his going,* see FUSED PARTICIPLE; for the use of the apostrophe in forming plurals (*1920's*), see PLURAL AND SINGULAR. See also SAKE.

**possible, possibly.** Bernstein and Copperud warn against the expression *possibly may* as redundant, since *possible* includes the contingency expressed by *may.* Bernstein and Evans caution against such constructions as "I will charge you no more than possible," where *possible* illogically displaces *necessary.* Bernstein and Copperud disapprove of the construction, common in newspapers, on the model *a possible fractured jaw; possibly* is required here. Bernstein argues for limiting *possible* to its strict sense of *capable of being done,* and on this basis criticizes the common tribute to those who are said to have made something possible, when in fact they brought it about; Fowler is more lenient.

**postmaster general.** See GENERAL.

**postmistress.** See FEMININE FORMS.

**postprandial.** Objected to by Evans, Flesch, and Fowler as polysyllabic humor.

**pother.** Considered a literary word by Evans and Fowler.

**pound(s) sterling.** See LB., LBS.

**pour.** See PORE, POUR.

**practicable, practical.** Sometimes confused. What is practicable is capable of being done or accomplished: "Construction of cities under the seas is now considered practicable." What is practical is useful or adapted to use or to actual conditions: "Practical solutions are better than theoretical ones" (Bernstein, Copperud, Evans, Follett, Fowler). Follett and Fowler give the negative forms as *impracticable* and *unpractical,* respectively; Fowler states and Follett implies that *impractical* (as the negative of *practical*) is wrong. Yet *impractical* is given as standard by both unabridged dictionaries, and it is incontrovertible that in America, at least, *impractical* is far commoner than *unpractical*.

**practically.** In the sense *almost, virtually, in effect* (*it is practically worn out*), considered objectionable by Copperud, Evans, and Fowler; Bernstein concludes that the words have become all but, or practically, interchangeable. Both unabridged dictionaries recognize *practically* as standard for *nearly, almost;* these terms are recommended as preferable by Copperud, Evans, and Fowler. The American Heritage panel narrowly (51 per cent) accepts *practically* for *in effect* and rejects it (64 per cent) for *nearly, almost,* though these expressions are often interchangeable, as in one of the examples cited to illustrate the supposed difference. Opinion is thus divided on the acceptability of *practically* in these senses.

**practice, practise.** The first is the American form of the verb and the second is the British form (Copperud, Evans, Fowler).

**pre-.** Copperud (following American dictionary practice) says the prefix is generally solid: *prearrange, preempt, preheat, preprint,* etc. Fowler holds the same view but prescribes the hyphen to prevent doubling the vowel: *pre-empt.* This, however, appears to be British practice. *Pre-* is sometimes redundantly affixed to words that already possess the meaning *previous, before: a precondition* (to a treaty); *preplanning.*

**precede, proceed.** Sometimes confused; *precede* means *go ahead of; proceed* means *go forward* (Copperud, Evans). Some common misspellings: *preceed, preceeding, procede.*

**precipitate, precipitous.** Sometimes confused. The first means *rash,* the second *steep: a precipitate decision, a precipitous roof* (Bernstein, Evans, Follett, Fowler, American Heritage).

**predicate.** Bernstein objects to *predicate* in the sense *base on,* as in "Several senators had predicated their misgivings on what effect it would have on European security." This sense is regarded as standard, however, by Copperud, Evans, Random House, Webster, and four current desk dictionaries as well as the American Heritage panel. The use of *predict* for *predicate,* which some authorities warn against, is apparently a British error. Copperud and Flesch recommend *based on* as simpler than *predicated on.*

**predominate.** Considered an error as an adjective by Copperud (*the predominate characteristics*); considered standard by Webster, and not listed by Random House. The usual form is *predominant.* Both dictionaries recognize *predominately* alongside *predominantly.* There is, of course, no question about *predominate* as a verb.

**preface.** See FOREWORD, etc.

**prefer.** The usual idiomatic forms with *prefer* in comparing two things are illustrated by *prefer* (*to do*) *this rather than* (*to do*) *that* (to avoid the double infinitive of *prefer to do this to to do that*); *prefer this to* *that; prefer doing this to doing that. Prefer than,* as in "They prefer going to the show than dancing," is not acceptable (Bernstein, Copperud, Evans, Follett, Fowler, American Heritage).

**Prefixes and Suffixes.** See HYPHENS 5.

**premier.** Aspersed by Flesch and Fowler as pretentious for *first, foremost: a premier musician.*

**premiere.** Rejected as a verb (*premiered a new film*) by American Heritage; considered standard by Random House and Webster.

**premise, premises.** The singular form means *a basis for reasoning or argument;* its plural is *premises.* Only *premises,* which is always a plural, may be used in the sense of *property:* "Trespassers were warned off the premises" (Bernstein, Copperud, Evans, Fowler).

**preparatory to.** Criticized by Copperud, Flesch, and American Heritage as a pretentious displacement of *before:* "He put out the cat preparatory to going to bed." What is preparatory to should be in preparation for (Bernstein, Copperud, Flesch).

**prepared.** Criticized by Evans and Fowler when it displaces more direct expression as in "The senator was not prepared to admit his part in the affair." *not willing, would not* (Evans, Fowler, Flesch).

**Prepositions. 1.** Piled-Up Prepositions. Bernstein and Copperud agree that prepositions are often unnecessarily doubled, and sometimes tripled,

when a range is being specified, especially in newspaper writing: "The weatherman predicted a low temperature of between 75 and 80 degrees" (omit *of*); "The airlift is expected to speed up the delivery of mail by from twenty-four to forty-eight hours" (omit *from*); "Investments of from two to four million dollars were reported" (omit *from*). Sometimes a single preposition is superfluous: "A low temperature (of) near 45 degrees is expected"; "The Sierra received (from) two to four inches of slushy snow"; "(At) about nine o'clock last night."

**2.** Bernstein and Follett give extensive information on the idiomatic prepositions that go with various verbs, e.g., that *acquiesce* takes *in, grate* takes *on,* etc.; Bernstein gives them in their alphabetical places and Follett in a list under the entry *Prepositions.* Another extensive list is to be found in the book *Words into Type* by Gay and Skillin. Evans deals with the problem less extensively, in the entry *Prepositions.* Such information is perhaps most conveniently and exhaustively available in examples appearing in the unabridged dictionaries, especially Webster.

**3.** Preposition at End. Six of the seven authorities being compared in this book agree that avoidance of ending a sentence with a preposition is a superstition based on Latin, rather than English. (Follett unaccountably does not mention this problem.) It is agreed further that the construction with the preposition at the end is often more natural and more vigorous, and not to be avoided except in the rare instances when the sentence will read more smoothly by placing the preposition earlier. Some examples of the preposition at the end, followed by the less desirable versions in which the word-order has been changed to place it earlier: *Make the world a better place to live in* (*a better place in which to live*); *What are we coming to?* (*To what are we coming?*); *There was nothing to talk about* (*nothing about which to talk*). The conclusion of this entry represents the consensus of Bernstein, Bryant, Copperud, Evans, Flesch, Fowler, and American Heritage. See also ALL OF; OFF OF.

**prescribe, proscribe.** Sometimes confused; to prescribe is to lay down a direction; to proscribe is to forbid, denounce, or outlaw (Copperud, Evans, Fowler, Random House, Webster). A doctor prescribes medicine; he may proscribe tobacco.

**present incumbent.** Redundant; delete *present.*

**presently.** In the sense of *at present, now, currently,* the word is grudgingly considered acceptable by Bernstein, Copperud, Flesch, and Fowler, all of whom think it would best be reserved for the sense *by and by, before long.* Follett complains that it has displaced *now,* and American Heritage narrowly rejects it in that sense. *Presently* for *now* is actually a revival of a long-abandoned usage. Both unabridged dictionaries give the sense *now* as standard; this is the consensus. *Presently, at present,* and *currently* are often redundant, however, with a verb in the present tense unless the desire is to express contrast or give emphasis: "He is (presently) living in Brooklyn."

**present writer.** See EDITORIAL (AND ROYAL) WE.

**pressure.** As a verb in the sense *exert influence, pressure* is newly arrived in the dictionaries "The mayor was pressured to fire the chief of police."

**prestige, prestigious.** The archaic sense (as designated by Webster) of *prestigious* is "of, relating to, or marked by illusion, conjuring, or trickery." This is likely to come as a surprise to most Americans, to whom the word means *possessing prestige. Prestige* itself has a corresponding history. Of the authorities being compared, only Follett disapproves of *prestigious* as still carrying its old connotation; Copperud, American Heritage, Random House, and Webster consider it standard and unexceptionable in the current sense, which is the only one given by Random House. There is reason to conclude that *prestigious,* particularly, in the sense *possessing prestige,* is new and an Americanism. Fowler approves *prestige* in the modern sense but neither he nor the Oxford dictionaries give *prestigious* in the sense *possessing prestige.* No authority asperses *prestige* for *status.*

**presumptive, presumptuous.** *Presumptive,* a technical term having to do usually with heirs (an heir presumptive being one whose right might be lost by the birth of another heir), sometimes is misused for *presumptuous,* which means *pre-*

*suming*: "It was presumptive of him to sit down at the head table." *presumptuous* (Bernstein, Evans; interchange of these terms is designated archaic or obsolete by Random House and Webster).

**Pretentiousness.** See POMPOSITY.

**pretty.** Considered acceptable by Bryant, Copperud, Evans, and Fowler as an adverb in the senses *somewhat, moderately; a pretty good bargain, a pretty reasonable explanation;* Random House and Webster also regard this use as standard.

**prevent.** Constructions on the pattern of *prevent me leaving* (instead of *prevent me from leaving* or *prevent my leaving*) are criticized by Bernstein, Fowler, and American Heritage but considered acceptable by Evans. See also AVERT; FUSED PARTICIPLE.

**preventative, preventive.** The second (and shorter) form is considered preferable by Bernstein, Copperud, Evans, Flesch, and Fowler as both adjective and noun: "He took preventive measures"; "This medicine is a preventive." This form is also considered predominant by Random House and Webster. See also INTERPRETATIVE, etc.

**previous to.** Criticized by Copperud, Flesch, and Fowler as pretentious where *before* will do.

**prewar.** The use of the word as an adverb (*the conditions prevailing prewar*) instead of exclusively as an adjective (*prewar conditions*) is criticized by Fowler but considered standard by Webster; Random House and American Heritage give only the adjectival use.

**principal, principle.** Often confused. *Principal* is an adjective meaning *chief* or *leading,* as in *the principal reason;* it is also a noun meaning *chief* or *leader,* as in *the principal of the school. Principle* is a noun only, meaning *a rule,* as in *a principle of conduct* (Bernstein, Copperud, Evans, Flesch, Fowler, American Heritage).

**prior to.** Considered pompous in the sense of *before* by Bernstein, Copperud, Flesch, Follett, and Fowler: "Prior to attending the theater, we all had dinner." *before.*

**prise, prize.** Follett recommends and Fowler recognizes the first spelling to differentiate the act of forcing by leverage ("The brick was prised out of the wall") from that of valuing highly ("He prized the view from his living room"). However desirable the distinction may be, it is not generally observed in America; *prize* is given by both unabridged dictionaries as the primary spelling in both senses.

**probe.** Use of the term as a noun or a verb to mean *an investigation* or *to investigate* undoubtedly comes from newspaper headlines, where space is at a premium. Copperud, Flesch, and Fowler discourage its general use in this sense; Evans considers the use acceptable, and it is regarded as standard by both unabridged dictionaries. Opinion is thus divided.

**proceed.** Bernstein, Copperud, and Evans warn that the word is pretentious when it displaces *go, come, travel, walk, move.* It is suitable only to express the idea *go forward. Proceed to* is often superfluous; e.g., *proceeded to open the meeting* for *opened the meeting.* See also PRECEDE, PROCEED.

**procure.** Pretentious where *get* will serve: "They interrupted their house-hunting long enough to procure a marriage license" (Copperud, Flesch).

**profession.** Copperud and Evans agree that, though the original professions were the law, theology, and medicine, the word is now commonly and properly applied to any occupation that is not manual and requires learning. Random House and Webster, while giving specialized senses, allow extension of the term in reference to any occupation.

**progression.** See ARITHMETICAL, GEOMETRICAL.

**prohibit.** Takes *from,* not *to:* "The audience was prohibited to smoke." *prohibited from smoking* (Bernstein, Copperud, Fowler).

**prone.** Bernstein would confine the meaning to *lying face downward* (in distinction to *supine, face upward*), but Copperud, Evans, and Fowler say it may also mean lying flat in any position. So do the two unabridged dictionaries, Webster's New World, the Standard College, and the American College dictionaries. The same is true of *prostrate,* in the view of Evans, Fowler, Random House, and Webster, though the original sense was (like that of *prone*) *face downward.* Bernstein, Evans, Fowler, and the dictionaries agree, however,

that *supine* means *lying face upward.*

**Pronouns.** More or less extensive discussions of faults involving pronouns are to be found in Bernstein, Copperud, and Fowler under that heading, and in Follett under *Antecedents.* In general, the writers agree that the antecedent (the noun to which a pronoun refers) must be stated, and that there must be no indecision over which of two preceding nouns a pronoun refers to. An example in which the antecedent is absent: "He was operated on immediately, and it was successful in spite of haste." Here *it* refers to *the operation,* which should have been stated. An example in which the antecedent is uncertain: "If the dog does not thrive on raw meat, it should be cooked." *the meat* should replace *it.* The antecedent should usually precede the pronoun: "The senator was the true heir, if indeed he had an heir, of Lyndon Johnson." *He* refers to *Lyndon Johnson,* but the reader may momentarily take it as referring to *the senator.* Preferable: "The senator was the true heir of Lyndon Johnson, if indeed he had an heir" (placing *Lyndon Johnson,* the antecedent, before *he*).

In this book other difficulties having to do with pronouns are dealt with under more specific headings, such as I, ME; HE, SHE; ANYBODY, ANYONE, etc. See also POSSESSIVE PRONOUNS; ELLIPSIS 4; VARIATION; IT'S ME; THEY, etc.; COLLECTIVE NOUNS.

**propellant, propellent.** Evans and Random House say *propellant* is a noun only (*a solid* *propellant*) and that *propellent* may be used as both an adjective (*a propellent force*) and a noun. Copperud and Webster consider the forms interchangeable as both noun and adjective. Opinion is thus divided on the use of *propellant* but there is full agreement that *propellent* may be used in both ways.

**prophecy, prophesy.** Often confused. *Prophecy* is the noun ("He uttered a prophecy") and *prophesy* is the verb that describes what the prophet does ("He prophesied rain"). "It takes no gift of prophesy to see the outcome." *prophecy* (Copperud, Evans, Fowler). Webster, however, considers the forms interchangeable; Random House does not. The consensus favors the distinction. Bernstein sees *prophesy* as necessarily connoting inspiration or the supernatural, but both unabridged dictionaries give also the senses *predict, foretell*.

**proportion, proportions.** The first figures in a number of pretentious redundancies, which would usually be better replaced by *most, more, a large part: the greater proportion, the larger proportion, in greater proportion* (Copperud, Evans, Flesch, Fowler).

*Proportions* is commonly used in the sense of *dimensions, size, extent:* "A storm of cloudburst proportions." Bernstein objects to this on the ground that a proportion indicates a relationship and has nothing to do with size. This use is considered standard, however, by Copperud. Evans, American Heritage, Random House, and Webster.

**proportional, proportionate.** In their usual sense, *in proportion,* the terms are interchangeable (Copperud, Fowler, Random House, Webster). This applies also to the adverbs *proportionally* and *proportionately*. But some expressions take one or the other: *proportional representation* (never *proportionate*).

**proposition.** As loosely used for *proposal, task, job, project, enterprise* ("The contract was a questionable proposition"; "a paying proposition"; "a tough proposition"), the expression is deplored by Bernstein, Evans, and Fowler. Random House regards this usage as informal, Webster as standard. As a noun or verb meaning to suggest sexual relations, *proposition* is considered slang by Bernstein and Copperud, standard by Evans, Random House, and Webster, and all but standard by Fowler. The consensus is that this sense is now standard.

**proscribe.** See PRESCRIBE, PROSCRIBE.

**prosecute.** See PERSECUTE, PROSECUTE.

**proselyte, proselytize.** Both forms are standard as a verb, Copperud, Evans, Random House, and Webster agree; Follett's dictum that only the second is acceptable as a verb represents what Evans reports to be British practice. But even this apparently is no longer true, to judge by the Concise Oxford Dictionary.

**prostrate.** See PRONE.

**protagonist.** The sense *proponent, champion of* is, etymologically speaking, a corruption, since by derivation from the Greek the meaning is *principal actor;* the term had to do primarily with drama. Bernstein and Evans insist on this sense, and so did Fowler in the original. American Heritage accepts *leader* but vaguely disapproves *champion.* But as Gowers, Fowler's reviser, points out, the misuse has become far commoner than the original sense and he concedes that the fight against it is lost. So does Copperud, and the senses *spokesman, leader, champion* are considered standard by both Random House and Webster. The consensus favors full acceptance of the newer and more frequently used sense.

**prototype.** Bernstein, Copperud, Evans, and Fowler agree that it means *earliest form* or *first model,* not, as so often intended, *a predecessor, sample,* or *example:* "Babbitt was the prototype of the businessman of the 20s." *Babbitt exemplified* . . . Nevertheless, the broader (and more commonly used) sense *exemplar* is considered standard by Random House and Webster.

**proven.** Bernstein, Flesch, Follett, Fowler, and American Heritage object to *proven* as the past participle of *prove:* "The mine has proven worthless." Bryant, Copperud, and Evans consider *proved* and *proven* equally acceptable, and both Random House and Webster regard *proven* as standard. Opinion is thus divided.

**provided, providing.** As a conjunction meaning *on condition that* ("Water will be supplied free of charge providing the rent is paid promptly"), *providing* and *provided* are considered equally acceptable by Bernstein, Bryant, Copperud, and Evans; American Heritage and Fowler prefer and Follett insists on *provided.* *Providing* is considered standard by both Random House and Webster; thus the consensus overwhelmingly approves of it. Bernstein, Copperud, Evans, Flesch, and Fowler all discourage either *provided* or *providing,* however, when *if* will serve: "We shall have a picnic provided it does not rain." *if.*

**psychological moment.** Criticized by Copperud, Evans, and Fowler as pretentious and trite in the popular senses *at the critical moment* or *in the nick of time.*

**pulling (my) leg.** See PUTTING (ME) ON.

**Punctuation.** Discussions of punctuation will be found in entries naming specific marks; see also DOUBLE PUNCTUATION. Extensive treatments of the subject are to be found in Bernstein under the heading *Punctuation* and in Fowler under the heading *Stops.* An appendix is given over to the subject by Follett.

**Puns.** In entries under this heading, Bernstein and Fowler spiritedly challenge the widespread assumption that puns are the lowest form of wit.

**pupil, student.** In general, *pupil* is applied to those attending elementary school, and *student* to those attending high school or college (Bernstein, Copperud, Evans, Follett). While Random House and Webster recognize this distinction, they also give the terms as synonyms.

**purchase.** Considered pretentious where *buy* will do (Evans, Flesch, Fowler).

**Purist.** Discussions of what constitutes purism will be found under the heading *Purist* in Bernstein, Copperud, and Evans, and under the heading *Purism and Pedantry* in Fowler. In general, the opinions are derogatory.

**purport, purported.** Bernstein, Evans, and Fowler agree that the verb is improperly used in the passive: "The vase is purported to date from the Ming Dynasty." *purports.* They hold also that the subject of *purport* may not be a person considered as such: "The minister purported to set a good example for his parishioners." *pretended, attempted,* or whatever is suitable. The first restriction conforms with dictionary definitions of *purport* as a verb. There is, however, the adjective *purported,* which as Webster gives it may apply to either people or things: *purported spies; purported original oils.* Fowler insists that *purport* as a noun may not be used in the sense of *purpose: the purport of his journey was to collect antiques.* Both unabridged dictionaries recognize

this as standard, however, and Evans calls it commoner in Britain than in the U.S.

**purpose.** Such expressions as "*With* (or *for*) *the purpose* of advancing," or whatever, are redundant for *to advance.* "He is studying with the purpose of bettering himself." *to better* (Copperud, Flesch).

**putting (me) on.** The popularity of this expression in the sense *kidding, fooling, making fun of,* is another example of the new admiration for British slang and other mannerisms of speech. The noun *put-on* ("I thought it was a put-on"—i.e., sham, pretense) is recorded in the *Smaller Slang Dictionary* by Eric Partridge, an Englishman, in a slightly different sense. The verb appears in the revised (1967) edition of Wentworth and Flexner's *Dictionary of American Slang,* which traces it to jazz, student, and swinger origins. *Pulling my leg,* which carries the same sense as *putting me on,* is another import from Britain. Still others, which will be found in this book: *early on, not too, not all that.* The theatrical world seems particularly fond of such expressions. They may sound affected.

# Q

**qua.** The use of the Latin term where *as* will do is discouraged by Copperud, Flesch, and Fowler ("A woman *qua* mother").

**quandary.** Often misspelled *quandry.*

**quartet.** See TRIO.

**query.** Bernstein and Evans

disapprove of using the word for *investigation*, or for *inquiry* in the sense of *investigation* (but not in the sense of *question*). This accords with dictionary definitions.

**question as to (of) whether.** Bernstein, Flesch, and Fowler discourage the use of the words intervening between *question* and *whether* when they can be done without, which is nearly always.

**Questions.** The indirect restatement of a question does not make the restatement itself a question: "He asked the director of the museum whether the paintings on display were originals?" The question mark is wrong. The error occurs also with speculative statements, as "I wonder whether my application has been considered?" The statement is declarative, not interrogative, though it describes a state of indecision. Another error: "What he would like to know is how the police found out about this?" "Guess what I did today?" is an imperative, not a question (Bernstein, Copperud, Fowler).

Evans and Fowler disparage the use of the question mark in parentheses to indicate sarcasm: "He received his education (?) in the South."

**quick.** Rejected as an adverb ("They move quick in this place") by American Heritage; Random House and Webster equate it with *quickly*.

**quieten.** Bernstein regards this verb as a Briticism, and as a conspicuous affectation when used in America, but Fowler rejects it for Britain too in favor of *quiet*. Both unabridged

dictionaries corroborate that the form is chiefly British.

**quip, quipped.** Often criticized as used in newspapers, either to characterize as a quip a remark that possesses no perceptible humor, or to nudge the reader in the ribs. An example of the first: "*This street has gone to hell," the mayor quipped;* and an example of the second: *The actress gave her age as thirty-seven, but later quipped to newsmen, "Confidentially, I'm fifty-seven."* This applies to *gag, gagged,* and *crack, cracked* (as a clipped form of *wisecrack, -ed*).

**quite.** The word may mean either *entirely, wholly, altogether;* or *somewhat, to a considerable degree.* Both senses are considered standard by both unabridged dictionaries; Bernstein and Copperud regard the second as colloquial. The second sense now seems predominant, Copperud and American Heritage agree, and its Usage Panel approves it. *Quite all right* is criticized by Fowler as a redundancy but defended uncertainly, on differing grounds, by Bernstein and Evans; American Heritage approves of it. *Quite a,* as in *quite a few, quite a little,* is found to be well established informally by Bryant and Bernstein, and defended as good English by Fowler; both American Heritage and Random House regard it as standard.

**quiz.** Bernstein and Fowler object to the use of the term, which occurs principally in headlines, to describe a formal interrogation of some kind, as in legal proceedings; Random House gives *a questioning,* but

Webster does not recognize *quiz* as a noun in this sense. Yet both Random House and Webster give *to quiz suspects* (by the police). The American Heritage panel accepts the noun and rejects the verb, both by narrow margins.

**Quotation. 1.** Bernstein, Copperud, and Flesch protest against the excessive and meaningless use of quotation marks, which is most conspicuous in newspaper writing, to set off informal expressions or slang. Just as often they are ignorantly placed around words used in standard senses. Examples: *Some "swapping" may be necessary; Winston Churchill once gave Basic English a "plug" over the radio; The professor is likely to "hedge" in his answers on this subject.* The consensus is that if the writer finds it to his purpose to use slang or colloquialisms, he should do so forthrightly, without the apology indicated by quotation marks. And in any event it would be well to ascertain whether what the writer suspects is slang is not really a standard term, like *hedge* in the last example.

**2.** Bernstein, Copperud, and Follett criticize the annoying and usually meaningless practice known as fragmentary quotation, also endemic in newspapers. This consists in breaking back and forth between indirect and direct quotation in the same sentence, for no perceptible reason. Example: *The secretary of the treasury told Congress today that the nation "will get into serious difficulty" if the present tax burden "is continued over a long period."*

Either the whole sentence should have formed a direct quotation, or the quotation marks should have been removed altogether to make one continuous indirect quotation. This criticism is not aimed at fragmentary quotation that is skillfully employed to give the sense of a long passage by combining a portion of it with indirect quotation, for the sake of brevity.

**3.** A fault that has been called wrong person in quotation is pointed out by Bernstein and Copperud. An example: "In point of fact," the historian remarked, "he couldn't bear to go—he was too immersed in the production of his fourteenth book." Since, as the context made clear, the historian was referring to himself, *he* should have been *I;* the writer was hopelessly mired between indirect and direct quotation. Another example, with the mixture of direct and indirect quotation that is more likely to show this fault: *Stevens said he "feels in his heart that the responsibility was entirely his."* Either dispense with the quotation marks, making the sentence an indirect quotation, or use first-person forms within the quotation marks, since the reference was to Stevens.

**4.** Copperud, Evans, and American Heritage agree that the comma and the period go inside quotation marks, and the colon and semicolon outside. Fowler favors placing the comma and the period outside. This is a matter, in general, of the difference between American and British printing practice. Almost universally in America the quotation marks go outside the comma and period. See also ATTRIBUTION 5.

**quote, quotes.** *Quote* for *quotation* ("He interpolated a quote from Shakespeare") is deplored by Bernstein, Follett, Fowler, and American Heritage, but considered standard by both unabridged dictionaries.

*Quotes* for *quotation marks* is regarded by Bernstein and Fowler as acceptable only as a technical term in the printing and publishing fields; Copperud believes the convenience of the clipped form is irresistible;

Random House accepts *quote mark* and Webster accepts both *quote* and *quote mark* in this sense.

*Quoted* for *quoted as saying,* as in *"There was no connection between that charge and my administration,"* the President *was quoted,* is denounced by Bernstein but considered acceptable by Copperud.

**quoth.** Regarded by Flesch and Fowler as archaic (a judgment in which Random House and Webster concur) and thus unsuitable to a modern context.

# R

**rabbit, rarebit.** See WELSH RABBIT, RAREBIT.

**rack, wrack.** Evans and Follett regard either *rack and ruin* or *wrack and ruin* as correct; Fowler chooses *rack and ruin.* The versions are considered interchangeable by Random House. In general it is agreed that *wrack* means *wreck* and *rack* means *stretch* or *strain.* By this reasoning (Bernstein, Evans, and Follett), the phrase is *nerve-racking* (not *-wracking*). Dictionaries give both forms but regard *-racking* as predominant. Since a rack is a frame, clothes hangers and the instrument of torture are *rack.*

**racket, racquet.** The first is considered preferable for the bat used in tennis and other games by Copperud, Evans, and Fowler. *Racquet,* however, is not wrong; Random House and Webster consider the terms

interchangeable in this sense. Bernstein and Evans warn against the jocular use of *racket* to describe legitimate occupations or businesses, since its standard meaning in this sense is *an illegal activity.*

**railroad, railway.** The second is seldom used in Britain; the terms are more or less interchangeable in the U.S. (Evans, Fowler). Random House and Webster indicate that *railway* is applied to the tracks, but *railroad* is not, and that as applied to the system *railway* designates a shorter line and lighter equipment.

**raise, rear, rise.** At one time it was earnestly argued that children are *reared,* animals *raised.* Bernstein, Bryant, Copperud, Evans, and Fowler, however, regard *raise* in reference to children as now standard, a judgment concurred in by American Heritage, Random House, and Webster.

For an increase in pay, the word is *raise* in America and *rise* (though *raise* is winning acceptance) in Britain (Bernstein, Bryant, Copperud, Evans, Fowler, American Heritage, though Bryant surprisingly reports a considerable incidence of *rise* in this sense in the U.S.).

*Raise* is transitive (that is, it requires an object, as in *raise the window*); *rise* is intransitive. Thus such constructions as "The curtain will soon raise" are wrong. *rise* (Bernstein, Copperud, and, by a narrow margin, American Heritage).

**raison d'être.** Since this French phrase translates *reason for existence*, it is pretentious and wrong where only *reason* is called for (Evans, Fowler).

**rambunctious.** Accepted as standard by American Heritage, Random House, and Webster.

**rampage.** A stereotype of journalism in reference to flooding; rivers are almost invariably said to *go on a rampage*, just as forest fires *blacken acres*, storms *pack winds*, and snow and rain are described as *dumped*. See also JOURNALESE.

**rara avis.** Flesch and Fowler disapprove of the phrase (Latin for *rare bird*) for *rarity*.

**rarebit.** See WELSH RAREBIT.

**rarefy.** *Rarify* is likely to be regarded as a misspelling; only Webster gives it as a variant.

**rarely ever.** Considered established colloquial idiom by Bryant; rejected by American Heritage. Preferable: *rarely*, or *rarely if ever*.

**rate.** As a verb in the sense *deserve* ("This letter rates a reply") rejected by American Heritage, not recognized by Random House, but considered standard by Webster, which quotes *Harper's;* in the sense *have rank, influence, position* ("She really rates around here") rejected by American Heritage but considered standard by Random House and Webster.

**rather.** The use of the term in the sense *somewhat* (which is misused in the same way) and coupled with strong, affirmative adjectives, as in *rather astonishing, rather amazing, rather superb* is criticized as illogical and as watering down the effect by Copperud, Flesch, Follett, and Fowler. The same is true of *somewhat, pretty, slightly,* etc. *Had rather* and *would rather* are defended as idiomatic by Bryant, Evans, Follett, Fowler, and American Heritage.

**rattle.** For *unnerve* ("The accusation rattled him"), approved by American Heritage and considered standard by Random House and Webster.

**ravage, ravish.** Sometimes confused. To ravage is to damage or destroy; to ravish is to rape, abduct, or enchant (Bernstein, Copperud, Follett). A building may be ravaged by fire; a woman may be ravished, ravishing, or ravaged (ordinarily by age).

**re.** This Latin term for *concerning, in reference to* is inappropriate in ordinary contexts and best left to legal documents (Bernstein, Copperud, Evans, Flesch, Fowler). This applies also to *in re* (*in* *the matter of*). *Re* is not an abbreviation and thus does not take a period.

**re-.** The prefix is generally solid, even when followed by *e: redo, retell, reelect* (Copperud, Fowler). Care should be exercised in distinguishing, by use of the hyphen, such pairs as *recreation* (*amusement*) and *re-creation* (*creation again*), *recollect* (*remember*) and *re-collect* (*collect again*) (Copperud, Follett, Fowler).

**reaction.** Bernstein, Evans, Flesch, Follett, and Fowler object to *reaction* in place of *opinion, reply, response, feeling,* and the like: "What was the reaction to the charge?" *response.* In general, their view is that *reaction* is primarily a technical term belonging to science, and is not properly applicable to people. Nevertheless, Random House gives *the nation's reaction to the President's speech* and Webster gives *her reaction to the news.*

**readjust.** See EUPHEMISMS.

**real.** *Real* for *really* ("I was real tired") is considered colloquial and unsuitable in writing by Bryant, Copperud, Evans, and Fowler. Random House and Webster consider *real* as an adverb informal. *Real* for *serious,* to provide an unnecessary emphasis, as in *real trouble, real danger,* is considered objectionable by Evans and Fowler. It is questionable, however, whether *real* in such contexts is not intended to mean *actual* as contrasted with *supposed* or *imaginary,* in which event the usage is not open to question.

**real facts.** See FACT, FACTS.

**realistic.** This descriptive and its opposite, *unrealistic,* are often misused, in the opinion of Copperud, Follett, and Fowler, not in reference to realism, but to mean *true, correct, sensible, acceptable,* etc., indicating approval or disapproval, as for example in collective bargaining, when one side describes its own proposals as realistic and the other side's proposals as unrealistic. Random House, however, gives *practical* as one definition, and Webster gives *not impractical.* See also EUPHEMISMS.

**realtor.** .The term was invented and registered as a trademark by the National Association of Real Estate Boards in 1916. In observance of this proprietorship, it should properly be capitalized and applied only to members of the organization. Its convenience in place of *real estate agent,* however, has caused it to be widely and indiscriminately used. Random House recognizes only the proprietary sense; Webster also recognizes the general sense of *real estate agent.* Owners of trademarks can protect their proprietary interest by exertions to inform the public about them (usually by means of advertisements aimed at the editors of newspapers and magazines, and also by writing remonstrative letters to those who have misused the trademarks). But the owner has no other recourse against a publication that has used a trademark improperly. The proprietary interest in some trademarks has been lost for want of effort to preserve it. Among these are *zipper, aspirin, milk of magnesia,* and *shredded wheat.*

**rear.** See RAISE, REAR, RISE.

**reason is because.** This common expression, in place of *reason is that,* is denounced as redundant by Bernstein, Copperud, Follett, Fowler, and American Heritage, and defended as standard and idiomatic, despite frequent criticism, by Bryant, Evans, and Flesch. The score here is 5 to 3, with the edge for *reason is that.* See also SIMPLE REASON.

**reason why.** Rejected as redundant by American Heritage, but defended by Evans as having been standard English idiom for centuries. Evans adds, "As a rule, it is better to be natural than to be correct according to theories that other people have never heard of."

**receipt, recipe.** In America, *recipe* has displaced *receipt* for the cooking formula (Copperud, Evans).

**recipient.** Disapproved as pretentious in such constructions as "He was the recipient of an award" (for "He received an award") by Flesch and Fowler.

**reckon.** Regarded now as dialectal or rustic in the senses *guess, suppose, consider* (as distinguished from *calculate*), though it has respectable literary precedent (Bernstein, Evans, Fowler). The unabridged dictionaries concur in this judgment.

**recollect, re-collect.** *Re-collect* (*collect again*) should be distinguished by the hyphen from *recollect* (*recall, remember*) (Evans, Fowler). See also RE-; REMEMBER, RECOLLECT.

**record.** *All-time, new high,* or even *new* is usually redundant with *record* in reference to an unprecedented level of achievement; therefore, *set a record,* not *new, new high,* etc., *record* (Bernstein, Copperud).

**recourse, resource.** The usual confusion is using *resource* for *recourse* in the set phrase *have recourse*: "When he needed encouragement, he had recourse (not *resource*) to liquor" (Evans, Fowler).

**recreate, re-create.** The hyphen is necessary to distinguish *recreate* (*amuse, divert*) from *re-create* (*create again*), and especially *recreation* from *re-creation* (Evans, Follett, Random House, Webster).

**recrudescence.** Fowler holds that the term should be used only concerning the renewed breaking out of something that is objectionable, such as disease; Evans argues that in the U.S. *recrudescence* is neutral, and means simply *a renewed breaking out.* Thus it may be applied to what is desirable. Random House defines the term neutrally, while Webster holds to Fowler's view, and opinion is divided. It is likely that some connotation of undesirability attaches to the term in the popular mind.

**recur, reoccur.** Bernstein sees a distinction between these forms to the effect that *reoccur* suggests a single repetition. Neither unabridged dictionary recognizes this difference, however; Copperud and Evans regard the forms *reoccur, reoccurrence* as superfluous, and the Concise Oxford Dictionary does not even list them. Nor does any American desk dictionary. The consensus is that *recur, recurrence* are preferred, and that in any event the two forms mean the same thing.

**redhead, redheaded.** Some newspaper stylebooks forbid the use of these terms to describe people having red hair. The prohibition is ignorant and quixotic, since all dictionaries recognize this application as standard.

**Redundancy.** Discussion of this rhetorical fault (using more words than are necessary), together with similar failings, are to be found in Copperud under this heading, in Evans under *Redundancy* and *Verbiage,* in Follett under *Pleonasm, Tautology,* and *Verbiage,* and in Fowler under *Tautology.* Perhaps the best explanation of why redundancy is objectionable was given by William Strunk Jr. in *The Elements of Style:* "A sentence should contain no unnecessary words, a paragraph no unnecessary sentences, for the same reason that a drawing should have no unnecessary lines and a machine no unnecessary parts."

**refer.** See ALLUDE, REFER.

**Reflexives.** It is a common error to set off reflexive pronouns with commas: "I, myself, am in complete charge." *I myself am in.* . . . See also MYSELF; COMMA 4; SELF.

**reform, re-form.** The hyphen is necessary to distinguish between *reform* (*correct*) and *reform* (*form again*) (Follett, Fowler, Random House, Webster).

**refute.** To *refute* is to *destroy by argument,* or *prove to be false or mistaken.* The word is often misused for *deny, contradict, reject, rebut, dispute.* A statement, for example, is not refuted simply by saying it is not so; evidence must be presented that effectively demolishes it for refutation to take place. To test whether *refute* is called for, substitute *disprove* (Bernstein, Copperud, Evans, Fowler, Random House, Webster).

**regard.** *With regard to, in regard to, regarding,* and *as regards* should be avoided where *about, on, concerning* will do: "He spoke to us with regard to the ceremonial." *about* (Copperud, Evans, Flesch, Follett, Fowler). The same reasoning applies to *relating to, relative to, in relation to. Regards* is wrong for *regard* in the first two phrases given above (Copperud, Evans, American Heritage). *Regard* takes *as:* "He was regarded as a failure," not *regarded a failure* (Copperud, Evans, Follett, Fowler, American Heritage, Random House, Webster). American Heritage rejects *in some regards* in favor of *in some respects.* See also AS. American Heritage approves *as regards* (apart from questions of succinctness) though conceding it is sometimes criticized.

**regrettable, regretful.** Sometimes confused; what is regrettable causes regret; *regretful,* applied to people, means *feeling regret.* Thus the thunderstorm that spoils the picnic is *regrettable,* not *regretful.* The distinction applies equally to the adverbial forms *regrettably* and *regretfully* (Bernstein, Evans, Flesch, Fowler).

**rehabilitate.** Follett insists that the word applies properly only to people (e.g., criminals), and not to things, but this view is not taken by either Random House or Webster. Follett's position appears to be supported by the definitions in American Heritage, but it seems untenable in view of the widespread application of the word to urban redevelopment.

**reinforce, re-enforce.** *Reinforce* predominates in the sense *strengthen* (Copperud, Evans, Fowler, Random House, Webster).

**relating to.** See REGARD.

**relation, relative.** Interchangeable in the sense *kinsman*, though there is an edge of preference for *relative* (Bernstein, Copperud, Evans, Fowler; the unabridged dictionaries give the terms as equivalents).

**Relative Clauses, Pronouns.** See RESTRICTIVE AND NONRESTRICTIVE CLAUSES; ELLIPSIS.

**relatively.** See COMPARATIVELY, RELATIVELY.

**relict.** Evans and Fowler say that the word (meaning *widow*) is not now in common use except in legal papers. This is corroborated by Random House, which calls it archaic; Webster gives it as current.

**remainder.** See BALANCE.

**remediable, remedial.** Sometimes confused. What is remediable is open to remedy: "A weedy lawn is remediable." What is remedial does the rem-

edying: "Weedkillers are remedial" (Evans, Follett).

**remember, recollect.** Evans, Fowler, Random House, and Webster hold that *recollect* implies an effort to bring to mind, and that *remember* denotes what is effortless or spontaneous. Both unabridged dictionaries, however, also give *remember* as a synonym of *recollect*.

**remind.** The verb is transitive, which means it must take an object. Thus such uses as "Taxes will be due April 1, the collector reminds" are wrong (Bernstein, Copperud; both unabridged dictionaries give *remind* as transitive, and so does American Heritage).

**remittance.** Considered pretentious where *money, payment* will do (Evans, Flesch). "The remittance for the books may be sent later." *payment.*

**remunerate.** Pretentious where *pay* will do (Copperud, Evans, Flesch, Fowler). Sometimes misspelled *renumerate*.

**renaissance, renascence.** Although they are synonyms and generally interchangeable, usage has pretty well settled on *renaissance* for the great revival of learning and things associated with it, and on *renascence* for rebirth in general (Copperud, Evans, Fowler). Webster concurs with this; Random House gives the forms as interchangeable, though it regards *renaissance* as predominant.

**render.** Considered pretentious for *sing* or *play* (*render a selection*) (Copperud, Evans).

**rendition.** Approved by American Heritage for *per-*

*formance (her rendition of the song)*, as distinguished from or not necessarily including *interpretation*, and considered standard by Webster; Random House does not give this sense.

**renege.** *Renege on*, in the sense *go back on* ("She reneged on her promise"), is approved by American Heritage and considered standard by Random House and Webster.

**renowned.** The correct form of the adjective; often erroneously given *renown*, which is noun or verb: "By 1926, he had become a renown pianist." *renowned*. Not even Webster, which is hospitable to many once erroneous usages, recognizes this one. *Renown* and *renowned* are sometimes misspelled *reknown, reknowned*.

**reoccur.** See RECUR.

**repast.** Considered quaint or pretentious for *meal, dinner,* etc. (Copperud, Evans, Flesch).

**repel, repulse.** To repel is to cause aversion, drive or force back, keep at arm's length; *repulse* also means *drive back,* and is the stronger term. The usual error is to associate *repulse* with *repulsive,* but there is no relation here. One may be *repelled* (not *repulsed*) by an idea; a suitor may be *repulsed* (Bernstein, Evans; Random House and Webster give the terms as synonyms).

**repellent, repulsive.** Both mean causing aversion, but the second is much stronger (Evans, Fowler). It is difficult to deduce this from the dictionary definitions, however, which appear to make the terms equivalents. Both Random House

and Webster give the variant spelling *repellant*.

**repertoire, repertory.** More or less interchangeable in the sense of compositions, plays, etc., available for performance, though the first is usually used for this meaning, especially in reference to music: "Her threadbare repertoire included only a few arias." *Repertory,* as both noun and adjective, is favored in connection with the theater in other senses than that described above, as *a small repertory house* (Copperud, Evans, Fowler). Random House and Webster appear to concur in general, though they give the terms as synonyms.

**Repetition.** Discussions of the repetition of words or sounds or both are to be found under that heading in Copperud, Evans, Flesch, and Fowler; Fowler's is by far the most circumstantial examination of the fault. The essence of their views is that while repetition is undesirable, conspicuous efforts to avoid it are worse. This subject is closely related to VARIATION, which see; see also ELLIPSIS.

**replace.** The word has two common senses, which must be carefully differentiated: *put back into place,* and *succeed* or *substitute for.* Thus the word may be ambiguous; unless the context makes the meaning clear, "The king was replaced on the throne" may be taken to mean he was put back or someone else was substituted (Copperud, Evans, Fowler). See also SUBSTITUTE, REPLACE.

**replete.** Evans and Fowler say the word does not mean *complete* or *filled with,* but only *abundantly supplied with.* Both unabridged dictionaries give both senses, however.

**replica.** To begin with, the term has a technical meaning in the fine arts: an exact copy by the maker of the original. This is so specialized, however, that the layman is unlikely to be aware of it, though Bernstein and Fowler will admit no other use for the word. Copperud says that the commonest misuse is in the sense of *model* or *miniature;* Evans regards *replica* for *copy* as loose. Both unabridged dictionaries give *copy* or *reproduction* as one meaning of *replica,* however, and the American Heritage panel also accepts it. This is the consensus. *Exact replica* is redundant.

**reportedly.** Although acknowledging its recognition by dictionaries, Follett deplores *reportedly* on grounds that are difficult to credit. Copperud defends it as useful in journalism, and both unabridged dictionaries consider it standard. It is, however, a relatively new term. Webster II relegated it to the limbo it maintained for questionable terms at the bottom of the page.

**represent.** Follett and Flesch object to the displacement of *is, are,* by *represent:* "The figure represents half his income." *is.*

**repulse.** See REPEL, REPULSE.

**repulsive.** See REPELLENT, REPULSIVE.

**require.** Objected to by Flesch and Follett where *want* or *need* will do.

**reside.** Regarded by Copperud, Evans, and Flesch as pretentious where *live* will do.

**resin, rosin.** *Rosin* is not, as is sometimes supposed, an error for *resin;* rosin is a distilled solid form of resin used to make the bows of string instruments tacky, among other purposes (Copperud, Evans, Fowler, Random House, Webster).

**resistance.** Sometimes misspelled *resistence.*

**respect.** See IN RESPECT TO.

**respective, respectively.** Often used unnecessarily: "They returned to their respective homes." The reader will not otherwise assume that they returned to each other's homes. The words should not be called into play unless there is a need for sorting out: "Mrs. Jones and Mrs. Smith selected carnations and snapdragons, respectively," which matches the women with the flowers in the order given. Words like *former, latter* (which see), as well as *respective, -ly,* which oblige the reader to match things up, are to be avoided. Sometimes used unnecessarily: "Shavers big and small will thus get a chance to compare the respective blades." No need for *respective.* The test is to leave out *respective, -ly* and observe whether the sense is affected (Copperud, Evans, Flesch, Follett, Fowler).

**responsible.** The applicability of the word to things as well as to people is approved by American Heritage: "Inattention was responsible for his ignorance." Webster apparently concurs, though it is not entirely explicit on this point; Random House explicitly concurs.

**rest.** See BALANCE.

**restaurateur.** The awareness that this word does not contain an *n* was once regarded in newspaper offices as distinguishing the seasoned reporter from the cub. Webster now admits *restauranteur* as a variant but no other dictionary does.

**restive.** Evans, Follett, and Fowler hold that the word can only mean *resistant to control* (a dog on a leash or a horse in a corral thus might be restive) and that the sense *restless* is wrong. Nevertheless, Random House gives *restless* and Webster gives *fidgety*. It is obvious here that popular misuse has added another sense.

**Restrictive and Nonrestrictive Clauses.** Failure to distinguish these by proper punctuation may mislead the reader as to the meaning intended or may result in ambiguity. Restrictive and nonrestrictive clauses are relative clauses, which means that ordinarily they begin with *which, that, when, where, who, whose,* or *whom.* A restrictive clause is one whose meaning is essential to the sentence; that is, it defines the subject of the main clause: "I waved at the girl who was standing on the corner." The same clause may be made nonrestrictive by being set off by commas: "I waved at the girl, who was standing on the corner." The girl in this example must have been previously identified. The example illustrates, too, that whether a clause is restrictive or nonrestrictive may depend on the writer's intention. Relative clauses depending on proper names ("He next performed in Chicago, where he was well received") are invariably nonrestrictive, except in the rare case where the purpose is to distinguish between two places or persons having the same name. Very frequently the comma in such sentences, when there is no question whether the clause is nonrestrictive, is omitted, even in generally well-edited publications. It is impossible to say whether this reflects ignorance of what is considered correct punctuation, or a feeling by the writer that the clause could not be understood as restrictive and thus the comma is superfluous. In the most carefully edited material, however, the comma is used to set off nonrestrictive modifiers.

Restrictive clauses are essential to the meaning and are never set off; nonrestrictive clauses are not essential, but merely descriptive or additive, and are always set off. The *whose*-clause in "No woman whose clothes make her conspicuous is well dressed" is inescapably restrictive, since the sentence no longer makes sense if it is dropped. An example of ambiguity caused by failure to punctuate correctly: "The rule exempts commercial lots where there is no restriction on all-night parking." The writer intended to convey that commercial lots are unaffected because they do not restrict all-night parking, but by omitting the comma before *where* gave the impression that the rule affects only commercial lots where there is no restriction on all-night parking (Copperud, Evans). See also THAT 4; APPOSITIVES.

**reticent.** The word sometimes displaces *reluctant* ("He said so many actors come to Hollywood that he was a little reticent to do so." The word usually means *disposed to keep silent;* it may also mean restrained in general, as in speaking of a reticent piece of writing, or a reticent musical performance. Neither Random House nor Webster gives any definition that justifies the use of the word in the sense *reluctant,* as in the sentence quoted.

**retire.** Evans and Fowler consider *retire* pretentious for *go to bed.*

**reveal.** See ATTRIBUTION 2.

**Revelations.** Evans and Fowler both consider this form acceptable in casual reference to *The Revelation of St. John.* Random House also sanctions this usage but Webster does not give it.

**Reverend.** Strictly speaking, an adjective meaning *deserving of reverence.* Bernstein, Evans, and Follett prescribe the forms *the Reverend John Jones* (*the* plus the first name) and *the Reverend Mr. Smith* (*the* plus *Mr.* with the last name alone). In addition to these forms, Copperud, Evans, and American Heritage also accept *Reverend John Jones* (omitting *the* with the first name). Evans and Copperud accept *Reverend* with the last name alone—*Reverend Jones*—and they accept *reverend* as a noun: "The reverend was standing on the porch." Both Random House and Webster also admit this usage as standard. Bernstein and Fowler will not permit

the plural forms *the Reverends Smith and Jones;* either the *Reverend Smith and Jones* or *the Reverend Smith and the Reverend Jones.*

**Reversal of Sense.** See NEGATIVES; DOUBLE NEGATIVE; NOT . . . NOT; NOT UN-.

**review, revue.** *Revue* is preferred for the stage performance, *review* in other senses, including reports on books, concerts, etc. (Copperud, Evans, Random House).

**revision (upward, downward).** See EUPHEMISMS.

**Rhyme.** As a fault in prose, see JINGLES. See also RIME, RHYME.

**rid.** The preferred form for the past tense and present participle is *rid* rather than *ridded,* though both are correct: "He rid the lawn of crabgrass last week"; "We rid the closet of moths" (Evans, Fowler, Random House, Webster).

**right.** In the sense of *very much,* or *greatly,* or *much, right* is not now standard: "We were right surprised" (Copperud, Evans, Fowler; neither Random House nor Webster even gives the sense). See also IN (HIS, HER) OWN RIGHT.

**rile.** For *anger, annoy* ("The inattention in the classroom riled him") approved by American Heritage and considered standard by Random House and Webster.

**rime, rhyme.** *Rhyme* is preferred in the sense *identity of sound* (Copperud, Evans, Fowler, Random House, Webster).

**ring.** The past form *rung* ("He rung the bell") is standard, but *rang* is preferred, Evans, Random House, and Webster agree; Evans and American Heritage consider *rung* nonstandard.

**rise.** See RAISE, REAR, RISE.

**rob.** What is robbed is the person or place from which something is taken, not the thing itself; thus a bank is robbed, but not the money that is stolen. This is the view of Bernstein, Evans, and Random House, but Webster quotes Dryden, "rob the honey." This, however, may be archaic, since Webster's treatment otherwise conforms with the limitation set by the others.

**robber, robbery.** See BURGLARY.

**rock, stone.** *Rock* generally connotes large size and *stone* small size, but *rock* is often used of what may be thrown: "They threw rocks at the squirrels" (Copperud, Evans). Random House gives for *rock* "a stone of any size" and Webster gives "ranging in size from a boulder to a pebble."

**role.** Evans and Fowler recommend dispensing with the circumflex and italics (*rôle*) and accepting the term as fully naturalized English. Both dictionaries also indicate this preference. *Role* is sometimes used when *roll* is meant (*relief roles*); though as Fowler notes, the words have the same origin, differentiation is now fully established.

**rooftop.** Bernstein asperses the term, asking what it means. Both unabridged dictionaries and some smaller ones give it as standard for *roof*. Though American Heritage asked its Usage Panel's opinions on this expression, the word was omitted from the dictionary.

**Roman Catholic.** See CATHOLIC.

**Roman Numerals.** Their use is discouraged by Copperud and Flesch.

**romance.** In the sense *make love* ("They were romancing in the moonlight"), considered nonstandard by Copperud and Evans, but this judgment may be outdated. Webster recognizes the sense as standard, and Random House gives "to think or talk romantically," and American Heritage gives "woo" as informal.

**rosin.** See RESIN, ROSIN.

**round.** The apostrophe (*'round*) is not required in such expressions as *the year round* (Bernstein, Evans, Flesch). Random House and Webster concur. See also ALL-AROUND.

**row.** The use of the word for *dispute,* especially in headlines, to describe serious differences, for example in international relations, is criticized by Bernstein and Evans. It is accepted as standard by both Random House and Webster, however, for *noisy dispute* or *quarrel.*

**rung.** See RING.

# S

s, 's, s'. See POSSESSIVES.

**Sabbath.** Not necessarily Sunday; to Jews and Seventh-day Adventists it is Saturday, and to Mohammedans it is Friday (Copperud, Evans).

**sabotage.** Evans and Fowler insist that the word should be used figuratively *(sabotage the legislation)* only when it is intended to imply malice, not simply obstruction, destruction, etc. Random House, however, gives "any undermining of a cause" and Webster gives "any act or process tending to hamper or hurt"; these broader definitions are among others.

**sacrilegious.** Often misspelled *sacreligious* through a mistaken connection with *religious* (Copperud, Evans, Fowler).

**Sahara Desert.** Though *Sahara* means *desert* in Arabic, and thus *Sahara Desert* is technically redundant, Copperud and Evans agree that there is no point in proscribing it. American Heritage concedes *Sahara Desert* is widely used but calls *Sahara* or *the Sahara* preferable.

**said.** Described by Copperud and Fowler as legalese in the sense *aforesaid, aforementioned: the said editor; said contractor;* American Heritage and Random House concur that its use is chiefly in legal connections. Thus the term is to be avoided in ordinary writing. Almost always the definite article *(the)* suffices in reference to what has already been specified. "The editor of the local newspaper, together with members of clergy, refused to take a position in the controversy. Said editor would not give his reason, however." *The editor.* See also SAY, SAID; ATTRIBUTION.

**sake.** Evans and Fowler agree that in such expressions as *for goodness sake, for conscience sake,* and others where the word preceding *sake* ends in a sibilant, it may be written without an apostrophe and should be written without *'s.* Webster, however, gives *goodness' sake.*

**salad days.** Criticized by Evans and Fowler as a cliché.

**saloon.** Once the general designation for what is now commonly called a bar or cocktail lounge, but it is now considered disreputable, as a result of the campaign conducted against such places before Prohibition (Copperud, Evans). In New York the designation is illegal.

**same, the same.** *Same* as a pronoun displacing *it, they, them* ("He collected the money and deposited same"; "The publication will be mailed regularly and costs for same will be charged to member organizations") is not good usage (Copperud, Evans, Flesch, Follett, Fowler, American Heritage).

239

Evans and Follett agree that either *as* or *that* may be used after *same* as an adjective: *the same thing as (that) I heard.* See also SUCH.

**sanatorium, sanitarium, sanitorium.** Bernstein, Copperud, and Evans agree that the first two are generally interchangeable forms today, though at one time the distinction was made that the first was more of a health resort and the second more of a hospital. *Sanitorium* is regarded by Evans and Fowler as an error, though Webster recognizes it, together with *sanatarium,* as an alternative spelling. Random House gives the original distinction, but also gives *sanatorium* and *sanitarium* as synonyms. It does not recognize *sanitorium* or *sanatarium. Sanatorium* appears to be the predominant general-purpose form.

**sanction.** Attention is called by Evans, Follett, and Fowler to the fact that in ordinary connections, *sanction* means *permission, approval* ("The administration gave its sanction to the wage increase") but that in international relations, sanctions are penalties or deterrents ("Sanctions were voted against the aggressor").

**sanctum, sanctum sanctorum.** Criticized as clichés in ordinary use in the sense *private place* by Flesch and Evans.

**sank.** See SINK.

**sans.** Objected to by Flesch and Fowler as a pretentious displacement of *without.*

**Santa Ana, santana (winds).** *Santa Ana* is the correct name for the strong, hot, dry foehn wind from the north, northeast, or east in Southern California, Copperud, Random House, and Webster agree; the designation comes from the mountain range and canyon through which they are channeled. *Santa Ana* is also the form sanctioned by the U.S. Weather Bureau. It is sometimes said that the term should be *santana,* from a supposed Indian word for *devil wind,* but anthropologists say no such word existed.

**sartorial.** Objected to by Flesch and Fowler as pretentious.

**satisfied.** Although the word can mean *convinced,* Evans and Fowler warn against using it in contexts where the meaning *content* may be ambiguously understood: "The police were satisfied that no one could have survived the crash."

**savant.** Objected to by Copperud and Flesch as a random variant for *scientist, professor, scholar, expert.*

**save.** *Save* for *except* ("All save the fisherman had departed") is regarded as affected by Bernstein, Copperud, Evans, Flesch, and Fowler; all but Evans comment that this usage is commonly an attempt to pretty up newspaper writing. See also POESY.

**saving, savings.** As a modifier in such connections as *savings bank, savings bond,* the plural form is required. *Savings* as a noun requires a plural verb: "His savings were disappearing." The corollary, as pointed out by American Heritage, is that one may not properly speak of *a savings of five dollars (a saving).* The correct form is *daylight-saving* (not *savings*) *time* (Bernstein, Copperud, Evans, Random House, Webster).

**say, said.** Bernstein, Copperud, Fowler, and Flesch all criticize the mannerism, oftenest seen in newspapers, of seeking variety by displacing *said* in favor of conspicuous and often inexact variants. Some of them are *affirm, assert, declare, asseverate, state, contend, insist, emphasize, avow, aver, claim.* See ATTRIBUTION 4 for a discussion of the tricky displacement of *said* by *grimaced, smiled, frowned,* etc.; see also QUOTATION.

**scan.** For *look through hastily* (*scan the newspapers*), approved by American Heritage and considered standard by Random House and Webster. American Heritage makes the useful point that the context should show that another sense of the word, *examine minutely,* is not meant.

**scarce, scarcely.** *Scarce* as an adverb for *scarcely* ("She was scarce out of her teens") is considered affected by Evans and Fowler. *Scarcely . . . than* (displacing *scarcely . . . when* or *before*) is criticized by Copperud, Evans, Follett, Fowler, and American Heritage: "Scarcely were the words out of his mouth *when* (not *than*) the music began." Bryant considers *scarcely than* informal. Bernstein, Bryant, Copperud, Evans, Fowler, and American Heritage point out that *scarcely* is a negative and should not be used with another negative: *scarcely enough,* not *not scarcely enough.* Sometimes the fault is not so obvious: "It was impossible to see scarcely

anything through the fog." *Impossible* is another negative. See also DOUBLE NEGATIVE; HARDLY; NEGATIVES.

**sceptic.** See SKEPTIC, SCEPTIC.

**scholar.** The term is no longer applied to schoolboys like the ten o'clock scholar, but rather is reserved for specialists at universities and the like who are deep in their subjects (Copperud, Evans, Follett, Fowler; Random House and Webster, however, give also *student, pupil*).

**Scientific English.** The practice of inappropriately using technical terminology and of attempting to impress the reader by using longer or more difficult expressions than are necessary is dealt with by Bernstein under *Inside Talk,* by Copperud under *Technical Terms,* by Evans under *Scientific English,* by Follett under *Popularized Technicalities* and *Scientism,* and by Fowler under *Popularized Technicalities.* In general, the advice is to avoid such language when everyday synonyms are available, and when they are not, to explain such technical terms as are used in writing aimed at a general audience.

**scientist.** See ENGINEER, SCIENTIST.

**Scot, Scotch, Scotchman, Scotsman, Scots, Scottish.** All are standard, but the Scots themselves prefer *Scot, Scots, Scottish* for people, and reserve *Scotch* for things (whisky, plaid). They prefer *Scotsman* to *Scotchman* (Copperud, Evans, Fowler, American Heritage).

**scotch.** Follett and Fowler concede that the original meaning of the verb, *put out of action temporarily,* has been supplanted in general use by *kill, destroy, thwart (scotch the snake; scotch the rumor),* but they are reluctant to approve. Random House recognizes both senses, and Webster no longer gives the original meaning.

**scrip, script.** Certificates used in place of money and certain other fiscal documents are known as *scrip,* not *script:* "The workers are paid in scrip" (Copperud, Evans, Fowler, Random House, Webster). *Script* has a number of senses, none of which give difficulty.

**sculp, sculpt, sculpture.** The first two are derogated by Bernstein as back-formations from *sculpture,* an allegation denied by Random House, which says *sculp* comes from the Latin verb *sculpere* and *sculpt* from the French *sculpter.* Copperud, Flesch, Random House and Webster consider *sculpt* the commoner term today. Follett approves only of *sculpture.* All three forms are recognized by the dictionaries as verbs.

**seasonable, seasonal.** What is seasonable comes at the right time or is appropriate to a season; what is seasonal is merely connected with a season. Snow in winter is seasonable; some jobs are seasonal. "The unemployment rate is always seasonably adjusted." *seasonally* (Bernstein, Copperud, Evans, Fowler, American Heritage, Random House, Webster).

**second, secondly.** See FIRST-LY, SECONDLY.

**secure.** Considered pretentious and inexact where *get* or *obtain* will do (Bernstein, Copperud, Evans, Flesch).

**seeing as how.** See AS HOW.

**seem.** See CAN'T SEEM.

**see where.** This common locution ("I see where the Mets won") is rejected by Bernstein, Evans, and American Heritage in favor of *see that.* Nevertheless, it is so firmly established in speech, particularly, that it is unlikely to be dislodged by the more formal *see that.* Partridge also rejects it, though describing it as "astonishingly common."

**seldom ever.** Rejected by Copperud and American Heritage as self-contradictory. Preferable: *seldom, seldom if ever.*

**self.** Not good usage for *I* or *me:* "Please reserve tickets for self and family" (Copperud, Fowler). Random House and Webster, however, consider it standard. See also MYSELF.

**self-.** Bernstein, Follett, and Fowler warn against compounds with *self-* (*self-confessed, self-deprecating, self-conceited,* etc.) when *self-* adds nothing to the meaning. The test to apply is to delete *self-* and see whether anything is lost.

**-self, -selves.** For the usage of words with these terminations (that is, reflexive pronouns) see MYSELF; REFLEXIVES.

**senior, junior.** See JR., SR.

**senior citizen.** Decried as a euphemism by Bernstein, Copperud, Flesch, Follett, and American Heritage. Random House gives it as standard; Webster, curiously, omits it.

**sensational.** Criticized by Bernstein, Evans, and Fowler as overworked.

**sensual, sensuous.** Bernstein, Copperud, Evans, and Fowler agree that when a distinction is made, *sensual* connotes something gross, *sensuous* something refined or intellectual. This view is borne out by Random House and Webster.

**Sequence of Tenses.** A subject with many ramifications, various of which are explored under this heading by Bernstein, Copperud, Follett, and Fowler, and under the heading *Tense Shifts* by Evans. A good deal of wordage is devoted to explaining idiomatic distinctions that are much more likely to be acquired by ear than by precept or example. In any event, many of the points discussed do not correspond and are not susceptible of comparison. Before going further it may be well to say what is ordinarily meant by sequence of tenses. It is that the tense of the verb in the main clause of a sentence usually governs the tense in a subordinate clause; this is sometimes referred to as attracted sequence. An example to illustrate the principle: "He said he was tired of everything." The verb in the main clause, *said,* is in the past tense, so the verb in the dependent clause, *was,* naturally falls into the past tense. Most of the time it is not necessary to stop and think about this relationship.

Bernstein, Copperud, Follett, and Fowler agree, however, that an exception to the rule is called for when the subordinate clause expresses a continuing or timeless fact: "He said the world is round" (rather than *was*); "The surveyor reported that the terrain is (rather than *was*) rugged." Fowler terms this the vivid sequence. It accords with logic, but common sense must be used in applying the exception, as Evans points out: "The ancients believed the world is not round" is palpably absurd; *is* should be *was.*

**Serial Comma.** See COMMA 6.

**service.** The use of *service* as a verb where *serve* will do is criticized by Bernstein, Copperud, Fowler, and American Heritage: "The bus line services the northern suburbs." *serves.* Evans, however, is indulgent toward this use. The critics agree that *service* is useful, if not indispensable, in the sense of providing maintenance to a machine: *service an automobile, a TV set,* etc. This view corresponds in general with the definitions given in Random House and Webster.

**set, sit.** In general, *set* is transitive (takes an object): "Set the package down"; *sit* is usually intransitive (takes no object): "They sit and rock on the porch." *Set* for *sit,* as in "They set on the porch," is not considered standard. There are numerous idiomatic exceptions to these principles, however: a hen *sets,* the sun *sets,* an object may *sit* on another (a book, for example, on a shelf); by the same token, *sit* is sometimes transitive; a rider *sits* a horse, one may *sit* oneself (Bernstein, Bryant, Copperud, Evans, American Heritage).

**sewage, sewerage.** *Sewage* is the waste material, *sewerage* the system used to carry it off or the process of carrying it off, Bernstein, Copperud, and Fowler agree. Evans concurs, but with Random House and Webster accepts *sewerage* as a synonym for *sewage*, and this usage is observably common.

**sex.** Follett disapproves of *sex* in the sense *sexual organs,* as used by Frank Harris in his autobiography, as a French term that is inappropriate in English. The word has also been used this way in the writings of James Baldwin. Neither unabridged dictionary recognizes this sense.

**shake down, shakedown.** In the sense *extort, extortion (a shakedown of customers)* approved by American Heritage and considered standard as verb and noun by Random House and Webster.

**Shakespeare, Shakspere, etc.** Copperud and Fowler agree that *Shakespeare* has indisputably established itself against all its rivals; Random House and Webster consider it predominant.

**shall, will, should, would.** The traditional rule for the use of *shall* and *will* is that to express the simple future, or to indicate a simple intention, *shall* should be used with the first person and *will* with the second and third persons. Examples: "I (we) shall grow old one day"; "You (he, she, it, they) will grow old one day." To express determination or insistence, the pattern is reversed: "I will demand my share, no matter what they

say"; "You shall obey the law like everyone else." In the United States, however, this distinction is almost universally ignored, and *will* is used indiscriminately with all persons to express both the simple future and determination. This is the consensus of Bernstein, Bryant, Copperud, Evans, Flesch, Fowler, and American Heritage; only Follett insists on the traditional usage, which is still observed, more or less, in Britain, though Fowler concedes that the American practice has made enormous inroads there and that insistence on the traditional pattern may soon be considered pedantry.

The same thing applies to *should* and *would. Should* is generally used in the U.S. only in the sense of *ought to* ("We should put the car in the garage before it rains"), and not to discriminate between the first person and the others.

A confused notion of what is right and wrong, or what is sometimes described as overcorrectness, leads to absurd displacement of *will* (where it is called for under the traditional rules) by *shall:* "I look forward to the time when delegates like yourselves shall meet in every country of the world." *will.*

No fewer than twenty pages (in an appendix) are devoted to discussing the ins and outs of *shall, should, will, would* by Follett. It is a complicated subject, but most of the questions that arise in this connection are readily solved by ear, since idiom shows the way. For example, the survival of *shall* in questions: "Shall I answer the phone?" *Will* is impossible here, even to those ignorant or uncaring of grammar, and the prescription of *shall* seems hardly worth making.

**shambles.** The word originally designated benches or stalls where meat was sold, and later a place of carnage. The argument today is whether *shambles* can properly be used to mean a scene of wreckage, or even simply a mess, disregarding any idea of bloodshed. Bernstein and Fowler say no; Copperud, Follett, American Heritage, Random House, and Webster say yes, while Evans gives qualified acceptance.

**sharp.** In reference to time idiom calls for *sharp* as the adverb, not *sharply: At 7 o'clock sharp* (Copperud, Fowler, Random House, Webster).

**she.** Reference to nations as *she* and *her* ("Britain must guard her traditions") is approved by Bernstein and Fowler with certain qualifications excluding incongruities and inconsistencies; American Heritage calls the usage traditional. *It* is preferred by Copperud and Flesch.

**shibboleth.** Originally, a test or password; by extension, a peculiarity distinguishing a sect or group. Flesch, Fowler, and Webster permit the senses *catchword* or *slogan;* Evans and Random House do not.

**shop.** As a transitive verb ("She shopped all the stores in town"), considered questionable by Copperud but accepted as standard by Random House and Webster.

**should, would.** See SHALL, WILL, etc.

**show.** Bernstein considers the term unacceptable in the sense *show up* or *appear:* "Several holders of reserved seats failed to show." Random House considers this usage informal, and Webster regards it as standard.

**showed.** Not incorrect, but rarely used, as a past participle: "We left after they had showed the movies." More commonly, *shown* (Bernstein, Bryant, Evans, Fowler).

**shrink.** *Shrank* predominates for the past tense ("The sweater shrank in the laundry") but *shrunk* is acceptable (Bryant, Evans, Random House, Webster). This is American usage, as Evans and Fowler point out; *shrunk* is now archaic in Britain.

**sibling.** This expression, meaning a brother or sister not a twin, is regarded by Flesch and Fowler as a technical term of anthropology and sociology, unsuitable for ordinary contexts. The criticisms appear to be aimed at its pretentious use when *brother* or *sister* would do.

**sic.** The use of the term (Latin for *so, thus*) should be restricted to assuring the reader that what has gone before is correctly quoted when there is reason to think the reader might question its accuracy, and not to jeer at grammatical errors, to call attention to jokes, nor (in place of quotation marks) to indicate ironical use of a word. *Sic* is often used (correctly) to indicate that a misspelling in quoted material appears in the original (Bernstein, Fowler).

**sick.** In British usage, the term means *sick at one's stomach:* in America, *sick* and *ill* are interchangeable. It is therefore an affectation in the U.S. to restrict *sick* to the sense *nauseated* (Copperud, Evans, Fowler; Random House and Webster both give the general as well as other senses). American Heritage slightly prefers *sick at* to *sick to*. *Sick* for *morbid (sick humor)* is considered standard by American Heritage, Random House, and Webster.

**sideswipe, sidewipe.** The second form is an artificiality (Bernstein, Copperud) and is to be found in neither of the unabridged dictionaries.

**similar.** Copperud and American Heritage point out that the word is often used where *same* or *identical* is called for: "Rice exports through the first seven months of this year were 20 million pounds greater than during a similar (actually, *the same*) period last year." "The cottages are occupied by children of similar age and sex." *the same. Similar* should not be used as an adverb: "The oboe sounds similar to the English horn." *like* (Copperud, Fowler, American Heritage; examples in Random House and Webster corroborate this). See also LIKE, AS.

**simple reason.** *For the simple reason that* is verbose for *because*. There is usually no occasion to point out the simplicity of a reason when this phrase is used; its effect often is to make the reader feel patronized (Bernstein, Copperud).

**simultaneous.** The only point that the American Heritage panel agreed on unanimously was that *simultaneous* may not be used as an adverb: "The ceremony was held simultaneous with the dinner." *simultaneously.* Bernstein, the only one of the writers on usage who took up this point, concurs, as do Random House and Webster.

**since.** It is a delusion that *since* may be used only as an adverb in a temporal sense ("We have been here since ten o'clock"). It is also a causal conjunction meaning *for* or *because:* "Since it is raining, we had better take an umbrella" (Copperud, Follett, Random House, Webster). The perfect tense is called for with *since* in the temporal sense: "He has not returned since he resigned" (not *did not return*), because *since* brings the time referred to up to the moment of speaking (Bernstein, Evans, Follett). See also AS VS. BECAUSE, SINCE; AGO.

**sine qua non.** Ordinary English (e.g., *essential*) is preferable to the Latin phrase (for *without which nothing*) (Evans, Flesch).

**sing.** *Sang* is now preferable to *sung* for the past tense: "She sang a lullaby" (Evans, Fowler).

**Singular and Plural.** See PLURAL AND SINGULAR.

**sink.** The past tense is either *sank* or *sunk:* "The boat sank (sunk) in three fathoms" (Copperud, Evans, Fowler; the dictionaries give *sank* as predominant).

**sir.** The British title is used correctly only with the full name or the first name, never with the last name alone: *Sir Winston Churchill* or *Sir Winston,* never *Sir Churchill* (Copperud, Flesch, Fowler). See also DAME.

**sit.** See SET, SIT.

**situate.** See LOCATE.

**skeptic, sceptic.** The first is the preferred American spelling and the second the British (Copperud, Evans, Fowler, Random House, Webster). Fowler recommends that the British adopt *sk-.*

**skills.** Follett calls *skills* a false plural, but it is recognized as standard by Random House, Webster, and Fowler.

**slander.** See LIBEL, SLANDER.

**Slang.** Discusions of various aspects of slang are to be found under that heading in Evans and Flesch, and under *Jargon* and *Rhyming Slang* in Fowler. See also QUOTATION.

**slash.** Journalese, particularly in reference to prices (Copperud, Evans).

**slate.** Often criticized in journalism (where it is oftenest used, especially in headlines) in the sense *schedule: Conference Slated.* The argument is usually that the word can only mean *berate.* This meaning, in fact, is British, and so the criticism is more or less inapplicable in the U.S. Copperud calls it undeservedly aspersed in the sense *schedule.* Both Random House and Webster give it as standard; all Webster's examples, however, come from news publications, indicating that the word has a journalistic flavor. Though American Heritage asked its panelists for their opinion on

*slate* for *schedule,* that sense is not included in the dictionary.

**slay.** Criticized as overused in newspapers, especially in headlines, by Evans, Flesch, and Fowler.

**sleep the sleep of the just.** Criticized by Evans and Fowler as a cliché.

**slow, slowly.** *Slow* is equally an adjective and an adverb, so that *go slow* is just as correct as *go slowly.* Most of the commentators say that *drive slow* is almost invariable (Bernstein, Copperud, Evans, Fowler, American Heritage; Bryant finds that *slowly* predominates in writing, however.)

**small in size (number).** Redundant; omit *in size, in number.* Similar lapses: *few, large, many in number; rectangular* (etc.) *in shape* (Bernstein, Copperud).

**smell.** Fowler says that *smell* as a verb meaning *give off an odor* should be followed by an adjective, not an adverb: *smell bad, sweet, sour, good;* American Heritage concurs, but inconsistently prescribes *smells disgustingly.* Evans allows *smell sweetly,* which American Heritage disapproves.

**so.** The use of *so* as an intensive meaning *very* ("It's so cold today"; "You're so funny") is considered informal and more suitable to talk than to writing by Bryant, Copperud, and Fowler. Bryant and Copperud say it is often feminine; Fowler regards it as silly. *So* as a conjunction should be followed by *that* ("He got an education so that he could succeed"), Copperud, Fowler, and American Heritage hold;

Evans and Flesch say that the usage omitting *that* is standard. *So that* is at least more formal than *so* alone. See also AS . . . AS; THAT 5.

**so . . . as.** See AS . . . AS, etc.

**so as to.** Considered redundant by Copperud and Flesch: "We took the train (so as) to save time." See also IN ORDER TO; FOR THE PURPOSE OF.

**so far as.** See AS (SO) FAR AS.

**so far from.** Defended by Fowler as an idiom, though illogical, for *far from:* "So far from dominating the field, he finished in last place," but he leaves to the writer a preference for *far from.*

**solicitor general.** See GENERAL.

**solon.** Copperud and Flesch discourage the use of the term, usually found in journalism, for *senator, representative, congressman,* etc.

**so long as.** See AS LONG AS, SO LONG AS.

**some, -odd.** Should be used only with round numbers to indicate an approximation: *some sixty-nine horsemen* is absurd. *Some 70 horsemen.* This is true also of the suffix *-odd:* "Waco is 94-odd miles south of Dallas." If the figure is exact, give it alone; otherwise, *90-odd* or *95-odd.* When any other indication of inexactness is given, as by *about, approximately, estimated,* or the like, either *some* or *-odd* is superfluous. Sometimes the offense is compounded by using both *some* and *-odd: some 70-odd horsemen* (Bernstein, Copperud).

**some, somewhat.** *Somewhat* is preferable in such examples as "He is somewhat better today" (Copperud, Evans, American Heritage; Random House considers this usage informal; Webster gives it as standard). See also RATHER.

**somebody, someone.** With *they, their, them,* see ANYBODY, ANYONE. See also -ONE.

**someplace.** Considered standard in the U.S., despite some criticism that the preferable form is *somewhere,* by Evans, Flesch, Fowler, Random House, and Webster; Bryant calls it colloquial; American Heritage rejects it for writing.

**sometime, some time.** *Some time* is an adverbial phrase meaning *an interval or period:* "He stayed some time" (not *sometime*). *Sometime* is an adverb indicating an indefinite occasion: "He will come sometime, I am sure" (Bernstein, Copperud, American Heritage; the definitions of *sometime* in Random House and Webster substantiate this view). The same distinction applies to *someday, some day.*

**sometimes.** For misuse of the hyphen with *sometimes,* see ALMOST.

**someway.** Considered standard by Random House and Webster but rejected by American Heritage.

**somewhat.** See RATHER.

**somewheres.** Considered unacceptable in writing by Bryant, Copperud, and Evans; Webster calls it chiefly dialectal.

**sooner.** See NO SOONER.

**sophisticated.** The use of this term, which once was ordinarily applicable only to people or their direct expressions, is now standard in the sense of *complex* or *far advanced*, as used to describe mechanical devices or systems (Bernstein, Copperud, Random House, Webster).

**sort.** See KIND.

**sort of.** See discussion of *kind of* under KIND.

**sound out.** Approved by American Heritage for *test opinion* (*sound out the electorate*). Neither Random House nor Webster gives it, which may indicate it is newer than it seems to be.

**Source Attribution.** See ATTRIBUTION.

**Soviet, Soviets.** The use of *Soviet* to mean *Russia,* and of *Soviets* to mean *Russians,* is sometimes criticized in stylebooks. Only the Concise Oxford Dictionary gives the former; Random House and Webster give the latter.

**sox.** Called not standard by Evans, but recognized as such nevertheless by American Heritage, Random House, Webster, and the Standard College Dictionary.

**Spanish.** See MEXICAN, SPANISH.

**spark.** In the sense *cause, prompt* (*sparked a revolt*), approved by American Heritage. Neither Random House nor Webster gives it, which indicates that it must be new; both, however, give a near sense, *kindle enthusiasm: sparked the players to a comeback.* There is little question

that *spark* for *cause* is predominantly journalistic usage.

**spate.** Regarded by Bernstein, Evans, and Flesch as a bookish or vogue word for *sudden flood, rush,* or *outpouring.*

**speak to.** In the sense *speak about, on,* parliamentary jargon that is creeping into general use. *Speak to* means *address* ("I'll speak to Master Rackstraw in the morning") except in the technical sense of commenting on a motion in parliamentary procedure. There seems no warrant, and none is given in any current dictionary, for "Resource leaders at the conference will speak to the theme, 'Waging Peace in Southeast Asia.'" *speak on.*

**special, especial, etc.** See ESPECIAL, etc.

**specie, species.** Often confused. *Specie* is coin: "The payment was made with a combination of specie and paper money." A *species* is a distinct scientific category of animal or plant: "Monkeys of this species are found only near the equator." *Specie* is sometimes given when *species* is meant, but *species* is both singular and plural (Copperud, Evans).

**Spelling.** Extensive discussions of various aspects of the subject are to be found under this heading in Copperud, Follett, and Fowler. See -IZE, ISE; -OR, -OUR.

**spell out.** Approved by American Heritage but derogated by Bernstein as overworked. Both, however, asperse *spell out details* as redundant. Random House considers *spell out* informal; Webster gives it as standard; both its examples, however, are from newsmagazines.

**spiral.** In the sense *move up* (*prices spiraled all week*), as distinguished from *spiral up*, or *upward*, approved as standard by American Heritage and Webster; rejected by Bernstein; Random House does not give this form.

**spite.** See IN SPITE OF.

**spitting image.** Authorities mostly agree that this is a corruption of *spit and image*, but *spitting image* is now recognized by the dictionaries as predominant.

**Split Infinitive.** See INFINITIVES 7.

**Split-Verb Constructions.** See ADVERBS; INFINITIVES 1.

**spoof.** Approved as standard as both noun (*a spoof of Broadway*) and verb (*spoofing Congress*) in the sense *parody* by American Heritage, Random House, and Webster.

**spoonfuls, spoonsful.** See -FUL.

**Sportswriting.** Discussions of the language used in sportswriting are to be found in Copperud under that heading, in Evans under the heading *Sports English*, and in Fowler in the middle part of the entry *Sobriquets*.

**spouse.** Regarded by Evans, Flesch, Follett, and Fowler as bookish, legal, or jocular.

**Sr., Jr.** See JR., SR.

**stage.** The use of the word as a verb in the senses *present, exhibit, offer, put on, perform, accomplish,* etc., is discouraged as loose or journalese by Copperud and Evans, who agree that *stage a comeback* is a cliché. The criticized senses are given as standard in Random House and Webster.

**stalling for time.** Technically redundant, though in common use. Stalling is inevitably for time. *Stall* in this sense, as well as *stall off* (*stall off bill collectors*), is considered standard by American Heritage and Webster, informal by Random House.

**Standard.** The term is often used in this book to describe usages that are, in Webster's definition, "substantially uniform and well-established . . . in the speech and writing of the educated and widely recognized as acceptable and authoritative." Random House has a similar definition. The descriptive has come into fairly wide use in this connection. Conventional dictionaries ordinarily do not use *standard* as a status label; the implication is that unless otherwise labeled, e.g., *dialect, slang, informal, colloquial,* etc., a term is standard. Webster does use *substandard* to describe a usage differing from that of "the prestige group"; *nonstandard* describes similar usages that are more widespread than those designated *substandard*. See also COLLOQUIALISMS.

**state.** Often inappropriately used, simply for variation, where *say* would be preferable. *State* means to set forth in detail or to make a formal declaration (Bernstein, Copperud, Evans, Flesch). See also ATTRIBUTION.

**stationary, stationery.** Often confused. The first is the adjective that means *standing still* or *in a fixed position;* the second is the noun that means writing materials (Copperud, Evans, Fowler).

**statistic.** Follett disapproves of the word as a false singular derived from *statistics.* Evans, however, recognizes it as now standard, and so do Random House and Webster. See also -IC, -ICS.

**statuesque.** Journalese as used to describe beauties of larger than average size (Copperud, Flesch).

**Status Labels.** See COLLO-QUIALISMS; STANDARD.

**stave.** In nautical connections ("The hull of the tug was stove in") the preferable form for the present participle and the past tense is *stove,* it is agreed by Evans, Fowler, and Webster. In other connections, either *staved* or *stove* is acceptable, though *staved* is usual.

**stem from.** Evans and Fowler say that *spring from* is preferable in Britain; Flesch regards the expression as literary and overused, but both Webster and Random House consider it standard. The consensus is that in American usage it *is* standard.

**step up.** Bernstein objects to the expression as a fad; Evans defends it as vigorous (*step up the power*). Random House and Webster recognize it as standard. The phrase is in such wide use and so well established that criticism of it seems unreasonable.

**still and all.** Objected to by Bernstein and Copperud as dialectal and redundant (for *nevertheless, even so*) but recognized as standard by both Random House and Webster.

**still remains (continues, persists).** Though *still* may sometimes add a desired emphasis, such phrases are oftener thoughtlessly redundant, except when *still* is used in the sense *nevertheless.*

**stink.** Bryant, Evans, and Fowler consider *stank* (rather than *stunk*) the usual form for the past tense; Random House and Webster give it as predominant. Copperud favors *stunk* and considers *stank* bookish. Both forms are standard.

**stoic, stoical.** Evans and Fowler agree that the first is more appropriate in reference to the Stoic philosophy, the second to impassivity in general.

**stomach.** See BELLY.

**stomp.** In the sense *stamp on,* considered standard by Bryant, Random House, and Webster, dialectal by Copperud, and informal by Random House ("The thief was beaten and stomped"). The consensus is that there is some doubt whether the expression is standard since Bryant reports that it is often labeled dialectal in dictionaries.

**stone.** See ROCK, STONE.

**stove.** See STAVE.

**straddle.** For *equivocate* (*straddled the issue*), approved as standard by American Heritage and Webster; labeled informal by Random House.

**strait-, straight-.** The circumstances that are constricting are

*straitened,* not *straightened*
(Copperud, Fowler, Random
House, Webster). The confin-
ing garment is *straitjacket,* not
*straight-,* in the view of Bernstein, Follett, and Fowler,
though Random House and
Webster recognize both forms
as standard.

**strata.** See STRATUM, STRATA.

**strategy.** Technically, as applied to military operations,
strategy is the overall plan, and
tactics the specific means by
which it is carried out (Copperud, Evans, Fowler, Random
House, Webster).

**stratum, strata.** Bernstein and
Copperud hold that *strata* is
the plural of *stratum;* this follows the Latin (for *layer*) from
which the words are taken.
Evans allows *strata* as a singular, with the plural form
*stratas,* but no other authority
recognizes this obvious misuse.
Copperud, Evans, Random
House, and Webster accept
*stratums* as a plural. The consensus is that the allowable
singular form is *stratum,* the
allowable plurals are *strata* and
*stratums.*

**strew.** *Strewed* and *strewn*
are both standard as the past
participle (Evans, Fowler, Random House, Webster).

**stricken.** As the past participle of *strike, stricken* is standard in the sense *afflicted* in
such phrases as *stricken with
disease, poverty-stricken, the
stricken population* (Bryant,
Evans, Fowler). Bryant and
Evans allow *stricken* or *stricken
out* for *deleted* ("The remark
was stricken from the record").
Random House and Webster
recognize the first use but not

the second, indicating that
*struck, struck out* now predominate for *delete.*

**strived.** As the past and past
participle of *strive, strived* is
being driven out by *strove* and
*striven* (Bryant, Fowler, Random House, Webster; Evans
says *strived* is still heard and
acceptable).

**structure.** As used in place of
*build, form, organize, set up,*
etc., particularly in the writings
of academia, the word is criticized as pretentious by Copperud and as jargon by Follett.

**student.** See PUPIL, STUDENT.

**stunning.** Often inappropriately used to indicate approval,
especially in reviews of per-
formances (Bernstein, Copperud).

**Subject and Verb Agreement.**
Only general cases are dealt
with here; cases dealing with
specific expressions are in their
alphabetical places.
1. Subject Disagreeing with
Complement. Ordinarily, the
subject, rather than the complement, governs the number of
the verb. Thus "Potatoes are a
vegetable" (not *is*); "Letters to
the merged corporations are
(not *is*) the next topic"; "The
cargo was watermelons" (not
*were*) (Bernstein, Follett, Fowler). Apparent plurals designating periods of time ("A few
months was spent")—not *were*
—and sums of money ("The
delinquency was $56 million, of
which $44 million was owed by
the Communist bloc")—not
*were owed*—take singular verbs
(Copperud, Follett, Fowler).
See also NUMBER IN ADDITION.
2. Compound Subjects with
*and.* Fowler declares it a mis-

taken idea that when one part of a compound subject is plural and the other singular, the verb follows the nearest. All compound subjects with *and* are plural and take plural verbs: "The bonds, the stocks, and the money are in the safe-deposit box" (not *is*). Bernstein, Fowler, Follett, and Evans agree, however, that if the sense of the subject is such as to form a single idea (*food and drink; toast and jam*), a singular verb is preferable.

**3.** Compound Subjects with *or*. With subjects of different number, Fowler and Evans recommend either recasting the sentence or using the number of the subject nearest the verb.

**4.** Attraction of an Intervening Phrase. Bernstein, Flesch, Follett, and Fowler all warn against the common error caused by losing sight of the subject and giving the verb the number of a phrase that intervenes: "The height of the buildings was (not *were*) limited by city ordinance."

**5.** Inversion. The problem here resembles that of (3), in that some element other than the true subject leads the writer astray, and he is the more easily distracted when the verb precedes the subject. Bernstein, Flesch, Follett, and Fowler warn against the error of such constructions as "After the reception comes dancing and refreshments." *come.* See also ONE OF THOSE WHO; COLLECTIVE NOUNS; THERE; WITH.

**Subjunctive.** Extensive discussions of the subjunctive mood, used most commonly to describe conditions contrary to fact, are to be found in Bern-

stein, Evans, Follett, and Fowler. All agree that the use of the subjunctive is sharply on the decline in English, a fact easily observable. The points taken up here are those considered by two or more commentators.

**1.** In sentences expressing a condition contrary to fact and calling for a choice between *was* and *were* ("If I were king"; "If she were you"), Bernstein, Copperud, and American Heritage insist on *were;* Evans considers *was* preferable, except in *If I were.* Fowler does not admit any usage but *were* in such circumstances, and Follett regards it as the mark of education. Flesch restricts the use of *were* to what is not merely contrary to fact but impossible or out of the question, a distinction that seems impossible to apply in any practical way. The consensus, then, overwhelmingly favors *If I were* over *If I was* for conditions contrary to fact. But, as Bernstein, Flesch, Follett, and Fowler warn, the writer must distinguish between a statement of a timeless condition contrary to fact and the statement of a simple condition relating to the past: "If he was (not *were*) absent from the meeting he did not vote." Clauses beginning with *if,* then, do not necessarily take a subjunctive verb (*were, be*).

**2.** Mixing subjunctive and indicative verbs in the statement of a condition and the result of its fulfillment is described as an error by Bernstein and Fowler. An example: "If he *went* to college, he *will have* an advantage over the others." Either "If he *went* . . .

he *would have*" (both subjunctives) or "If he *goes* . . . he *will have*" (both indicatives, expressing a simple condition). The second form is considered preferable; the use of subjunctive forms where the indicative will serve is considered unnecessarily formal and even pretentious.

**subsequent, subsequently, subsequent to.** The first two are described by Copperud and Flesch as pretentious for *later*, and the last is described by Bernstein, Copperud, and Flesch as pretentious for *after*. American Heritage lists these uses without aspersing them.

**Substandard.** As a status label, see STANDARD.

**substitute, replace.** *Substitute,* which means *put in the place of,* is followed idiomatically by *for; replace,* which means *take the place of,* is followed by *by.* Careful attention to the choice of the appropriate prepositions will prevent the usual misuse, which is that of *substitute* for *replace.* "Natural rubber has been largely substituted by synthetic rubber." *Natural rubber has been largely replaced by;* or *Synthetic rubber has been largely substituted for* (Bernstein, Evans, Flesch, Fowler).

**succeed.** May not be followed by an infinitive: "He succeeded to keep the place to himself." *succeeded in keeping* (Evans, Fowler).

**such.** Considered objectionable when used as a personal pronoun (for example, in place of *it* or *them*) or in place of such indefinite pronouns as *any, all, one,* or in place of demonstrative pronouns like *this, these.* "Dues are used for political purposes, but a dissenting member or minority group is without protection against such." *this,* or *this practice.* "As long as stores sell toys that encourage violence, and parents place such in children's hands . . . " *place them.* "The government will grant asylum to members of the crew who request such." *request it* (Bernstein, Copperud, Evans, Flesch, Follett, Fowler). In spite of the nearly unanimous disapproval by commentators on usage, both Random House and Webster give examples indicating they regard this use of *such* as standard, as does Bryant.

*Such* as an intensive ("We had such a good time"; "It was such a nice day") is considered feminine by Copperud, but regarded as standard by Bernstein, Bryant, Evans, and Fowler (who, however, recommends substituting *so* when this is possible without artificiality, e.g., *so trifling an objection* vs. *such a trifling objection*). This usage of *such* is also considered standard by both Random House and Webster.

The correct form is *no such,* not *no such a:* "There is no such beast as the Loch Ness monster" (Bryant, Evans).

**such as.** *Like* is often preferable to *such as:* "Sudden and totally unexpected upheavals such as that in Guatemala . . ." *like* (Copperud, Follett). *Such as* for *those who* (*such as frequent these places*) is considered colloquial by Bryant, standard by Evans; no other work cites this construction, which, however, occurs frequently and seems likely to establish itself as standard if it is not already so.

Bernstein and Follett point out that in constructions like "The banks refuse to make such loans that are not backed by sufficient collateral" *such* must be followed by *as,* not *that: such loans as are not.* However, *make loans that are not* would be better. When *that* introduces a clause of result, *such that* is correct: "His surprise was such that he refused to believe the letter."

**such is the case.** See CASE.

**such that.** See SUCH AS.

**sudden (death).** Often criticized on the curious ground that death is always sudden. This is obviously not so (Copperud; the expression is specifically recognized by American Heritage and Webster).

**suffer from, with.** American Heritage rejects *suffer with* in relation to ailments: "He suffered with dandruff." *from.* The examples in Webster confirm this preference; Random House is not explicit.

**sufficient(ly).** See ENOUGH.

**Suffixes.** See HYPHENS 5.

**suggestive.** Usually used in the sense *improper* or *indecent,* and thus the writer who intends merely the primary sense *offering a suggestion* had better be on his guard (Copperud, Evans).

**suit, suite.** The correct form is *suite* in such connections as a musical suite, a suite of rooms, a suite of furniture, though the terms are actually the same (Copperud, Evans, Fowler; Random House and

Webster make the distinction but also give *suit* as a synonym of *suite*). *Suite* is pronounced *sweet.*

**Sums of Money.** See COLLECTIVE NOUNS.

**sung.** See SING.

**sunk.** See SINK.

**Superlatives.** See COMPARISON 2, 4.

**supine.** Means *lying face upward,* Bernstein, Evans, Fowler, and the dictionaries agree. This is of interest in connection with the broadened sense of *prone,* which see.

**supplement.** See AUGMENT, SUPPLEMENT.

**surcease.** Evans, Fowler, Flesch, and Random House agree that the noun is archaic, and the implication is that its use is affected. Webster, however, labels only the verb obsolete, thus strengthening the suspicion that the noun, though it may have fallen into disuse for a time, is now experiencing a revival ("There followed a surcease of political accusations").

**sure.** *Sure* as an adverb ("That sure was a good dinner") in place of *surely* is considered substandard by Copperud and Evans, colloquial by Bryant and Random House, and standard by Webster. The consensus is that this usage is questionable. *Sure enough,* however, is regarded as standard by Bryant and Evans. Compare REAL.

**suspected.** See ACCUSED.

**Suspensive Modifiers.** See COMMA 9.

**suspicion.** As a verb ("Police suspicioned the vagrant"), considered substandard by Copperud, Evans, Fowler, Random House, and Webster.

**sustain.** Commonly used in newspapers in connection with injuries (*sustained a broken leg*). *Suffer* and *receive* are considered preferable by Bernstein, Evans, Flesch, and Fowler; the term is considered standard in this sense by Copperud, American Heritage, Random House, and Webster.

**swap.** Bernstein deprecates the use of the word in serious contexts, but both Random House and Webster consider it standard.

**swum.** *Swam* is the preferred form for the past tense, not *swum*, and *swum* is correct for the participle: "She swam (*has swum*) the English Channel" (Bryant, Copperud, Evans, Fowler).

**Synonyms.** For the use of synonyms as a stylistic fault, see VARIATION; ELEGANT VARIATION.

# T

**tablespoonfuls, tablespoonsful.** See -FUL.

**tactics.** See STRATEGY.

**take.** See BRING, TAKE.

**take it easy.** Sometimes, out of overcorrectness, mistakenly given *take it easily* (Bernstein, Copperud).

**take off.** For *depart* or *leave* in ordinary connections not associated with aircraft ("He took off for the suburbs"), considered slang by Copperud and American Heritage, informal by Random House, and standard by Webster.

**take place.** See OCCUR, TAKE PLACE.

**taps.** The bugle call is said by Bernstein to be plural and thus to require a plural verb ("Taps were sounded"); Webster says it is usually singular in construction and American Heritage says flatly "used with a singular verb," a conclusion that appears to be supported by general usage.

**target.** The use of the word in the sense *quota, goal, deadline, objective,* which became popular in World War II, is discouraged as tiresome and often inaccurate by Bernstein, Evans, and Fowler. An example: "Contributions have exceeded the target," in which *goal* or *quota* would have been a better choice; at any rate, a target would be *missed,* to pursue the metaphor consistently, not *exceeded.*

**teaspoonfuls, teaspoonsful.** See -FUL.

**Technical Terms.** See SCIENTIFIC ENGLISH.

**telecast, televise.** Copperud and Evans point out a technical distinction, that the first means to broadcast by television and the second to record and then to broadcast. Copperud adds that the distinction has no meaning to laymen, *televise* being used interchangeably with *telecast* in the sense *broadcast,* a conclusion supported by the definitions in both unabridged dictionaries, neither of which recognizes the restricted sense of *televise*.

**temblor.** The word for an earthquake; sometimes misspelled *tremblor* (Copperud, Evans).

**temperature.** Bernstein and Evans are critical of *temperature* for *fever,* as in "The patient has no temperature." Evans and Fowler speculate that this is a euphemism, an idea that Bernstein rejects. Fowler regards the expression as firmly established colloquially and beyond cavil. This sense is also recognized as standard by every current dictionary without qualification.

**tend to.** Rejected by Fowler and American Heritage in the sense *apply attention:* "The lawyer said he would tend to the matter." *attend.* Considered dialectal by Evans, standard by Random House and Webster.

**Tenses.** See SEQUENCE OF TENSES.

**terminate.** *Terminate* where *end* will do is pretentious (Evans, Flesch, Fowler).

**terrible, terribly.** See AWFUL- (LY).

**than.** An extremely detailed exploration of the difficulties attending *than* is to be found under that heading in Fowler, and a less extensive one in Evans. The topic common to

these discussions is whether *than* shall be considered a conjunction or a preposition in sentences like "He is taller than me." If it is a conjunction, the sentence should read *than I.* Fowler concedes that *than me* is very common in speech, and both he and Evans recommend sidestepping the question in writing by recasting in some such form as *than I am.* Flesch considers the objective case idiomatic with *than;* this, however, is an oversimplification. The analysis of this problem is tortuous, and more confusing than helpful. In general, the tendency is to regard *than* as a conjunction (Bernstein, Evans, Fowler, American Heritage) and thus to have the pronoun following it in the subjective case ("He is better informed than I") unless the pronoun has an antecedent or a word closely linked with it in the objective case ("We have hired less honest men than him"). All the commentators point out that ambiguous statements are likely with *than* and a preposition: "He likes the teacher better than her" (better than he likes her, or better than she likes the teacher?). Obviously, *she* is called for here, but it sounds pedantic. In all such cases, recasting is recommended ("better than she does") to avoid both ambiguity and artificial construction.

*Than whom* in such constructions as "An architect than whom none is more reputable" is correct, instead of *than who,* Bernstein, Copperud, Flesch, Follett, Fowler, and American Heritage agree, but the latter three consider the expression clumsy and recommend avoiding it. For other hazards involving *than,* see COMPARISON; see also HARDLY and SCARCE, SCARCELY for the use of those words with *than;* for the inversions *than is, than are,* see AS IS, AS ARE.

**than any, than anyone.** "He has more readers than any financial writer on a New York newspaper"; "He is more interested in the capture of his wife's murderer than any person on earth." In both instances, logic requires *any other.* As pointed out by Perrin, the rule is that *other* is required in the comparison of things in the same class. Fowler calls sentences like "She is the best-dressed woman of anyone in town" idiomatic but adds that those who object to the construction as illogical may recast.

**than is, than are.** See AS IS, AS ARE.

**thankfully.** Increasingly misused (like *hopefully,* which see) to indicate thankfulness by the writer, rather than by the subject of the sentence: "The decision, thankfully, was in our favor." To put it another way, the word is used to mean *we* (or *I*) *feel thankful,* rather than *in a thankful manner* (Flesch, Follett; neither unabridged dictionary recognizes the misuse.)

**thanking you in advance.** To Copperud, the phrase is overeager and sophomoric; to Evans, it is presumptuous and insolent.

**thanks to.** Considered standard in the sense *due to, because of* by Bernstein, Bryant, Follett, Random House, Webster ("Thanks to early registration, all classes began on schedule"). The phrase is sometimes also used ironically: "Thanks to your help, I failed the course."

**than whom.** See THAN.

**that.** 1. As a conjunction. All the authorities being surveyed in this book agree that *that* may be omitted as a conjunction, and most of them agree that this is stylistically preferable when there is no reason for its inclusion: "He said (that) he was starving." The tendency to omit *that* is too strong, however; it is agreed equally that the conjunction is often omitted when it should have been used. This is mainly a matter of having a sensitive feeling for correct construction. Usually, *that* is best omitted in short sentences, and when the relation of the elements it would otherwise connect is immediately clear. Some examples of undesirably omitted *thats* will be given here.

"Metzman said on Jan. 1 the fleet stood at 1,776,000 cars." *That* is required after *said* to indicate that Jan. 1 was the date on which the fleet stood at the figure given; as it is, *Jan. 1* may be taken as the date on which Metzman made the statement. "The speaker said last November the outlook improved." "Said *that* last November . . ." for the same reason.

"He added the proposed freeway could follow the existing route." "Added *that* the proposed freeway . . ."; *that* is necessary to keep the reader from going off on a false scent and assuming that *freeway* and not the entire clause is the object of *added*.

"The deputy foreign minister said last night that Panama does not receive its fair share of Panama Canal revenues, and sentiment for a 50 per cent increase is likely to grow." "And *that* sentiment . . ."; parallel construction and unambiguous expression require *that* with both of a pair of coordinate clauses. In this instance, doubt is raised whether both clauses are attributable to the speaker.

"The board was told the point is really one of economics, and that if the ordinance were repealed, meat markets would be driven out of business." "Was told *that* . . ." for the sake of parallel construction.

**2. Before Direct Quotation.** *That* is excessive before a direct quotation: "The Point Four director in Iran reported that 'More than half the population of the village have been killed under the falling walls of their homes.'" *reported, 'More than* . . .

**3. Doubled.** *That* is sometimes unnecessarily doubled: "It is hard to realize that as he lives in quiet retirement at the age of 88 *that* a generation is coming up that knows him only by reputation." The italicized *that* is superfluous; its work has already been done by the first *that*.

**4. As a Relative Pronoun:** *that* vs. *which*. All the authorities surveyed except Bryant deal with this question, and except for Evans they agree that *that* is preferable to begin a restrictive clause ("The rule

exempts commercial lots that place no restriction on all-night parking") and that *which* is preferable to begin a nonrestrictive clause ("Los Angeles, which dates back to Spanish days in California, is an exception"). (More information on the distinction between restrictive and nonrestrictive clauses—sometimes called limiting and nonlimiting, or defining and nondefining—may be found under the heading RESTRICTIVE AND NONRESTRICTIVE CLAUSES.) It is generally conceded, however, that *which* is often used to introduce restrictive clauses ("We attended the reception which followed the concert") and that this cannot be considered an error. It may be a useful reminder at this point that nonrestrictive clauses are set off by commas, and restrictive clauses are not. A rule of thumb may also be useful. If *that* will fit comfortably, it is correct, and furthermore the clause is restrictive. *That* introducing a nonrestrictive clause is a blunder: "The sun, that had a murky orange color, soon burned off the fog" (Copperud, Fowler; Evans unaccountably says *that* may introduce nonrestrictive clauses in current usage, but cites examples dating from times long past, when this practice was acceptable). In "It was easy to find the house which was on fire," *that* can be substituted for *which*, and in accordance with our rule of thumb it thus is preferable. The chief use of the distinction given here between *that* and *which* is that it helps in distinguishing between restrictive and nonrestrictive clauses, a far more important matter than any arbitrary preference of pronoun. The punctuation, however, remains decisive in indicating the distinction. American Heritage offers the helpful comment that a nonrestrictive clause theoretically is capable of being enclosed in parentheses.

**5.** As a Relative Pronoun: *that* vs. *who*. Evans and Follett consider *that* freely interchangeable with *who* in restrictive clauses where it fits smoothly "The man that was walking in the park yesterday." Fowler prefers *who* for particular persons *(you who)* and *that* in generic references *(a man that)*, but concedes there is a strong tendency to use *who* out of politeness in generic references *(ladies who)*. *That* for *who* is sometimes objected to, but the objection has no basis. Random House says *that* may refer to a person, and so do American Heritage and Webster.

**6.** As a Pronoun: Omission. The tendency is strong to omit *that* as a relative pronoun when it is the object in a restrictive clause: "The apple (that) I was eating . . ." Both Evans and Fowler consider this usage standard.

**7.** *That* for *so* ("He was that rich he didn't know how much money he had") is considered colloquial by Bryant and dialectal by Evans. See also ALL THAT; SAME; SUCH AS; ELLIPSIS 4.

**that of.** See FALSE COMPARISON; POSSESSIVES 3.

**the.** Bernstein, Copperud, Flesch, and Follett deplore the journalistic mannerism of omitting *the* when idiom or grammar requires it, in the mistaken idea that by doing so the writing is made brighter or breezier. Necessary *thes* are oftenest omitted in newspaper writing at the beginning of a story, or at the beginning of any sentence. The reader is not sped on his way, as the writers hope, by the omission; rather, he is caused to stumble, and to choose between the possible shades of meaning that the writer has neglected to specify. An example: "Crux of the situation is belief expressed by board members that legislation should govern the use of the reservoir by the public." If the object is to be telegraphic, why not go all the way: "Crux of situation is belief expressed by board members that legislation should govern use of reservoir by public"?

Evans, Flesch, and Fowler agree that it is preferable not to capitalize *the* even though it may form part of the title in constructions like "I read it in the *New York Times.*"

Exhaustively circumstantial discussions of the use and misuse of *the* are to be found under that heading in Follett and Fowler, and somewhat shorter ones in Copperud and Evans.

Copperud and Follett warn about carelessly using *the* where *a* or *an* is required. This may suggest a distinction that is either inaccurate, unintended, or both. Referring to John Jones as *the vice-president of the Smith Corporation* implies that the corporation has only one vice-president. *Laurence Olivier, the actor* is acceptable on the assumption that he is well enough known so that his name will be recognized. On the other hand, referring to a movie starlet, Hazel Gooch, lately of Broken Bottle, Iowa, as *the* (rather than *an*) *actress* leaves the reader with a rattled feeling that he has not recognized a name he should know, though the fault is in fact the writer's.

**thee, thou.** *Thou* is the nominative and *thee* the objective form of these archaic pronouns; the difference is the same as between *I* and *me,* or *he* and *him.* (The modern equivalent of both *thou* and *thee* is *you,* which has the same form for the nominative and the objective cases, and for that matter for the singular and the plural.) The usual error is to use *thee* where *thou* is ordinarily called for: "Thee art my ideal." Quaker usage, however, is specialized, and calls uniformly for *thee* (Copperud, Evans). For related problems, see -ETH.

**theft.** See BURGLARY.

**their.** See THEY (THEIR, THEM); COLLECTIVE NOUNS.

**their's.** An error; the correct form is *theirs* (Copperud, Evans).

**them.** See IT'S ME, etc.; THEY (THEIR, THEM).

**themselves.** See MYSELF; REFLEXIVES.

**then.** Follett disapproves of *then* as an adjective (*the then mayor*), but this usage is given as standard in Random House, Webster, and other dictionaries.

**there.** Care is required in choosing the number of the verb in a clause having *there* as a false subject. Attention should be fixed on the true subject, which governs the verb: "There are (not *is*) six flowers in the vase"; "There were (not *was*) an outing and a dance after the golf tournament" (Bernstein, Copperud). Bernstein says a plural verb is preferable in the following case, but Bryant finds that the singular verb predominates overwhelmingly in standard usage when the first part of a compound subject following *there* is singular: "There was a sausage, an orange, and a piece of cheese on the table (rather than *were*). Evans and American Heritage concur.

At one time there was frequent criticism of starting a sentence or clause with *there* on the ground that this construction is indefinite or weak. Only one of the works surveyed deals with this question, which may be taken to mean that beginning with *there* is no longer regarded as a fault, if indeed it properly ever was. Copperud cites numerous quotations from literature to show that the usage is frequent, and objects only to constructions like "As in the previous ruling, there was no jail sentence imposed," which could be more economically and forcefully put *no jail sentence was imposed.* Hook's *Guide to Good Writing* says, however, that sentences beginning with *there is, there are,* etc., may be wordy; Perrin's *Writer's Guide and Index to English* says frequent use of the construction tends toward a lack of emphasis.

**thereafter, etc.** The use of such words as *thereafter* (instead of *after that* or *then*), *thereby, therefrom, therein,* etc. instead of modern alternatives

is discouraged by Flesch and
Fowler as stiff.

**therefor, therefore.** Sometimes confused. *Therefor* means
*for that* or *for it:* "He explained the cause of action and
the basis therefor" (that is, *the
basis for it*). *Therefore* means
*consequently, as a result:* "The
conclusion, therefore, is that
we have no case" (Copperud,
Fowler, Random House; Webster gives *therefore* as a synonym for *therefor*).

**these.** See THIS.

**these kind, sort.** See KIND.

**they (their, them).** In reference to singular pronouns like
*anybody, anyone, each, either,
everybody, everyone, neither,
nobody, no one, somebody,* and
*someone,* see ANYBODY, ANY-
ONE; EACH; EVERYBODY, EVERY-
ONE, etc.; COLLECTIVE NOUNS.
*They* as an indefinite subject
("They say the climate is getting colder"; "It's what they
are wearing this season") is
sanctioned by Bryant, Evans,
Random House, and Webster.

**thief.** See BURGLARY.

**thinking man.** This expression as used in such sentences
as "Every thinking man must
agree that . . ." is criticized
as insidious by Flesch and as
offensive to the reader by
Fowler.

**this.** Follett protests at length
about the use of *this* to summarize a preceding clause or
sentence, but this usage is
considered correct by Bryant,
Copperud, Evans, and American Heritage: "Because of in-
herited venereal disease, their
population remains static. This
worries the elders of the tribe."

Follett would insist on *this
problem* or something of the
kind. The consensus is heavily
against him. Webster says *this*
is "often used with a general
reference to something stated
or implied in the previous context but without particular reference to a noun or noun
equivalent in that context." Perrin too says *this* is regularly
used to refer to the idea of
a preceding clause or sentence.
Bernstein admits *this* in some
such instances but prefers *that*
in reference to what has been
stated; Bryant finds this usage
more frequent, adding that the
summarizing *this* has been
common since the time of
Shakespeare, and quotes, "This
above all: to thine own self
be true."

Bernstein, Copperud, Follett,
and American Heritage object
to the growing tendency to use
*this* where *that* or some other
pronoun seems more appro-
priate: "The Senussis established what has been called a
theocratic empire, spilling over
political frontiers. This was
then broken up." Better: *It* or
*The empire.* "We were much
impressed by the chief. This is
an able and progressive citizen." Better: *He* or *This man.*
*These* (the plural of *this*) is
often misused in the same way:
"She digs up whole pages of
evidence and serves these hot."
Better: *them.*

**this reporter, this writer, etc.**
See EDITORIAL WE.

**tho.** Not a generally accepted · curtailment of *though*
(Bryant, Copperud).

**thoroughbred, pedigreed,
purebred.** The tendency, Evans
and Fowler agree, is to restrict

the first to horses and to apply the second and third terms to other animals. *Pedigreed* is applied particularly to dogs.

**those kind.** See KIND.

**thou.** See THEE, THOU.

**though, although.** *Although* once was considered the more emphatic, but the words are now synonymous and interchangeable where either will fit (Bernstein, Bryant, Copperud, Evans, Follett, Fowler). Some commentators cite examples of constructions where only *though* will go, such as *as though, even though,* and "The sky was still cloudy, though," but it is inconceivable that anyone would attempt to use *although* in such instances. American Heritage objects to *though* for *however,* as used in the preceding example, usually at the end or in the middle of a sentence; Random House and Webster consider this usage standard. Usually idiom, sometimes rhythm, sometimes the tone of the writing will dictate the choice. Follett has an extended and useful discussion of pitfalls attending the use of these words that are not taken up by any other commentator. Fowler and Follett point out that *though* or *although* should be used only to indicate concession: "Though some students did not meet the standards for admission to the college, the requirements have been changed." These ideas are not opposed, and should be stated as a sequence. "Earthquakes are infrequent, although little damage has been done by them." Flesch objects to the comma preceding *though*

in the sense *however:* "The audience did not respond, though." This is in accord with the modern tendency toward open punctuation; see COMMA 1. For *as though* see AS IF, AS THOUGH.

**through.** Accepted as standard for *finished (through with the book)* by American Heritage, Random House, and Webster. In the senses *having no further relationship, done for* ("We're through"; "He's through in politics") considered informal by American Heritage, standard by Webster, and not given by Random House.

**thus.** See FOR.

**thusly.** Regarded by Bernstein, Copperud, Flesch, Follett, and Evans as a superfluous variant of *thus;* rejected almost unanimously by the American Heritage panel.

**till, 'til, until.** There is no difference between *till* and *until* (Bernstein, Bryant, Copperud, Evans, Fowler; Bryant considers *till* somewhat more formal, a distinction no other commentator makes; Fowler considers *till* the more usual form). The forms *'til* and *'till* are wrong (Bernstein, Copperud; American Heritage considers *'til* unnecessary and *'till* nonstandard). Fowler and American Heritage object to *till* or *until* for *before:* "It was not five minutes until the rain stopped." But this is a British quibble, and such constructions, which are always negative, are sanctioned by Evans, Random House, and Webster.

**Time Elements.** The misplacement of time elements too early in the sentence is a conspicuous gaucherie of much newspaper writing, despite continual criticism. The usual version that appears in print is something like "The City Council last night voted a street improvement program" (instead of *voted a street improvement program last night*) or "John Jones Thursday shot his mother-in-law (instead of *shot his mother-in-law Thursday*). The natural place for the time element is generally after, rather than before, the verb, and sometimes at the end of the sentence. The journalistic idiosyncrasy of placing it immediately after the subject perhaps has two causes: eagerness to put it in a prominent position, and a disinclination to pause and consider where it would fit most smoothly, for this is a matter that does sometimes require a moment's consideration. The reflex action of placing the time element after the subject obviates any such consideration, and the damage this placement does to the flow of the sentence apparently is not regarded as counting for anything. Sentences on the model of the "John Jones Thursday" example given earlier have been endlessly ridiculed as suggesting that *Thursday* is the subject's last name. Placement of the time element immediately after the verb and before an object can also be awkward: "An American novelist was awarded today the Nobel Prize for Literature" (*was awarded the Nobel Prize for Literature today*). Sometimes the element will go as well first as last: "World War II veterans next year will collect $220 million in divi-

dends on their government life insurance." Either *Next year veterans will* or *on their government life insurance next year;* as it stands, the sentence is clumsy.

**times less, times more.** "This procedure is 100 times less effective." The sentence does not convey a clear meaning, since *times* implies multiplication, not division or diminution. Better: *one one-hundredth* (if that is what it was) *as effective.* "The new star is probably 25,000 times fainter than the sun." Baffling. *One twenty-five thousandth as bright;* or "The sun is 25,000 times as bright as the new star." *Times more* is ambiguous; "His income is four times more than it was last year." This may be taken to mean quadrupled, or quintupled. *four times as much as* (Copperud, Evans, Fowler). See also ALMOST MORE, LESS.

**tinker's dam, damn.** Authorities differ, or decline to state a preference, as to which of these forms is correct. The Oxford English Dictionary, however, says that the theory that the expression refers to a small dam of putty erected by tinkers to contain solder is "an ingenious but baseless conjecture." If this conclusion is correct, it appears that the *tinker's dam* is nothing more than a bowdlerization of *tinker's damn.*

**-tion, -ion.** Warnings against writing sentences that contain a series of words ending in this sound are given by Bernstein, Copperud, Flesch, Fowler, and Follett. An example: "The educa*tion* of the popula*tion* of the na*tion* is substandard." The repetition is annoying, and such sentences should be recast. This kind of writing exemplifies the style that tends toward abstractions rather than the concrete; the concrete is always to be preferred as more vigorous and effective. The sentence quoted could be improved to "Education in this country is substandard."

**'tis.** See POESY.

**Titles.** See FALSE TITLES.

**to all intents and purposes.** A windy way of saying *practically, in effect.* Derives from a legal expression, *to all intents, constructions, and purposes* (Copperud, Evans).

**together with.** See WITH.

**token.** The expression *by the same token* is derogated by Copperud, Fowler, and Flesch as pompous and archaic.

**Tomb of the Unknowns.** This form of reference to the Tomb of the Unknown Soldier gained a certain lasting popularity after the Army used it for a time on guide signs in Arlington National Cemetery. It was dropped after protests, however, and the Army verifies that the correct term is *Tomb of the Unknown Soldier.*

**tome.** A conspicuous journalese variant of *book,* as *white stuff* is of *snow, yellow metal* of *gold,* and *pachyderm* of *elephant. Tome* is properly applied to a volume forming part of a larger work, or to any book, but it has been found in bad company too often (Copperud, Evans, Flesch).

**too.** Setting off *too* with commas is old-fashioned: "They, too, depend on cash flow to finance their activities." *They*

*too depend . . .* (Copperud, Flesch). See NOT TOO; COMMA 1.

**top.** Bernstein objects that the word is overused as an adjective *(top singer, top administrator, top prices)* in the senses *foremost, principal, highest,* etc., especially in journalism. Fowler takes notice of this use without expressing any criticism except such as may be implied in the comment that it appears mostly in journalism and advertising. Evans also deals with the word but only to differentiate it from others of similar meaning, and says only that it is used more freely than the others. The use is recognized as standard by both Random House and Webster.

**tortuous, torturous.** Sometimes confused. *Tortuous* means *twisting, winding (a tortuous road up the mountain); torturous* means *causing torture (a torturous stiff collar)* (Bernstein, Copperud, Evans; Webster, however, allows *torturous* as a synonym of *tortuous*).

**to the manner born.** See MANNER BORN.

**touch.** See FINISHING TOUCH.

**toward, towards.** The second form is generally considered preferable in Britain, the first in the United States (Bernstein, Bryant, Evans, Fowler; American dictionaries consider *toward* predominant). Both, of course, are standard; Bryant and Copperud find the second gaining in favor in this country.

**Trade Names.** See REALTOR.

**tragedy, tragic.** What is termed a tragedy should have impressive or at least respectable dimensions: "The tragedy is that there is seldom complete agreement as to which direction change should take in yielding to progress." An inconvenience, no doubt, perhaps a stumbling block, but hardly a tragedy. Devaluation of *tragedy* to describe ordinary misfortunes is one of the marks of the overwriting common in journalism (Bernstein, Copperud, Evans; the definitions in Random House bear out this distinction; Webster, however, gives as synonyms *bad luck, misfortune*, though the examples nearly all conform with the distinction).

**trans-.** Solid as a prefix: *transarctic, transoceanic, translocate,* etc.; but *trans-American, trans-Mississippi* (followed by capitals). *Transatlantic* and *transpacific* are solidly established, however.

**transcendent, transcendental.** Evans and Fowler agree that *transcendent* is the word for *surpassing, supreme (of transcendent importance); transcendental* means *visionary, outside experience,* etc. *(transcendental idealism). Transcendental* is oftenest used in its strict sense in religious or philosophical contexts. Random House and Webster, however, both accept *transcendental* as a synonym for *transcendent.* Opinion is thus divided, but the view of the dictionaries indicates at least that the words are well on the way to becoming interchangeable in the sense of *surpassing.*

**transpire.** Formerly the only meaning was *leak out* or *become known;* commonly the word is now used in the sense *happen, occur, go on:* "No one would say what transpired at the meeting." *Transpire* in the new sense is considered established as standard by Copperud and Evans; Evans, however, warns that its use may prompt criticism. *Transpire* for *happen* is considered unacceptable by Bernstein, Flesch, Follett, Fowler, and American Heritage. Webster's Second Edition said *transpire* for *occur* or *happen* is (or was—the book was published in 1934) "disapproved by most authorities but found in the writings of authors of good standing." Webster's Third Edition omits the caveat and quotes several authors as using the word in the formerly disapproved sense. *Occur, happen, take place* is the first sense given in Random House. Thus opinion is almost evenly divided, which in itself is a strong indication that the new sense is well on the way to acceptance as standard, especially since both new dictionaries recognize it. Writers who are unsure of themselves, however, or fearful of being taken to task, may limit their use of *transpire* to mean *become known.* In the strictly correct sense it is regarded by Copperud, Flesch, and Follett as somewhat pretentious for *become known.*

**tread, trod.** Ordinarily, *trod* is the past tense of *tread* ("They trod the straight and narrow") and *treading*, not *trodding*, is the participle. There are occasional instances of the use of *trod* for *tread* ("She will trod the boards tomorrow") and of *trodding* for *treading* ("He's trodding softly, meanwhile, on that borrowed oriental rug"). It seems safe to regard this as a misuse, though Webster does give for *trod, trodding* "to follow as a chosen course or path." This, however, is not the same as *step* or *walk on,* and at *tread* Webster does not give *trod* as an alternate form for the present tense, nor *trodding* for the participle. Evans and Random House do not recognize *trod* except as the past of *tread*.

**trek.** Evans and Fowler object to the use of the term to describe other than mass migration (like those of the Boers in South Africa, where the expression comes from), and to its loose extension to mean simply *go* or *travel*. The definitions in Random House and Webster in effect concur with this, allowing *trek* for *journey* only when difficulty or hardship is present. This is also the view of the American Heritage panel.

**tribute to.** In the sense *illustrative of (a tribute to his perception),* approved as an idiom by American Heritage and considered standard by Webster; Random House does not give this sense, and Fowler disapproves.

**trigger.** Bernstein, Copperud, and Follett object that the word is overused as a verb displacing *cause, start, begin, produce, signal, precipitate, initiate,* and others that the reader may easily think of. The American Heritage panel sanctions this usage but considers it informal. Its popularity is traced by Bernstein and Follett to the advent of the atomic bomb and its triggering mechanisms. Perhaps its vogue was inevitable in an age of armament races, wars, and rumors of wars.

**trio.** Journalese as used in reference to three of anything whether they have any relationship or not (Bernstein, Copperud). The same is true of *duo, quartet, quintet,* etc.

**triple, treble.** Interchangeable as both verb and adjective in the sense *three times (triple, treble one's savings: triple, treble damages)* though *triple* is perhaps more used in the U.S.; British usage prefers *treble* as the verb (Copperud, Evans, Fowler).

**triumphal, triumphant.** *Triumphal* means expressing or celebrating triumph; *triumphant,* feeling or experiencing triumph. *Triumphal* often applies, for example, to *procession;* a procession could be described as triumphant, however, if its participants were exultant. Usually *triumphant* applies to people, *triumphal* to things; *the triumphant victors; a triumphal arch* (Copperud, Evans, Fowler). Random House gives *triumphant* as a synonym for *triumphal* in the sense *exultant;* and Webster gives it as a general synonym.

**trod.** See TREAD, TROD.

**trooper, trouper.** Sometimes confused. A *trooper,* in its commonest senses, is a *cavalryman* or a *mounted policeman;* a *trouper* is an *actor,* or *member of a troupe* (Copperud, Evans, Fowler, Random House, Webster).

**troublous.** Evans and Fowler agree that the word is now archaic for *troublesome*. Random House labels it thus, but Webster considers it standard.

**truculent.** Bernstein holds that this word, which dictionaries define as meaning *savage, cruel, ferocious,* is rarely found used in that sense today, but that instead it is intended to mean *challenging, sulky, disagreeably pugnacious,* or *aggressively defiant.* No observant reader can deny that he is right. American Heritage, which appeared after the foregoing was written, became the first dictionary to recognize the new sense, and its Usage Panel explicitly approves it. Evans warns against the senses *base, mercenary* as a misuse but, as Bernstein adds, it is difficult to find examples of this.

**true facts.** See FACT, FACTS.

**trustee, trusty.** Both are people in whom trust has been reposed; confusion oftenest arises in the plural forms: *trustees, trusties.* A trusty is an inmate of a prison who enjoys special privileges because of his trustworthiness. Irresponsible trustees, however, sometimes end as trusties (Copperud, Evans).

**try.** As a noun for *attempt, effort (give it a good try),* narrowly approved by American Heritage; considered standard by Random House and Webster.

**try and.** As severe a critic as Fowler in the original described *try and* (displacing *try to*) as an idiom that should not be disapproved when it comes naturally; he regarded it as meeting the standard of literary dignity. Bryant finds the phrase to be informal standard English; it is considered standard by Copperud, Evans, and Follett. Bernstein grudgingly allows that it has its uses in certain contexts, but remains suspicious of it on the whole. American Heritage rejects it. Bernstein, Follett, and Fowler discern shades of difference in meaning between *try and* and *try to;* their examples show that the writer is likely to make the right choice by instinct.

**tubercular, tuberculous.** Fowler insists that the terms should be differentiated, the first having to do with tubercules and the second with tuberculosis. Evans recognizes them as interchangeable in reference to the disease, and so do Random House and Webster; Webster, in addition, recognizes them as interchangeable in reference to tubercules. The distinction prescribed by Fowler may represent British usage, but it is not recognized in American practice. Evans concurs with Fowler's rule, however, for what is described as strict usage; to judge from the context, this apparently means technical usage.

**tummy.** See BELLY.

**turbid, turgid.** Sometimes confused. *Turbid* means *muddy (turbid water); turgid* means *swollen, inflated,* and is oftener used figuratively, perhaps, than literally *(turgid prose)* (Bernstein, Fowler).

**turn in to, into.** See INTO, IN TO.

**'twas, 'twere, 'twill, etc.** See POESY.

**tycoon.** Considered standard by American Heritage, Random House, and Webster, informal by Evans, and colloquial by

Fowler, who notes that it is taking hold in Britain after having been first applied in the popular sense in the U.S., where, Partridge remarked, it is overdone.

**type, type of.** *Type* as an adjective displacing *type of* *(the intellectual type employee, athletic type persons)* is considered unacceptable in writing by Bernstein, Copperud, Evans, and American Heritage; Bryant says *type of* is preferred in formal written English though *type* is frequent in speech and business prose; neither Random House nor Webster recognizes *type* as an adjective. *Type* forming part of a compound modifier (*American-type gad-* *gets, family-type burlesque*) is regarded as verging on respectability but most suitable in technical connections (*V-type engine, O-type blood, cantilever-type bridge*) by Bernstein and Copperud; Follett considers it unacceptable; Bryant gives the same judgment on this form as on *type* in place of *type of*. The problem is apparently unknown in Britain, for Fowler does not comment on it.

**typhoon, hurricane.** Both are tropical cyclones but *typhoon* is applied only to those occurring near the Philippines, the China Sea, or India (Copperud, Evans, Random House, Webster).

# U

**uh-huh.** This interjection, common in speech and sometimes reproduced in writing, is defined by Webster as used to indicate affirmation, agreement, or gratification. Paul Trench, writing in the magazine *Editor & Publisher* (June 14, 1969), protested that the spelling should be *mm-hm*, or something of the sort. He pointed out also that the negative version, which by analogy with the positive form would be written *huh-uh*, is not recorded in Webster (nor is either form to be found in Random House).

**unapt, inapt, inept.** *Unapt* and *inapt* are generally interchangeable in the senses *inappropriate, not suitable, not apt;* *inept* is sometimes used in those senses, but generally is reserved for the meaning *foolish, incompetent* (Evans, Random House, Webster).

**unaware, unawares.** Fowler holds that *unaware* is the adjective *(they were unaware of the joke); unawares* the adverb *(observed unawares)*. American Heritage explains and thus apparently endorses the distinction. But the majority view (Evans, Random House, and Webster) is that *unaware* may be either adjective or adverb *(taken unaware, unawares)*. Evans considers *unawares* the preferred form for the adverb, a view that appears to be corroborated by observation of usage.

**unbeknown, unbeknownst.**
Evans and Fowler regard these
expressions as rare, but neither
Random House nor Webster
gives any indication of this,
and there is reason to believe
that though they may have
fallen into disuse for a time,
they are now fairly common.

**unbend, unbending.** Evans
and Follett are concerned over
possible confusion as the terms
are applied to people. One who
unbends relaxes, loses his stiffness of manner; one who is
unbending remains stiff and inflexible in his attitude.

**uncomparable, incomparable.**
Evans says the first means *incapable of being compared,* the
second either that or *matchless,*
and adds that *incomparable* is
most likely to be used in both
senses. *Uncomparable* is in fact
rarely seen; Random House
merely includes it in a list of
*un-* compounds without definition; Webster does not give it
at all. Both dictionaries give
both senses for *incomparable.*

**uncooperative.** See COOPER-
ATE, etc.

**underestimate.** "It would be
a mistake to underestimate the
Russian leadership," com-
mented a newsmagazine. Well,
yes; a mistake is indeed a mistake. "The role that his wife
played in the importance of
the office cannot be under-
estimated" should read *overestimated.* Such reversals of
sense result from inattention by
the writer (Copperud, Flesch).
See also DOUBLE NEGATIVE;
NEGATIVES.

**underprivileged.** This term
was disparaged some years ago
by Henry George Strauss,

Baron Conesford, a captious
and often wrongheaded critic
of American usage who unfortunately had a faulty grasp of
American idiom, as a leading
example of "American pretentious illiteracy." This harsh
judgment was based on the
Latin meaning of *privilege*—
that is, *a private law.* It is
stupid, he said, to pretend
favoring equality before the
law and at the same time use
a word like *underprivileged,*
which complains, in his view,
that there is not enough inequality. The fundamental
error here is the reliance on
the original meaning of the
word in another language from
which it was derived to determine what its meaning should
be in current English. Many
English words that have been
adopted from other languages
have departed considerably
from their original senses, and
it is well recognized that etymology, or derivation, is a poor
guide to present usage. Fowler,
for example, has remarked on
this subject (under *True and
False Etymology*) that a writer
should be much less concerned
with a word's history than with
its present meaning and idiomatic habits; yet he comments
on *underprivileged* in a way
that implies disdain for the
term, obviously having taken
his cue from Lord Conesford.
Flesch criticizes it from another
direction, as being a euphemism for *poor,* an objection that
has some merit. The word is
recognized as standard, however, by all current dictionaries;
Webster defines it as "deprived
through social or economic
oppression . . . " The British
scorn for *underprivileged* ap-

parently arises, as is often true in such instances, from the fact that the term was fabricated in America. This appears to be an instance in which an American expression has not been widely taken up in Britain; it is not given in the 1964 Concise Oxford Dictionary. But apparently it is making headway there, or Fowler would not have commented on it at all. H. L. Mencken traced its origin to the New Deal of Franklin Delano Roosevelt. Raven I. McDavid Jr., as editor of the abridged edition of Mencken's *American Language*, which appeared in 1963, quotes the *New York Times* as having protested in an editorial (Oct. 6, 1961) that *underprivileged* and *culturally deprived* are euphemisms for *slum dwellers. Underprivileged* is in such wide use now, however, that it may no longer be a euphemism, but rather may have become a literal term, since of course euphemisms cease to be euphemisms when awareness of them as such is lost. Whether or not that time has arrived, there is no question that *underprivileged* is standard in America. It may be significant that no American writer on usage but Flesch has even raised a question about its acceptability.

**under the circumstances.** See CIRCUMSTANCES.

**under way.** The correct form; not *under weigh*. The confusion perhaps arises from another nautical term, *weigh* (meaning *raise* or *lift*) *anchor* (Bernstein, Copperud, Evans, American Heritage). Though the adverb (*let's get under way*) is often given as one word (*underway*),

both Random House and Webster give it as two words. Webster gives the adjective (*underway refueling*) as one word.

**undue, unduly.** Often used redundantly and, indeed, absurdly, as in "The situation does not warrant undue concern." This says that the situation does not warrant unwarranted concern. More logically, "The situation does not warrant concern"; or, if this is not strong enough, "The situation does not warrant great (or any of a number of other adjectives) concern" (Copperud, Evans, Flesch, Follett, Fowler). See also DOUBLE NEGATIVE; NEGATIVES.

**uneatable, inedible.** Fowler makes the distinction that the first applies to what cannot be eaten because of its condition (e.g., spoiled meat) and the second to what is unsuitable for food (e.g., grass). This is borne out to some extent by the definition in Webster, but *inedible* is given as a synonym for *uneatable*. In general, it appears that *inedible* is likely to be used in both senses in the U.S. *Uneatable* does not appear in desk dictionaries, and Random House lists but does not define it; the implication is that it is the opposite of *eatable*.

**unexceptionable, unexceptional.** See EXCEPTIONABLE, EXCEPTIONAL.

**unhealthful, unhealthy.** See HEALTHFUL, HEALTHY.

**unhuman, inhuman.** The first is simply the negative of *human*, meaning *not possessing human qualities;* the second goes beyond this, meaning *cruel, barbarous, savage,* etc., according to Fowler. But *inhuman* is used in both senses in the U.S., Evans points out, a view that is corroborated by the dictionaries. American Heritage makes a general distinction of words beginning with *un-* and *in-*, corresponding with Fowler's dictum; that is, that the prefix *un-* is neutral, the equivalent of *non-,* while *in-* implies an adverse judgment. *Unhuman* is rare.

**uninterested.** See DISINTERESTED, UNINTERESTED.

**unique.** For MORE UNIQUE, MOST UNIQUE, etc., see COMPARISON 3.

**United Kingdom.** See GREAT BRITAIN, etc.

**unless and until.** Disparaged as redundant by Bernstein, Flesch, Follett, Fowler, and American Heritage; one or the other is considered enough. See also IF AND WHEN.

**unlike.** Like *like,* often figures in FALSE COMPARISON, which see.

**unmoral.** See IMMORAL, etc.

**unpractical.** See PRACTICABLE, PRACTICAL.

**unprecedented.** Bernstein and Copperud warn that the word is often loosely used, especially in newspaper writing, where *uncommon, unusual* would be more appropriate. What is unprecedented has never happened before. This view is borne out by Random House and Webster. See also JOURNALESE.

**unrealistic.** See REALISTIC.

**unreligious, irreligious.** The distinction that the first means merely having no connection with religion and the second lacking in religion, sinful, is observed primarily in Britain, Evans and Fowler agree. In the U.S., according to Evans, Random House, and Webster, the primary sense of *unreligious* is *irreligious,* and its secondary sense is *nonreligious, lacking in religion.* The distinction may perhaps be made clearer by saying that *irreligious* is disapproving, if not derogatory, and that *unreligious* in its primary sense is equated with *irreligious. Unreligious* in its secondary sense is neutral. Examples: "Public schools are supposed to be unreligious" (secondary sense). "The irreligious (unreligious) scoffed at the bishop's interpretation."

**unsanitary, insanitary.** As Evans points out, *unsanitary* is the customary form in the U.S., and the words are considered synonyms, a view substantiated by Random House and Webster. The distinction, set forth by Fowler, that *insanitary* implies danger to health while *unsanitary* means merely *lacking in sanitation* is not observed in the United States.

**unsolvable, insoluble.** The usual term in the U.S., as Evans points out, is *insoluble* for both *incapable of being dissolved* ("It was insoluble in water") and *incapable of being solved* ("The problem was insoluble"), and the words are considered synonyms. This view is corroborated by Random House and Webster. But *unsolvable* would not be used to mean *incapable of being dissolved.*

**until.** See TILL, etc.

**until and unless.** See UNLESS AND UNTIL.

**untimely end.** Objected to by Evans as hackneyed and by Flesch as illogical. Whether an end is untimely is, of course, a matter of opinion, but there is such a thing as a reasonable consensus in such matters, which perhaps justifies the phrase from the standpoint of logic.

**unthinkable.** Evans, Follett, and Fowler all consider it necessary to explain that in ordinary (i.e., nontechnical) use the word does not mean that which cannot be thought, since as Follett puts it anything that can be named can be thought. They agree that it now ordinarily means *unacceptable, preposterous, improbable, out of the question,* etc. Random House and Webster, however, both give *unimaginable* as the first sense. Fowler protests that *unthinkable* is often loosely and inappropriately used in place of *objectionable.*

**upcoming.** Considered objectionable for *forthcoming, coming, approaching,* etc., by Copperud, Follett, and American Heritage; Copperud regards the expression as journalese. It is considered standard, however, by both Random House and Webster.

**upon, on.** See ON, UPON.

**up tight, up-tight, uptight.** This expression, which originated in hippie and teen-age argot, is so new that it is to be found only in the American Heritage dictionary. The usual meanings are *tense, nervous* and *conforming rigidly to convention,* but American Heritage gives also *destitute* and *on intimate terms with another person.* Though the term is unquestionably slang, as American Heritage classifies it, it has quickly spread into general use and is often to be found without either explanation (not that any is still needed) or apologetic quotation marks. American Heritage's designation of the two-word form as predominant may be open to question; many well-edited publications use the one-word form, which seems preferable as conveying its sense as a compound. So does the hyphened version, which appears occasionally.

**upward, upwards.** The first form is generally preferred in the U.S. *Upwards* may not be used as an adjective: *an upwards slope. upward* (Bernstein, Evans, Random House, Webster). American Heritage disapproves *upward(s) of* for *less than, about,* or *almost;* this seems an imaginary misuse.

**upward revision.** See EUPHEMISMS.

**us.** See IT'S ME, etc.

**usage, use.** *Usage* relates to a customary practice or manner of use: *usages of the church, rough usage.* In reference to language, for example in this book, it relates to a standard of use. Follett makes a curious and obvious error, as any dictionary will show, in saying that *usage* has no use outside the subject of language. *Use* relates to the act of employing something. Copperud, Flesch, Follett, Fowler, and American Heritage protest against *usage* where *use* is called for: "He didn't like the word *no* and wouldn't permit its usage by others"; "This custom is no longer in usage"; "Year-round usage of the schools is recommended." In each instance *usage* should be *use*. In general, the misuse of *usage* is laid to pretentiousness.

**use to, used to.** The phrase is now used only in the past tense: "We used to go skating every Saturday." Negative statements and questions with *did*, however, take the form *use to*: "We didn't use to build a fire unless it was bitterly cold"; "Did there use to be trees along here?" These latter constructions are considered clumsy by Bernstein and Copperud. Fowler describes *didn't*

*use to* as an archaism in England, but recognizes it as accepted usage in the U.S. American Heritage accepts this as well as the negative and interrogative constructions illustrated here.

**utilize.** Criticized by Flesch, Follett, and Fowler as a long and usually unnecessary substitution for *use*. Evans says *utilize* means make a practical or profitable use; Fowler concedes this distinction of senses once existed but says it has now disappeared. Random House and Webster both give *use* as a synonym, but also give Evans' version as one sense.

**utopia.** See A, AN.

# V

**vaccinate.** See INOCULATE, VACCINATE.

**vacuity, vacuousness.** Evans and Fowler agree that the first is the commoner except in reference to facial expressions.

**van, von.** In proper names, see DE, DU, etc.

**variance.** Takes *with*, not *from: at variance with previous ideas* (Bernstein, Fowler, Random House, Webster).

**Variation.** Conspicuous variation to avoid repeating a term is not only worse than repetition, as Fowler said, but may suggest a distinction that is not intended and thus mislead or confuse the reader. The problem is often neatly solved by ellipsis: "He played with

Charlie Barnet's Orchestra and worked with Red Norvo's Sextet." By changing from *played* to *worked* the writer was merely straining to avoid repeating the same word. Yet he might have said "played with Charlie Barnet's Orchestra and with Red Norvo's Sextet." "Russia's army newspaper *Red Star* claims there are now 33 million Communist Party members in seventy-five nations. The breakdown gave Indonesia one million. France was said to have five million Red voters; Italy, 1.8 million card-carriers." Are Communist Party members, Red voters, and card-carriers all the same thing? The writer assumed this to be so, but of course it is not. The changes are rung obtrusively and unnecessarily.

Once it had been established that *Communist Party members* is the subject of the discussion, the writer might have trusted the reader's memory beyond Indonesia to "France was said to have five million; Italy, 1.8 million." "About 76 per cent of Russia's doctors are women, while in the United States only 6 per cent are female." *Women* would have sounded better repeated; or *but the proportion in the United States is only 6 per cent.* "Cigarette smokers puffed a record 205 billion cigarettes in the first six months of this year, 4.4 per cent more than they lit up in the same time last year." Lighting up and puffing are different things, and the variation is absurd: *4.4 per cent more than in the same period last year.* "In cases where both parents are obese, 72 per cent of the offspring also are fat. When one parent is fat, 41 per cent of the children are overweight. When neither parent is obese, only 4 per cent of the offspring are fat." The writer danced an ungainly dance between *obese, fat,* and *overweight* on one hand, and between *children* and *offspring* on the other. He might have put it "When both parents are fat, 72 per cent of the children are. When one parent is fat, 41 per cent of the children are. When neither parent is fat, only 4 per cent of the children are."

One aspect of variation might be called the geographical fetish, since it requires that the second reference to a place be in the form of a geographical description. In Southern California, under these ground rules, it is permissible to name

San Francisco once, but the second time it is mentioned it must become *the northern city.* Other samples of this aberration: "The caravan plans a dinner in Podunk and an overnight stop in the Razorback County city" and "A three-day international convention opened today in Nagasaki on the anniversary of the atom bombing of the southern Japanese city." Desirable information about locale should be offered for its own sake and not made a device to avoid naming a place again. In the first instance *there* should have been used in place of *in the Razorback County city* and in the second *the city* would have been preferable to *the southern Japanese city.* "Children who want to enter a frog in the event may pick up an amphibian at the Chamber of Commerce office." *may pick one up.* "A search for a mountain lion was abandoned when no sign of such a carnivore was found." *Such a carnivore* is a pompously stupid substitute for *such an animal* or even *one.* Some synonyms that are popular with journalists in their quest for variation: *simian* for *monkey, jurist* for *judge, bovine* for *cow, feline* for *cat, quadruped* for any four-legged animal, *equine* for *horse, optic* for *eye, tome* for *book, white stuff* for *snow, bivalve* for *oyster, pachyderm* for *elephant, yellow metal* for *gold, solon* for *legislator, savant* for *professor.*

"To use a vulgar expression, they were spitting with the wind, whereas in Italy, which has enjoyed a persistently favorable balance of payments, they were expectorating against the wind." It is surely inexcusable to use a word one considers it necessary to apologize for and then obstrusively sidestep it a moment later.

Reluctance to use pronouns also figures in variation. "Three governors planning to attend the conference have stated their intention of turning public schools over to private hands. The three are . . . " Better: *They are* . . . The writer must be careful that the antecedent is clear, but when it is, he should take advantage of the terseness, naturalness, and ease that come from writing *he* instead of *the official, she* instead of *the housewife,* and *it* instead of *the proposal under discussion.* Points similar to those in this entry, as well as others bearing on the problem, are made by Fowler under the headings *Elegant Variation, Repetition of Words and Sounds,* and *Sobriquets;* by Bernstein under *Monologophobia and Synonymomania;* and by Flesch under *Synonyms.* See also ELEGANT VARIATION and JOURNALESE in this book.

**various.** Fowler, like Follett and American Heritage, objects to the word as a pronoun, as in "Various of the specimens were imperfect," though he concedes that it may become established. Webster recognizes this use, but Random House gives *various* only as an adjective (*various books on the subject*). See also DIFFERENT.

**vastly.** Fowler objects to the use of the term where measurement or comparison is not at issue, as in "We were vastly amused." Evans regards this as standard American usage, and

so do Random House (by extension from a definition of *vast*) and Webster.

**vault.** Bernstein holds that *vault,* in the sense of *a place of safekeeping,* is a permanent part of a building and generally large enough to walk into, but both Random House and Webster also apply the term to a compartment, cabinet, or strongbox.

**venal, venial.** Sometimes confused. *Venal* means *mercenary, corruptible, open to bribery* (*a venal official*); *venial* means *excusable* (*a venial transgression*) (Bernstein, Evans, Fowler).

**verbal.** See ORAL, VERBAL.

**Verbiage.** Discussions of this rhetorical fault (the use of excessive words) are to be found under this heading in Evans and Follett. See also REDUNDANCY.

**Verbs.** Diverse problems of usage affecting verbs are discussed under that heading by Copperud and Evans. For the division of compound verbs by adverbs, see ADVERBS; see also WHO, etc.

**veritable.** Bernstein, Evans, and Fowler complain that the word is often used for excessive emphasis: "It was a veritable cloudburst."

**verse.** Evans complains that the word is misused for *stanza,* but both Random House and Webster give *stanza* as a synonym, and this is widespread standard usage. The distinction Evans insists upon, that a verse is a line, is not general usage but part of the technical terminology of prosody.

**very.** The main point at issue is whether *very* (rather than *much,* or *very much*) may be used before a past participle, as in "We were very inconvenienced by the strike" and "Jones was very pleased to be invited." Fowler and American Heritage hold that only participles that have come into common use as adjectives may be preceded by *very;* this means that *very pleased* is acceptable, and *very inconvenienced* is not. The test of whether a participle is commonly used as an adjective is to place it in the attributive position, that is, directly before a noun: *a pleased expression* sounds unexceptionable, but *an inconvenienced public* sounds less so. The difficulty is that even grammarians are likely to disagree whether a given participle has become an adjective. Bernstein, like Fowler and Follett, favors the distinction, though he admits it is not always easy to apply; Copperud, Evans, and Flesch take a more liberal view and allow *very* wherever it will not affront the ear. Random House, perhaps sidestepping the question, gives no example of *very* used as described here; Webster gives *very pleased, very separated.* Opinion thus is evenly divided on this usage.

*Very* is sometimes used in attempts to strengthen that in fact have the effect of weakening. *Very wonderful* is an example; the writer has overstrained, and would have done better to say *wonderful.* A *very lovely singing star, a very splendid performance, a very excellent dinner*—all these descriptions are diminished by the presence of *very.* The writer in these instances gives the impression of reaching for an effect he does not quite believe in. A *very great man* sounds to the reader less great than *a great man;* the writer is trying to convince himself, and, giving himself away by his use of *very,* loses the confidence of the reader (Bernstein, Copperud, Follett). For similar faults, see RATHER; QUITE.

**via.** The word, which comes from the Latin, meant in that language *by way of.* If derivation is strictly observed, then, it would be correct to say "We traveled to San Francisco from Chicago via Los Angeles," but not "we traveled via train," nor "They talk to their friends via ham radio." That is, *via* is often used in the sense *by means of,* and sometimes it displaces *by* or *through.* The use of *via* in any but its original sense is more or less severely criticized by Bernstein, Copperud, Flesch, Follett, and Fowler; Evans condones it. The extended meaning is also sanctioned by Random House, which gives *a solution via scientific investigation,* and by Webster, which gives several similar examples as standard usage. The consensus is slightly in favor of restricting *via* to *by way of.*

**viable.** The term is criticized by Flesch, Fowler, and Follett as overworked and misused. In its primary sense, *viable* means *able to live and grow,* but it need not be restricted to things possessing life; it could as well be applied to a city or a country. The critics tend to limit *viable* to this meaning, but

Random House and Webster also give *real, workable, vivid, practicable, important,* definitions that seem only to confirm the critics' complaints that the word has had the edge hopelessly ground off it. The criticism that *viable* is overworked is hardly open to question. What is intended by the word in the following is anybody's guess: "It's not that the present system can't work. It's just that it's not very viable." There is reason to suspect that *viable* sometimes displaces *valid,* which may have been intended here.

**vice, vise.** A vice is an evil ("He knew all the vices before he was 18"); a vise is a clamp, usually mounted on a workbench ("The subassembly is held in a vise while braces are welded on it"). The occasional confusion is aggravated by the fact that *vice* is an alternate spelling of *vise,* though *vise* is preferred and, it might be added, more frequent (Copperud, Evans, Random House, Webster).

**vicinity.** See IN THE (IMMEDIATE) VICINITY OF.

**vicious, viscous.** Sometimes confused. *Vicious* means *depraved, immoral; viscous* means *oily* or *syrupy in consistency,* and is said usually of liquids (Copperud, Evans).

**victuals.** The term is discouraged by Evans and Flesch as quaint.

**view.** Bernstein and Fowler agree that *with a view to* is preferable to *with a (the) view of;* Evans and Fowler agree that a participle rather than an infinitive should follow *with a*

*view to,* e.g., *with a view to succeeding* rather than *with a view to succeed.*

**viewpoint.** American Heritage reports that some writers and grammarians consider *viewpoint* inferior to *point of view,* but no such opinion is expressed by any of the other authorities surveyed for this book. The American Heritage panel sanctions *viewpoint.* See also POINT OF VIEW.

**violoncello.** Evans and Fowler point out that the term is sometimes incorrectly given *violincello.* The fact is, however, that the long form has been all but forgotten in favor of *cello,* and the form *'cello* is now considered fussy.

**Virgin Birth.** See IMMACULATE CONCEPTION.

**virile.** Although the word comes from *vir,* Latin for *man,* it is no longer exclusively associated with maleness as such; its standard senses now include *strong, vigorous, forceful* (Copperud, Fowler, Random House, Webster). Copperud, Evans, and Fowler agree that in any event *virile* is inappropriate where *male, masculine* will not do, and the dictionaries appear to bear this view out. This means that above all it should not be applied to women. Partridge curiously warns against using the term to describe sexual power in women.

**virus.** *Virus* for *disease* or *illness* ("He is in bed with a virus") is incorrect, Bernstein points out, because the virus is the organism causing the disease; neither Random House nor Webster allows *virus* in the sense he criticizes.

**vis-à-vis.** The expression (from the French) means *face to face*, and is sometimes misused in English to mean *concerning, regarding,* and in other ways (Bernstein, Follett). Random House, however, gives also *in relation to, compared with,* and Webster gives *in relation to, in comparison with, toward,* definitions that seem to indicate that the phrase has been Anglicized and thus protests based on its original meaning are irrelevant.

**visa, visé.** Evans says the British use *visé* for what in America is called a *visa,* but Fowler says *visa* is now established in Britain.

**vise, vice.** See VICE, VISE.

**visitation.** A formal or official visit, as of an inspector; thus not interchangeable with *visit* (Evans, Follett, Fowler). The dictionary definitions bear out this distinction, though Random House gives as one sense *the act of visiting.*

**visit with.** The term refers primarily to conversation, not necessarily to physical presence, and so it is possible to *visit with* by telephone. Thus, too, it is not a displacement of *visit* (Bernstein, Copperud; American Heritage calls it informal). For that matter, however, both Random House and Webster give *converse* (as by telephone) as one sense of *visit* alone. Probably no question concerning the standing of *visit with* would have arisen except that it was one of numerous expressions denounced by Henry George Strauss, Baron Conesford, on a visit to the United States, in the course of which he exhibited a lamentable ignorance of the American idiom he made bold to criticize. In this instance, Lord Conesford mistook *visit with* for a useless elaboration of *visit* in its primary sense. Thus it may be in Britain, for Fowler asperses *visit with* on the same grounds. As with *underprivileged,* Fowler's reviser, Sir Ernest Gowers, has evidently taken his cue from Lord Conesford.

**vocal cords.** See CHORD, CORD.

**Vogue Words.** See FAD WORDS.

**Voice.** See PASSIVE VOICE.

**voice.** For *express, state (voiced objections),* considered objectionable by Copperud and Flesch. This sense is given as standard by Random House and Webster, however. Evans explains that in Britain *voice* is considered impermissible for *express* except for what is spoken, as contrasted with what is written. This view apparently is outmoded, however, for the Concise Oxford Dictionary specifically recognizes *voice* as applied to what is printed.

**von.** See DE, DU, etc.

**vow.** A journalese variant of *say* or *promise,* and as often used in newspapers it implies an inappropriate solemnity (Copperud). Definitions in both Random House and Webster agree that the term has this connotation.

# W

**wage.** Copperud regards the term as likely to be applied to payment for work at the lower end of the scale in terms of prestige, as indicated by the saying that a job pays a wage and a position pays a salary; Evans feels that this distinction is being lost. Webster, however, says that *wage* denotes payment for chiefly physical labor, and this sense perhaps is encouraged by the terms *wage scale, wage worker,* and *wage slave,* all of which suggest that kind of work. Random House says the term applies to payment for work done by the hour, day, or week. The consensus thus is that *wage* primarily connotes manual or menial labor.

**wait on.** Dialectal or regional for *wait for:* "I'm waiting on the bus" (Bernstein, Bryant, Copperud, Follett, American Heritage, Random House, Webster).

**waive, wave.** Sometimes confused; the first is used in the sense belonging to the second. *Waive* means to relinquish or forgo *(he waived the privilege); wave* denotes motion *(we waved goodbye; the flag waved above). Waive* for *wave* is obsolete (Evans, Fowler).

**wane.** Evans says that what wanes, except as the word is applied to the moon, declines or decreases permanently, but there is no sign in the diction-

ary definitions that this is necessarily the meaning.

**want.** In the sense *should, ought to* ("You want to listen carefully"), *want* is considered conversational by Bryant and standard by Evans. Neither dictionary gives this sense. The consensus is that it is questionable in writing.

**want in, out, off.** These expressions, which telescope *want to come (go) in, out* or *want to get off,* are considered regional by Bryant, Copperud, and Evans. American Heritage and Random House label this usage informal; Webster considers it standard. The consensus is that it is not fully acceptable.

**warm (and cold) temperatures.** Strictly speaking, a temperature, as a reading, can only be higher or lower, not warmer or cooler.

**warn.** There is a notion in journalism that *warn* cannot be used transitively: "The Better Business Bureau warns of unscrupulous magazine sellers"; "Taxes will go up, the legislator warned." There is no basis for this; *warn* is given as both transitive and intransitive in American Heritage, Random House, and Webster. This, however, may be a relatively new usage; Fowler calls it "now common in journalism," and the Century Dictionary and Cyclopedia, an American work published in 1897, gave *warn* only as transitive. The criticism that *warned* is often used as a random displacement of *said*, in reference to a statement that could not be considered a warning, may have more validity. *Warn* takes *of*, *about*, *concerning*, *against*, not *on*.

**was, were.** See SUBJUNCTIVE.

**was a former.** The phrase is illogical in reference to a living person: "Like Hull and Padrutt, Johnson was a former Progressive." Once a former, always a former. *Was a former* (and *was a onetime*) can be sensibly used only of a dead person to describe a condition that ceased to exist before he died. Even then, the meaning is more clearly expressed with different wording: "The late governor was at one time a Farmer-Laborite."

**was given.** The frequent criticisms of this construction appear to have originated in the strictures of Ambrose Bierce, who argued that a sentence like "The soldier was given a rifle" is inadmissible because "What was given is the rifle, not the soldier . . . Nothing can be 'given' anything." Regrettably, Bierce broke his own rule by using *was given* in the very lines he composed to forbid its use. "The soldier was given a rifle" is a variant arrangement of "A rifle was given to the soldier." Curme writes that sentences in which the accusative becomes nominative "are often preferred in choice expression" and cites as an example "They were given ample warning." Simeon Potter, in *Our Language*, says, ". . . in

spite of loud protests from prescriptive grammarians, 'Me was given the book' has become 'I was given the book' by the most natural process in the world." The Oxford English Dictionary quotes as an example of the uses of *give* "He was given the contract." Random House and Webster have similar examples. The criticism of *was given* thus is obviously superstition.

**was graduated.** See GRADUATE.

**wave.** See WAIVE, WAVE.

**way, away.** *Way* as an adverb, for *away*, *far*, *as far as*, was found by Bryant to be common in ordinary and educated speech and in informal writing: "Way back in the good old days"; "We went way to Chicago"; "That's way too much." Bernstein grudgingly accepts the usage; Copperud calls it idiomatic; Evans considers it standard in the U.S., and Fowler describes it as an Americanism that is becoming established in Britain. Both Random House and Webster give the sense as standard; this is the consensus.

**way, ways.** *Ways* as a noun in place of *way* (*a long ways*) is considered unacceptable by Bernstein and American Heritage and loose by Copperud, but given as standard by Random House and Webster.

**way, weigh.** See UNDER WAY.

**we.** See EDITORIAL WE; I, WE.

**wean.** Bernstein points out that the word is sometimes misused in the sense *bring up* or *raise on*: "He was weaned on the old rules," rather than in its proper meaning of *deprive* or *end dependence on,* as derived from the primary sense of *accustom to loss of mother's milk.* This objection is borne out by dictionary definitions.

**we at.** See HERE AT, WE AT.

**weather.** Copperud and Evans agree that the overpopular saying "Everybody talks about the weather, but nobody does anything about it" is generally miscredited to Mark Twain, and that the author of it was probably his friend, the editor Charles Dudley Warner.

**wed.** Except for newspaper headlines, *wed* is considered obsolescent for *marry* by Evans, Flesch, and Fowler. Neither Random House nor Webster gives any such indication.

**weigh.** See UNDER WAY.

**weird.** Bernstein and Fowler complain that the word has been devalued by inappropriate and trivial use. Dictionary definitions give *supernatural, unearthly, fantastic, bizarre,* etc.; the usage referred to by the critics substitutes *weird* for *unusual, strange, out of the ordinary.*

**welch.** See WELSH, WELCH.

**well.** Fowler says flatly that the combination of *well* with a participle ( *well-read, well-tuned,* etc.) is hyphened only when used attributively and not when used predicatively. That is, it may be hyphened, but not necessarily, when it stands before the noun modified (*A well-tuned piano*) but not after (*The piano was well tuned*). American usage, however, as Copperud points out,

and as is indicated by Random House and Webster, is inconsistent in the use of the hyphen in the predicate construction. The best advice perhaps is to follow the dictionary example for such *well-* terms as may be found there. Fowler is right, however, when he says that the hyphen grammatically serves no purpose in the predicate construction, and so it may well be omitted; in such instances, *well* can modify nothing but the verb form following it.

**well-known.** There is a widespread idea in journalism that *widely known* is preferable to *well-known.* Like many other journalistic assumptions about language, it has no basis. This usage is specifically sanctioned by Copperud, American Heritage, Random House, and Webster, and is criticized by no authority.

**well-nigh.** Considered objectionable, primarily because it is archaic and thus affected, by Evans, Flesch, and Fowler.

**welsh, welch.** Fowler says *-sh* predominates for the form meaning *pertaining to Wales,* but cites established exceptions; Webster and Random House give *-sh* as the primary form. *Welsh* is also preferred for the verb meaning *to swindle someone in a bet,* or *to go back on a commitment* (Copperud, Fowler, Random House, Webster), though *welch* is acceptable.

**Welsh rabbit, rarebit.** The original form was *Welsh rabbit,* and is said to have been a joke at the expense of Welsh hunters. (The dish is melted cheese poured over toast or crackers.) *Rarebit* represents an attempt to dignify that caught on; the form is now commoner than *rabbit*. Evans and Fowler disapprove *rarebit* as a corruption, which indeed it is; Copperud and Follett regard it as established; Random House and Webster consider *rabbit* the basic form. The consensus favors *rabbit*, though as Follett points out, *rarebit* predominates in cookbooks and on menus.

**were, was.** See SUBJUNCTIVE.

**we, the people.** See I, WE.

**wharf.** See DOCK.

**what.** Long discussions of the number of the verb to be used with *what* when it is followed by a plural predicate—"Let me point out what seem(s) to be some misplacements of emphasis"—are to be found in Bernstein and particularly in Fowler, who devotes nearly three pages to various ramifications of the problem in his characteristically hairsplitting style. It is difficult to compare these discussions, since they approach the question from different directions. On this much there is agreement (by Bernstein, Bryant, Copperud, Evans, Fowler, Follett, and American Heritage): *what*, despite the assumptions of some writers, is not necessarily singular, but may be plural. Copperud and Evans say that *what* may be followed by either a singular or plural verb, so that in the example given at the outset, either *what seems to be* or *what seem to be* is correct. In constructions like "What remains are a few trees" Fowler favors *is* or *what remain*, but Bryant

finds that *are* is commoner. Copperud and Follett say that with a linking verb (chiefly forms of *to be—is, was*, etc.), *what* is considered singular: "What I saw *was* eight white horses." Beyond this, the reader can only be referred to the authorities themselves for explanations of what they consider good usage in various constructions involving *what*.

**whatever, what ever.** In questions, the second form is proper, Evans, Follett, and Fowler agree: "What ever (not *whatever*) can he be thinking about?" Follett concedes, however, that the distinction is often ignored; Random House and Follett both admit *whatever* as an interrogative without qualification. The consensus slightly favors *what ever* in questions. The distinction is clear enough to anyone who stops to analyze the forms, but it seems well on the way to being forgotten. Follett disputes Fowler's further insistence that the interrogative *what ever* is colloquial, and in this has the support of the two dictionaries, neither of which gives any such indication. Bernstein and Fowler point out that *whatever* should not be followed by *that:* "Whatever is decided that should be final." Omit *that*. This error seems rare.

**when.** See WHEN, WHERE; NO SOONER.

**when and if.** See IF AND WHEN.

**whence.** See FROM HENCE, etc.

**whenever, when ever.** As with WHATEVER, WHAT EVER

(which see), Evans, Fowler, and Follett hold that the interrogative form should be two words ("When ever will you be ready?"); Evans and Fowler consider the form colloquial, but Follett says it must now be regarded as standard. Random House accepts the one-word form in questions, but Webster considers two words preferable. The consensus, then, is that two words are preferable in questions and that the expression is not colloquial. Otherwise, as a conjunction ("We saw him whenever we chose") or as an adverb ("Whenever shown, the painting attracted crowds"), the one-word form is standard (Evans, Follett, Fowler, Random House, Webster).

**when . . . then.** See IF . . . THEN; the same comments apply.

**when, where.** Used in definitions ("Music is when there is a concordance of pleasing sound") the words mark an immature style, Bernstein, Copperud, and Evans agree; American Heritage calls this usage unacceptable. Bryant finds the construction defensible but says many educated people avoid it.

**where.** As used for *when* or *if*, criticized by Copperud and Flesch: "Employees of the company are given compensatory time off, or where this is not possible, they get extra pay." *when, if.* See also WHEN, WHERE; FROM WHENCE; SEE WHERE.

**whereabouts.** Though it looks like a plural it is a singular, Bernstein and Evans hold, but both Random House and Web-

ster say it may be construed as either singular or plural. Thus opinion is evenly divided: "His whereabouts was (or *were*) unknown."

**whereas.** Flesch objects that the word is stuffy and prescribes *while* instead, but Follett points out that *while* is stretched when it is used in the sense of *whereas (but by contrast).* Flesch's opinion of the word seems captious and is perhaps based on the fact that some *where-* combinations, as Fowler points out, have been displaced in modern use. But *whereas* is not one of them.

**where . . . at.** See AT VS. IN.

**whereby.** Flesch and Fowler agree that the word is being displaced in modern use by *by which* or other constructions.

**wherein.** The term is becoming archaic and thus sounds pompous (Flesch, Fowler). *In which, where, when* are displacing it.

**wherever, where ever.** The form should be two words in stating questions, Follett and Fowler agree. See the similar cases of WHATEVER and WHENEVER.

**wherewithal.** Flesch and Fowler agree that the word is quaint for *means:* "We wanted to make a trip but we lacked the wherewithal."

**whether.** See AS TO; DOUBT-(FUL); IF, WHETHER.

**whether or not.** Bernstein, Copperud, Evans, and Flesch say *or not* should be omitted when this is possible, a matter easily determined. When an alternative is clearly posed, as in "The program will be placed in effect whether the council decides or not," *or not* is clearly indispensable. Random House and Webster both give examples omitting *or not*. Fowler does not discuss omission, but his examples in other connections include *or not*. The consensus favors omission.

**which.** Copperud, Bernstein, and American Heritage warn that *which* may be ambiguous in reference to the whole clause preceding it, rather than to just the nearest noun or pronoun: "Styles of the 1920s did nothing to set off the female figure, which frustrated girl-watchers." *figure; this frustrated.* Flesch concedes that this construction is generally frowned on, but approves it anyway as idiomatic. Follett objects to it. Webster says that it is widely used by speakers on all educational levels and by many reputable writers, though disapproved by some grammarians. The consensus is that it should be used with care. See also THIS.

Fowler inveighs against *which* for *who* or *that* ("the finest poet which the nation has produced"). Webster calls this usage archaic but adds it is still occasionally seen in current writing; Random House says *which* may never be applied to people. *That* is freely interchangeable with *who;* see THAT 3. For *which* vs. *that* see THAT 4; see also AND (BUT) WHICH, etc.; IN WHICH; ELLIPSIS 4.

**while.** The word is best reserved to mean *at the same time* or *during the time that,* and is often objectionable in the senses of *and, but, although,* or *whereas,* Bernstein, Follett, Fowler, and American Heritage agree. ("One brother was born June 9, 1898, at Oakland, while the other was born July 19, 1893, at San Jose"; "The cannon will be based on Okinawa while the rockets are being sent to Japan"; the examples are ambiguous.) Bryant says that *while* is standard in the senses *whereas* and *although,* but concedes the possibility of ambiguous construction. Evans approves *while* for *although* or *but,* but not for *and.* The consensus favors restricting the use of *while* to its temporal sense, particularly when there is danger of ambiguity or looseness. See also AWHILE, A WHILE.

**whiskey, whisky.** Although the forms are often used interchangeably in reference to Scotch (and sometimes Canadian) whisky, the preferred form for these varieties, as distinguished from bourbon, is *whisky,* a fact expounded at some length in *The New Yorker* of Nov. 14, 1964. The distinction is corroborated by American Heritage, Random House, and Webster.

**white.** The word is not capitalized in reference to race (nor are the names of other colors used in this way: brown, yellow, red, black). This is the consensus of Copperud, Random House, and four current desk dictionaries; Webster says sometimes capitalized.

**whither.** Flesch calls the word pompous, and Fowler regretfully concedes that it is obsolescent; Random House's classification is "archaic." The consensus is that the word is questionable in ordinary contexts.

**who, whom; whoever, whomever.** *Who* and *whoever* are the subjective forms and *whom* and *whomever* the objective. Strictly speaking, the choice depends upon a moderately sophisticated understanding of grammar, and it seems as if the detailed explanations that are offered by the strict constructionists on this subject represent wasted effort, because if their readers can follow such an explanation they are unlikely to need it. All the authorities agree that in speech, at least, *whom* is disappearing, and that this tendency is evident in print. In both speech and writing, moreover, *who* is likely to be used when it occurs toward the beginning of a clause, because this is the normal position of a subject, regardless of whether *whom* may be required by the grammatical construction. Confusion over what may be the object of a nearby verb often results in the use of *whom* where *who* is called for. *Whom* is used uniformly after a preposition (*to whom, for whom, with whom,* etc.), though Webster allows *who* here. *Than whom,* though strictly speaking an ungrammatical form, is established beyond cavil as an adjective. The strict constructionists among the authorities compared for this book, who insist on *who's* and *whom's* based on grammar, are Bernstein, Follett, Fowler, Random House, and American Heritage, which, however, permits *who* for *whom* in speech. The liber-

tarians, so to speak, who are willing to accept as standard the usage that actually predominates, are Bryant, Copperud, Evans, Flesch, and Webster. The libertarians thus slightly outnumber the strict constructionists. Many examples from the works of writers of unquestioned skill and fame can be cited to illustrate supposedly erroneous choices of *who* and *whom.* The following examples are offered to illustrate the instances in which the strict constructionists would say the wrong choice was made.

"He summoned the officer, whom he said had just been commissioned." Strictly, *who,* as the subject of *had been commissioned;* but apparently misconstrued as the object of *said.*

"She explained her presence to the Hussar, whom she hoped would fall in love with her." Strictly, *who,* as the subject of *would fall,* but apparently misconstrued as the object of *hoped.*

"Who are you going with?" Strictly, *whom,* as the object of the preposition *with. Whom* sounds precious when spoken, however, and even strict constructionists allow *who* in speech, while insisting on *whom* in writing. Webster quotes Raymond Paton: "Of who I know nothing," with the preposition standing before *who;* even the libertarians generally agree that in this position the word should be *whom.*

Webster's comment on this problem perhaps best sums up the consensus: "[Who is] used by speakers on all educational levels and by many reputable writers, though disapproved by some grammarians, as the object of a verb in the clause that it introduces (old peasants who, if isolated from their surroundings, one would expect to see in a village church—John Berger) or less frequently as the object of a preposition in the clause that it introduces." Of *whom* Webster says, "Sometimes used as the subject of the clause that it introduces esp. in the vicinity of a verb of which it might be mistakenly considered the object (a recruit whom he hoped would prove to be a crack salesman—Bennett Cerf) (people whom you never thought would sympathize—Shea Murphy)."

The verb following *who* should agree with its antecedent in person and number, Bernstein, Follett, and Fowler point out: "It is perfectly clear to me, who has given much study to the matter." *have*, to agree with *me: I have.* See AND (BUT) WHICH, etc.; RESTRICTIVE AND NONRESTRICTIVE CLAUSES; for *who* vs. *that* see THAT 5; for *who* vs. *which* see WHICH; for *than whom* see THAN; ELLIPSIS 4.

**whodunit.** Considered informal by Random House and slang by Fowler. That it is nonstandard is also the consensus of desk dictionaries. There is no uncertainty about the form or spelling, however, and thus no excuse for *whodunnit, who dun it,* etc. Webster gives it as standard.

**whoever, who ever.** Evans distinguishes between the interrogatory *whoever* ("Whoever did he choose?") and the combination of *who* with the adverb *ever,* as in "Who ever would think of such a thing?" and prescribes the one-word and two-word forms accordingly. Follett apparently does not make quite the same distinction but requires two words in any question, and Fowler concurs. Compare WHATEVER and WHEREVER. But both unabridged dictionaries give the one-word form for what other authorities would regard as the interrogative, or pronoun with the separate adverb. Such distinctions seem hairsplitting and a waste of effort.

**whom.** See WHO, WHOM.

**whose vs. of which.** It is a superstition that *whose* as a possessive form of the relative *who* may refer only to people (*the tree whose leaves were falling*). The *of which* that is sometimes prescribed instead is avoided as clumsy (cf. *the tree of which the leaves were falling*). That is to say, *whose* is a standard and preferable substitute for *of which* (Bernstein, Bryant, Copperud, Evans, Fowler, American Heritage, Random House, Webster). The erroneous idea concerning the application of *whose* apparently grew out of the fact that the nominative, *who,* does ordinarily apply only to people, though it is sometimes applied to animals, particularly those having names, and occasionally to organizations.

**why.** See REASON WHY.

**wide-, -wide.** Usually hyphenated as a prefix: *wide-angle, wide-awake, wide-open* (as part of a compound adjective standing before the noun modified). But *widespread.* Solid as a suffix: *citywide,* *countywide, nationwide.* Evans dissents from this, but both unabridged dictionaries give the solid form.

**widow of the late.** A redundancy common in newswriting; *widow of* (Bernstein, Copperud).

**wife, widow.** Whether a man should be described as survived by his wife or his widow is a subject of disagreement in journalism. The definition of *survive* ("to remain alive or in existence") seems to argue for *wife.*

**will.** See SHALL, WILL, SHOULD, WOULD.

**win.** Criticized by Bernstein as needless as a noun ("a win over great odds"). Considered standard in this sense by Copperud, Random House, and Webster; American Heritage would restrict it to sports contests.

**-wise.** The fad of forming adverbial modifiers by tacking *-wise* onto nouns ("Dollarwise, sales are up") is deprecated by Bernstein, Copperud, Follett, Flesch, and American Heritage; all, that is, except one of those who comment on this mannerism. The exception is Fowler, surprisingly enough, since his criticism of such affectations is usually scathing. Fowler (or, to be more specific, Gowers, his reviser) merely notes that such compounds "made for the occasion from nouns" exist. Occasionally such terms may be convenient: "This scheme is clumsy productionwise" is surely easier than *with respect to production* or *when it comes to production,* though perhaps *for production* is possible. Usu-

ally, as the critics point out, the *-wise* compound displaces direct English: "Solano is the largest county populationwise and assessed valuationwise." *in population and assessed valuation.* The *-wise* used to make an adverbial modifier is not to be confused with the suffix *-wise* meaning *possessing wisdom (weather-wise, worldly-wise)* nor the one that is joined to a noun to produce an adjective meaning *in the manner of (clockwise, crabwise); lengthwise,* too, is beyond criticism. Such terms are solidly established.

**wisecrack, -ed.** See QUIP, QUIPPED.

**wish.** *Wish* for *want* ("Do you wish some more potatoes?" "What do you wish?") is considered objectionable by Evans, Flesch, Fowler, and American Heritage; both Random House and Webster, however, consider this usage standard.

**wishful thinking.** The phrase is disparaged by Evans as a cliché and admired by Fowler as a useful neologism. Another illustration of how the soothsayers disagree.

**with.** Bernstein, Follett, and American Heritage hold the traditional view that parenthetical phrases beginning *along with, together with,* or *with* do not make an otherwise singular subject plural: "The apple, together with the orange, was (not *were*) shrunken." Copperud and Evans say such constructions may take either singular or plural verbs, just as the number of the verb with collective nouns depends on what the writer intends to stress.

Partridge (*Usage and Abusage*) also expresses this view concerning *with*, and cites Onions' *An Advanced English Syntax*. Curme says in *Syntax* that a plural verb may be used if the idea of number is prominent. The same reasoning applies to such connectives as *as well as, besides, in addition to, and not alone, like*. See also SUBJECT-VERB AGREEMENT; COLLECTIVES: AS WITH.

Copperud, Flesch, Follett, Fowler, and American Heritage deplore the habit, most conspicuous in the loose writing of journalism, of using *with* to tack elements of sentences together with no clear indication of their relationship. Some examples, with suggested emendations: "Smith was struck in the chest and right hip with the third shot going wild" (*hip; the third shot went wild; or but the third shot . . .*); "The United States ranks ninth in infant mortality with Sweden having the best record" (*mortality; Sweden has . . . or and Sweden has . . .*).

with a view to. See VIEW.

within the framework. Deplored by Follett and Fowler as pretentious.

without. *Without* for *unless* ("I won't go without he does") is disparaged as substandard by Bryant, Evans, Follett, and Fowler, and as dialectal by Random House and Webster, though Bryant reports it is occasionally heard in cultivated speech. This usage is actually a revival.

with regard to. See REGARD.

with respect to. See IN RESPECT TO.

with the exception of. Often redundant for *except, except for* (Bernstein, Copperud, Flesch).

with the purpose of. Verbiage in place of an infinitive construction. *With the purpose of circumventing* equals *to circumvent* (Copperud, Flesch).

witness. Misused, Bernstein, Copperud, and Evans agree, when it displaces *see, watch, observe* (*witness a ball game, witness a school play*), as it does in journalese.

woman, lady. The conflict between *woman* and *lady* in American usage is curious. In one widely accepted view, *woman* suggests commonness, if not vulgarity, while *lady* suggests breeding and refinement. It is this idea, no doubt, that has led to the rejection of *women's* in such designations as *Ladies' Aid* and *Ladies' Auxiliary*. A few notches up the social scale will be found organizations with names like *Woman's Club* and *Women's Alliance* and *League of Women Voters*. This choice is common among the country-club, study-group, and college-alumnae sets.

Newspapers commonly forbid the use of *lady* in their columns as a synonym for *woman*, holding that *lady* belongs only in titles (*Lady Astor*) and in references to their holders. Even so, no newspaper has been known to insist that ladies' aids must be referred to as women's aids. At the same time, *neighbor woman, widow woman*, and *the Smith woman* are discouraged as disparaging (see MISS).

*Lady* is in general use as a courtesy, as in the salutation *ladies and gentlemen.* Most people, addressing a group of women, would say *you ladies* rather than *you women. Lady* remains useful when a touch of courtliness is desired, but *woman* is the workaday word, and the idea that it contains a hint of disparagement is mistaken and generally held by the uneducated.

These comments represent in general the views of Bernstein, Copperud, and Evans. Fowler deals with peculiarly British applications of *lady,* and frowns on such designations as *lady doctor,* preferring *woman doctor.* This is unquestionably in accord with educated American usage, which prefers *woman* in the absence of any overriding reason to use *lady.* It is interesting, however, that the impulse to dignify lowly occupations, which has made the *janitor* a *sanitation engineer,* has produced *saleslady* and *charlady* to replace *saleswoman* and *charwoman.* See also FEMALE; FEMININE FORMS.

**Word Order.** See ADVERBS; MODIFIERS 6; DANGLING MODIFIERS; INFINITIVES 1; INVERVERSION; TIME ELEMENTS.

**worsen.** Despite some criticism, the word is standard as both an intransitive *(become worse)* and a transitive verb *(make worse)* (Copperud, Fowler, Random House, Webster).

**worst to worst.** Bernstein and Copperud point out that the correct form of the quotation is "let the worst come to the worst," not "worse to worst."

**worthwhile.** Bernstein, Copperud, Follett, Random House, Webster, and three of five current desk dictionaries give the one-word form as preferred; British preference, however, as pointed out by Fowler and some of the dictionaries, is *worth-while.* Flesch, Follett, and Fowler complain that the word is overused and misused, and there can be no doubt that, as Fowler says, it has become a fad for the description of any kind of merit.

**would, should.** See SHALL, WILL, etc.; SUBJUNCTIVE.

**would appear, would think, would seem.** This way of expressing oneself, in place of more direct statement ("It would seem that someone is at fault" vs. *it seems* or even flatly *someone is*), is deplored by Flesch as timid and described by Evans as extremely cautious or very modest. The conclusion to be drawn is that framing statements in this way is to be avoided and should not be allowed to become a habit, because of the weakening and mealymouthed effect it produces.

**would have.** *Would have* is erroneous for *had* in a conditional statement ("If a doctor would have been on the premises, a death certificate would have been signed"). *If a doctor had been . . .* (Copperud, Evans, Follett, American Heritage).

**would like, should like.** See SHALL, WILL, etc.

**would rather.** See RATHER.

**wrack.** See RACK, WRACK.

**wrath, wrathful, wroth.** Evans and Fowler agree that *wrath* is the noun ("His wrath was awe-inspiring"), *wrathful* the attributive adjective *(a wrathful reply)*, and *wroth* the predicate adjective ("The king was wroth"). Both Random House and Webster, however, allow *wrathful* and *wroth* as adjectives in both positions (that is, before and after the noun modified).

**writ large.** The correct form of the phrase (sometimes *written large*). "Ireland's contributions to peace and the noble aspirations of the human effort are written largely on the pages of history, Johnson said." This sentence, from a news dispatch, illustrates a not uncommon

error. *Writ large,* the usual form of the archaic expression, means *written in larger form, more clearly. Writ largely,* on the other hand, means *written for the most part,* a different matter altogether (Copperud, Fowler, Webster).

**writer, present.** See EDITORIAL WE.

**wrong, wrongly.** The preferred usage of *wrongly* is before the verbal modified: "The wrongly identified man stood up." Otherwise, *wrong:* "The word was spelled wrong" (Evans, Fowler, American Heritage, Webster).

**wroth.** See WRATH, etc.

# X

**xerox.** Recognized as a verb by Random House and the American Heritage Dictionary, but not by Webster, probably because the term is so new ("They xeroxed several copies of the letter"). It means, of course, to reproduce by xerography, and comes from the invented trade name *Xerox.* See also REALTOR.

**Xmas.** The use of this form (which derives from a reverent form used in the early Greek church, on the basis that X represents the first letter of Christ's name in Greek) is discouraged by Bernstein, Copperud, Flesch, and American Heritage; it is considered demeaning or irreverent by many.

# Y

**yankee.** Fowler says the British err in applying the term to other than New Englanders or Northerners in the Civil War. The fact is, however (as reported by Random House and

Webster), that the expression is widely used to denote any inhabitant of the U.S. This usage was firmly established during the World Wars.

**yclept.** The use of this expression (an obsolete word for *called, named*) is discouraged as worn-out humor by Bernstein, Evans, Flesch, and Fowler.

**ye.** Bernstein and Fowler hold that *ye* as an article meaning *the (Ye Olde Tobacco Shoppe)* should have its original pronunciation, *the.* (*Ye* in fact results from an error, in which a now disused printing character for *th*, known as *thorn*, was mistaken for *y*.) This, however, is information possessed usually only by scholars; Copperud, Evans, Random House, and Webster approve the pronunciation that is heard everywhere: *ye.*

**yet.** *Yet* as a conjunction beginning a sentence, meaning *but* ("Yet he continued to hope"), is disparaged as pompous by Flesch. This judgment seems quixotic in the light of widespread use in this way in all contexts, and considering also that in detailed discussions of various uses of *yet* neither Evans nor Fowler makes any such objection. Both recognize *yet* as a conjunction, as do Random House and Webster, and in general there is no reason why conjunctions may not begin sentences, as Flesch himself recognizes.

**Yiddish.** The name of a language, really a variety of German, spoken by many European Jews and often written with Hebrew characters, and not to be confused with Hebrew, a totally different language, Evans and Fowler point out.

**you.** Bernstein and Copperud agree that the use of *you* to address the reader ("If you want to have a good time, try to be agreeable") conduces to informality and directness. Follett and Fowler warn against mixing the indefinite *you* with *one*: "If one wants to succeed, it helps if you know the right people." Either *one* and *one* or *you* and *you*. See also ONE.

**you-all.** Southerners often become indignant when it is suggested that they use the expression *you-all*, which is indigenous to their region, as a singular, that is, to address or refer to a single person. Bryant says that though *you-all* may be addressed to one person, it implies others; Evans says merely that it is a respectable plural of *you*, and does not take up the possibility of its use in the singular. Random House gives only the plural use, and Webster's definition concurs with Bryant's. Copperud, hopelessly outnumbered, says the expression is sometimes used in the singular.

**your.** Copperud objects, but Evans, Random House, and Webster approve of *your* in place of *a, an,* or *the,* or when no article at all is necessary, as in "Your water is a sore decayer of your whoreson dead body" (*Hamlet*).

**your's.** No such form (Copperud, Evans).

**yourself, yourselves.** See MYSELF; REFLEXIVES.

# Z

**zoom.** The original meaning, still in use, was *to make an aircraft climb briefly at a sharp angle*. Bernstein and Evans insist that only this sense remains correct; thus it would be wrong to say "The car zoomed down the incline." Copperud accepts *zoom* as applied to motion in any direction, and Random House gives cars *zooming by on the freeway*. There appears to be some confusion here between *zoom* in its original sense as a technical term of aviation and the echoic *zoom*, having to do with the sound produced (*to move with or make a loud but low hum or buzz*—Webster). The distinction is thus necessarily based on what the writer has in mind. American Heritage accepts *zoom* for motion on the level, especially with the suggestion of accompanying sound, but rejects it for downward motion.